CONTINENTAL DRIFT

Continental Drift
Australia's Search for a Regional Identity

RAWDON DALRYMPLE
University of Sydney, Australia

LONDON AND NEW YORK

First published 2003 by Ashgate Publishing

Reissued 2018 by Routledge
2 Park Square, Milton Park, Abingdon, Oxon OX14 4RN
711 Third Avenue, New York, NY 10017, USA

Routledge is an imprint of the Taylor & Francis Group, an informa business

Copyright © Rawdon Dalrymple 2003

Rawdon Dalrymple has asserted his right under the Copyright, Designs and Patents Act, 1988, to be identified as Author of this Work.

All rights reserved. No part of this book may be reprinted or reproduced or utilised in any form or by any electronic, mechanical, or other means, now known or hereafter invented, including photocopying and recording, or in any information storage or retrieval system, without permission in writing from the publishers.

Notice:
Product or corporate names may be trademarks or registered trademarks, and are used only for identification and explanation without intent to infringe.

Publisher's Note
The publisher has gone to great lengths to ensure the quality of this reprint but points out that some imperfections in the original copies may be apparent.

Disclaimer
The publisher has made every effort to trace copyright holders and welcomes correspondence from those they have been unable to contact.

A Library of Congress record exists under LC control number: 2002028145

ISBN 13: 978-1-138-72531-7 (hbk)
ISBN 13: 978-1-138-72529-4 (pbk)
ISBN 13: 978-1-315-19195-9 (ebk)

Contents

Introduction		1
1	Living With Vulnerability – From the Beginning to 1983	4
2	Approaching an Independent Australian Foreign and Defence Policy	32
3	The Persistence and Decline of Dependence	53
4	Promoting Australia's Asian Future	74
5	Commitments and Hesitations	97
6	Development, Values, Solidarity and Fault Lines	111
7	Australian Efforts to Qualify	133
8	Dealing with Indonesia	162
9	East Timor and the Watershed in Policy	185
10	Opportunities and Constraints	211
Bibliography		*234*
Index		*238*

Introduction

This book is about Australia's search for a sustaining and sustainable identity and place in the world, and particularly in the region of the world where it is located. Few peoples have had so much difficulty in defining themselves in regional terms or in reconciling themselves to their location as have the Australians. These uncertainties became more acute after the Second World War when the European, American and Japanese colonies in the region achieved independence. But before that there was always a sense of unease at the core of Australians' nationhood, a clinging to Britain as the more fundamental identity and a sense of being a small lodgement in a part of the world which was alien to the British identity.

Necessarily the book draws on Australia's history in its examination of Australia's attempt to establish its regional identity. But its purpose is not primarily historical or narrative. Nor does it seek to be comprehensive. Thus it does not examine closely Australia's bilateral relations with the United States, China or Japan, whereas it does pay closer attention to relations with Indonesia, the country which has been at the heart of the attempt to engage closely with East Asia. There is little attention to functional aspects of foreign policy such as arms control, resources issues, conflict resolution and the many other matters which take up most of the time of foreign ministries and diplomats abroad. The purpose is rather to examine some of the main strands which Australia has sought to weave into its national goals and foreign policy, to ask whether those strands make a whole cloth, and, concluding that so far they do not, to consider Australia's options in a new century.

In the second half of the twentieth century Australia opened itself to non-British migration and became a much less provincial society. It gradually rid itself of the White Australia policy which had been so affronting to the inhabitants of the region in which Australia is located. It engaged in a deliberate, persistent and, until 1996, increasingly intensive attempt to forge links of all kinds with the countries of East Asia, especially in trade after it became clear that Britain was moving into the European community whose protectionist wall would virtually bring to an end large parts of Australia's export trade and decimate some Australian industries. But Australians retained some images or myths concerning themselves which seem to have been resistant to reality. For example there has been little or no questioning of the popular myth that Australians have a matchless record of battlefield heroism and that where they have not been successful (as at Gallipoli) that was due to the incompetence of others. In fact the Australian record in World War Two is rather patchy and it would be a healthy corrective to complacency if it were acknowledged that Asian soldiers (Japanese) inflicted major reverses on Australians in Malaya, in New Guinea and elsewhere.

On the other hand one former strong Australian preoccupation seems to have diminished to perhaps an excessive extent. Australians seem almost to have ceased to have a concerned awareness about the small population base of the country in relation to the massive and growing populations nearby. It seems extraordinarily unrealistic that there should be a significant lobby in Australia which favours a *reduction* in the population when the issue for much of the rest of the world will probably be whether a mere twenty million people are entitled to enjoy prosperous sole occupancy of a continent nearly as large as the United States in a world moving towards an expected peak population of nine billion. Migration of course will not solve population pressures elsewhere, but that is not really relevant to the likely politics of the issue.

Australia's search for a sustainable place in its regional context is also of wider relevance. Australia can be seen as an example of a country which is located in a different cultural or civilizational setting from that to which it inherently belongs and which faces stresses as a result. It has been argued (by Samuel Huntington) that Australia is in this regard a 'torn' country which has sought to cross over a civilizational fault line, leaving the Western civilization from which it sprang for a regional East Asian hybrid. That was at the time strongly contested by Australian policy makers. But Australia's situation could well become a test case of whether a nation that is labelled 'different' – and manifestly is different – can be accepted by and live on good collegiate terms with its Asian neighbours in a region which has begun to create its own collective image. It relates to one of the great issues of our time: whether differences of race, religion and income can at last be subsumed in shared commitments to universal values and opportunities for improvement of the human condition.

Australians have still not resolved basic issues which stand in the way of arriving at a clear sense of their identity. They have deferred or tried to ignore other issues which nevertheless overshadowed their thinking about their place in the world and, to the extent they think at all about this fundamental question, still overshadow their thinking about the nation's future. The most recent attempt to provide Australians with a new vision, or a greatly intensified version of a vision with a pedigree going back some decades at least, ran out of steam in the last three or four years of the twentieth century. That vision was of an Australia which would succeed in taking an important and fully accepted place in a region of democratizing and liberalizing states stretching from China in the north to Indonesia in the south. Australian governments never committed unequivocally to that vision. They equivocated between commitment to 'the Asia Pacific' (that is the Pacific Basin including the United States) and commitment to East Asia. Even so it became clear in 1996 that many Australians were uncomfortable with the speed at which the Keating government had sought to implement the policy of strengthening engagement with East Asia.

At the same time there was uncertainty and opposition in the region. That was strengthened with the disruption of the Australian relationship with its most important neighbour, and the principal state of South East Asia, Indonesia, from

1998. In 1999 Australian forces were placed in East Timor under United Nations cover and the Indonesian military (which had fought a campaign there against independence guerrillas since 1975) withdrew along with the Indonesian administrative structure and many Indonesians who had been living in the territory as a province of Indonesia. The Australian government at the time represented this as removing the major impediment and problem in relations between the two countries and made much of the professionalism with which the Australian force carried out its task. But for the Indonesians involved it was a humiliation. Even for many of those who had favoured the ending of Indonesia's rule in East Timor, what they saw as Australian triumphalism left a bitter taste and deep resentment.

The vision of Australian engagement or 'enmeshment' with East Asia and Australian membership of an emerging regional institutional network has been set back by these events. It has been heavily discounted as the prime objective of Australian foreign policy which now claims to be more 'realistic'. It has less support in East Asia than it did in the first half of the 1990s.

One of the main concerns of this book is to examine that vision and to assess whether it is still realistic, if indeed it ever was. At the beginning of the twenty-first century it seems questionable. But it involves most of the key Australian dilemmas and indeed other dilemmas and issues whose importance and relevance in the new century have implications stretching beyond the particular case of Australia. If that vision for the future of the region and Australia's place in it is now questionable it becomes all the more important for Australians to develop expertise and capacities for dealing successfully with East Asia. Cultivation of good relations wherever they can be developed in East Asia becomes even more important. Acceptance by key East Asian states is essential for Australia's long term security. That should still be the primary focus of Australian foreign policy, and the development of supporting public opinion, along with the appropriate intellectual resources, is one of the keys to Australia's future.

Chapter 1

Living With Vulnerability – From the Beginning to 1983

The Sense of Vulnerability

For much of Australia's modern history, that is to say since 1788, a sense of vulnerability was a prominent feature of its attitudes to the outside world. Indeed it can be argued that it remains in changed forms, and still exerts an important influence on Australian attitudes and foreign policy.

The nature of the apprehension of vulnerability evolved and became more complex as the colony itself evolved, spread, reproduced itself in other parts of the continent and developed its own characteristics. The surrounding circumstances changed too. The original fear of being overwhelmed by a foreign enemy came back in acute form 154 years after the beginning of the settlement but since then it has receded and become hardly visible, although no doubt it still lies dormant in the Australian mind – or in many Australian minds. Certainly it plays almost no part in current public discussion of foreign policy and has been heavily discounted in official discussion of foreign and defence policy. But the wariness about Indonesia which shows up in opinion polling[1] suggests that the fear of actual attack could recur and influence political consideration. Beyond that fear of being overwhelmed by force, other grounds for feeling vulnerable developed. But these too have receded, although remaining strong enough still to be exploitable in domestic politics. At the beginning of the twenty-first century Australia seems to have more confidence in its capacity to survive and prosper largely on its own terms than at any time in the past, and the old concerns about vulnerability to threats from outside seem to trouble Australians far less than used to be the case. But some of the grounds for feeling vulnerable which influenced policy and discussion in the past have not gone away. The issues which produced them have not been resolved and indeed the various problems which have come to be included under the rubric of 'border security' have attracted more attention than for many years. That is especially the case with what the Government describes as attempted illegal entry mainly by people from Iran, Iraq and Afghanistan. Their movements are typically arranged by 'people smugglers' and terminate in dangerous and sometimes fatal journeys in small boats from Indonesia. The treatment of these people under the increasingly stringent Australian immigration regime has become politically contentious both domestically and internationally.

It seems moreover inherently unlikely that the sense of vulnerability which was for so long an important influence on Australian attitudes and Australian policy has not retained some hold even though the old grounds for feeling vulnerable have all diminished. Indeed the diminution has almost become a reversal in some senses. Whereas the smallness of the population used to be a major factor in the sense of vulnerability, it is now seriously argued in some quarters in Australia that the population is too large for ecological sustainability, even though it is only 19 million in an island continent nearly as large as the United States of America. Australia's sense of remoteness has greatly diminished with the ease and rapidity of travel and the instant capacity to communicate with all of the rest of the world including especially Australia's cultural homelands of Europe and North America. That capacity will expand even more rapidly in the early decades of the twenty-first century. But already an Australian who is conversing by e-mail with people across the world, browsing web sites everywhere, and aware that the great cities of Asia are only between eight and twelve hours away, while in twenty four hours she or he can be in London or New York, is unlikely to have a sense of remoteness such as young Australians had in my youth when it took five weeks to reach London and most of what lay between Australia and Europe was ignored. Moreover the fear of being overwhelmed by foreign force, while it can perhaps still be summoned up by questions about Indonesia for example, is not at all acute or urgent in the absence of any identifiable potential enemy with the present intention and power to dominate Australia. And the sense of racial isolation which fed into vulnerability in various ways has greatly diminished. But all of these factors still have some presence in the Australian consciousness, even though much changed and reduced, and another kind of isolation and vulnerability may be emerging. A Prime Minister of noted political sensitivity, on a visit to Washington in mid-2002, still spoke in terms which Menzies could have used of the strength of Australia's commitment to the United States. Though uttered to the Congress of the United States such ringing statements are addressed indirectly to an Australian audience. Mr Howard knows that the alliance continues to give comfort to Australians. The influence on Australian thinking and action of the sense of vulnerability is therefore worth further exploration.

In 1979 Alan Renouf wrote a book entitled *The Frightened Country* reflecting his critique of the dominance of Australian policy by the perceived 'threat of international communism', especially during the Vietnam war period. Recently David Walker has written *Anxious Nation* with a wide historical and cultural sweep based on extensive research which illustrates Australian anxieties about Asia. He shows how, despite the anxiety, there was a growing Australian interest in Asia and over many years the development of links of many kinds. He calls for a sympathetic understanding of the sense of vulnerability which 'the four million insecurely established and predominantly Anglo-Celtic settlers of 1900' felt towards Asia: 'The idea that Australia was a continent under threat seemed all too rational for those who saw the world as a place in which the strong preyed upon and eliminated the weak. Australia's distance from Europe, tiny population, high levels of urbanization and declining birth-rate seemed unmistakable signs of a community at risk either of takeover or of an accelerating exposure to Asian influences'[2].

Nor has the perception that undercurrents of fear and uncertainty have strongly influenced Australia's view of the world been limited to Australian writers. For example, in the 1940s and 1950s the American historian Werner Levi conducted studies of Australian foreign policy and wrote of an Australian fear of 'the Asian peoples swooping down over Australia and appropriating the empty lands for their impoverished masses...The assumed hostility of these "masses" was usually made more frightening by pointed emphasis to the "loneliness" of Australia, a psychological factor dating back to colonial times, a haunting obsession which [in the Second World War] seemed to turn into reality'[3].

The manifestation of the sense of vulnerability in attitudes and policies from the beginnings of modern Australia is surveyed briefly in this chapter as a necessary preliminary to the examination of the main themes of this book. It raises questions which will be addressed in what follows.

The Last of Lands

When Captain Arthur Phillip arrived at Botany Bay on 18 January 1788 after eight months and one day at sea he had a total complement of 1030 people to found the new settlement. Three quarters of them were convicts. Finding Botany Bay unsuitable, Phillip moved the fleet a few miles north, through the entrance to Port Jackson, and raised the British flag on the site of what is now Sydney. The tiny remote settlement survived with difficulty and on the edge of starvation until the second fleet arrived in July 1790. Even then its isolation and smallness meant that it remained vulnerable to Britain's imperial rivals or enemies and especially the French. A French expedition under Baudin in 1801-03 caused alarm and prompted expansion of the colony to the south with settlements in Tasmania and on Port Phillip, in what was later Victoria. Those and subsequent outlying settlements remained conscious of their extreme remoteness from the metropolitan country and their very small population. In an age of European expansion and rivalry, the colonists looked apprehensively at the presence in regional waters of French and then Russian naval units. Anxious reactions to a subsequent French expedition prompted the establishment of further settlements including in Western Australia where a colony was established in June 1829. It was concern about the Russians in the 1850s which led to the construction of Fort Denison, the little stone fort which still stands in Sydney Harbour. The extension of the colonizing phase to include the United States and then Japan added to the sense of potential turbulence. In 1863 the Admiral in command of the Russian Pacific fleet visited Melbourne and Sydney and it was claimed that he carried plans for Russian attacks on the Australian colonies in the event of an outbreak of war between Russia and Great Britain[4].

In the beginning the infant colony with its complement of a thousand people, its remoteness from home, and its very precarious supply of food and other necessities of life was vulnerable to attack by an enemy force. Intelligence about the presence of French or other potentially hostile visitors was lacking or late and there was an obvious basis for anxiety about survival. That direct sort of anxiety about the possibility of being overwhelmed by sea-borne invasion has never entirely disappeared from Australia. From time to time it was stimulated by the presence of actual or perceived threats and was at its most acute in 1942 under Japanese attack. As a ground for perceived vulnerability the possibility of invasion persisted for most of the first two centuries. but other grounds emerged alongside it. The most influential of these were closely related. One was the perceived need to retain the whole of the continent and its approaches in British (Australian) hands and the other was the determination to ensure that the population remained British. Both of these objectives were seen as threatened by non-British of one kind or another and the settler British at times feared, and greatly resented, that they did not have whole-hearted support from the homeland on the other side of the world.

The territorial integrity argument was based on the belief that security would be compromised if the island continent were to be shared with an alien and possibly rival power. The argument that vulnerability would be reduced, and future opportunity increased, by holding the whole continent developed strong roots in the colony. When later it was extended to demands that British or Australian control be asserted over New Guinea and other South Pacific islands, because they were seen as essential to the integrity of Australia's security, there were rather sharp disagreements with the imperial government in London.

Governor Phillip's commission had not covered the whole of the continent, excluding most of the parts already discovered by the Dutch. Phillip's commission extended from longitude 135 degrees east, that is a line through the continent a little to the east of present day Alice Springs. The primary and indeed decisive reason for establishing the colony of New South Wales was to create a place far away from England to replace the lost American colonies as a repository for convicted criminals and for that purpose half a continent would no doubt have seemed sufficient. With time and the emergence of a sense of identity and long term interest among the settler population, there emerged a determination to make Australia a new country, to be populated by British but with its own character. With the debate over federation of the separate colonies came the call for 'a continent for a nation and a nation for a continent'. Already in 1826 the decision had been taken to claim the western side of the continent and in 1829 Captain James Stirling took settlers there to establish Australia's first non-convict colony.

Practical interest in the north of the continent was much slower to develop and was desultory until South Australia claimed administrative control in 1863. The economic advantages which had been expected failed to materialize and 'By the late nineteenth century, accusations of inertia, ineptitude or downright incompetence were routinely levelled at [South Australian] politicians and bureaucrats responsible for the Territory'[5]. David Walker has recently shown how 'deeper anxieties' developed in Australia about the 'Empty North' and the failure of the South Australian administration to develop and populate it. 'Australia could not afford to run the risk of appearing indifferent to the mounting pressures and restless energies of emerging Asian nations in its immediate neighbourhood'[6].

Authorities including President Theodore Roosevelt of the United States were invoked; there were grave warnings by prominent Australians, and novels were written which depicted the traumatic consequences of imagined Asian invasions. Not much less imaginative were some of the contributions in the debate which preceded passage of the Northern Territory Acceptance Bill in December 1910, ending South Australia's administration and transferring responsibility to the Commonwealth. Some proponents spoke in extravagant terms of the development potential of the territory, others of its alleged attractions to countries to the north, especially Japan. But in fact when the South Australians had made representations to the Japanese government in the late 1870s to undertake government sponsored immigration into the territory the proposal was rejected. The debate on the Northern Territory Acceptance Bill precipitated increased attention to the perceived threat to the British character of Australia of burgeoning Asian populations and rising Asian nations thought to be looking on Australia's 'Empty North' with covetous eyes.

Already in the 1880s the issue of Chinese immigration had generated a sharp disagreement with the Imperial government and begun to figure in the movement for a federation of the Australian colonies. Sir Henry Parkes, Premier of New South Wales, made a series of speeches in 1888 explaining what he saw as the Chinese threat and justifying action taken to prevent Chinese immigration. In the Legislative Assembly in Sydney on 3 April 1888[7], he recalled that in November of the previous year he had sent a circular letter to 'all the Australian governments', in which he had invited them to join in a general measure 'for the virtual prohibition of Chinese immigration'. He then explained that in February 1888 he had written separately to the premier of South Australia (because it had been exploring the possibility of bringing Asian immigrants into the Northern Territory) 'that it appeared a very likely fact that the Chinese government were privy to what was taking place in the Northern Territory, and that very probably it might be the design of a considerable number of Chinese to form a settlement in some remote part...where they might become strong enough to form, in the course of time, a kind of Chinese colony'. Sir Henry concluded that if the British government did not take the action he was demanding 'it will be the duty of this government, without the loss of a single day, to ask Parliament to take the necessary steps to protect this colony once and for ever from the influx of Chinese'. A few days later, on 9 April in a speech[8] at Wagga Wagga, the Premier sought again to drive home the message about the threat from China. He spoke at length about the transformation of China in a relatively few years from 'a mysterious and sealed country' to 'one of the most formidable Powers in the world' with 'considerably more than one quarter of the whole population of the globe' (contrasting China's 403 million with a total of 3,500,000 for 'all the Australian colonies including New Zealand and Fiji') and massive armies, large fleets with modern ships and a growing national armaments industry. He went on to extol the qualities of the Chinese people and especially 'their endurance and their patient labour' and said that 'It is for these very qualities that I do not want them to come here'. It was 'because I believe our first duty...[is] to preserve the British type against all other nations, that I do not want these people to settle amongst us'. Sir Henry endorsed the assertion, attributed to Napoleon, 'that if the Chinese nation once learnt the art of shipbuilding and the use of European arms, they would be able to conquer the world', another reason for not wanting to 'see the imprint of a Chinese settlement on the fair face of these Australian colonies'.

The British government was disconcerted to find itself the recipient of representations by the Chinese Minister in London on instructions from his government protesting the discrimination by the colonial authorities in Australia against immigrants of Chinese race. In the end the Australians got their way on the issue. The British government was also concerned about Australian attitudes towards Japan, a rising power which was being cultivated for reasons of Imperial policy and trade. In Australia there were doubts and worries about these developments. While there was a recognition of commercial opportunities in trade with Japan there was also a disposition to see the Japanese through the same anxious eyes which looked with alarm on Chinese immigration. In August 1894 Great Britain and Japan ratified a Treaty of Commerce and Navigation which they had signed the previous month in London. In the New South Wales Legislative Assembly a question was asked under the title 'Immigration of Japanese'[9]. 'In view of the warlike events in the East, and the great success attained by the Japanese nation, will the Government consider the advisability of immediately introducing legislation to prevent Japanese immigration into New South Wales similar to that passed into law against the influx of Chinese'[10]? The question went on to ask that the recent Treaty between Great Britain and Japan be tabled in the House along with relevant correspondence, and this was done by the government. The most important element in the correspondence from Downing Street was its reference to Article XIX of the Treaty 'from which you will observe that, if it is desired that the Colony under your Government should come within the operation of the treaty, notice to that effect must be given to the Japanese Government within two years from 25th August, 1894, the date of the exchange of ratifications of the treaty'. Article XIX stated that the treaty did not apply to the (listed) self-governing possessions of Great Britain unless notice was given on their behalf to the government of Japan within two years. The list included New South Wales, Victoria, Queensland, Tasmania, South Australia, and Western Australia. All of these except Queensland refused to become parties to the treaty.

The opposition to Japanese immigration hardened despite a recognition that it was causing resentment in Japan and hindering the Australian efforts to develop exports to that country. In May 1901 the Japanese Consul in Sydney sent an official letter[11] to the Prime Minister of Australia asking that Japan not be included in the ambit of legislation proposed to keep all non-white people out of Australia. He began by saying that 'The friendship that exists between the Empires of Great Britain and Japan leads me to suppose that your Government would not willingly take steps calculated to wound the feelings of the people whom it is my privilege to represent' and then argued that Japan's 'standard of civilization' is so much higher than that of 'Kanakas, Negroes, Pacific Islanders, Indians or other Eastern peoples, that to refer to them in the same terms cannot but be regarded in the light of a reproach, which is hardly warranted by the fact of the shade of the national complexion'[12]. Japan had no interest in finding an outlet for her population in

Australia and therefore 'any arrangement by which all that Australia seeks, so far as the Japanese are concerned, would be at once conceded'. It was therefore suggested that the Australian government propose a means of achieving the same end without including the people of Japan in any legislation on the grounds of colour. But in parliamentary debate it was asserted by both government and opposition that it was because the Japanese were regarded as superior, while being prepared to work for much lower wages than Australians, and because 'they are incapable of being assimilated' that they must be kept out.

That this Australian ambivalence towards Japan, this blend of respect and apprehension, was not solely pretence to soften the racist message is suggested by the vogue for Japanese decorative arts and the influence of Japanese models on taste in various ways. It is also suggested by the Australian response to the Anglo-Japanese alliance of 1902, the signing of which was welcomed in Australia. *The Sydney Morning Herald* of 14 February 1902 reported that 'The general opinion expressed in political circles is that the alliance is of the greatest importance to Australia, because it gives the protection of the Japanese fleet to our commerce. The alliance will, it is contended, offer to Australia effectual protection against possible attacks from a Russian fleet at Vladivostock or Port Arthur, or from a German fleet in the Chinese Sea. Australia is most vulnerable in the north, so that an offensive and defensive alliance with Japan will, it is contended, not only protect the northern portion of the Commonwealth, but will secure the trading interests of Australia in the Far East'[13]. But the most striking evidence of respect for Japan was shown by the reception Australians gave to the visits in 1903 and again in 1906 by the Japanese naval training squadron[14]. Large crowds went to see the ships and their complements, there were extensive official programs and generally highly favourable editorials and other comment in the main newspapers. The second visit was especially notable because it followed the Japanese victory over Russia which ended the long-standing fear in the Australian colonies of the 'Slav menace'.

At the same time there were undercurrents of concern about this dependence on Japanese naval power and uneasiness about British policy in that regard. This was a time when racist theories about 'white' and 'yellow' races were in vogue and when the influence of *The Bulletin* with its masthead slogan 'Australia for the White Man and China for the Chows'[15] was strong. Many Australians believed in the inevitability of conflict between the 'white' nations and the Asians and, as a small country remote from the centres of 'white' power, felt far from reassured by an arrangement which placed them under the protection of the Japanese navy. The Australian Prime Minister, Alfred Deakin, understood the political importance of this sentiment and indeed appears to have shared it. He had been working for some time for Australia to have its own navy, an arrangement which was eventually agreed by the British government in 1909. When he became aware that the United States 'Great White Fleet' was to visit the Pacific he made determined efforts to have Australia included in the itinerary. He successfully lobbied the United States representatives in London and Melbourne and a visit to Australia was included in the itinerary. The visit, in August and September 1908, was very successful and the Australian response 'exceeded the welcome given to the Japanese squadrons;

indeed it was generally conceded that the event drew bigger and more enthusiastic crowds than anything in Australian history, including the ceremonies that ushered in the inauguration of the Commonwealth in January 1901'[16]. Accounts by American visitors at the time emphasize the Australians' fear of the 'yellow peril' and their determination to keep Australia for the 'white man' as the major reason for the intensity of the Australian welcome to the American fleet. Accounts in the press both in Australia and in the United States emphasized the role of the visit in balancing and checking Japanese power and ambitions in the Pacific. That was the clear policy perspective of the commander of the Great White Fleet, Admiral Charles S. Sperry who wrote[17] to his wife that 'we are the only power in the Pacific which can hold Japan in check' and it was recognized by Australia as well as by Chile and others 'we alone stand between the Japanese and a career of adventure'. He thought that the cruise of the fleet had established 'a curious sort of protectorate – a new Monroe Doctrine'.

Prime Minister Deakin in a personal letter[18] also put very directly his view of the contribution of the visit of the Great White Fleet in diminishing Australia's vulnerability: 'The visit of the United States fleet is universally popular here...because of our distrust of the Yellow Race in the North Pacific and our recognition of the "entente cordiale" spreading among all white men who realise the Yellow Peril to Caucasian civilization, creeds and politics'. Possibly encouraged by his talks with Admiral Sperry, Deakin in the following year wrote to the British Colonial Secretary proposing that the United States be invited to extend the Monroe Doctrine to the Pacific in a formal way 'supported by guarantees of the British Empire, Holland, France and China'. This would have been a very 'curious sort of protectorate' indeed and, as Deakin seems to have expected, it was politely turned down by the British. Leaving out the Japanese, with whom the British continued to develop their relationship, would have made all too clear against whom the project was directed.

The Near North

This Australian feeling of vulnerability towards Japan coexisted with efforts to develop Australian exports to that country and with various steps to develop Australian understanding of Japan. But the dominant strand in policy continued to be a determination to prevent Japan obtaining a position of influence over Australia or in Australia's region. That was evinced repeatedly in the years before and during the First World War and then in the strongest possible terms through the Armistice and Peace negotiations. The Australian Prime Minister, W.M. Hughes, strenuously disputed policy towards Japan and over the former German possessions in the Pacific with the British and with President Wilson of the United States. Hughes was dogged in his assertion of what he took to be Australia's interests. Australia had only five million people, but it had made a disproportionately large contribution to the allied victory and it had made a major sacrifice, 60,000 war dead, a greater number than had been lost by the United States. Hughes fought hard to obtain Australian control of as large a share as possible of the former German possessions in the Pacific, to minimize the Japanese role and to keep it as far to the north as possible. On his return to Australia from the Peace Conference he was ready to proclaim what W.K. Hancock[19] described as 'Australia's Monroe Doctrine against the world' in the following terms: 'While the Monroe Doctrine exempts the two Americas from the jurisdiction of the League of Nations we would not allow anything relating to our sphere in the Pacific to be regarded as a proper subject for submission to the tribunal'.

This was an ambitious claim for a relatively small country to make and stands in some contrast to the litany over the years about Australia's vulnerability vis-à-vis very large countries such as Russia, China and then repeatedly Japan. Hancock, writing in 1929, evidently recognized as much. He followed the above account of Hughes's position with an interpretation of Australian policy. 'These, then, are our policies of security. A continent for a nation and a nation for a continent. Since federation we have asserted that claim with increasing emphasis. We intend to keep Australia "ninety-eight per cent British". We will not permit any strong Power to establish itself in our vicinity. We ourselves must hold the islands which cover our continent. But we ourselves are a small nation, a weak people'[20].

Hancock, who was Australia's most eminent historian and whose 'little book', first published in Britain in 1930 was the standard general text on Australia for many years, went on to argue that this security dilemma of being small and weak while demanding not only a continent for the maintenance of British race purity, but also the islands screening it to the north, was to be resolved within the framework of the British empire. His argument was that because Australia had these requirements while being small and weak its security was a liability not only on itself but upon the whole British Empire. If Australia tried to deny the liability and shirked the responsibilities it remained 'a colony'; but if it recognized the liability and shouldered the consequent responsibilities 'we are a nation'. He exemplified what he meant by the Australian record on New Guinea and in the exercise of its responsibilities there. He argued that in terms of defence too Australia had acted as a nation, shouldering the responsibilities for its defence (despite ending compulsory military training in 1929). In the event of war Australia would stand on its own feet, but as a member of the British Commonwealth of Nations it would not stand alone. Seventy years ago it was not unrealistic to write in such terms and indeed Australia had no better option. Ideas such as those with which Deakin toyed in 1908 of taking Australia under the umbrella of an extended Monroe Doctrine would have had no attraction for the United States in the 1930s. The turning to the United States for protection was only feasible after Pearl Harbor and *in extremis*.

Hancock judged that 'The strategical position of Australia is less secure than that of any other member of the British Commonwealth except New Zealand' (an exception which he did not explain and which seems surprising). Her awareness of that had perhaps caused her to cling closer to the British connection than would otherwise be the case:

> Australia's physical vulnerability, her close economic relationship with Great Britain, and her intense British race-consciousness, have made her less eager than some other

Dominions to claim every fact and form of national status. Perhaps we do not yet completely realise in Australia that we act as a nation and that the world accepts us as a nation[21].

There were at that time some leaders in Australia who thought that it was indeed time to claim rather more of the 'fact and form of national status'. In 1930, the year when Hancock's book was published, the Australian Prime Minister, J.H. Scullin, was in London insisting directly to King George V, against His Majesty's strong objections, on the appointment for the first time of an Australian, Sir Isaac Isaacs, as Governor-General. There were also other differences and resentments especially on the political left in Australia as the country was struck hard and early by the world recession. In regard to foreign policy matters which impinged on Australian interests the Australian government was seeking more effective consultation by Whitehall. But overall the course of Australian foreign and security policy in this period was less assertive than during the latter part of the nineteenth century and the first decade or so of the twentieth. In the aftermath of the 1914-18 war and the peace settlement there was for a time less sense of vulnerability.

The Australian forces had played a prominent role in key campaigns and had won a high reputation. The nation grieved the terrible losses and it has often been said that there was not a place in Australia which did not have its bereaved families. It is less often remembered that in addition to the 60,000 who died, tens of thousands of young Australians came back from that war crippled or permanently incapacitated because of poison gas, wounds, frostbite and so on. Many of those who were physically unharmed carried with them for the rest of their lives memories and feelings which marked them permanently and produced a bond between all 'returned' men (and women) which was far deeper and stronger than the institutional links provided by the influential veterans' association, the RSSAILA[22] (later RSL), for example. Much of the residue of war thus constituted was profoundly anti-war and deeply sceptical of the sort of Empire loyalist rhetoric which had been part of the currency of Australian politics before the war and which had been employed by Parkes and even by Deakin when pressing Whitehall to take more effective steps to protect a vulnerable Australia. Much of the jingoistic element was bled out of Australian politics by the First World War. Victory in the war had enabled the British and their allies to reach a peace settlement which, while much contested and with manifest weaknesses, provided an expectation that there would be a period of peace. And Hughes's return to a hero's welcome after his remarkable campaign at the Peace Conference recognized success in consolidating the buffer zone between Australia's northern approaches and Japan.

Hughes himself retained his suspicions of Japan and it can no doubt be said that events proved him right. But elsewhere in the government a different view was taking shape. The Department of External Affairs, which had existed since Federation had never exercised the responsibilities of a modern foreign ministry. It was abolished by Hughes in 1916. In 1919, while Hughes was away in Europe, a Pacific Branch was established in the Prime Minister's Department to fill a gap which its first director, E.L. Piesse, had identified as the absence of any 'adequate arrangement for obtaining information from abroad of matters affecting the external relations of the Commonwealth, or for furnishing advice to Ministers on questions of external policy'[23]. Consistent with what had been the Australian threat assessment since federation and earlier Piesse's work at first 'concentrated almost exclusively on Japan'[24]. Piesse recommended a softening of the application of the White Australia policy to Japan and similar treatment of the Japanese as for 'the less advanced European nations'. On this Prime Minister Hughes minuted simply: 'Rot'[25]. Piesse attended the Washington Conference in 1921-22 which reinforced his view that Australia's interests vis-à-vis Japan were protected by the Anglo-Japanese Alliance, British policy and the treaties agreed at Washington. He recommended against continuing the close study of Japan which he had been directing. (Years later, in 1935, Piesse wrote a book recalling 'the dead hopes of the 1920s' and calling for Australia to face and prepare for the possibility of war with Japan.)

With the victory in the long and exhausting war, the threat to the Empire had been seen off. Australia was thus not vulnerable, through defeat of the British Empire, to fall under the suzerainty of another European imperial power. The main Australian fear in the Pacific region had been of Japan and that subsided for the time being in the light of the post-war arrangements and British assurances. The national mood was disinclined to foreign policy. The war had been a terrible experience 'over there'. People wanted to focus on making real lives in Australia again, not on the troubles or complications overseas. Peter Edwards has described Australian foreign policy for most of the period between the wars as being 'almost undiscernible': 'The increasing confidence in external affairs that had been demonstrated by Australian leaders before World War I, consecrated at Gallipoli and personified by Hughes at Versailles, underwent a remarkable reversion in the 1920s. Perhaps it was sacrificed with the "lost generation" of leaders slaughtered in the war, for during both the 1920s, when the catchcry was for "men, money and markets", and the 1930s, when markets crashed, money was scarce, and men stood blankly in dole-queues, Australians thought of little but their economic fortunes'[26].

Events in the Pacific from 1931 onwards made it more difficult to take a complacent view although the record suggests that Australian governments were far from eager to face emerging realities. Australian trade with Japan was developing, there were official missions from that country and a developing awareness in some quarters that there were opportunities for Australia, as well as potential dangers, in the region to its north. With Japan in mind, the British decided to build a naval base at Singapore, which Australia supported in principle but not with any practical contribution. When Japan invaded and annexed Manchuria in 1931 the Australian government was preoccupied with the depression and wanted to do nothing which would disturb the exports of wool and wheat to Japan. The United Australia Party government under J.A. Lyons which replaced the Labor government at the beginning of 1932 was at least as concerned not to cause offence to Japan[27].

In 1934 the Lyons government sent the Minister for External Affairs, J.G. Latham and an accompanying party on a mission to the Far East, the principal purpose of which was to have discussions with Japan which had been pressing for a treaty of commerce and navigation. Latham's report to the Prime Minister[28] referred to Manchuria as 'the critical issue to-day in the Far East', advocated acceptance of the Japanese creation of the puppet state of Manchukuo as a fait accompli and proposed efforts to find a formula under which both Japan and the League of Nations, from which she had resigned, could 'save face'. The Chinese, Latham observed, would not accept that, 'but that could not be helped'. Reporting on his conversation with Foreign Minister Hirota, Latham said he believed that Japan was genuinely afraid of Russia and that it was in that area that 'the most immediate possibilities of conflict in the East arise'. But he could not see that there was 'any necessity for the other nations of the world to concern themselves directly with such a conflict'. Then, addressing the subject of 'Japan and the South' the Minister canvassed in apparently frank and open terms with Mr Hirota the possibility that Japan might undertake 'military adventures to the south' including the invasion of Australia. He said that 'in the case of any attack on a white Power it could not be assumed that America would be completely acquiescent and that, dependent as Japan was upon sea-borne supplies...it would obviously be unwise for Japan to engage in war with the British Empire'. The Japanese minister agreed and even 'further developed some of the points which I had mentioned'. Latham adds that 'Incidentally, I said that if Japan were to go as far as to attempt to land an army in Australia, and succeed in the enterprise, she would then find that she had in her hands a very lively nest of hornets'. Latham concluded:

On the whole I think that the ambitions of Japan are at present confined to trade on the mainland of Asia, and the protection of Japan against attacks from Russia probably by seizing the maritime provinces if an opportunity should present itself.

Latham's account indicates that the possibility of a threat from Japan was still very present in Australian policy thinking. But he hoped that Japan would continue to be preoccupied with expansion on the Asian mainland to its north and west rather than looking south. The task for Australian policy was to minimize the risk of a war which might have that effect. A few days after making his report to the Prime Minister Latham made a statement in the Parliament in which he made a famous call for greater attention to what he said was for Australia not the 'Far East' but the 'Near East':

It is inevitable that the relations between Australia and the Near East will become closer and more intimate as the years pass. Therefore, it is important that we should endeavour to develop and improve our relations with our near neighbours, whose fortunes are so important to us, not only in economic matters, but also in relation to the vital issues of peace and war...if war takes place there on a major scale, it is bound to affect Australia profoundly...The whole of our interests, therefore, lie in doing everything in our power to prevent the risk of war in the East from becoming a pulsing reality[29].

The following year Latham's successor as Minister for Foreign Affairs, Sir George Pearce, explained Australia's policy concerns in terms which were recorded by the United States Consul-General in Sydney, J.P. Moffat[30]. Noting that there was a feeling in Australia at large that she could not count on American help in case of Japanese attack, Pearce said he did not share that feeling but it was colouring Australia's policy towards Japan.

> The Government remained suspicious of [Japan's] ultimate intentions, but with British naval strength reduced below the safety point, and with American aid discounted, there was no policy open to her other than trying to be friendly with Japan, to give her no excuse to adopt an aggressive policy vis-à-vis the Commonwealth, and to rejoice (irrespective of the moral aspect) every time Japan advanced more deeply into Manchukuo and North China. He hoped that her energies would be absorbed there for a generation, and so did the Government of the Netherlands East Indies, with which the Australian Government kept in close and constant contact. But the feeling he described existed throughout Australia, and so [as] probably most Australians would be too polite to explain it to me in so many words, he felt that it was his business to tell it to me with all candour.

Presumably Pearce's motive in presenting matters to Moffat in these terms was to try to generate some assurance from the American side that they would not stand aside should Australia be threatened. That might have led him to present Australian government policy in starker terms than were really the case. But there was rising concern about Japan and about the adequacy of the British defence arrangements based on Singapore. At the same time the government was disconcerted by public statements of the seriousness of the position such as those made by Hughes and Piesse (of course quite separately) in 1935[31].

Australian policy in these years leading to the outbreak of war in Europe in 1939 was neither purposeful nor clear. There was a growing feeling of vulnerability and a mixture of appeasement and belated and inadequate attempts at preparation for the inevitable. The Lyons government muddled the issue of trade preferences for Great Britain, incurring resentment from Japan and annoyance from the United States. Lyons then raised without adequate prior consultation and preparation at the Imperial Conference in 1937 a proposal for a regional Non-Aggression Pact in the Pacific. It was decided by the Conference that Great Britain would pursue the idea with Japan. The Japanese were not responsive and the proposal lapsed. The month following the London Conference saw the Japanese launch a major attack on China. The Australian government subsequently advised the British government on several occasions of its view that every effort should be made to accommodate Germany in Europe and Japan in the Far East. Appeasement was the diplomacy while appropriations for defence expenditure were increased and consultations with the British on defence policy in the Far East intensified. The government did not lack advice from its Departments of External Affairs and Defence about the threat from Japan but, even after the invasion of China in 1937, it was reluctant to depart from its policy of seeking to appease or at least avoid antagonizing Japan by speaking frankly to the Australian people about the deteriorating situation, Australia's potential vulnerability and the need for more urgent defence preparation. It was also reluctant to do anything which might curtail valuable Australian exports to Japan including those of strategic importance.

As the situation in Europe deteriorated and the danger of war increased there was growing concern in Australia about Britain's capacity to meet a threat to

Australia in the Pacific if Britain were already engaged in a major war with Germany. There were reassurances from the British side which continued after the outbreak of war in September 1939. R.G. Menzies, who had succeeded to the Prime Ministership on Lyons's death, declined to give any immediate undertakings about providing Australian forces for the war against Germany until the government had a clearer idea about Japanese intentions and about British planning in the light of their assessment of Japanese intentions. The British assessment was that the Japanese would continue to be preoccupied with the campaign in China and would want to bring that to a successful conclusion while the other major powers were involved in war in Europe. Japan was expected to sit on the fence in regard to the war with Germany. Japan would court United States opposition if it tried to expand beyond the China Sea zone. The British naval appreciation was also reassuring. It started with the assessment that a Japanese attack on Singapore would require at least 50,000 troops and a siege of four to five months and long lines of communication which could be interrupted. Invasion of Australia was regarded by the Navy as even less likely because of the expected position of the United States, and because it would involve the despatch of a large army with very long lines of communication which would be liable to be cut at any time by a British fleet. It was 'needless to suppose such an enterprise would be attempted'. In conclusion 'The Admiralty accept full responsibility of defending Australia or Singapore from a Japanese attack on a large scale and have forces at their disposal for these essential purposes'[32]. When twelve days later Menzies announced that the Sixth Division would be sent overseas he said 'adequate assurances have been given to the government with respect to the capacity and availability of the Royal Navy, which is, after all, our first line of defence, to give to us protection against any major aggression'[33].

Those assurances were to prove hopelessly inadequate a little more than two years later. If they were based on serious assessments then those assessments must have been very flawed in terms of their estimation of Japanese strength in the area and especially in terms of air power. While at the time they seemed to reassure Casey and Menzies, the fall of France led to further doubts about the British capacity to send a fleet to Singapore in the event of a Japanese move which could threaten Australia. Churchill then sent a telegram to the Australian government, on 11 August 1940 giving a categorical assurance that if Japan 'set about invading Australia or New Zealand on a large scale' Britain 'would proceed in good time to your aid with a fleet able to give battle to any Japanese force which could be placed in Australian waters, and able to parry any invading force, or certainly cut its communications with Japan...'[34]. This assurance 'greatly comforted the Australian Government'[35]. However all these doubts and assurances were to lead before long to Australia's greatest crisis when 'our first line of defence' proved quite unable to provide us with any effective protection, and when Australia was left dependent on the United States navy to stop the Japanese advance. They led too to the sharp disagreement between Churchill and the then Australian Prime Minister Curtin about the disposition of Australian forces returning from the Middle East. Churchill's tough message to Curtin on this was sent on 20 February 1942, the day after a large Japanese air armada raided Darwin. On 19 February there were two large air raids on Darwin[36] involving more aircraft than had been deployed in the attack on Pearl Harbor. There was no effective opposition. Not surprisingly, part of the population of Darwin panicked, discipline was lacking and people attempted to flee down the road south to Katherine. The government did not wish to publicize this disaster, but Curtin must have been deeply concerned and in no mood to accede to Churchill's decision to divert, to a probably doomed attempt to defend Rangoon, forces which were on their way back for the defence of Australia. The attacks on Darwin demonstrated Australia's extreme vulnerability especially in the absence of modern aircraft capable of fighting the Japanese naval and land-based attackers. The effects of the raids on the defenders and populace of Darwin also suggested that there was a good deal of bravado in Latham's assertion some years before to the Japanese foreign minister that if Japan invaded Australia they would find they had a hornets' nest in their hands.

The problem for the Australian government in 1939 lay in the possibility that Japan might launch a campaign of expansion in the Pacific which could threaten Australia directly. In that event, and even in anticipation of it, most difficult issues would arise if, as might be expected, British resources were fully committed to the war against Germany so that adequate provision for the defence of Australia by the British Empire could not be made. Yet Australia could not even develop and concentrate its own small resources on the looming threat from Japan. It was obvious that Australia had a direct interest in joining Britain against Germany as in the 1914-18 war because defeat of Britain by Germany would have grave consequences for Australia. While all parties recognized that Australian interests should not be submerged in the overall effort because of uncertainty whether the overall British effort would be willing or able to save Australia in the event of all-out war by Japan, the Menzies government possibly invested too much of Australia's limited resources in the war against Germany. In hindsight they accepted too readily the assurances which they were given by the British in 1939. But they did not have much room for manoeuvre in the circumstances of the time, and all previous Australian policy and practice pointed to prompt and practical engagement in the common struggle against Germany. The sense of Australia's vulnerability gave signals which were not easily compatible in these circumstances. Without its membership of what Menzies, in his announcement to the Australian people that the country was at war, called 'a great family of nations' and 'the entire British world' Australia still perceived itself as small, remote and vulnerable. Moreover its perception of its own identity still involved for most people a more or less strong sense of Britishness. The course of the war, and the way it later bore down on Australia, helped to bring about change which Menzies in the post war world resisted. But in 1939 it would have been hard for an Australian government of any persuasion to have failed to give large scale support to the British cause. Nor would it have been easy to adapt that support so as to provide better for the direct defence of Australia. For example, when Japan struck, Australia had only obsolete and ineffective aircraft in its air force in Australia, and few trained air crew. But under a scheme put in place soon after the beginning of the war over 40,000 Australians were trained for air force service and they were deployed, largely in the British air force, in the defence of Britain and later in the air war over Europe where they remained after the Japanese entered the war. Perhaps Australia might then have insisted that more of them, with modern aircraft such as they were flying in Britain, should be redeployed promptly to Australia. In the exigencies of the time that might well have been difficult; but planning which left Australia defenceless against Japanese air power must be open to criticism.

Australia no doubt made a useful if modest contribution to the overall British war effort against Germany; but the Empire contribution to the war against Japan and the defence of Australia, to which effective assistance had been pledged, was notably inadequate. If Australia had had to rely on the British navy as its 'first line of defence', as Menzies had called it when announcing that Australia was sending the Sixth division to join the British war effort, then it would have been virtually defenceless against Japan. Two powerful British warships were despatched to Singapore before Pearl Harbor but without any accompanying aircraft carrier and with very inadequate land-based air cover they were quickly sunk by Japanese aircraft after hostilities began while attempting to prevent Japanese landings in Malaya. The British-planned and led defence of Malaya was easily overcome by a Japanese invading force which was numerically inferior to the defending force. Singapore, for which claims of invulnerability had been made, proved very vulnerable to attack from the landward side and it was there that the largely demoralized British force, including the two Australian brigades, surrendered. As the Japanese advance continued through the Netherlands East Indies and on to New Guinea Australia was dangerously exposed. The new Australian Prime Minister[37], John Curtin, published a famously controversial New Year message on 27 December 1941 in which he said that 'Without any inhibitions of any kind, I make it quite clear that Australia looks to America, free of any pangs as to our traditional links or kinship with the United Kingdom'. He recognized the problems faced by the United Kingdom and the dangers of dispersal of strength, 'but we know, too, that Australia can go and Britain can still hold on. We are therefore determined that Australia shall not go, and we shall exert all our energies towards the shaping of a plan, with the United States as its keystone, which will give to our country some confidence of being able to hold out until the tide of battle swings against the enemy'[38].

Curtin proceeded to place his confidence in General MacArthur, in command of the Allied forces in the South West Pacific based in Australia, an imperious leader who paid little attention to any other Australian including General Blamey, the Australian Commander-in-Chief. By May of 1942 Curtin, his government and the Australian people appeared to face the possibility which they most dreaded – a Japanese invasion of Australia. Japan had no actual plan to invade Australia. Rather their immediate purpose was to establish a position across the sea lines between Australia and MacArthur's command and the United States. If the large fleet they despatched via the Coral Sea to seize Port Moresby on the South coast of Papua opposite Australia had not been stopped they would have been perilously close at least to cutting Australia off and in effect rendering her helpless. The crucial factor at this point was that the Americans had broken the Japanese naval code and were thus able to intercept the Japanese expeditionary force of eleven transport ships, three aircraft carriers, six cruisers and six destroyers in the Coral

Sea on the way to Port Moresby. The ensuing battle was indecisive and costly to both sides but its result was that the Japanese turned back from Port Moresby and subsequently tried to take it by land offensive from the north over the mountain ranges. After long and hard fighting against the Australians they eventually came within sight of the sea but were halted and forced back all the way with heavy losses. A month after the Battle of the Coral Sea American intelligence detected the movement of a powerful Japanese carrier force involved in a plan to take the American base at Midway. The ensuing engagement, fought entirely with carrier-based aircraft, resulted in a defeat from which the Japanese navy never recovered. They lost carriers which they could not replace while the Americans were rapidly building new ships which were to give them an overwhelming advantage at sea and in the air.

Thus already by the middle of 1942 the air and seaborne threat to Australia had been blunted when the war with Japan was still only some seven months old. Yet it had been a real threat and indeed more than a threat if we recall the big and very destructive air raids on Darwin on 19 February which were followed by repeated attacks. Shipping on the east coast of the continent was sunk by Japanese submarines and there were observation flights by Japanese naval aircraft over Sydney. At that time Australia had little or no effective air defence. In Sydney air raid shelters were built and other preparations made for air attacks. The Coral Sea and Midway battles made them unnecessary. The land campaign in New Guinea continued to cause both Curtin and MacArthur considerable anxiety for much longer. After victory there, achieved mainly by Australian forces, the Australian role became peripheral to the American campaign which was built up to the recapture of the Philippines and then on to the doorstep of Japan in Okinawa before the decision was taken to use the nuclear weapons on Hiroshima and Nagasaki.

The experience of the Pacific War left a deep sense of dependence on the United States but political developments in Australia delayed the expression of that in Australian foreign policy. Curtin, who had embodied the dependency association, died in 1945 before the end of the war. Chifley, who took his place, although the undisputed leader with corresponding responsibility for policy, left the actual conduct of foreign policy largely to Dr H.V. Evatt, the Minister for External Affairs. Evatt had an agenda which, while having clear links with the internationalist and idealist traditions of Labor thinking on international affairs, was largely his own. It brought him into frequent and sometimes sharp disagreement with the United States, and perhaps even more so with the United Kingdom, in the course of the end-of-war and post-war diplomacy dealing with the Pacific area and the early stages of the United Nations Organization. The very active Australian role up to the end of 1949 when Labor was defeated and replaced by Menzies as head of the Liberal Party in coalition with the Country Party pushed the sense of vulnerability and of dependence on the United States at least temporarily into the background.

In two respects the immediate post-war phase of Australian foreign policy, which is identified with Evatt, was reminiscent of the Hughes phase after the 1914-18 war. Evatt was a forceful, indeed aggressive, advocate for Australia at the infancy of the United Nations just as Hughes had been at the negotiations at the end of the first war. Both men were very ready to stand up to the large powers and demand that Australia's point of view be heard and respected. Again Evatt, like Hughes, was concerned to limit Japan's post-war opportunities to occupy a powerful position in the Pacific which could enable it to bear on Australia's security or other interests. But the circumstances with regard to Japan were different. Hughes had a strong sense of Australia's potential vulnerability in the face of growing Japanese power and the disposition of British policy makers to welcome a larger Pacific role for Japan. That determined his position on major issues at the Conference. Evatt no doubt also had a recognition of the potential for a resurgent Japan to cause trouble if not constrained and restricted, and he favoured a hard settlement with Japan. But by the time that issue came to a head he was already out of office. Moreover the position in terms of Australian opinion was different from that in Hughes's day. Japan had been an ally in the first war and was on good terms with Great Britain. At the end of the second war the Australian attitude towards Japan was one which could be described as hatred. Some 23,000 Australians had been prisoners of war of Japan and had been treated with brutal cruelty. Many died in captivity as a result of exploitation and maltreatment. Moreover Australia itself had for the first time in its history been directly attacked and had faced what seemed in 1942 an imminent threat of invasion by Japan. In those circumstances any Australian foreign policy would have had to take a hard line on a post war settlement with Japan[39].

In a wider sense Hughes and Evatt had radically different attitudes to foreign policy. Hughes was a classical realist, always with an eye to the power relations and sceptical of international idealism and its manifestations in the League of Nations and elsewhere. Evatt was driven by a sense of mission to contribute to the building of a new edifice of international cooperation and justice in which the small and middle sized nations would have equal voice with the big and powerful[40]. Hughes was driven by a sense of Australia's vulnerability in terms which had been present from the beginning and which persisted into the 1930s (Hancock's analysis being an example of the latter). Evatt appears not to have shared that sort of preoccupation with the vulnerability of Australia. He saw all small and medium nations as vulnerable to exploitation and injustice by big and powerful nations, whatever the latters' ideological orientation. No sense of a specifically Australian vulnerability, deriving from smallness, geographical location, cultural isolation and so on, qualified for him the overriding objective of winning acceptance for the principles and institutions which he believed would be the basis for a just and peaceful world in which human progress could flourish.

In the Australian federal elections of December 1949 the Labor Party was defeated and the Liberal-Country Party coalition came to office under the Prime Ministership of R.G. Menzies. They had a very different view of the world from Dr Evatt's and a very different view of what was the prudent and responsible foreign policy for Australia. The Coalition remained in power until 1972 and reintroduced the idea of vulnerability as one of the bases of Australian foreign policy, but for the most part in a different context from the past and with different policy consequences. It is true that, under Menzies, but mainly on the initiatives of his ministers for External Affairs, Spender and Casey, the foundations were laid for the later much more comprehensive policy of engagement with Asia[41]. However it is also clear that, especially in its early stages, the Menzies era was influenced by the sources of concern about vulnerability which, as we have seen, influenced Australian attitudes to the outside world, especially Asia, and their own situation in it up to the Second World War. Australia was seen as isolated and vulnerable, with a small population (at that time only seven million) over which loomed the huge numbers of emerging Asia[42]. The Japanese campaign, which had brought the perception of imminent invasion and the recognition that only the United States could save Australia, was fresh in Australian minds and a first priority was to ensure that Japan would never again be able to mount such a threat. But it was soon made plain to the new government in Australia that there was a deep divide between preferred United States policy on the peace settlement with Japan and what Australia saw as essential safeguards. Within less than a year the Menzies government was engaged in a difficult negotiation with the Truman administration on this issue.

Vulnerability and the Cold War Rationale

The Cold War and the Korean war now strongly influenced United States policy on Japan and when the Australian External Affairs minister P.C. Spender went to Washington in September 1950 Secretary of State Dean Acheson and the latter's Consultant, John Foster Dulles, told him that 'Japan had to be denied to the U.S.S.R. and attracted to the side of the Western democracies. The treaty accordingly should be one which would not engender Japanese resentment but rather one which would tend to attract their adherence to the Western world'. Dulles said that the Treaty of Versailles after the First World War had shown the uselessness of restrictive treaty provisions in these circumstances. Such provisions would engender resentment and hostility. 'He made it explicit – and this was to be reiterated in the Canberra discussions more than once – that the U.S.A. was not, in any case, prepared to police any such provisions – and if they were not – who, then, would be?'[43] This was a stage in what became a protracted negotiation involving also Australia's objective of a Pacific Pact which would provide a long-term assurance of United States engagement in Pacific and Australian security. Alan Renouf put the outcome with characteristic directness: 'the Pact was the price extracted by Australia and New Zealand for their acceptance of the "soft" treaty with Japan'[44]. Alan Watt, also characteristically, took a more qualified view: 'The Peace Treaty favoured by the United States would have come into existence whether or not Australia opposed it. It remained for the Australian Government to seek security by other means. By accepting a treaty which in some important respects it did not approve, Australia was able the more effectively to press the United States to agree to become a party to a security treaty designed, *inter alia*, to guarantee the territorial integrity of metropolitan Australia, and its island territories, against armed attack'[45]. In Watt's discussion of these developments he makes two other important points. One is that the Korean war changed the American view of the post-war world by bringing the focus more to Asia and the

Pacific whereas it had been heavily centred on the Atlantic, and the second is that Australia's prompt and helpful decision to give active and practical support in military terms in Korea had created a remarkably positive and favourable atmosphere for Australia in Washington. The Menzies government seized the opportunity.

The government's motivation was the perceived need to find compensating arrangements to offset Australia's vulnerability and when Spender launched his Washington campaign on these issues with a call on President Truman he 'pointed out the isolation and vulnerability of Australia in the Pacific'[46]. The negotiations which followed, and which produced the ANZUS Treaty on 1 September 1951 and the peace treaty with Japan a week later, brought a shift of focus of the idea of vulnerability in Australian foreign policy. ANZUS was not the control on Japan which Australia had wanted, but it was seen as a very valuable substitute and it gave Australia reassurance against being vulnerable and exposed again should Japan follow the example of Germany twenty years after the latter's defeat in the First World War. Uneasiness about Japan diminished steadily and especially after the signature of the Trade Agreement in 1957. Japan, which had been seen as the most likely threat to a vulnerable Australia since the latter part of the previous century, was replaced by concern about the expansion of 'international communism'.

To some extent the two things ran together because the communist threat which most directly concerned Australia was that from and through Asia. In the election campaign in December 1949 this was used by the leader of the Country Party, Arthur Fadden, who became Deputy Prime Minister in the Menzies coalition government. Campaigning for votes in North Queensland Fadden said that the recent war had proved beyond doubt the strategic importance of North Australia as a bastion of national defence and criticised the Labor government for claiming there could be no war for fifteen years while 'a major war is already raging on the battlefronts of China, where Communist forces are thrusting their Red spearpoints towards Australia'. Mr Fadden said that Labor were 'blind to the fact that advance guards of Communist forces have been extremely active in the pattern of guerilla war through Burma, Siam, Malaya and Indonesia, which has already resulted in the cold-blooded murder of Englishmen and Australians' and he claimed that 'Nobody can deny a similar fifth column is operating in Australia as part of a conspiracy for world conquest, sabotage of our industries and defence activities'[47]. Fadden's election rhetoric, with its alarmist exaggerations and McCarthyite overtones, was the product of particular circumstances rather than the considered view of the Coalition, although Fadden was of course not alone among prominent conservatives in using it[48]. But it does give the flavour of the times and it is not far from the repeatedly stated views of Menzies as Prime Minister and of other Ministers in his government. Menzies believed, as did many in the West at the time, that there was a grave danger of a third world war launched by 'international communism' and he introduced conscription for national service and provisions for Australian regular troops and volunteers to serve overseas in the 'common front against Communism'.

The Menzies government's foreign and defence policies were based on the belief that 'World Communism' was a more or less monolithic movement pursuing coordinated policies around the world in a 'cold' war to subvert and convert to communism one country after another. If at some point they assessed that the odds of winning a 'hot' war on a global scale had turned strongly in their favour they might resort to that. Australia was not under immediate direct threat, but its security depended on the overall struggle and it therefore had vital interests in Europe and the Middle East as well as nearer at hand in Korea, Malaya and the rest of South East Asia. In May 1951 Menzies told the Australian House of Representatives that it was his solemn belief that Australia had 'not a minute more than three years at the very best to be ready' for a third world war, this time against 'Imperialist Communism'. Despite these dire warnings the Menzies government showed very little urgency in terms of any practical preparations of the nation for participation in a new world war. Nor did the Prime Minister ever later explain why such a war did not eventuate. But the government's foreign policy continued to be based on fear of communist expansion.

A little over three years after Menzies' speech calling for Australia to be ready for world war in three years time, in September 1954, Australia signed the Manila Treaty establishing SEATO, the South East Asia Treaty Organization. Its genesis was a British desire to maintain a serious role in the region, having not been invited to participate in the ANZUS Treaty. The 1954 Indo-China crisis provided the opportunity to re-introduce the proposal for a NATO type organization in the region, but the South East Asia Defence Treaty which was the outcome reflected American determination to have an organization to resist communist aggression whereas the British had wanted something broader and including the non-aligned Asian states. SEATO became the institutional vehicle for much of Australia's policy in the region in what was seen as the struggle to contain the spread of communism, including communist subversion, in South East Asia. This interpretation of the political and strategic outlook for the world and the region underpinned Australian foreign policy throughout the long Menzies ascendancy in Australian politics. It was replaced by a different view when Gough Whitlam eventually brought the Labor Party to government in 1972 and it has been trenchantly criticized not only by political opponents but also by a range of others who have analyzed and commented on Australian foreign policy during that period. It is not the place here to attempt a detailed assessment of the Menzies era in Australian foreign policy. It will be necessary to comment on aspects of it in Chapter 2. What concerns us here is those aspects of Australian thinking about the nation's situation which reinforced the sense of vulnerability and isolation and, as we have noted, there was a shift in that regard as Menzies took up the reins in the early years of the Cold War. The fear of Japan was not altogether abandoned but was set aside after offsetting arrangements were made with the United States, and a new basis for concern, the perceived threat of 'Imperialist Communism' was introduced. Alan Renouf discussed this extensively in terms of the influence of fear of communism, and of the alleged global communist strategy, on Australian policy, thus the title of his book *The Frightened Country*.

As in the past, and notably with both World Wars when Great Britain itself was challenged and under threat, there were two strands to the dangers which the Menzies government saw confronting Australia. One was the danger posed by the global communist threat to the whole fabric of the world support system to which Australia adhered and on which it was seen to depend. Menzies saw this in terms primarily of the British Commonwealth, bolstered by the American alliance and all in the framework of the values and institutions which he personally valued above all else and which he saw as essentially British. If communism, led by the Soviet Union, were to triumph in the great world struggle the whole system of which Australia was a dependent part would be overturned. Secondly there was the more localized danger to Australia of the spread of communism down through South East Asia, like a series of falling dominoes on Eisenhower's analogy. Indo-China and Burma, Malaya and then Indonesia could all fall to communism leaving Australia isolated at the bottom of South East Asia with its lines of communication and its trade and political lifelines threatened.

R.G. Casey, Australia's Minister for External Affairs for most of the Menzies period produced in 1958 a widely-distributed book entitled *Friends and Neighbours*[49], sub-titled 'Australia and the World' which gives an account of the elements in the government's foreign policy. It is a valuable guide to the thinking and attitudes which influenced Australia's policy for a generation. Australia's national outlook was 'based on the fact that we are a homogeneous British community' which between the world wars came to realize that what was the Far East to London and Washington was the Near North to Australia, that Australia was a Pacific power, and that it must actively concern itself with Asia and especially South East Asia. 'We are a European community living alongside and working with Asia'. Casey's book was aimed partly at explaining and promoting the policies and activities which were aimed at building relations and 'working with Asia'. But all of that was threatened by the 'political warfare' being waged against the democracies by Russia and Communist China. It was a 'carefully thought out campaign of political warfare'. Casey discussed Korea and Indo-China in this context and Australia's position based on ANZUS and SEATO. Collective security was a major part of the defence against the spread of communism in Asia.

Casey's outlook as expressed in *Friends and Neighbours* and as advanced in his activities as Minister was in fact a rather robust one. Certainly he saw the free world, the broad association of democracies of which Australia was an integral member, as engaged in a great global struggle against communist expansion. And he saw Australia's efforts to build friendly and neighbourly relations with Asia as threatened by communist infiltration. But he thought that there were practical steps which could be taken to win those struggles and to develop for Australia a viable place in the region. He did not leave an impression of a 'Frightened Country'. Nevertheless, the world outlook and foreign policy of the Menzies Government was based on perceptions of threat, and specifically the perceived threat of communism. In that struggle Australia was vulnerable because it was isolated and relatively small. Menzies was more prone than either Spender, his first and most innovative foreign minister, or Casey, to seek to make Australian flesh creep with depictions of the dangers faced. He was also more inclined to see communism behind most of the problems of the world. As Renouf pointed out, the problems of the Middle East for example were not, as Menzies asserted, derived from communism.

At the beginning of the twenty-first century the concerns which drove Menzies and his governments in their assessments of Australian vulnerability in a threatening world may seem exaggerated and mistaken. Certainly they misunderstood the relationship between the Soviet Union and China at critical points, and they misunderstood the relationship between the Vietnamese communist leadership and the Chinese. They underestimated the role of nationalism in South East Asia and over-estimated the attraction of western values. Their policy on Indo-China and the Vietnam War is obviously open to criticism. But it remains true that the Cold War was a reality. There *was* a huge struggle in a largely bipolar world power structure for forty years and there was never any doubt as to which side the bulk of the Australian people preferred. Since that struggle was real, and since the outcome was long contested, it is understandable and indeed obvious that Australia was in some sense threatened by it. It is another matter whether conservative governments in Australia at the time well understood its subtleties and whether and how they used it somewhat crudely in domestic political terms as a weapon against the Australian Labor Party.

It is also more contested whether Australia was threatened by the possibility of South East Asia, all or much of it, coming under communist dominated governments. In retrospect the threat as depicted at the time was often exaggerated and over-simplified. But was it just chimerical? A stronger version of Renouf's 'frightened country' thesis had been presented twenty years earlier by Dr John Burton who had been Dr Evatt's Secretary of the Department of External Affairs. Burton argued that Australia had nothing to fear from Communism because it had already progressed along the road to the welfare state, had minimized economic injustice, and was able to prevent widespread unemployment. He argued that Australian fears were not really about communism but about the threat of invasion. 'In the mind of almost every Australian is the thought that one day the open spaces of the Australian continent will attract the great and rapidly growing populations of Asia which already suffer from inadequate resources' and 'Australia's fear that sooner or later the country will be invaded from Asia is the reason for its seeking American military assistance...'[50]. That fear did still exist in many Australian minds in 1954 when Burton wrote *The Alternative* from which the above statements are taken. But there was also a fear that, if South East Asia fell under communist rule, the prospect of Australia establishing friendly and neighbourly relations would be much reduced. Indeed such a South East Asia might be actively hostile. Two questions arise: was there a possibility that South East Asia would be 'taken over by communism'? And would that have constituted a threat to Australia?

The domino theory picture of the 'communist threat' to Asia and especially South East Asia, was of a high degree of coordination between the communist parties of the region so that if, for example, Vietnam became communist Cambodia and Laos would follow, and then Burma, Malaya, and Indonesia. The extent of coordination was exaggerated and communism proved to be far less contagious in the region than was feared to be the case in the 1950s and 1960s. But it did seem to have powerful momentum through its organizational advantages, its nationalist credentials in some countries and its appeal to the exploited, landless or other potential beneficiaries from its proclaimed policies. In Indonesia for example, the case of most immediate interest to Australia, the Communist Party, the PKI, by the 1960s had a claimed membership of some six million with a network of associated organizations for farmers, journalists, students, and so on. The PKI had strong links with the Chinese party and government, as well as with other regional parties and it was becoming increasingly influential with the President, Sukarno. In the climate of the times it would have been impossible for an Australian government not to look uneasily at these developments. There did seem to be a possibility that South East Asia, or important parts of it, would be taken over by communism. As to whether that would have constituted a threat to Australia it was reasonable for the government to conclude that communist neighbours would feel antipathy towards a capitalist, European-populated ally of the United States and would in various ways at least make life difficult and uncomfortable for Australia. In the context of the bipolar world of the Cold War there was also the fear that such a development would bring to Australia's borders the influence and reach of the Soviet Union or perhaps China, stirring both current and ancient anxieties.

To make these points is not to defend but to seek to explain. The anti-communist orientation of the foreign and security policies of Australian conservative governments from 1949 to 1972 can easily be criticized especially in the light of what we now know. But they were more plausible in the context of the times, reflected some reasonable concerns, and drew also on long-standing fears about Australia's isolation, relative size and potential vulnerability.

By the time the Labor Party election victory in 1972 eventually ended 23 years of Liberal-led Coalition government, the picture of the world which had driven Australian foreign and defence policy since 1949 had lost plausibility and indeed viability. Post Vietnam, post Sukarno, with communism now perceived to be not monolithic but with major differences between Moscow and Beijing, the times required an extensive revision of Australian policy. Under the last and least effective of the Liberals who succeeded Menzies before the Labor victory in 1972, William McMahon, Australia had been embarrassingly left behind by the United States shift of policy towards China. Indeed United States policy in the region was in the process of major change, especially after President Nixon on Guam in 1969 proclaimed that the United States would now expect regional countries to look after their own defence, looking to the United States only if threatened by the other superpower.

In 1972 Gough Whitlam came into office as Labor Prime Minister with the intention of revolutionizing Australia's view of the world, of the neighbouring region, and of Australia's place in both. The appeal to Australian vulnerability as a justification for close adherence to United States policy was dropped and, to the extent that vulnerability figured at all, it was rather in the sense that Australia must resist exploitation by powerful American and other western commercial interests.

Whitlam ended Australia's involvement in Vietnam, opened diplomatic relations with China, and sought a closer relationship with President Soeharto of

Indonesia. Whitlam and his colleagues sought to approach all foreign policy issues from an independent Australian perspective rather than from the perspective of a loyal ally of the United States engaged in a team effort to oppose 'world communism' led by the Soviet Union, the perspective that had often characterized the Liberal-Coalition governments which had been in power for the previous 23 years. The sense of vulnerability which had always influenced Australians' views of their place in the world was much less prominent under Whitlam. While he acknowledged the value of the alliance relationship with the United States he also appeared to have much sympathy for the non-aligned nations and took Australia some way in their direction. Whitlam was much less doctrinally and diplomatically opposed to the Soviet Union than his Liberal Party predecessors and successors. There was a sense in much of the Labor movement, shared by some members of the Whitlam government, that communism was a legitimate alternative to the system which we in Australia preferred. He formally recognized Soviet sovereignty over the occupied Baltic States.

Whitlam was displaced by Malcolm Fraser and another Liberal-coalition government in 1975. Fraser returned to the Cold War alliance with the United States as the central feature of Australian foreign and defence policy. But he was different from all of his Liberal predecessors in his sense of solidarity with the third world of developing and largely non-aligned states. He shared their view that, as commodity producers, they were exploited by the leading industrialized powers and he had sympathy for their efforts to climb out of poverty by achieving a better deal in world trade and finance. But he was strongly anti-communist and was in no doubt of the need to resist the Soviet Union. For example he took a very strong line against the Soviet incursion into Afghanistan and in protest largely prevented Australian participation in the Moscow Olympic Games in 1980.

Fraser's sense of Australia's vulnerability had a somewhat different focus from that of the Liberal Prime Minister Sir Robert Menzies who dominated Australian politics from 1949 to 1968 and in whose last government he served as Minister for the Army. For Fraser there was for Australia not only the threat of international communism. There was the danger that the intransigence of the major industrial powers, and especially the Western Europeans in the European Economic Community, would prevent or fail to promote the development of the poor countries of the world. The outcome would be chronic discontent and instability which would endanger Australia. To Fraser the world was a threatening place for Australia and he sought to ameliorate that by trying unsuccessfully to persuade the EEC to change its protectionist policies particularly in agriculture, by standing firmly with the United States against the Soviet Union and by seeking to forge links with the Third World countries, including China. But these elements did not cohere into a productive whole, partly because the Third World was so influenced at the time by anti-capitalist and anti-United States thinking and, on much of the Fraser agenda, more closely aligned to the Soviet Union than to the West.

Although Fraser was a conservative and strongly anti-communist there was a sense in which he echoed Evatt's belief that Australia's interests lay in exercising a vigorous role with the emerging nations. He seemed to feel more solidarity with the African and Asian developing countries than with the Europeans or Americans.

But his policies did not succeed in finding a solution to the Australian search for a place to belong, nor a salve for the sense of isolation, of being out of our proper context in an unfamiliar world. The attempt to make a break with the past and strike out towards a different future was to follow under Labor which displaced the Fraser-led Coalition government in 1983.

Notes

1. See for example Jones, Roger, McAllister, Ian, Gow, David (1996), *Australian Election Study, 1996* [computer file], Social Science Data Archives, The Australian National University, Canberra. Also subsequent election studies from SSDA.
2. Walker, David (1999), *Anxious Nation: Australia and the Rise of Asia 1850-1939*, University of Queensland Press, St Lucia, p. 231.
3. Levi, Werner (1958), *Australia's Outlook on Asia*, Angus and Robertson, Sydney, p. 69. Levi also wrote *American Australian Relations*, University of Minnesota Press, Minneapolis, 1947.
4. A report was prepared by Severin Rakowski (the author's great grandfather) and sent to the Colonial Secretary for transmission to London
5. Walker, *op. cit.* p. 113.
6. *Ibid.*
7. New South Wales, *Parliamentary Debates, Legislative Assembly*, Vol. XXXII, pp. 3787-8, reproduced in Meaney, Neville (1985), *Australia and the World: A Documentary History from the 1870s to the 1970s*, Longman Cheshire, Melbourne, pp. 93-5.
8. Text in Meaney, *ibid.*, pp. 96-9.
9. See Meaney, *ibid.*, pp. 108-12 for full text and for text of Treaty.
10. *Ibid.*, p. 108.
11. *Ibid.*, p. 122 for text from which the extracts here are quoted.
12. Millar, T.B. in *Australia in Peace and War*, Australian National University Press, Canberra, 1978, pp. 47-8, quotes a relevant letter from Kato Takaaki, the Japanese Minister in London, to Lord Salisbury in 1897 which Millar reproduces from a paper by D.C.S. Sissons, 'Immigration in Australian-Japanese Relations 1891-1971' published in J.A.A. Stockwin (ed.), *Japan and Australia in the Seventies*, p. 194: 'The point which had caused a painful feeling in Japan was not that the operation of the prohibition would be such as to exclude a certain number of Japanese from immigrating to Australia, but that Japan should be spoken of in formal documents, such as Colonial Acts, as f the Japanese were on the same level of morality and civilisation as Chinese and other less advanced populations of Asia'.
13. Meaney, *op. cit.* p. 125.
14. See Walker, *op. cit.* Chapter 7.
15. Horne, Donald (1964), *The Lucky Country*, Penguin, Adelaide, p. 127. Horne records that the slogan had already been reduced to the first five words when he got rid of it altogether on becoming editor of the 'Bulletin' in 1960.
16. Walker, *op. cit.* p. 94.
17. Meaney, *op. cit.* p. 174.
18. Meaney, *op. cit.* p. 173.
19. Hancock, W.K. (1945), *Australia*, Ernest Benn, Sydney, p. 203. (The first edition was published in London in 1930.)
20. *Ibid.*, p. 202.

21 *Ibid.*, p. 219.
22 Returned Soldiers', Sailors' and Airmen's Imperial League of Australia.
23 Edwards, P.G. (1983), *Prime Ministers & Diplomats*, Oxford University Press, Melbourne, p. 53.
24 *Ibid.*, p. 54.
25 *Ibid.*, p. 55.
26 *Ibid.*, p. 67.
27 Millar, *op. cit.* p. 56, summarises his account of the Australian reaction as follows: 'The Australian position over Manchuria was thus a triumph of immediate self-interest and pusillanimity over principles of any kind, of political and economic appeasement'.
28 See Meaney, *op. cit.* pp. 388-90.
29 *Ibid.*, p. 391.
30 *Ibid.*, p. 397.
31 Hughes wrote in 1935 'With our small population, our great territories, our far-flung coast-line, we are of all nations in the Pacific the most vulnerable and the most open to attack. Yet although other Pacific nations are armed to the teeth, we are practically defenceless...'. Meaney, *op. cit.* p. 399.
32 *Ibid.*, p. 465.
33 *Ibid.*, p. 466.
34 See Watt, Alan (1967), *The Evolution of Australian Foreign Policy 1938-1965*, Cambridge University Press, pp. 53-4. Watt gives an excellent succinct account of the issue of Australian concerns about Singapore and about British intentions and capacities including the matter of the 'Beat Hitler First' strategy.
35 *Ibid.*, p. 53.
36 The first of these comprised 81 medium bombers, 71 dive bombers and 36 fighters and the second, two hours later, comprised 54 land based bombers. The shipping in the harbour was destroyed, as were 23 Australian aircraft, and the town was shattered.
37 Menzies had stepped down in favour of the Country Party leader, A.W. Fadden, on 28 August 1941 but the Government was defeated in the Parliament during discussion on the Budget and Curtin, as leader of the Labor Party, was commissioned to form a government on 3 October.
38 Meaney, *op. cit.* pp. 473-4.
39 Watt, *op. cit.* p. 211, leaves no doubt of Evatt's strong commitment to a 'rigid' Australian commitment to ensuring 'that Japan should never again have the capacity to commit another act of aggression' and records that in the Far Eastern Commission, and through his representative on the Allied Council in Tokyo, Evatt had no hesitation in opposing strongly (less rigid) American policy towards Japan. But Evatt's position was modified after a visit to Tokyo in 1947 as guest of General MacArthur.
40 See Chapter Two.
41 This became an issue in the 1996 election and subsequently between the Labor Party and the Coalition with each claiming the foundation stones of Australian policy towards Asia. Labor emphasized Evatt's role in Indonesia's independence and in the General Assembly and contrasted that with Menzies. The Liberals emphasized Spender's initiative with the Colombo Plan and Casey's Asian diplomacy. Labor had apparently intended to name the new building of the Department of Foreign Affairs and Trade 'Evatt House' but when the Coalition won the election in 1996 Casey's name was substituted for that of Evatt and the opening ceremony, addressed

by Howard and Downer place the Liberals' stamp on the policy as well as on the building.

42 See, for a succinct contemporary statement of 'The strategic factors upon which [Australia's] existence depend' the essay 'Foreign Policy' by Sir Frederic Eggleston (who had been Australian Minister to China and to the United States and had a long and influential involvement in Australian foreign policy) which was published as Chapter IX of Grattan, C. Hartley (ed.) (1947), *Australia*, University of California Press, Berkeley and Los Angeles, p. 135.
43 Meaney, *op. cit.*, p. 569 from Sir Percy Spender, *Exercises in Diplomacy*.
44 Renouf, Alan (1979), *The Frightened Country*, Macmillan, Melbourne, p. 93.
45 Watt, *op. cit.* p. 123.
46 Spender, Percy (1967), *Exercises in Diplomacy*, Sydney, p. 40.
47 *The Sydney Morning Herald* report, 6 December 1949, in Meaney, *op. cit.* p. 596.
48 See for example the Liberal Party's election publicity in 1966 reproduced in Meaney, *op. cit.* p. 698.
49 Casey, R.G. (1958), *Friends and Neighbors*, Michigan State University Press, East Lansing. The book was in fact largely written by James Plimsoll (later Secretary of the Department of Foreign Affairs).
50 Meaney, *op. cit.* p. 590.

Chapter 2

Approaching an Independent Australian Foreign and Defence Policy

Independent Australian Britons

Even before the federation of the British colonies to create the Commonwealth of Australia in 1901 there was a strongly emerging sense of independent Australian foreign policy concerns which were different from, and at times at odds with, those of the imperial government in London. These arose largely from the sense of vulnerability explored in the previous chapter. Especially as expressed frequently from the early 1890s by Henry Parkes, the Premier of New South Wales, there were concerns that the British government was not making sufficient provision for the security of its Australian colonies in the face of interest in the region by other European imperial powers, and potentially by Japan. There was also an acute concern to ensure the preservation of the British composition of the population and prevent the establishment of an Asian component in it. For the British government, which had other interests to pursue with China and Japan, it was an unwelcome inconvenience to receive protests and representations against this discrimination from the governments of the affected major Asian powers. These nineteenth century concerns produced assertions of an independent Australian point of view and independent Australian interests at variance with imperial policies, while at the same time emphasizing the strongest possible attachment to the British composition of the population and the British character of the Australian colonies. It was a dichotomy which produced in time a qualified and curtailed nationalism. The Australians wanted to have and to be seen to have their own voice, and they had an increasingly vigorous sense of their separate identity. But that identity was asserted as a *British* identity and the assertion of their own interests took the form of assertion of the rights and interests of loyal *British* subjects.

That Australian sense of being British was widespread even up to the Second World War, and indeed beyond. It is often discussed, for example in the context of the attitudes and policies of Australia's longest-serving Prime Minister, R.G. Menzies, in terms of an *attachment* to Britain. But such a formulation conveys an impoverished impression of the relationship as it was felt by many Australians who actually saw themselves as British. They felt themselves to be at once British and Australian. It could be said that Americans of British stock also might have seen themselves both as British and as citizens of the United States. But Australians saw both their immediate Australian identity and a British one as having the quality of continuing membership of a society or a nation. They had British passports and saw themselves as subjects of the British monarch. Their institutions were close derivatives of British models. Most of them saw Australia as an offshoot of Britain which had Britain at its core even when they were conscious of quite sharp differences between Britain and an Australia which, during the latter part of the nineteenth century and the first part of the twentieth. had developed strong distinctive characteristics.

Already before the 1914-18 war some of those distinctive characteristics had been recorded, and in some cases celebrated, in a nascent Australian literature and were part of the common discourse of ordinary Australians. But the war sharpened that awareness and added to it an enhanced sense of pride and confidence. About half a million Australians in a population of less than five million served in the armed forces. If it had not been for the war few of them would ever have left Australia's shores. The war placed them in a position to compare themselves with officers and men from Britain itself and reinforced their sense of difference. They were indeed different in obvious ways. It struck them immediately that in general they were physically larger. They then soon became aware that the British army reflected quite sharply the stratifications of a traditional European society in which the officers appeared often to be almost of a different race from the other ranks. In this regard the Australian army was very different. Independent observers as well as the Australians themselves believed that their more egalitarian and less hierarchical army generated greater initiative and drive than was the case in the British army. What they saw of the British army grated on the democratic and levelling values which were distinctive and highly valued features of life in Australia. Throughout the war there were disciplinary problems where Australian troops were expected to conform to British standards of deference to officers and adherence to rules with regard to saluting and such matters which to many Australians seemed to be irrelevant to performance. This became part of the Australian folk memory of the war, as well as of the historical record[1].

But for all that they did not cease to see themselves as British, albeit a special (and improved) sort of British. W.K. Hancock addressed this matter of the increasing sense of Australian nationalism which seemed able to coexist with a firm continuing sense of Britishness and attachment to Britain. The nationalism had emerged he thought largely from the earlier 'struggle between the landless majority and the land-monopolising squatters' who were backed by London banks. Nevertheless 'Among the Australians pride of race counted for more than love of country...Defining themselves as "independent Australian Britons" they believed each word essential and exact, but laid most stress upon the last'[2]. The experience of Australians in the 1914-18 war, the enhancement of Australia's reputation through a war in which the AIF (Australian Imperial Force) performed with distinction, and of the subsequent peace negotiations, in which the then Prime Minister, W.M. Hughes, robustly pushed what were conceived to be Australian interests in New Guinea, the South Pacific and especially with regard to Japan, all strengthened the Australian sense of nationhood. But they did not produce a more assertive separate Australian foreign policy. Australian foreign policy from the time of the peace settlement after the war up to the outbreak of the Second World War seldom diverged from that of Great Britain. And when it did the reason was usually to be found in Australian security concerns especially as Japan took on an expansionist role and developed a formidable strategic capacity. On most international matters the Australians saw themselves as British and were content to let decisions be made in London. But where the issues involved the Pacific and the region of Australian strategic concern they asserted Australian interests and made sure that they were heard.

During the inter-war years Australia urged the British government to maintain and develop a capacity to defend its possessions in East Asia and to defend Australia, but Australia's voice was still directed to London and little heard elsewhere. It was not until January 1940 that Australia opened its first independent diplomatic representation in a foreign capital when R.G. Casey was appointed Australian Minister in Washington. Although Deakin and others had at times made representations in Washington, Australia had lacked the machinery, in the form of a foreign ministry, to take a substantial role in international affairs. But that changed rapidly at the end of the war when Australia took a very active role in the new United Nations Organization and set up a network of representation in other countries.

To look back on the Australia of the 1930s and 1940s is to recall a time when Britain was the most important overseas influence on the Australian economy, when very few Australians had family names which did not stem from Britain or Ireland[3], and when indeed Australia was in some ways still a province of Britain. Although Britain was far away it was near in felt affinities including those of race and family, and in terms of the attention which was paid to it. My recollection of the conversation of my parents and their friends when I was a child are of some scepticism and complaints about Britain but at the same time an assumption that Australia was indissolubly tied to Britain. There was certainly a strong racial quality to this – the sense of being of British race and the sense that Australia must resist any intrusion of other races. My recollections of school days reinforce that. It was only with the big immigration program from Europe after the war that the complete dominance of the British influence on and British character of Australia began to be modified.

Shortly after the war, and before the immigration program had introduced many non-British into the population, a nation-wide Gallup Poll was held on the question: 'Do you think we should continue to have British nationality – or would you prefer separate Australian nationality'? The poll was held twice (with the same question), in June 1946 and in November/December 1947. On the latter occasion the results were as follows[4]:

Want British Nationality:	65%
Prefer Australian:	28%
No Opinion:	7%

In 1947 Australia was far more British than any of the other former British colonies with the exception of New Zealand. The ruling white race in South Africa comprised descendants of Dutch settlers as well as British[5], and in Canada there was a substantial minority of people descended from the original French colonists who remained attached to their French roots and language.

Australians' feeling of identity with Britain seems not to have been much if at all diminished by the events of 1942 touched on in the previous chapter, although as we shall see that period affected the quality of the relationship in the foreign policy context. The continuation after the war of the sense of identity with Britain may be attributable partly to admiration for the British role in the victory over Germany and a sense of shared triumph when the long war was brought to an end with the surrender of Germany and then of Japan. Australians identified strongly with the British especially in 1940 and 1941 when they had stood alone after the fall of Europe and had fought and won the Battle of Britain, defeating the Luftwaffe and frustrating Hitler's plans to invade Britain.

The apogee of what Hancock saw as the Australian sense of themselves as 'independent Australian Britons' came during the early period of the war when the Australian Prime Minister tried hard to influence the course of British policy on the future of Europe and of the Empire and indeed appears to have seen himself as a prospective replacement for the Conservative Prime Minister, Neville Chamberlain, and later as a rival to Churchill himself. In 1939 and early 1940 the Australian Prime Minister, R.G. Menzies, and the High Commissioner in London, S.M. Bruce, argued strongly against the Churchill policy of refusal to contemplate further attempts to appease Hitler. Menzies strongly opposed Churchill's policy and rhetoric of resolute defiance of Hitler at a time when there was still considerable support for a negotiated peace. There was support in the country and in the Conservative party for the ageing Lloyd George, who was in a deeply pessimistic frame of mind about the outlook for the prosecution of the war and was talking of a negotiated peace[6]. Less than three months before Churchill became Prime Minister Menzies described Churchill as a 'menace' who 'stirs up hatreds in a world already seething with them and he is lacking in judgement...'[7]. According to David Day in his book *Menzies and Churchill at War*, Churchill was already exasperated with Menzies before the fall of Chamberlain and Churchill's elevation to Prime Minister. But Day's work appears to show that the relationship developed a degree of acerbity which had at its base a disagreement about grand strategy. Churchill's tendency to embark on risky and inadequately considered ventures, and to fail to consult the Australian Prime Minister, seems to have played a part in the tensions which developed between the two. Day suggests that defence of Australian interests shaded across into advancement of other more personal agenda. But clearly it was, in the context of the times, perfectly natural and expected for the Prime Minister of Australia to play a role in the determination of the greater strategy especially on the great issue of whether the British Empire should insist on a war to the end in which Germany would surrender or whether there should be attempts to negotiate a settlement with Germany (that is essentially a continuation of the Chamberlain policy). Menzies saw the maintenance of the Empire as the most important strategic goal whereas for Churchill the over-riding goal was the defeat of Hitler.

In all of this Menzies saw himself as British, as a leader fitted and entitled to participate in the politics and strategy of Britain at the highest level, while at the same time remaining Australian. Within the category of 'independent Australian Briton', a national characterization which seems remote indeed at the beginning of the twenty-first century, there was a wide range or spectrum with Menzies at the British end of the spectrum but nevertheless a very recognizable Australian type. In Hancock's terms Menzies was certainly one of those Australians for whom 'pride of race', that is to say being British, 'counted for more than love of country'. A problem for those who shared Menzies' outlook was that it was not satisfactorily reciprocated. This was to be sharply demonstrated in 1942, and then increasingly after the war as Britain shifted gradually more and more towards identity with the rising movement for Western European cooperation and solidarity. There were Australians who went to Britain and became absorbed in British life and work at very high and influential levels. But on the whole the British establishment saw Australians as provincials and did not admit them to the inner councils of policy making.

Despite the problems between Menzies and Churchill, during the Battle for Britain the Australian sense of solidarity with Britain was strong. And despite the strains on the relationship at government level at the end of 1941 and in 1942 much of that sense of solidarity was preserved so that at the end of the war Australia still saw itself as British. But by then Australia was at least in partial remission from its sense of vulnerability and the perceived constraints on its independence had, in consequence, diminished.

The Great Pacific War and its Aftermath

Australia's experiences in the Second World War did not have the heroic, albeit grievous, resonance of those of the 1914-18 war which gave the country its sense of proud nationhood. The last years of the twentieth century saw a remarkable welling up of Australian feeling about the Australian participation in the 1914-18 war. Young people were going in large numbers to Gallipoli in Turkey to attend the dawn service of remembrance on Anzac Day, 25 April[8]. All over the country the Anzac Day ceremonies were attracting greater participation and interest than for many years. More Australians than ever before made the pilgrimage (as it is frequently called in the media) to the battlefields in France where Australia's army fought with great distinction and where many thousands lie in war cemeteries. There is also renewed interest in the Kokoda Track and the fighting in New Guinea in the Second World War; but that has not generated the reverence which is being shown to the first AIF and its deeds. Perhaps something similar will develop in regard to the Second war, and perhaps the greatly increased interest in the First World War is related to the fact that (in 2001) there is only a handful of survivors left.

There are indeed notable World War II Australian actions to remember. But the brave, though despairing, stands in Greece and on Crete, for example, which share with the Gallipoli episode the fact that they failed, seem unlikely ever to be seen in the same light as the ANZAC campaign. No doubt that is partly because Gallipoli came first and has a place in Australian history which no later event could rival. And no doubt the remoter event is always easier to mythologize.

To suggest that there has been an element of mythologizing in the view of Australia's participation in World War I which has led to such a resurgence of interest in recent years is not to suggest that there have been major exaggerations of the quality of Australia's performance or that pride in that performance is misplaced. But the popular view does contain some over-simplification and some exaggeration. For example, while it is true that the Gallipoli landings were mismanaged, the evidence does not suggest that the Australian commanders in that campaign were better than their British counterparts, even though it is the popular Australian view that the dashing and gallant Australians were let down by incompetent British commanders. And it was not until 1917-18 that the Australians established themselves as superior on the Western Front. The performance of the four[9] Australian divisions in 1916 was mixed, but was not helped by abject British leadership in their two principal actions, Fromelles and Pozieres, where their casualties were enormous. Two of the division commanders (Legge and M'Cay) were relieved of their commands. By 1918, when the leadership of the higher command was more professional and sounder, the battlefield performance of all five divisions was universally acclaimed as outstanding. By war's end the two Australian corps commanders, Monash in France and Chauvel in Palestine, were unsurpassed on the Allied side[10].

In World War II, not least because the conflict was being fought on a much larger and more diverse number of battlefronts, popular attention in Australia was never concentrated in one or two areas as it had been in the previous war. For that and other reasons, outstanding figures, such as Monash and Chauvel had been in the First World War, did not emerge with the same clarity, although by the end of the war the performance of commanders like Morshead, Vasey and Lavarack was of a similar standard.

But in the 1939-45 war there were Australian feats of arms which are now taking a place in the popular memory to match those of the 1914-18 war, for example the siege of Tobruk and the fighting on the Kokoda Track which eventually (after some anxious times) turned back the Japanese push on Port Moresby. The Australian troops at their best were widely acknowledged to be very good. It was because of the quality of the Ninth Division that the British sought so strongly to dissuade Curtin from bringing it back to the South West Pacific theatre before the battle of El Alamein. Their performance in that crucial battle justified the importance attached to their participation on the allied side. As soon as victory was assured the British commander, Bernard Montgomery, went to the headquarters of General Morshead the commander of the Ninth Division to thank him for what his troops had done[11]. They covered for the shortcomings of others and took as many casualties as the whole of Montgomery's Tenth Corps. The Australians did not always have such satisfactory relations with British commanders in North Africa and there was a strong view that in the Mediterranean theatre, where the Australians made a large contribution early in the war, the British passed over more experienced and competent Australian senior officers for appointment to top command positions in favour of less well-qualified British regular officers[12]. But lack of appreciation by the senior ally was to become a far greater problem with General MacArthur and his headquarters in the Pacific campaign.

El Alamein was a victory, and a famously important one. But the Australians had been involved in major reverses in the previous year, in Greece and Crete. It is questionable whether Menzies should have agreed to provide troops for the Greek campaign given the expectation that it could not be won against such odds, including in the air. Even more questionable was the decision to agree to the rearguard action in Crete. These were major strategic decisions by an Australian government which had the independence and the standing to take a firm position against the British Prime Minister on the issues. Certainly a decision by Menzies not to make Australian forces available for Greece and Crete would have had very adverse consequences on his relationship with Churchill who was personally attached to the project. And an Australian Prime Minister at the time would have had in mind that there was a looming possibility of Australia coming under threat should Japan enter the war. Then Australia, in its turn, would want to call on British help, although the extent of such help in Britain's then circumstances would have been limited and indeed was very limited when the time came in 1942[13]. Nevertheless it is surprising that the Australian government did not take a more robust and more *independent* stand on the matter even if it had in the end acceded to the British request.

As Australian concerns about the outlook in the Pacific deepened, and with troops including some who had recently been engaged in Greece and Crete now fighting in Syria, the Australian government recognized that the British were in no position to strengthen Malaya or send more supplies to Australia. In September 1941 the British were expressing optimism about Japanese intentions despite the available evidence[14]. The relationship was approaching a watershed. Menzies as Australian Prime Minister had asserted independence of Churchill's line on negotiations with Germany and had done so as of right as a leader of the British empire not just as the leader of a country that was itself under direct threat and imminently vulnerable. Now matters were to move quickly closer to home.

When a Labor government under John Curtin took office in Australia on 3 October 1941 it was still unclear whether or when Japan would launch new offensives or whether those offensives would be such as to bring on intervention in the war by the United States. The Japanese attack on Pearl Harbor on 7 December 1941 resolved these uncertainties and the following Japanese southward thrust also resolved the question whether the British navy and the Singapore strategy would be able to hold the Japanese at bay in South East Asia and the approaches to Australia. In September 1939 Australia had been remarkably ill-prepared for war. For most of the period since the First World War nearly two thirds of Australia's annual defence budget had been used for the navy, to the neglect of the other two services[15]. When the first regular army division was formed in 1939 it was numbered the Sixth, because on paper there were five militia or home defence divisions. After the war broke out in September 1939 Australia committed itself to a British scheme which in effect meant that Australia's military aviation capacity was developed mainly for service in the European theatre rather than for service in the RAAF in Australia and the Pacific theatre. The ships of the Royal Australian Navy were deployed in various places under the direction of the Royal Navy. Successive Australian governments had accepted the British strategy of using the Royal Navy and the Singapore base to contain Japan and protect Australia. Increasing scepticism had not produced any Australian alternative and when the Japanese struck there was little Australian capacity to protect Australia or the approaches to Australia.

Throughout 1941 Australia watched uneasily as Britain and the United States took various steps which were far from reassuring in the light of the ascendancy of the war party under General Tojo in Japan. United States naval deployments reduced its forces in the Western Pacific, and the United States and Britain were unwilling to combine to deter Japan from moving south on Thailand or British or Dutch possessions in South East Asia. Eventually on 2 December the United States gave Churchill an assurance to that effect[16]. On 8 December the Japanese landed troops at Kota Bharu in Malaya and at two points in Thailand. At that stage the Australians had two brigades of the Eighth Division in Malaya and three divisions, the Sixth, Seventh and Ninth, in the Mediterranean theatre. Churchill raised the question whether one of the Australian divisions should be sent to Singapore. This precipitated discussion which produced a decision on 5 January 1942 that both the Sixth and Seventh should be sent to the Far East. While they were still en route the Japanese swept through Malaya, took Singapore, and were poised to seize the Netherlands East Indies (NEI)[17]. At this point there occurred a major dispute between Churchill and Curtin about the deployment of the First Australian Corps (including the Sixth and Seventh Divisions). D.M. Horner describes it as the Australian government's 'most notable disagreement with the direction of allied strategy' and as 'the most important example of the way in which Australia could, if only in a negative fashion, influence allied strategy'[18].

On 14 February Wavell, the allied commander, and Lavarack the commander of the First Australian Corps, with the first ship carrying the Australians from the Middle East soon to arrive, sent appreciations and recommendations that the Australians not be landed in the NEI. Wavell suggested that they be diverted to Burma or Australia. On 15 February Singapore fell and the Australian Chiefs of Staff recommended that all the troops on the way from the Middle East be diverted to Australia. Curtin accepted that recommendation, sent a cable to Churchill asking that it be implemented, and it was confirmed as government policy at a War Cabinet meeting on 18 February.

Churchill however saw the Australians as the only available force which could be deployed to reach Rangoon in time to seek to prevent its capture by the Japanese and on 20 February he gave instructions for the convoy carrying the Australians to alter course for Burma. For the Australian government this was a particularly critical time. Darwin had been subjected to massive bombing attacks on 19 February and the Japanese landed in Koepang and Dili in Timor on 20 February. Ambon had already been taken, as had Rabaul. In both places and in West Timor the three Australian battalions had been heavily outnumbered and had given up the fight after brief resistance. There followed an exchange of cables in which Curtin insisted that the convoy come on to Australia but sweetened the pill for Churchill by agreeing that two of the three brigades of the Sixth Division be diverted to bolster the defence of Ceylon.

In effect Curtin had his way, asserting Australian independence at least to the extent of deciding in what theatre his land forces should be used. But even at that time the Australian navy was still effectively under the direction of the British admiralty and most of what Australia could contribute to the air war was under the control of the Royal Air Force and deployed far from its homeland which was virtually defenceless against the formidable Japanese air power.

The fall of Singapore was a major turning-point. It had been the key to the British Empire strategy to protect the approaches to Australia and the Dominion itself. It had been the subject of repeated assurances by British political and military leaders over the years in the face of Australian concerns about the adequacy of the resources provided and the effectiveness of the strategy itself. A particular Australian concern was the inadequacy of the air defences. The RAF and the smaller RAAF contingent had only 158 front line aircraft with 88 in reserve in Malaya and Singapore and these were slower, less well armed and less manoeuvrable than the Japanese aircraft despite British assurances to the contrary[19]. The Australian front line squadrons were equipped with the inadequate Brewster Buffalo fighters[20] and Lockheed Hudson bombers. The commander of the Australian Eighth division, Major-General Bennett, had warned before the Japanese attack about the inadequacy of air defence of Malaya and Singapore and had said that he feared 'another Crete', that is a situation where the Australian army was left exposed to enemy air attack with no friendly air cover. Events rapidly proved him right. Churchill had sent out the newest British battleship, *Prince of Wales* and a battle cruiser, *Repulse*, which were quickly sunk by air attacks while attempting to stop Japanese landings, and by the second day of the fighting one third of the British aircraft were already out of service. From then on the Japanese were virtually unchallenged in the air over Malaya and Singapore and the defenders on the ground were exposed to constant harassment from above.

It is rare in the history of warfare for a smaller attacking force to overcome with ease a more numerous defending force; but that is what happened in Malaya, and Singapore which the British had claimed to be impregnable held out for only seven days. Australian historians and military analysts have pointed out that the British generalship and performance in the campaign were very poor and that the Australians took the largest number of casualties, suggesting that they did the bulk of what fighting was done by the defenders. There were actions in which the Australians performed well but no-one claims that this was a proud chapter in Australian military history. It was such an ineffectual performance overall that it would be difficult for any of the national contingents to avoid some loss of reputation. An Australian historian, John Robertson, called it 'the most humiliating defeat in [British] history' and argued that 'Because Britain had military and political responsibility, the explanation for this spectacular disaster belongs to British rather than to Australian history'[21]. But why did not Australia make a more determined and timely effort to persuade the British political and military leaderships to develop more effective defence planning and provision for Malaya and Singapore[22]? The planning appears to have been feeble and its execution worse. The air defence was obsolete and grossly inadequate, and some of the British-officered Indian units appear to have lacked the will to fight (although others performed well). Australia seems not to have been well informed about the internal situation in any detail, having appointed a Trade Commissioner rather than a political or military officer to represent it on the War Council the British established in Singapore[23]. The answer to the above question is presumably that Australian foreign and defence policy was still seen, including by Australian governments, as essentially subsumed by British Empire policy with the result that Australia was not expected to exercise significant independent influence. For many years the Australians had been querying the blue water, Singapore strategy – always being reassured that it was workable and reliable. That this was accepted points to a failure of Australian political leadership, especially given the dominant British presence in the Australian defence establishment at the time.

Finally the Malaya campaign cannot be left without mentioning other specifically Australian controversial aspects. General Bennett, the Australian commander, has been criticized not only for aspects of his leadership during the campaign but also for avoiding capture and making his way back to Australia instead of staying with his men. (He was the most senior officer of the Empire forces to escape). The other is the controversy about the role of Bennett's Australian Eighth Division in the defence of Singapore. Bennett's bad relations with the British commanders (and with nearly everyone else) and his planned decision to depart Singapore rather than be captured no doubt have contributed to the version of events propagated in some British circles[24]: that the Australians caved in on Singapore even before the Japanese assault and so ensured the collapse of the island stronghold. Australian opinion on the other hand was that Australia had been fobbed off for years by a British Singapore strategy which was fatally flawed, never taken seriously by Britain itself and, faced with the Japanese attack, left in the hands of incompetent leadership. The most authoritative and perhaps the most objective account of these matters, by a Canadian professor of military history at the National University of Singapore, Brian P. Farrell[25], notes that 'The Australians accused the British of deceiving them over the "Singapore Strategy", and thus their security against Japan, by covering up the risk they took in grand strategy to leave the area so weak. Now some Britons replied that the final defence of the island was fatally compromised by the collapse of the Australian division relied on to bear the brunt'. Farrell shows that the Australians did not cause the collapse of the defence by abandoning their positions before the major assault. He dismisses Peter Elphick's account and its most damaging indictment of the Australians. But he concludes that 'Nevertheless, the division did indeed fall apart in the end because it did not bring the straggler problem under control. From 10 through 12 February mass straggling turned into mass desertion, and only a rump formation fought in the final perimeter'. Farrell shows that the Australian official war history was disposed to cover up the breakdown of order and the incidence of indiscipline and panic at the end. It is a sorry story but his conclusion is that the blame for the Australian collapse rests on command failures: 'The GOC was barely functioning, looking instead to escape. One brigadier was defeatist. The other made plans based on the assumption the main plan would not succeed. The rank and file...could not have failed to note the attitudes of their commanders and the lack of clear direction and harmony in the chain of command'[26]. Sixty years later the subject is still sensitive enough to constrain critical and open discussion in Australia. Perhaps that will continue to be the case as long as the survivors of the Japanese captivity in which most of the Eighth Division spent the rest of the war are still alive. But it would be prudent for Australians to study dispassionately the various lessons in this sad chapter of their history. It should not be mythologized as a triumph over adversity by the Australian spirit and its code of mateship. No doubt there were elements of that both in the brief campaign and in the suffering of the Australians who endured the subsequent long captivity. But the whole thing was a disaster.

Curtin said the fall of Singapore had opened the battle for Australia. It is understandable that he would want to put behind as soon as possible a shattering defeat, humiliating surrender, and the capture of most of the Australian Eighth Division. At the turn of the year he had said that he looked to the United States as Australia's primary strategic partner. That became a stark reality with the total collapse of the British position in the area, the near approach of the Japanese and the arrival of General Douglas MacArthur in Melbourne on 21 March 1942. Now, as we saw in the previous chapter, Australia was manifestly vulnerable. Its survival depended on the United States and an American leader (MacArthur). As long as that was the case there was limited scope for independent Australian policy. General MacArthur saw Australia as a necessary base for the campaign in the South West Pacific and he was the Allied Commander of that campaign. Mr Curtin was Prime Minister of Australia and to MacArthur that meant he was responsible for motivating and ensuring the unstinting support of Australia for the allied effort based in Australia. MacArthur was the most political of Generals. In a World War not lacking in publicity-conscious and image-making Generals MacArthur had no peer. He was also extremely status-conscious, not to say egocentric.

The situation of Curtin and his government at this juncture exemplified a sort of inverse correlation between vulnerability and independence. Nevertheless, Curtin's dependence on MacArthur was from the beginning of their relationship quite remarkable. This was due no doubt in part to the fact that Curtin had no relevant experience or background. He and his colleagues in the Australian Labor Party tended to have an uneasy relationship with the military, stemming in part from the great conscription controversy of the First World War. General Blamey, who was recalled from the Middle East to become Commander-in-Chief of the Australian Army, never developed a close and trusting relationship with Curtin. Even before Blamey's return work was proceeding on strategic appreciations and planning for the expected Japanese offensive against Australia. In the meantime the government had been informed by the British that they could not divert capabilities from other commitments to come to Australia's help. There was a mood of desperation pending the return of Australian troops from the Middle East and the arrival of expected United States air force units. Information on Japanese planning was not to hand and defensive plans had to be based on inferences. There is no doubt that MacArthur's arrival in Melbourne had a calming effect on the political leadership.

His manner, confidence and air of authority impressed the Australian ministers and he was a visible manifestation of the commitment of the United States to the prosecution of the war against Japan. Within weeks MacArthur was appointed allied Commander-in-Chief for the South West Pacific with Blamey as C-in-C Allied Land Forces. Curtin directed that all members of the Australian forces should regard any order from MacArthur as coming from him, Curtin.

Curtin and his colleagues, who had no experience, no confidence and little in the way of resources now felt there was a reasonable chance that, with American help, Australia could be saved. In that situation MacArthur was in charge. Curtin saw no alternative and it was the role for which MacArthur's whole stellar career had prepared him. He could have accepted nothing less. It may be that the Curtin government exaggerated the vulnerability of Australia and the approaches in March 1942 and as a result gave away too much control to MacArthur. But that is to underestimate the devastating effect of the crushing defeat in Malaya and the collapse and surrender in Singapore. The Japanese had built a momentum and the very limited forces available in Australia appeared a frail barrier. Within weeks the urgency of the threat lifted with the naval battles of the Coral Sea and Midway. But if the invasion fleet heading for Port Moresby had not been intercepted Port Moresby would have been in grave danger and with its occupation by the Japanese much of Queensland would have been within bombing range. With the frustration of their attempt to take Port Moresby by sea the Japanese turned to a land campaign which was at first seriously underrated by MacArthur but became a source of deep anxiety to Curtin and MacArthur and a deeply contentious issue between MacArthur's headquarters and the Australians and also within the Australian high command.

This important episode for Australia in the war is examined in detail in D.M. Horner's *Crisis of Command*[7]. It has several aspects. There is MacArthur's denigration of the fighting spirit of the Australian army and his attempt to attribute to that cause the success achieved by the Japanese force which fought its way over the Owen Stanley Range to within some 30 miles of Port Moresby. There is MacArthur's criticism of the Australian commanders. There is MacArthur's manoeuvring of Blamey into command of the Australians in the field in Papua and the subsequent explosion in the relationship between Blamey and Rowell who had been commanding the operation to that time. But for the present purpose the most illuminating aspect is the support of Curtin for MacArthur and his direction to Blamey, at MacArthur's behest, to go to Port Moresby in effect abandoning his nominal position as C-in-C Allied Land Forces. Horner sees MacArthur's criticisms of the Australians as part of his tactics to protect his own reputation in the event that Port Moresby was taken despite his earlier underrating of the threat to New Guinea. In the meantime the Australians had inflicted on the Japanese at Milne Bay their first defeat on land in the Pacific War. In a letter to General Marshall MacArthur wrote:

> ...the Australians have proven themselves unable to match the enemy in jungle fighting. Aggressive leadership is lacking. The enemy's defeat at Milne Bay must not be accepted as a measure of relative fighting capacity of the troops involved. The decisive factor was

the complete surprise obtained over him by our preliminary concentration of superior forces[28].

The quality of the Australians at jungle fighting at that stage of the war may be contested, and indeed is contested. But the campaign, essentially Rowell's campaign, to stop the Japanese thrust to Port Moresby was successful, at considerable expense to the enemy, whereas MacArthur's subsequent plans for pushing American ground troops through to the coast on trails to the east of the Kokoda Track was impractical. It is at least doubtful whether there was ever good reason for the degree of concern which MacArthur generated about the threat to Port Moresby in September 1942. He was under pressure from the highest level in Washington over the matter and, according to Horner, 'believed that the one solution to the position he might find himself in if Port Moresby fell was to send Blamey to New Guinea, for not only did he expect Blamey to "energise the situation", but he could then claim that he had done all he could possibly do to save New Guinea'[29]. Blamey himself was under heavy pressure from his own ministers. He explained the situation to the Advisory War Council on 17 September emphasizing the Australian success at Milne Bay but analyzing the reasons for the retreat down the Kokoda Trail. He shared the view of the Australian commanders on the spot that, with 30,000 allied troops in the area and more on the way, and 10,000 Japanese troops, the latter would not be able to take Port Moresby. This turned out to be absolutely correct. The Japanese got to within sight of the sea but by then they were exhausted, sick, out of supplies and under the guns of the Australian field artillery. There were certainly some nervous moments along the way and mistakes were made. But in the end the Japanese were in the same position before Port Moresby that the Australians had been in at the northern end of the Kokoda Track – with attenuated supply lines and difficult communications. It could be argued that what the Australians did was to employ classically effective tactics of gradually withdrawing until the enemy was defeated[30]. But Curtin and his government showed inadequate confidence in their own military leadership and followed, apparently without question, the advice of MacArthur which cast doubt not only on the judgment of the Australian high command but on the fighting spirit of the Australian army. Of the various manifestations of the limitations on Australian self-reliance and independence during the war this had been one of the most remarkable.

Organized Japanese resistance in Papua ended on 23 January 1943 but the Japanese fought on in New Guinea where they retained considerable strength. This culminated in the campaign to retake the Huon Peninsula involving the Seventh and Ninth Australian Divisions. MacArthur's forces moved on up the north coast of New Guinea and at the end of July 1944 reached the Bird's Head peninsula at the extreme western end of the island. The direct threat to Australia had been repulsed but the task of accomplishing the defeat of Japan still remained and, with it, the question for the Australian government of the role Australia would play in the combined allied effort to force Japan to surrender.

By then MacArthur was focussed on reclaiming the Philippines and then invading Japan. His strategy was to seize island stepping stones from which each next assault could be launched. This 'island hopping' campaign required massive use of specialized equipment and transport and construction capabilities as well as munitions. Australian forces were not equipped to take an independent role in this new warfare and MacArthur presumably saw no great need to provide a major role for allies who did not have the equipment or resources to take a full part in the American campaign but who wanted to preserve their separate identity and command. He was under pressure from the Australians to find a role for the Australian force. In the end, and after considerable argument about their strength and the perennial issue of keeping them under Australian command, he gave them the rather thankless, but as it turned out quite dangerous role, of mopping up Japanese forces bypassed and left behind by the successful campaign in Papua and New Guinea and the American advance towards Japan.

The uses to which the Australian forces were put from 1944 have been the subject of much contention. That is partly because MacArthur had held out the prospect that Australians would be in the vanguard of the assault on the Philippines and there is a question whether he reneged on that in order to ensure that he and the American forces got all the credit for retaking the Philippines. Also contentious is the tasking of the Australian forces once they were recommitted to battle. It has been argued, for example by Peter Charlton[31], that many of the tasks they were in the end given were unnecessary, involving attacking Japanese forces in out of the way and non-essential places where they could equally well have been left to wither harmlessly on the vine until the final surrender, thus saving Australian casualties.

A third area of contention arising from the events of 1944 is the issue of the possibility of a major British offensive against Japan based on Australia to begin when Germany surrendered, and of Australia's role in such an offensive. Charlton and others have argued that Blamey deliberately held the Australian divisions back from participation in the main MacArthur campaign and kept them training unnecessarily long on the Atherton Tableland because he hoped to be given command of such an offensive. This 'middle strategy' was to have pushed from North Australia to Ambon on the western flank of the American line of advance and on to the Celebes, Borneo and Saigon. Then it became the 'modified middle strategy' when it was projected to launch from the north coast of New Guinea and, bypassing Ambon, aim for Borneo[32]. It is not clear what view Curtin had of this and related plans. There was ill-feeling on the part of H.V. Evatt, the Minister for External Affairs, especially that the British had been discussing future Pacific strategy at a high level with the Americans without including Australia, and Evatt suspected that the United States intended to try to keep permanently some places in the South West Pacific where they had set up bases for use against the Japanese. On the other side there was keen resentment on the part of the British and the Americans when subsequently Evatt negotiated an agreement on collaboration with New Zealand. But Curtin certainly looked forward to the despatch of a proposed British naval task force which had been agreed at the Cairo conference.

As late as mid March 1944 when MacArthur came to Canberra and met with Curtin and Shedden he said that three Australian divisions and an American paratroop division would be the spearhead of his advance on the Philippines[33].

Curtin went to London via Washington for a meeting on 3 May of Commonwealth Prime Ministers on the war with Japan. The ensuing discussions were inconclusive and unsatisfactory, concerning British requirements for basing forces in Australia to undertake the modified middle strategy (now modified again), should that be approved by Churchill, and Curtin's reminder that Australia was part of the United States South West Pacific Area of responsibility. The record left by the British military chief referred to Curtin being 'entirely in MacArthur's pocket'[34]. Even though Curtin had fully protected MacArthur's position the discussions in London about the Middle Strategy precipitated a sharp reaction from MacArthur who saw a threat to the area of his command. He distrusted Blamey in this and may have raised with both Curtin and Shedden the possibility of having Blamey replaced[35]. Although there were differences between Curtin and Blamey the Prime Minister was not about to take such a drastic step. Curtin wanted Australian troops used in the assault on the Philippines, but he was not prepared to make a critical issue of it. And it is not clear that either of the other main parties, MacArthur and Blamey, saw it as a priority from their points of view.

At the end of 1941 Curtin had recognized, and conveyed to his fellow Australians, the reality that Britain was not going to be able to save Australia despite all the assurances and reassurances. Australia therefore had no alternative but to turn to the United States. He did that wholeheartedly, in the sense that he made MacArthur entirely welcome and reposed great confidence and trust in the allied commander. During 1942 Curtin's difficulties with Churchill increased, while his relationship with MacArthur was a close working partnership – a partnership in which the Australian Prime Minister could hardly be said to have been the senior partner. He repeatedly sought MacArthur's advice either directly or through Shedden, the Secretary of the War Cabinet, and MacArthur naturally in response tendered advice which suited his or his country's interests. But as MacArthur moved geographically further away from Australia, first to Port Moresby and then to Hollandia, Curtin's contact with him became less immediate and MacArthur's interest in his Australian partner diminished as he planned and worked for the approaching day of his promised return to the Philippines and then the invasion of Japan. For Curtin the problem was that, despite a gradual and continuing shift of human resources from the armed forces to industry, agriculture etc after the ending of the threat to Australia, it was still necessary to have an honourable role for the Australian armed forces in the continuing war against Japan, if only to ensure Australia's voice in the post-war settlement. He spoke in Parliament about the importance of Australia ensuring that and of the need to establish by the Australian record in the South West Pacific the right to have a suitable voice in the post-war settlement. As the need or justification for Australian naval and air resources to be held away from the South West Pacific diminished he pressed the British for their return from other theatres and by October 1943 less than 5 per cent of Australian servicemen were outside that area. His determination in May 1944 not to enter into any arrangements for British participation in the region which might derogate from the command arrangements for the South West Pacific Area which placed Australia in MacArthur's command may have prejudiced the possibility of the provision of a substantial British task force there.

But the British had doubts about the capacity of the Australian economy to sustain such a force and Churchill's interest in the project was not unconnected with his desire to find suitable employment for Mountbatten.

But Curtin wanted to see an effective British presence in the war against Japan and he made that clear especially in relation to the proposal that a British fleet be provided to support MacArthur. That these projects were not implemented, or not fully, can hardly be laid at Curtin's door especially given the agreements which he had made in desperate circumstances in early 1942. After the Japanese invasion threat was blocked and the tide of the Pacific war began to ebb back against Japan Curtin, his government and his military and civilian advisers, began to look increasingly to the longer term. They knew that Australia had had no effective voice in major allied strategy decisions which bore on Australia's national interests, especially the crucial decision to prosecute the war against Germany as a priority with the Pacific war as a holding operation until Germany was defeated. Looking to the future it seemed clear that the British imperial connection and the British Commonwealth would again be one vehicle by which Australia could make itself heard.

The war ended with Australia still fighting in New Guinea and the other Australian possessions which the Japanese had seized in 1942 and which had been left behind after the victories against the Japanese in 1943 in the islands to the north of Australia. Although it is still argued by some that the Australian fighting to clear those possessions of Japanese control in 1944 and 1945 was unnecessary, from a political point of view Australia's standing would have been gravely damaged if the inhabitants had been left under Japanese suzerainty with no Australian attempt to free them. In terms of Australia's responsibilities and ambitions in the region there really was no alternative to prosecuting a campaign against the Japanese occupation. It was however a different matter in the British territories in Borneo where Australian forces were deployed in strength in 1944 and 1945. Those campaigns had little bearing on Australian interests but were expensive in Australian lives.

From the point of view of the main subject of this book the key issues for Australia late in the war were the efforts of the Prime Minister and the Commander-in-Chief to ensure the concentration of Australian forces in the area of main present and future strategic and political importance to Australia, the South West Pacific. That their respective efforts were not well coordinated and indeed were at odds from May 1944 is regrettable; but it is hard to know how much difference it made. If it were true that MacArthur never really intended to use the Australians as his 'spearhead' then it made little difference. If on the other hand a more determined and clearly focussed Australian political leadership could have ensured that role for the Australian forces it would have given a boost to Australian national feelings and would have reinforced the relationship with the United States, perhaps putting it on the map in a way that would have helped sustain it to this day. On the other hand the time was soon to come when Australian foreign policy, in Evatt's hands but in changed circumstances and after Curtin had passed from the scene, would be more assertively independent and on occasion irritating to the United States and Britain. Dr Evatt strove to ensure that the smaller countries had a far greater voice in the post-war United Nations than they had had in the wartime alliance when Curtin had had to fight even to get Australian troops deployed to defend their own country, when momentous decisions affecting Australia's survival were taken by Roosevelt and Churchill with no reference to the Australian government, and when Evatt himself had found his efforts to get modern warplanes from Britain given very low priority and virtually fobbed off.

Overall the Pacific war did enhance Australia's independence in terms of the relationships with Britain and the Commonwealth but obviously much less in terms of the relationship with the new ally, the United States. Australia did not establish a system of management which ensured that Australia's interests were kept paramount in Australian policy and that both the commitment of Australian resources and the engagement of allied forces were decided on the basis of those interests. The political management of the Australian war effort was second-rate and did not achieve the synergy with the military high command which was needed. As a result major decisions were sometimes confused and there was not the steadiness and consistency of objectives which the country should have had. There was a degree of subservience to the allied commander which was excessive and reflected the inexperience and insecurity of the Australian political leadership during the critical phases of the war. It can however be argued, as it has been for example by Horner, that Curtin as Prime Minister had to operate within the confines of the limitations inherent in the role of the smaller ally, 'especially when the greater ally has the ships and planes'[36].

The Basis for an Independent Foreign Policy

Australia emerged from the Second World War with a rather patchy record. The performance of its services was in some instances of a high order, in other instances ineffective for one reason or another. The Navy, on which two thirds of pre war defence expenditure had been spent, was effectively under the direction of the British Navy for the first part of the war and succeeded in sinking an Italian light cruiser. Later it lost 'three of its biggest and newest cruisers, three destroyers, two sloops and a corvette to enemy action, and another destroyer grounded in Timor'[37]. Australian ships were active against the Japanese in the South Pacific largely as elements in the United States operations, and sustained substantial losses. For their part they succeeded in sinking one Japanese submarine and contributing to the sinking of two others, but no Japanese surface ships. Of course the ships of the Australian navy contributed more than that tally would suggest by their work in escorting convoys, minesweeping and so on. But the heavy losses sustained at modest cost to the enemy leave the impression that the Australian navy did not perform at the level of the other combatants. Australia's contribution to the air war was, as already noted, during the first years of the war mainly under the Royal Air Force in the European theatre leaving Australia virtually defenceless against Japanese air attack. Later, Australian production of some more modern aircraft and the availability of front line aircraft (and especially the three British Spitfire squadrons Evatt extracted with so much effort) eventually gave the

Australian Air Force a capacity in the Pacific War. But their record against the Japanese was modest. We have already discussed the issues which confronted the Army and its performance. It was the largest element in Australia's war effort and it was the Army which in 1942 and 1943 bore the brunt of the fighting against the Japanese, in the end achieving notable success. But there were several factors which demand careful attention in assessing the performance and the outcome. Professor Horner has, as explained above, analyzed the problems which faced the Australian High Command under MacArthur's overall direction, ceded to him by the Australian Prime Minister. The abandonment of so much independence is unlikely to be either sought or conceded in any future defence of Australia in alliance with the United States or other allies. But the lesson is that Australia must have first class commanders of its own and political direction that has devoted time to studying defence issues. Neither of those can be produced without national awareness and planning. Another factor was the quality of the Japanese forces in all three arms. The British had denigrated to the Australians the quality of Japanese military and naval aviation which, at least in 1942, was far superior to that of the British and what little the Australians had. The feats of the Japanese army were beyond expectations. Their campaign in Malaya was imaginative, resourceful, economical and highly effective. In New Guinea they were generally extremely persistent, resourceful and resolute and they were able to function effectively with minimal supplies. All Australian successes against the Japanese were made in circumstances where the Australians were far better supplied, had more air support and were more numerous. The Pacific War should have taught Australians that racial (or racist) supremacist stereotypes of potential enemies are at all costs to be avoided. The subsequent policies and planning of the Defence Force (such as the initiatives taken for cooperation with other regional Defence Forces) suggest that that lesson was heeded. But it bears repeating so that it never slips from mind.

In terms of preparing the way for an independent foreign and defence policy for Australia the Second World War might seem to have left mixed messages. After the Japanese campaign began Australia was rapidly shown to be dependent on the United States. If it had not been for the United States navy Churchill's forecast that Australia would have to be 'mauled a little' would no doubt have been fulfilled a good deal more than it was in the event. And the Australian Prime Minister, recognizing accurately the extent of Australia's need to turn to the United States, turned to them more unreservedly than was probably necessary. Australia was excluded from the most important councils of the allies affecting the war in the Pacific. It played no significant role in the major campaign against Japan which pushed them back to their own islands. Its overall contribution to the allies' South West Pacific campaign was estimated by the Americans to have been eight per cent, a figure which the Australian historian John Robertson regarded as generous.

But the other message, which was more important and enduring, was twofold. At the end of the war Australia insisted, with success, on the leading Commonwealth role in the occupation and control of Japan and on an active and independent voice in the long deliberations on a peace treaty. Thus the basis was laid for an independent and active Australian foreign policy in the region. The building on that basis, after 1949, was somewhat sporadic for many years, but the wartime and immediate post-war experience provided the start. Secondly, the urgency and proximity of the Japanese threat, and the virtual shutting down of British assistance and supply until the defeat of Germany, forced Australia to develop industrial and other capacities which gave it greater independence than previously and opened the way for a planned expansion of the economy which was to enable the country to assume a much more active and important role in areas of international policy after the war. The lessons of the war were, or should have been, in some respects chastening. But the war left Australia a more important country with a leadership, at least in the immediate post-war years, which was determined to assert that importance in the new councils of the world. As noted in the previous chapter Australia had been very slow to develop a foreign service and a capacity to gather and assess information on relevant international developments. This omission now had to be rapidly addressed and, with considerable assistance from the British, there was a rapid development of the professional capacity to formulate and implement external policy. There was also a development of the wartime capacity to gather information by covert as well as overt means, and to assess it professionally.

Thus, despite having been in great danger for the first time, Australia came out of the war without suffering invasion, with relatively little damage, and with many fewer casualties than in the First World War. And it had developed capacities and learned lessons which would enable it to develop a more independent international stance than it had previously contemplated. That development has had its ups and downs since. But it was greatly advanced as a result of the war.

Notes

1 There is much contemporary evidence of these and related observations including the letters of Australian troops. I draw also on recollection of what I heard from my parents, both of whom served in France in the Australian army and both of whom spent periods in England in British training and hospital institutions.
2 Hancock, W.K. (1945), *Australia*, Ernest Benn, London, pp. 56-7. Not all Australian historians would agree with this. Manning Clark, for instance, probably Australia's most famous historian, would have argued that the independent Australian element was the authentic voice of the nation.
3 As late as 1947 more than 97 per cent of the population had been born in Australia or Britain. See Jayasuria, L. and Kee, P. (1999) *The Asianisation of Australia?* Melbourne University Press, Carlton, p. 11.
4 *Australian Gallup Polls*, No.s 470-77 (see Meaney *op. cit.* pp. 549-50).
5 The Dutch, known as Boers, had fought a bitter war against the British in the first years of the century and many of them sympathized with the Germans rather than the British in the two world wars.
6 Day, David (1993), *Menzies and Churchill at War*, Oxford University Press, pp. 11-12.
7 *Ibid.* (quoting Letter from Menzies to Bruce 22 February 1940).
8 Over 15,000 Australians went there in 2002.
9 The First, Second, Fourth and Fifth. The Third Division did not arrive from England until December.

10   The advice of General John Coates is gratefully acknowledged here.
11   Coates, H.J. (1999), *Bravery Above Blunder*, Oxford University Press, Melbourne, p. 20.
12   See for example Horner, D.M. (1982), *High Command – Australia and Allied Strategy 1939-1945*, George Allen & Unwin, North Sydney, pp. 92-3.
13   It might be argued that Menzies shared the responsibility for this limitation. When Hitler invaded the Soviet Union in June 1941, Menzies urged Churchill to build up strength in the Middle East to take advantage of Germany's new preoccupation. However Churchill really did not need much urging because that was his own inclination. In a sense Menzies was compounding his own problem because building up forces in the Middle East could only be done at the expense of the Far East. (I am indebted to General John Coates for this observation.)
14   Horner, *op. cit.* p. 132-3.
15   Robertson, John (1984) *Australia Goes to War*, Doubleday, Sydney, p. 12, gives the relevant figures for defence spending 1925 to 1937 and points out that the navy, not unnaturally, was a strong advocate of imperial defence while the more 'nationalistic' army was more critical of the concept.
16   Robertson, *ibid.*, p. 72.
17   Horner, *op. cit.* pp. 156-7.
18   *Ibid.*, p. 155.
19   Robertson, *op. cit.* p. 72, refers to a meeting between Air Chief Marshal Sir Robert Brooke-Popham with the Australian Advisory War Council in which he told the latter that the Brewster Buffalo (a second line American aircraft which was being supplied to the Far East) 'would probably prove more than a match for any Japanese aircraft' a claim which ran counter to the assessment of RAAF Intelligence.
20   So slow that later, over Singapore, they were unable to catch up with Japanese bombers after the latter had dropped their bombs.
21   Robertson, *op. cit.* pp. 89-90. The same point is made by General H.J. Coates in his *An Atlas of Australia's Wars* (The Australian Centenary History of Defence Vol. VII) p. 214: 'The reasons for the loss of Malaya and Singapore belong to British rather than Australian history' But they are nevertheless very relevant to Australian history and deserve to be more fully and openly examined than they have been to this point. Coates' assessment on p. 214 of the *Atlas* is important as a current, succinct summing up of the Malaya/Singapore disaster by an expert Australian who has studied it closely.
22   Horner addresses this issue in *High Command, op. cit.* pp. 145-6.
23   In the event V.G. Bowden, the Trade Commissioner, warned correctly that Singapore would not be able to hold out.
24   See for example Elphick, Peter (1995), *Singapore: the Pregnable Fortress. A Study in Deception, Discord and Desertion*, Hodder and Stoughton, London.
25   See his chapters in *Between Two Oceans, A Military History of Singapore From First Settlement to Final British Withdrawal*, Oxford University Press, 1999. Appendix 3 by Farrell deals with 'Controversies surrounding the Surrender of Singapore, February 1942'.
26   *Ibid.*, p. 359.
27   Horner, D.M. (1978), *Crisis of Command*, Australian National University Press, Canberra.
28   *Ibid.*, p. 149.
29   *Ibid.*, p. 162.
30   Discussion with Professor Horner 5 September 2000. He points out that this tactic was fine 'except that the government was having a nervous breakdown'.

31 Charlton, Peter (1983), *The Unnecessary War*, Macmillan, Melbourne.
32 D.M. Horner, *High Command, op. cit.* p. 316.
33 *Ibid.*, p. 308.
34 *Ibid.*, p. 321.
35 *Ibid.*, p. 18.
36 *Ibid.* Chapters 13 and 14 discuss in convincing detail the struggle over the commitment of Australian forces in the South West Pacific Area at the end of the war and especially the issue of the use of Australian divisions in the assault on the Philippines.
37 Robertson, *op. cit.* p. 214.

Chapter 3

The Persistence and Decline of Dependence

Britishness

It is not surprising, in the aftermath of the Second World War in which Australia found itself almost totally dependent on United States power, and through a deepening Cold War in which Australia's commitment to the Western side had the overwhelming support of the electorate, that Australian governments from 1949 to 1972 believed that Australia was essentially vulnerable because of its isolation and small population and that its long term security and prosperity were best protected by close alliance with the superpower leader of the Western world. While that policy was carried at times too far, to the point of submerging independent thinking and an independent voice, it is now seldom noted that during that period of 23 years Australian foreign policy also sought to build constructive relationships in the Asian region. But before examining that policy strand we need to look at the effects of the residue of Britishness and of the feeling that Australians were 'Australian Britons', and how the dilution of that feeling facilitated the development of a more open and wider Australian foreign policy.

Australian institutions were naturally for the most part derived directly from British antecedents. British professional and other bodies were, and to a large extent still are, the source of standards. After the war young Australians still aspired to go to London and they went in their thousands. Earls Court in London became known as 'kangaroo valley'. Queen Elizabeth made a triumphal visit to Australia in 1953 during which the Australian populace overwhelmingly welcomed her in an outpouring of affection. Australians had not lost the sense of Britishness which had produced the motto of their first university a hundred years earlier. The motto of the University of Sydney is *Sidere Mens Eadem Mutato* freely translated as 'The same spirit under a different sky'. In effect it was an expression of the belief and intention of the founders of the University that it should be a British institution on the other side of the world. It is a motto that would have served as well for most of the principal institutions of the Australian colonies and it reflects the main strand in the feeling of most Australians about their link with Britain from the settlement until the middle of the twentieth century. Australians had a strong sense of being British even when they were deliberately diverging from British attitudes and practices.

In the field of external relations *sidere mens eadem mutato* is particularly apposite because it was precisely the changed location, under the stars of the

Southern Cross, which gave rise to most of the differences and tensions which drove the long and slow evolution of an independent Australian foreign policy. As we have seen, Australian feelings of vulnerability and of concern to ensure exclusive occupation of the country caused them to press British governments to bear Australia's security concerns prominently in mind and to protect what Australians saw as their key interests in the conduct of the Empire's diplomacy.

The role of the sense of vulnerability in the development of an independent and characteristically Australian foreign policy has been contested. In August 1969 Dr Neville Meaney and Dr T.B. Millar had an exchange in the pages of the journal *Australian Outlook* (No. 23)[1] in which Meaney argued against what he said was 'the central myth about Australian foreign policy, that Australia has had no foreign policy of its own, that it has in international affairs acquiesced happily in British policy and assumed gratefully the all-saving virtue of the British navy'. Meaney went on to argue that from the end of the nineteenth century to the time at which he was writing, 'Australia's defence and foreign policy has been dominated by one idea – the search for security in the Pacific'. The search for security in the Pacific was one of the two elements in the long influence of the sense of vulnerability (the other being the exclusionist immigration policy) and it did, as Meaney stated, lead at times to independent action as when Australia decided to develop its own naval squadron or when Deakin successfully lobbied for the visit of the Great White Fleet. But more often, in the time frame in question, its defence and foreign policy manifestations were efforts to intensify dependence on Britain. New or renewed assurances of support were sought, assistance requested for Australian demands for control of nearby island territories, and so on. Nor could Australia have easily done otherwise as long as she persisted with the British race patriotism which was so strong a characteristic for so long and, as we have seen, persisted until well after the Second World War. As long as Australians saw themselves as British, even independent Britons, and as core members of the 'British world', as Menzies called it, they were bound to seek support primarily from Britain. Even when, in the hour of need, that was not forthcoming there was very little disposition to cut the painter and become really independent. The wartime association with the United States was mostly seen as without prejudice to Australia's Britishness and, as we have seen, late in the war the Australian High Command was attracted to a plan to develop a British Western Pacific strategy separate from the Americans. The sequel was the era of seeking close engagement and protection through two 'great and powerful friends'.

In the early part of the war, while Menzies was Prime Minister, the main obstacle to the development of independent Australian policy in the Pacific area was the preoccupation of the Australian Prime Minister and Government with the Imperial global foreign policy and strategy. There was an independent and energetic Australian foreign and strategic policy at the global and imperial level pursued by Menzies. But it had little effect, and indeed little merit to the extent that a central element in it was the belief that the British empire would be able to reach a satisfactory accommodation with Hitler. Moreover this policy and activity depended for such influence and effect as it had on the personal standing and force of argument of Menzies and the Australian High Commissioner in London, previous Prime Minister Stanley Melbourne Bruce. That was to change with the defeat of Menzies and the elevation of Curtin to the Prime Ministership in Canberra.

The alliance with the United States then assumed much greater importance in the war strategy than the relationship with Britain. After the war the ascendancy of British people and attitudes in Australia was gradually diluted as a consequence of the decision of the Chifley government, with Arthur Calwell as its Immigration Minister, to open Australia to a wave of immigrants from Europe. This was itself a consequence of the extent to which Australia's vulnerability had been demonstrated by the war. Seven million people, in a few concentrations around the periphery, could not hold a continent against a modern major power. A bigger and more industrial economy was seen to be necessary with a significant manufacturing capacity. If Australia were to be made less vulnerable and less dependent than in 1942 the population must be increased and that would require a large immigration program. The immigrants must be European, to preserve the White Australia Policy, but not enough could be obtained from Britain alone. So the net was cast wider across Europe.

The new mass immigration policy was taken up and amplified by the Menzies government after it defeated Labor in 1949. It fuelled the great expansion of the Australian economy, and 'nation-building' public sector infrastructure development. Many of these immigrants were British but of the nearly two million who settled in Australia in the twenty years after the end of the war about half came from other European countries. This was perhaps Menzies' greatest contribution to the development of Australia, but inevitably it had some diluting effect on the British character of the Australian population which he himself valued so much. As we have seen[2], the evidence of contemporary opinion polling is that, at the end of the war, the attachment to Britain was still very strong. But the ties of state had been loosened by the war and would slip further or be cast off altogether in later decades, although some continue into the twenty-first century, notably the retention of the British monarch as Australia's head of state.

From the end of the war Australia acted in many ways as an independent agent in international affairs and under Chifley and Evatt it was a vigorous independence. But for the rest of the period until 1972 that independence was significantly curtailed by the perceived requirement to keep in step with Britain and then with the United States. On the face of it this continued attachment to the British links is in retrospect surprising, especially after the period in the later years of the war and in its immediate aftermath when Australian foreign policy was largely conducted by the formidable idiosyncratic figure of Dr H.V. Evatt and when the relationship with London was rather sour. The Curtin government had had a difficult relationship with Churchill. On the Australian side it was felt that Britain's undertakings concerning the naval defence of Australia had not been kept and that the British had sought to keep Australian forces committed in Europe and the Middle East and North Africa rather than have them return to fight in the Pacific theatre and in the defence of Australia. Then Australia, when under air attack from the Japanese, failed to obtain more than a handful of modern combat aircraft from Britain while thousands of Australian air crew were kept in Europe even when Australia was under threat. There was resentment and ill feeling on both sides in the aftermath of the enormous and rather shameful military disaster of the collapse in Malaya and the surrender of Singapore. Evatt in particular was strongly disliked in London, a dislike which carried over post-war, and even intensified, under the British Labour government and its Foreign Secretary, Ernest Bevin.

Curtin and the British Commonwealth

Yet Curtin appears to have seen his leadership, which brought him into conflict with Churchill, as a 'successful struggle to assert Australian sovereignty as a Self-Governing Dominion'[3]. David Day, commenting on this, says 'It was not a struggle to assert independence but a struggle for recognition within the Empire'[4]. Thus Curtin could be represented as continuing the position of Parkes and his contemporaries: despite differences and disagreements with Imperial authorities Australia was British and demanded that British policy reflect Australian interests as of right. Of course Curtin's position on Australia and the British Empire was more complex and qualified than Parkes's fifty years earlier. But the core of it was the same: Australia's place in the world was determined mainly by its British character and its membership of the British Empire. The Australian military leader, General Blamey, took the same view in January 1944 in looking to the future of Australian defence planning: 'Australia should seek its protection by a means which may be anticipated will stand the test of time, and will allow considerable development of strength and the continued recognition of our place as a member of the British Empire. This envisages a closer degree of cooperation, and a closer alignment of common interests in the Empire than ever before in our history. This aspect is so paramount as to require no further elaboration'[5]. Curtin's most famous statement on Australia's defence orientation is his New Year message published in the *Melbourne Herald* on 27 December 1941 after Pearl Harbor – 'Without any inhibitions of any kind, I make it quite clear that Australia looks to America, free of any pangs as to our traditional links or kinship with the United Kingdom'. But after three years of the Pacific war, in February 1945, in a major address in the House of Representatives, he emphasized the importance of the British Commonwealth context for Australian policy. After Australia's experiences in 1942 and Curtin's own struggle with Churchill it may seem surprising that Australia's political and military leadership should so unequivocally reassert the Commonwealth link at the end of the war. Two main explanations have been offered. One derives from the discomfort of working under MacArthur and the latter's sometimes dismissive attitude towards the smaller ally and its limited military effectiveness. The other lies in the changing circumstances in which Australia was placed in 1945 as compared to the last days of 1941. Both are discussed in Coral Bell's study of Australia's relations with the United Kingdom and the United States[6]. She writes that 'This disillusioning experience of the discomforts in wartime of an excessive strategic dependence was one of the factors responsible for a sort of half or three-quarter turn back towards the British connection, as against the American one, in Australian policymakers' attitudes from about the end of 1943'[7] and she refers to major policy statements by Curtin to his Party Conference in December 1943 and to the Commonwealth Prime Ministers' Conference in London in May 1944 to which he took Shedden and Blamey as his principal advisers, but not Evatt. By then the Prime Minister and Evatt had a rather strained relationship, not least because Evatt's ambition to replace Curtin had become manifest.

In the absence of Evatt or any External Affairs advisers at the 1944 Conference Curtin relied on Shedden, the civilian Head of the Defence Department, for advice. His long and close association with Sir Maurice (later Lord) Hankey, who had been Secretary to the British Cabinet and of the Committee of Imperial Defence, had largely formed Shedden's views. This influence through Shedden and his successors, seeing the Commonwealth at the core of Australian foreign policy, persisted in the Australian Department of the Prime Minister and Cabinet for some forty years, into the Prime Ministership of Malcolm Fraser, though by then much diminished. In 1943, with no countervailing influence in the Prime Minister's delegation, it led to Curtin pushing for a new Secretariat to enhance the role of the Commonwealth. But this was strongly opposed by Canada, South Africa was lukewarm and Churchill did not even bother to attend that part of the agenda. The failure of this initiative, and Curtin's declining health, were to mean that the foreign policy field was now largely Evatt's, although the Prime Minister, in his report on the Conference to Parliament on 17 July sounded the trumpet for the Commonwealth in language which could have been used by Menzies:

> It will be gathered from what I have said that it is as an integral part of the British Commonwealth that Australia can most influentially express itself in the world organisation, and I have no doubt whatever that the unity of the British Commonwealth will, in the problems of the future give to His Majesty's subjects everywhere, an authority in the consultations with other countries that will enable our concept of life to influence greatly the decisions which have to be made so that all we have fought for can be achieved. The relationships of the Dominions to each other and the Mother country many even now not be completely understood by the rest of the world. But our influence, historically great, is at this stage greater than it has ever been and, I am confident, will not grow less[8].

This, and similar statements which Curtin made at the time, suggest more of a full turn back towards the British connection and the British Commonwealth than the half or three quarters turn suggested by Bell. But in any case they were not realistic and events turned out quite differently. It would not be long before Evatt would be involved in bitter differences of policy in the United Nations with the 'Mother Country', itself now with a Labour government and with a Foreign Secretary, Ernest Bevin, who was a product of the working class and the trade union movement.

The explanation of Curtin's turning again towards the British and Commonwealth connection which Bell gives – his experience of working with MacArthur – loses something in plausibility from reflection on the nature of the relationship which Curtin had with MacArthur. It may be that Curtin instinctively felt that the degree of dependence Australia had perforce had on the United States and its regional commander during the war needed balancing. But one of the obstacles in the way of British ambitions to develop a major Commonwealth thrust against Japan late in the war was Curtin's insistence that Australia was part of the United States' South West Pacific Area of responsibility which produced the British reaction mentioned in the last chapter that he was 'entirely in MacArthur's pocket'[9]. Resentment towards treatment by MacArthur seems likely to have been a more important factor with Blamey than with Curtin, and to the extent that Australian leaders were discomfited by lack of consultation by the Great Powers the British record towards them was hardly better than that of the Americans. Moreover Curtin had shown more than any Australian leader that he was not constrained by sentiment to follow Britain. The other factor mentioned above, of changed circumstances, seems more persuasive. Bell argues that 'As Curtin gained more experience in diplomatic matters and developed more independence of his difficult colleague [Evatt], he seemed to develop also a feeling that there might be much to be said for the traditional or pre-Evatt notion of Australian foreign policy as part of a unified Commonwealth policy'[10]. Curtin could never be described as a Commonwealth man in the way this was said about Menzies, including by himself. But Curtin was pragmatic and it would be natural, as he turned his mind to the post-war future, to assume that Australia would be more influential and more able to protect and advance its interests as a significant member of the Commonwealth than on its own. His view of Australia's place in the world still did not envisage it as wanting or being able to strike out on its own. Its place in the British Commonwealth was still a given and one which was still seen naturally by Australians as offering support, opportunity and status which Australia would not otherwise have. This view was manifested for example when Australia successfully laid claim to appoint the senior Commonwealth representative in the Allied occupation of Japan. It was manifested too in the following years by the assistance given by Britain in the development of Australian intelligence and diplomacy, both of which acquired a professionalism and capabilities which owed much to British advice and cooperation. The new relationship with the United States, which had been founded in Australia's dire need at the end of 1941, did not have the basis in common roots and derivation, in shared culture and long familiarity which still characterized the relationship with Britain. Even the disappointments and resentments arising from the ignominious failure of British strategy in the Pacific and what was seen through some Australian eyes as desertion when the dominion was in greatest need, left in place much of the old relationship, and much of the over-arching and pervasive institutional structures and habits. Thus it was natural that Australia's great wartime leader should seek to deploy this again to Australia's advantage as the end of the war came in sight.

Evatt in the Limelight

As it had been after the 1914-18 war Australia was very active in the negotiations at the end of the Pacific War and in the early days of the United Nations

Organization and positioned itself to engage diplomatically in what were then the world's major capitals as well as in the newly emerging post-colonial countries in Asia and elsewhere. But the immediate post-war years to 1949 turned out to be uncharacteristic. Australian foreign policy was of course heavily influenced by Dr Evatt who shared the determination which W.M. Hughes had shown after the previous war to stand up to the great powers. But in most respects his views and objectives were rather different. Hughes was a realist in international relations and a sceptic, while Evatt had a vision of a world largely governed by the United Nations Organization in which the small and medium nations would have a major influence and all would work together in great enterprises of peace and prosperity. As already pointed out, the prominence and influence Evatt achieved for himself and for Australia at the beginning of the United Nations could not have continued at so high a pitch if only because of the emergence of an increasing number of newly-independent countries, some of them obviously larger and more important than Australia. In 1949 Chifley and Evatt lost office to Menzies and the reconstituted conservative (Liberal) party in coalition with the Country party. Whereas Hughes had lived on into an active and influential old age Evatt suffered a sad decline and then an early death. Even as Minister for External Affairs Evatt had earned a reputation for intolerance, impatience and self-promotion. Leading Australian public servants such as Paul Hasluck and Alan Watt, who worked for Evatt, subsequently wrote in terms which, while recognizing his achievements, conveyed major reservations about his methods and some of the results. Thus Watt:

> Evatt was no man to rest content with being a power behind the throne; he sought the limelight, the full glare of favourable publicity, and, being avid for power, when acquired he used it to the full. His natural abilities certainly made it possible for him while Minister to influence events and people, but in the process he made few if any friends. The status, therefore, which he succeeded in winning for Australia during his overseas visits was diminished by his aggressive and thrusting manner, which took small account of the susceptibilities of other countries, including the United Kingdom[11].

Hasluck, 'whose departmental functions (in External Affairs) and conference responsibilities involved close working relationships with his Minister'[12] later wrote extensively on the San Francisco Conference, the negotiation of the United Nations Charter and related issues at which Evatt exercised a major influence. Hasluck afterwards became a political opponent of Evatt in the Federal Parliament but his views on Evatt's style and methods and the effects on international perceptions of Australian diplomacy were formed before he entered politics and were shared by most of his External Affairs colleagues at the time. Hasluck criticized Evatt's direction of Australian foreign policy as activist for the sake of activism and insufficiently selective. 'We have also stamped the foot and thumped the table a little too often...Then we have sometimes butted unnecessarily into other people's arguments without waiting to consider whether the argument was getting on all right without us. We are not as considerate of other people's honour as we are of our own and are rather careless of other people's corns'[13]. Evatt was probably the most influential figure in the effort at San Francisco to increase the role of the General Assembly in the formation of the United Nations and to limit the veto power of the Security Council. Indeed he sought generally to strengthen the voice of the medium and small powers at the expense of the great powers. Because of this and because of his abrasive style, constant activity, great forensic skills and huge industry, Evatt was bound to be an irritant to the Americans and the British (and not to them only). Leading figures in both Washington and London made no secret of that irritation.

This fuelled criticism by Labor's and Evatt's political opponents in Australia. There was an *ad hominem* element in this but also an issue of substance. Thus in his speech in the debate in the House of Representatives on the ratification of the Charter John McEwen, Leader of the Country Party, who had been with the Australian delegation at San Francisco, complained that Evatt's public reproaching of and differences with the British government reduced the international authority of the voice of the United Kingdom and thus damaged Australia's security, which McEwen saw as depending on the strength of the British Commonwealth led by Britain. In effect Menzies, McEwen and others on the conservative side thought that Evatt had sought to make a reputation as a leading international statesman at the cost of damaging Australia's standing with what Menzies would later call 'our great and powerful friends'. Menzies was also of course much more sceptical of the United Nations and its Charter than was Evatt. While he paid tribute to the idealism of the Charter and supported its ratification, both then and afterwards he asserted the realist view that 'it would be a tragedy if we believed that the ratification of the world Charter would of its own force either create or protect the peace'. The smaller powers would have the opportunity to seek to use their influence on the great powers, but 'the vital issue of peace or war, so far as it concerns the world as a whole, will be determined by the Great Powers – by a core of alliances within the general structure of the Charter'[14]. These debates in 1948 defined the principal difference between the Evatt foreign policy and what followed after the 1949 election through the long reign of Menzies and beyond. Under Menzies, Australian activism in foreign affairs was considerably curtailed and much greater regard was had for the views and policies of the United Kingdom and the United States. But it is not to be overlooked that Evatt fought for principles and ideas which were important if the United Nations was to be more than a directorate of the great powers[15].

Menzies and the Return to Dependence

With the defeat of Labor in 1949 the Evatt foreign policy was replaced by a less active policy which had as its main guiding principle solidarity with the United States and Great Britain. Menzies, who was the dominant and formative figure of this era, was Prime Minister until 1966. Attention has been properly drawn by Menzies' successors in the Liberal Party in recent times to occasional statements he made emphasizing the importance for Australia of relations with Asia and of policy in the Pacific. Certainly, during his long tenure of the Prime Ministership the foundations were laid for later more comprehensive policies of engagement with Asia. But Menzies' own beliefs and instincts all tended to draw him towards the reinforcement of Australia's ties to Britain as the prime driver of foreign policy, and reinforcement of the alliance relationship with the United States. The latter was institutionalized early in his tenure with the conclusion of the ANZUS Treaty. Menzies' emphasis on the British connection, his repeated assertions that Australia was British, and his personal manifestations of loyalty to her British monarchy and to British institutions and interests, led to some errors of judgment and to some statements and actions which, even at the time, left him open to something close to ridicule, though his intellectual and personal dominance, and his formidable wit made ridicule a dangerous weapon for his opponents to attempt to use against him. In 1964 Donald Horne wrote scornfully that Menzies 'has taken pleasure in allowing the Queen of Great Britain (also constitutionally the Queen of Australia) to make him a Knight of the Thistle, as if he were some great Scottish gentleman, and allows himself to be surrounded by those who jostle for honours with some of the energy of nobles in a petty German court of the eighteenth century'[16]. Horne saw this and similar manifestations as 'the ceremonial clinging [which] is part of the delusional structure of the people who now run Australia. It is a symptom of an inability to recognise and to dramatise the new strategic environment of Australia and the present problems of Australia. The momentum towards concepts of independent nationhood has slowed down, or stopped'[17]. As to policy, Horne said in the same book a couple of pages later that 'throughout the fifties and until the shocks of the Common Market debate, Menzies was more British than the British, always running several years behind London, expressing dreams of Commonwealth that had something of the flavour of progressive debate in 1908'. This is invective but it is based on fact. For more than twenty years Australia's political leadership was committed to a very conservative attachment to the British connection and to following British and American leadership.

But, as was noted in Chapter 1, there were important steps towards Asia during Menzies' time, notably the Colombo Plan, work done through ECAFE (the United Nations Economic Commission for Asia and the Far East as it was then known), the development of Asian studies in Australia through government initiative and particularly the foundation of the Australian National University, the encouragement of Australian business interest in the region, and a substantial increase in diplomatic representation and activity as well as increasing government-initiated visits not only of Ministers and officials but of journalists and other professional groups. Some of Australia's Menzies-era Asian diplomacy turned out to be ephemeral because it was driven by Cold War and anti-communist objectives which produced alliances and institutional structures such as SEATO (the South East Asia Treaty Organization) and ASPAC (the Asian and Pacific Council) which were not very effective against the communist or independence movements they were designed to contain. This was partly because some of the member governments were authoritarian, and tainted by corruption and other abuses which rendered implausible the American claims that they represented the best choice for the peoples of the region struggling to emerge from poverty and underdevelopment. But it would have been difficult, especially in the nineteen fifties and early sixties, for an Australian government to stand aloof from the United States' efforts to develop alliance relationships in the region to resist the spread of communism, misconceived as that was in some cases. Moreover Australian diplomacy laboured under the effects which the White Australia policy had on regional perceptions of the country. Nevertheless Australian diplomacy during the period generally showed skill and patience. For example in the case of Indonesia in the later days of Sukarno Australia managed to preserve a working relationship even while Australian and Indonesian troops were clashing in the nascent Malaysia on and near the border in Kalimantan.

In the sixties the Menzies world in which the British Commonwealth was one of the key institutions and in which Australia was locked to Britain not only by myriad institutional and personal ties but by very close economic ties began to erode. As a result Australia's economic and trading context and opportunities shifted away from the dependence on Britain which had characterized them up to the war when 61 per cent of Australia's exports were taken by Britain. Milestones were the 1957 Australia-Japan Trade Agreement and the signature in Rome of the Treaty establishing the European Economic Community. Harold Macmillan, the British Prime Minister who was personally on good terms with Menzies, gave assurances that Britain would not join the EEC and repeated this when he visited Australia in 1958. But a couple of years later Macmillan changed his mind on Europe and there followed a long and often rather rancorous argument between the United Kingdom and Australia on the issue and on the subsequent arrangements which should be made in Australia's interest. These arguments continued well beyond the entry of Britain into the EEC in 1973 by which time the share of Australia's exports going to Britain had declined to not much more than one tenth of the 1940 figure. While there was considerable hardship in some industries in Australia (especially the dairy and fruit-growing industries) the rapid growth of the East Asian economies eased Australian adjustment and within twenty years that region was taking the same share of a much more diverse and valuable Australian basket of exports as had Britain at the outset of World War II. (By 1990 Britain's share of Australia's exports had fallen to four per cent, although that figure understates the relationship between the two economies in which the most important element was the substantial investment in both directions.)

Thus Australia was coming increasingly to depend on East Asia while her deeper affinities and allegiances lay still with the United States and Britain. The dilemma Parkes had faced a hundred years before seemed to be even sharper as Australia moved into the last quarter of the twentieth century; Australia's independent interests and Australia's comfort zone were a world apart. But now there were Australian voices calling for a national effort to assimilate to the Asia which Parkes had looked at only with apprehension and revulsion. Already, during the nineteen sixties, tensions and problems were emerging in the British connection for Australian foreign and defence policy. Menzies became increasingly disillusioned with the British Commonwealth, which for so long had been at the centre of his view of the world and of Australia's place in it. This had much to do with the increasing role of the former colonies and the treatment of South Africa, under growing pressure over apartheid. He also found himself largely out of sympathy with some of the thinking on both sides of British politics. The most fateful decision came the year after his retirement with the decision of the Wilson government to withdraw British forces from East of Suez.

Menzies' successor, Harold Holt, quickly formed a close personal rapport with US President Johnson, and the US/Australia alliance was at a high point during his brief Prime Ministership. Holt died at the end of 1967 and was followed by John Gorton, a former fighter pilot who had been in the Senate and had not previously held high ministerial office. Through the governments of Gorton and McMahon Australian policy seemed unpredictable and prone to discord with both the United States and Britain. Gorton craved independence and a new style for Australia but seemed unable to implant that in real substance. In terms of style especially he became increasingly a source of irritation and embarrassment for his colleagues and he was overturned in a party room revolt led by Malcolm Fraser which installed William McMahon as leader and Prime Minister. McMahon gave the impression of being out of his depth. He sought to reaffirm the Menzies and Holt role of loyal ally to the United States but in the end was caught trailing embarrassingly in the wake of Nixon and Kissinger as they moved to get out of the Viet Nam imbroglio and to establish a new relationship with China.

Whitlam Breaks Out

E.G. Whitlam led Labor to government in 1972 after the long run of Conservative Coalition governments since 1949. He was a commanding figure in the Parliament and in public and he reflected the widespread demand for change and for a break with old constraints, as well as the passions involved in the anti-war movement that had grown strongly in Australia in reaction to the Viet Nam involvement. Many on the Labor side of politics had been active in the Viet Nam war protest movement and the wider peace and anti-nuclear movements, including in some cases the more flamboyant manifestations of the 'make love not war' genre. Whitlam had already visited China as Leader of the Opposition and had met with Chou En-Lai on 6 July 1971, three days before Kissinger. On that occasion he promised that when Labor won office Australia would recognize the People's Republic of China, and as soon as he became Prime Minister Whitlam wrote to Chou En-Lai proposing the exchange of diplomatic representation[18]. In general Whitlam was committed to breaking away from the Cold War alliance parameters which had dominated Australian foreign policy and soon after assuming office there was sharp disagreement between Australia and the United States. The Australian Labor movement reacted strongly to the United States bombing of North Vietnam undertaken in an effort to force Hanoi to accept a peace settlement. Whitlam condemned the move as 'the murderous bombing of Hanoi', the Minister for Labour, Mr Cameron, called it an 'act of virtual genocide' and the Minister for Trade, Mr Cairns, said that the bombing was naked aggression and 'the most brutal, indiscriminate slaughter of defenceless men, women and children in living memory'[19]. Australian Trade Unions placed bans on American shipping and American companies. The United States protested formally and vigorously and threatened retaliation. There was a sharp change in the quality of the relationship between Canberra and Washington from the days of Menzies and Holt. When Whitlam visited Washington in July 1973 there was a question whether President Nixon would see him. In the end Nixon did so, as did Kissinger and the Secretary of State William Rogers. In these and other meetings and in his address to the National Press Club the Prime Minister explained his government's new policy directions for Australia and reaffirmed its commitment to the ANZUS alliance.

Whitlam's message was that his government's approach was neither anti-American nor isolationist. It strongly supported the ANZUS alliance. But that alliance was not the only element in the new Australian government's foreign policy and under Labor Australia would not be regarded as a satellite of the United States or any other country. In his National Press Club speech[20] Whitlam said 'My government wants to move away from the narrow view that the ANZUS Treaty is the only significant factor in our relations with the United States and the equally narrow view that our relations with the United States are the only significant factor in Australia's foreign relations'. He made it clear that Australia would cultivate a wide range of other relationships especially in its own region and that it would adopt a less ideological approach than its predecessors 'in our dealings with all the countries of that region we think it's time for an ideological holiday'. Whitlam said that for 20 years he had been 'appalled at the damage we of the West have done to ourselves and to other peoples by our Western ideological preoccupations, particularly in South-East Asia' and we shall see later how that view influenced his approach to Indonesia and the issue of East Timor.

Whitlam's approach to the 'countries of the region', seeking to escape the anti-communist, cold war ideological framework in which Australian policy had long been cast, had another aspect. As already noted, he and many of his supporters had been prominent in the Viet Nam war protest movement and the Labor movement in Australia had also very close links with the trade union movement which still contained communist and indeed pro-Soviet elements. Whitlam sought to finesse those well to his left on foreign policy while seeking to engage with regional leaders and governments of importance to Australia which were themselves to his right. This was especially the case with President Soeharto of Indonesia. In that case, and to a degree in regard to others, Whitlam showed himself prepared to set aside 'Western ideological preoccupations' of a different kind in the interests of developing relations in Australia's interests with a profoundly anti-communist regional leadership which was regarded with disfavour by prominent members of his government. To this extent then, Whitlam in practice interpreted the setting aside of 'ideological preoccupations' in relations with the countries of the region as both the breaking out of the constraints of the anti-communist, cold-war Western alliance ideology and circumvention of the ideological distaste of the left-leaning or non-aligned elements in his party for governments in the region which were seen to transgress other Western ideological standards. He cultivated the relationship with Mao's China but also that with Soeharto's Indonesia and was not much constrained by any revulsion from the authoritarian, anti-democratic, anti-human rights aspects of either.

Nevertheless, at the time, and especially in the early stages, Whitlam's foreign policy appeared to be locating Australia a good deal further away from the United States and a good deal closer to the Soviet Union in an overall Cold War context. On a range of issues he quickly showed that his government would not routinely follow American or Western policies in the United Nations and elsewhere. In general this was done with little regard for explanation to others who were affected and with an appearance of wanting to maximize the demonstration effect of Australia's increased independence. There was a natural determination to show how different the values, attitudes and policies of the new government were from those of its predecessors, as if the pent-up instincts and inclinations of all those years in opposition since 1949 needed at once to overturn the outdated policies of the conservatives. Australia's place in the councils of the West and especially in the Washington foreign policy and intelligence communities was called into question by all this, and there were those in Canberra of course who revelled in the greater attention shown to Australia as a result. The Prime Minister himself certainly never wanted or intended to put the alliance with the United States at risk, and went to some pains to limit any damage. But he clearly wanted to make a sharp break with the past and he certainly saw himself as unequivocally in charge of this large step forward in Australia's place in the world. Many Australians were inspired by his speeches on foreign policy issues and Australia's place in the world, saved as they often were from self-importance by wit, occasionally even at his own expense. Many others of course felt that the compass of the ship of state was being thrown overboard. Although Whitlam was at pains to retain control of foreign policy, and limited the role of his Minister for Foreign Affairs, Senator Don Willesee, he was unable to control the often strident voices of other senior members of the government and of those in the parliamentary party who saw the CIA behind every bush[21] and whose sympathies in the Cold War were at best ambivalent. For example, real damage was done to the intelligence relationship with the United States (and the United Kingdom) by the raid staged by the Attorney General, Senator Lionel Murphy, on the headquarters of the Australian Security Intelligence Organization.

In terms of the relationship with the region the Whitlam government made important advances. There was the ending of the freeze on relations with China, a policy which was of great political importance to the Labor Party and 'held topmost priority for the new government'[22]. It was of special importance to the Prime Minister himself who had visited China as Leader of the Opposition in 1971 against a chorus of criticism from the then government and for whom his 1973 visit as Prime Minister was a vindication and something of a triumph. There were costs and irritations subsequently in terms of Chinese complaints and comments on Australian affairs. The Prime Minister found it necessary to scotch larger ambitions held by some for Australia to assume the role of go-between for China with South East Asia. He made it clear that Australia should not seek for itself 'any grandiose, pompous role as a "bridge" between China and South East Asia but might occasionally and in a general way be "one honest broker among others"'[23]. Although there was not much early substance in the relationship with China the fact that it had been established was of great symbolic and practical importance in

Australia's foreign policy, both regionally and generally. The most ambitious regional move by the Labor government was to seek to promote the establishment of a wider Pacific regional association which would include the members of ASEAN and others as well as Pacific countries such as Australia. An active diplomacy towards ASEAN was pursued partly with a view to engaging the members of that Association in the project of the wider grouping. But the ASEAN response was lukewarm and nothing came of these efforts during the Whitlam government's term in office. However Australia's general standing in the region was raised by the elimination of the remaining elements of the White Australia policy and by a general demonstration of interest and involvement in the region. More than his predecessors, Whitlam sought to put substance into the notion that Australia's future was bound up with that of South East Asia and his policy towards Indonesia, especially on the East Timor issue was the clearest expression of that. It was therefore unfortunate that that policy became clouded in controversy and that it led in the end to recrimination and dispute within the Labor Party and in the wider Australian community.

Whitlam had no particular interest in the attachment to Britain and indeed at the centre of his policy approach was the need to escape from the shadow of Menzies' 'great and powerful friends'. But under his government there was perhaps more interest in the Commonwealth as an organization because the British role had diminished and a wide range of independent members had taken their places in it. It was a forum where Australian diplomacy could be pursued on issues in which the government was active in the United Nations, the place where Australia under Whitlam was most active. At the Commonwealth Prime Ministers meeting in 1973 Whitlam had a famous row with Lee Kuan Yew of Singapore, a leader as impatient with contradiction and as foreign to self-effacement as Whitlam himself. It was probably inevitable that these two would clash but they did so publicly as well as privately and in terms which made good copy. Whitlam impugned Lee's democratic credentials and Lee saw Australia, as he later explained in other contexts and in more detail, as a lazy, protected second-hand offshoot of Europe. But in general Whitlam and his government made good use of the multilateral organizations, and especially the United Nations, to show that Australia had a genuinely independent new foreign policy.

There is a sense in which Whitlam returned to the main themes of the foreign policy of the Chifley/Evatt era in that he was quite ready (and at times appeared almost eager) to defy the United States and was determined to assert Australia's independent interests as he saw them and, above all, Australia's right to an independent voice. But the times were very different and the Cold War imposed some constraints even on a government which was determined not to be as tied down by alliance with one side in that conflict as its predecessors had been. Moreover the association with Britain had lost much of its relevance and its efficacy by the time Whitlam came to power, whereas the need to engage with the region to which Australia was bound by geography and increasingly by trade was very clear to Whitlam and his main advisers. In these ways Whitlam's brief period as Prime Minister was a watershed. He and his associates threw away a number of old and irrelevant constraints on Australian policy and positioned Australia to engage in a more collegiate way with much of the world with which relationships had been characterized by mutual suspicion or indifference. But in the process the strains on the relationship with the United States worried parts of the electorate. What worried them more as the government pursued its somewhat erratic course were the economic policies, including especially the bizarre attempt of the super-nationalist Minister for Minerals and Energy R.F.X. Connor to raise vast loans through a Pakistani intermediary to finance massive resources investments. The government increasingly appeared to be creating disorder and indiscipline and the economy was suffering as a result. During the three years of the Whitlam government unemployment rose from two to nearly five per cent; inflation from four to 13 per cent, at one stage touching 18 per cent; federal spending as a proportion of GDP rose from 24 to 30 per cent and taxes went up as a consequence.

Mr Whitlam had explained his aims in his speech to the National Press Club on his first visit to Washington in 1973:

> My great hope for my Government, however long it may endure or as my opponents would say be endured, is that it will see the end of the old inhibitions, the self-defeating fears about Australia's place in the world, and the beginning of a creative maturity[24].

Certainly it moved to end some old inhibitions, but by the end the attempt to remove fears about Australia's place in the world began to take on an air of bravado, while the new creative maturity was at risk of being undermined by actions and statements of some ministers and others on the government side which appeared to many Australians reckless and irresponsible. In extraordinary circumstances the government was brought down, and in an election soon after, with a massive landslide, the Liberal/Country Party Coalition under Malcolm Fraser won office.

Fraser and Peacock

In the 1974 election campaign Whitlam and Willesee had tried to minimize foreign policy issues and had asserted that there was a basically bipartisan approach to foreign policy with Fraser leader of the Opposition and Andrew Peacock the spokesman on Foreign Affairs. As events showed later there were some substantial similarities and shared positions. But there was also a major difference which Fraser explained at length in his first major foreign policy speech as Prime Minister. In essence this was that Fraser set out to enshrine realism as the guiding principle of Australian foreign policy:

> We must be prepared to face the world as it is, and not as we would like it to be. Only in that way can we hope to perceive accurately possible problems for Australia and seek to overcome them. Only in that way can we effectively advance our objectives of peace and security. To point to possible problems and dangers is not to be gloomy or pessimistic. It

is an essential step in the development of realistic and appropriate policies. It is an essential step in enabling us to avoid problems and dangers which may arise.

And he contrasted this with the Whitlam approach as follows:

> In recent years, abroad as at home, lack of realism has inhibited Australia from the constructive role open to us. A government does a great disservice if it encourages acceptance by the people of an unrealistic view of the state of the world in which they live. At home, the costs of a lack of realism have become very apparent in the economic dislocation Australia has suffered. Abroad, unrealistic notions that an age of peace and stability had arrived encouraged a neglect of power realities – a neglect that did not serve our interests[25].

In practical terms this meant for Fraser that Australia should recognize the dangers of the world around it, be aware of its limitations and of its need to forge links with countries (such as the ASEAN members) with which it had common interests, not have illusions about détente and support the United States without prejudice to the pursuit of Australian independent interests.

This rather comprehensive statement by Fraser was in sharp contrast to the rhetoric of Whitlam on foreign policy. It was studiedly unemotional and indeed dour. The world was not an easy place. Australia's lot was not an easy one. It was irresponsible to be carried away by windy ideals. We needed to strengthen our defence. The United States was troubled by internal disputation and external criticism but we had closer links with it than with other great powers. South East Asia was important to us and we had a deep interest in 'maintaining sound and close relations with Indonesia'. But there were differences with Indonesia over East Timor despite which 'a major concern of our policy will be to continue the friendship we both value'. Australia would act to deepen the understanding it had with Japan.

An important element in Fraser's policy was that he flagged what he saw as the shared interest between China and Australia in ensuring a balance against Soviet power in the Pacific and South East Asia. He saw that (and believed he had China's endorsement of the conclusion) as entailing support for an effective American presence in the Pacific and Indian Oceans. Prime Minister Fraser's first overseas visit was made to Japan and China and in Beijing a record of what he said during a meeting with Hua Guofeng was obtained by the accompanying press party. This record was interpreted as indicating that Fraser had entertained the idea of an agreement between China, Japan, the United States and Australia to contain the Soviet Union in the Pacific and Asia. What the visit certainly showed was that the strong tilt towards China undertaken by Whitlam was to be continued and indeed enhanced by Fraser. But the motivation was of course different in that the Whitlam government was far less critical and suspicious of the Soviet Union than China and would not have sought to engage the latter to help contain the former.

The following year brought President Jimmy Carter to the White House and one of his early foreign policy announcements was that he had proposed to the Soviet Union the complete demilitarization of the Indian Ocean. This raised a large problem for Canberra because it appeared to derogate from the formula in the

ANZUS Treaty covering the metropolitan territory of the signatories. (A large part of Australia's littoral is on the Indian Ocean.) After strenuous Australian efforts (including by Fraser directly to Carter) the Secretary of State, Cyrus Vance, wrote a letter which gave an assurance that if the United States and the Soviet Union negotiated an agreement on the Indian Ocean it would not 'in any way qualify or derogate from the US commitment to Australia or limit US freedom to act in implementing our commitments under the ANZUS treaty'[26]. This was on the face of it a significant success for the Australian side. An advantage for the Fraser government was the access enjoyed by its Minister for Foreign Affairs Andrew Peacock in Washington. Peacock had developed a range of key contacts over a number of years and was liked by and accepted into key circles, especially on the Democrat side. When Carter assembled his Administration Peacock was well placed to use that access and he did so to good effect, rapidly establishing an easy rapport with Vance and with the latter's principal assistant for Asia and the Pacific, Richard Holbrooke. Peacock shared Fraser's realist outlook on the world. But his style and method were very different and at times this produced some chafing. To the extent that the two increasingly cultivated somewhat separate gardens this was limited.

Fraser was always preoccupied by the danger of Soviet expansionism but he was increasingly concerned with the injustices of the global trading system as he saw them and with exploitation of third world countries by the industrialized world. He sympathized with much of the resentment and discontent which were generated by protectionism practised by the advanced countries, especially in Europe, and by the low prices which the developing countries received for the products they could export. He had very strong views about the ending of colonial regimes in Africa and especially on the Rhodesia issue. This meant that he was attracted to the Commonwealth for much the same reasons as Whitlam – the very reasons which had led Menzies to become disillusioned with it and eventually to despair of it. He believed that it was very important for Australia to do all it could to help overcome what was being called the North-South divide and to build on shared interests in the reform of the world trading system. Australia was geographically remote from the countries of the 'North' – the industrialized and advanced countries – and was located in the 'South', that is in a region of developing countries with which, as a commodity exporter, it shared important interests. Fraser commissioned an enquiry into Australia's relations with the Third World by a conservative academic, Owen Harries. This was staffed by a task force in the Department of Foreign Affairs and absorbed a significant part of that Department's resources. The Harries Report seems to have found rather limited favour with the Prime Minister, possibly (as Alan Renouf in his book *Malcolm Fraser and Australian Foreign Policy*[27] asserted) because it said Australia should not rely on continuity in China's conduct of foreign policy and should avoid any prominence in Southern African affairs. However the Report was interesting in that it saw that 'It is now becoming increasingly clear that, from the point of view of the ASEAN countries, Australia's relevance to their sub-region will increasingly [be measured] in terms of our willingness and capacity to participate in a process of expanded economic exchange'[28] and argued that 'The combined population of the ASEAN countries gives them the potential to develop over coming decades into a market as important as that currently provided by the US or EEC'.

Fraser thought that Australia's relations with the Third World were of great importance but he was not especially interested in South East Asia and looked increasingly to the global economic arrangements for answers to the growing North-South divide and the growing tendency of developing countries, non-aligned in the Cold War context, to be fiercely critical of the West while basking in the approval of the Soviet bloc. At the same time Fraser himself deeply resented the treatment of Australia by the European Economic Community, including the role which had been played (or not played) by Britain since its belated entry. He saw the Community's Common Agricultural Policy (CAP) particularly as severely penalizing not only Australia but much of the developing world and as imposing huge costs on the consumers and taxpayers in Europe itself. He appointed a special Minister to conduct negotiations with Europe to seek reform of the CAP. This was John Howard, who twenty years later became Prime Minister. Howard was assisted by a specially selected team of the ablest young talent from relevant departments of the Commonwealth Public Service and they subjected the EEC system to rigorous scrutiny, placing the results and their critique before the Commission and all the member governments as well as briefing the European media. There was no doubt about the intellectual quality and validity of the work but they encountered what all others had encountered before them: the political deals underpinning the Community, both between the member nations and within influential member nations. While there were some who were prepared to admit that the CAP and other protectionist systems in the EEC imposed a cost on the rest of the world the senior politicians argued (as they always had) that this was an essential component of the glue which held the Community together and that, given the value to the world of bringing Europe's rivalries and conflicts to an end, this was a price well worth paying.

Fraser's attention turned to creating an impetus to reform the international economic system mainly to give a better deal to the developing countries. He worked with a group of other leaders including the President of Nigeria, the Chancellor of the Federal Republic of Germany and the Prime Minister of Jamaica to seek to put the so-called North-South dialogue on a less acrimonious and more productive footing. He was in sympathy with efforts to establish a New International Economic Order. A favoured vehicle for this purpose was the proposed Common Fund which was to be a massive bank of resources which would be managed on a price stabilization and price maintenance model. The model which the Prime Minister often quoted to illustrate the advantages of this management of the markets for commodities was the Australian wool price stabilization scheme with which he was well acquainted as an Australian wool producer[29]. The Common Fund idea had appeal to those developing countries which saw or thought they saw that it would be of benefit to them as commodity producers. But to those who already had for example special access privileges to the European Common Market or to the United States it was less interesting. In any case the times were turning against massive attempts to manage markets. The era of Ronald Reagan and Margaret Thatcher was about to begin and indeed for the last two years of Fraser's Prime Ministership his advocacy of these third world causes became something of an irritant in Washington. At the United Nations and in its specialized agencies, the Soviet Union and its satellites, along with non-aligned countries, often led by India, had for years subjected the United States especially to tendentious and often malevolent attacks for the alleged crimes and misdemeanours of its corporate citizens. They made long and doctrinaire speeches claiming that capitalism and the United States especially was exploiting the developing countries and perpetuating their backwardness by 'neo-colonialism'. Under the Carter Administration the United States and the West generally seemed to have little stomach for contesting this attack in a direct way. But it was inevitable that things would change and that there would be a strong reaction. When it came, with Reagan in 1981, there was no longer any disposition to submit relatively uncomplainingly to ideological attacks at the UN including denunciatory resolutions, nor to countenance either much of the rhetoric or the specifics of the New International Economic Order. Such ideas as the Common Fund were subjected to robust and sceptical analysis and criticism from an economic perspective which believed in minimal government, minimizing taxes and minimum interference with market competition.

Thus the Fraser approach to the North-South dialogue fell out of step with the times. But his years in government maintained a distinctively Australian foreign policy not only on the so-called global dialogue and the world trade agenda. He was also active on African issues, particularly Zimbabwe, was a stern critic of the Soviet Union and took a very robust position on their action in Afghanistan. There was steady but unspectacular development in Australia's relations with Asia but awkwardness persisted in the relationship with Indonesia following their invasion of East Timor in the first days of the Fraser government. Australia had growing capacities in foreign affairs and increasing interests around the world, both economically and in strategic terms. There were tentative beginnings of what became later the policy of seeking engagement with East Asia. But by 1983 when the Coalition lost office to Labor there was a need for new thinking and for a new approach to major issues of economic policy and to foreign policy issues which flowed from them, and especially to the central issue of regional policy.

As a young man Fraser had been a minister under Menzies and it was perhaps partly from Menzies that he drew his sense that the world was a hard and, for Australia, rather unsympathetic place. He conveyed the sense that Australia needed always to be on the watch for threats to its welfare or its security. But the threats he identified were largely those of the central balance, the great issues of the Cold War including the nuclear standoff between the superpowers. There were deep differences about these issues in the Australian domestic political context but Australia's international position on them was fixed under Fraser and for the wider electorate there was no sense that Australia was exercising a significant influence on these great issues, or that it could do so. Nor, after seven or eight years of Fraser in office, had more imminent and direct threats to Australia emerged. The Australian sense of vulnerability had greatly diminished, even though it was to some degree at least implicit in Fraser's concern about the North-South divide and the discontents and resentments of the Third World. Australia's need to be seen to be active and helpful in that context no doubt reflected a sense that Australia, because of its geographical position and its modest size, should seek to avoid those discontents and resentments to which the Europeans and the Americans could afford to be more indifferent.

Whitlam and Fraser, in their very different ways, established Australia's independence in foreign policy. In 1983 there was still valued consultation with Britain and vital security and other cooperation with the United States. But following great and powerful friends was no longer the basis of policy. It was recognized by key figures on both sides of politics and elsewhere in the foreign policy community that Australia had to develop new associations reflecting its location and its economic relations.

Notes

1. See Meaney, Neville (1985), *Australia and the World, A Documentary History from the 1870s to the 1970s*, Longman Cheshire, Melbourne, pp. 37-43, where the discussion is reprinted.
2. See Chapter 2 endnote 4.
3. Day, David (1993), *Menzies and Churchill at War*, Oxford University Press, Melbourne, p. 79, quoting Sir Frederick Shedden's unpublished manuscript. Shedden as Secretary of Defence was in a good position to understand the Prime Minister's thinking at the time.
4. *Ibid.*
5. Letter Blamey to Shedden quoted in Day, *op. cit.* pp. 184-5.
6. Bell, Coral (1988), *Dependent Ally, A Study in Australian Foreign Policy*, Oxford University Press, Melbourne.
7. *Ibid.*, p. 33.
8. Meaney, Neville, p. 505.
9. See Chapter 2 above.
10. Bell, *op. cit.* p. 34.
11. Watt, Alan (1967), *The Evolution of Australian Foreign Policy, 1938-1965*, Cambridge University Press, Cambridge, p. 46.
12. *Ibid.*, p. 94.
13. Hasluck, Paul (1948), *Workshop of Security*, Cheshire, Melbourne, quoted in Watt *op. cit.* p. 94.
14. Watt, *op. cit.* p. 96, quoting from *Commonwealth Parliamentary Debates*.
15. For a detailed discussion making this case see Waters, C.W.P. (1994), 'Anglo-Australian Conflict over the Cold War: H.V. Evatt as President of the UN General Assembly, 1948-49', *The Journal of Imperial and Commonwealth History*, Vol. 22 No. 2.
16. Horne, Donald (1964), *The Lucky Country*, Penguin, Adelaide, p. 98.
17. *Ibid.*
18. Bell, *op. cit.* p. 116.
19. Meaney, *op. cit.* p. 737.
20. For text see Meaney, pp. 747-50.

21 Although some students of the period are still concerned about what they see as gaps in information relating to alleged US intelligence involvement in some events which embarrassed the Whitlam Government.
22 Albinski, Henry (1977), *Australian External Policy Under Labor*, University of Queensland Press, St Lucia, p. 151.
23 *Ibid.*, p. 153.
24 Meaney, *op. cit.* p. 750.
25 Prime Minister Fraser's address from which both these extracts are taken is on pp. 781-6 of Meaney, *op. cit.*
26 Bell, *op. cit.* p. 150.
27 Renouf, Alan (1986), *Malcolm Fraser and Australian Foreign Policy*, Australian Professional Publications, Sydney.
28 Committee on Australia's Relations with the Third World (1979), Australian Government Printing Service, Canberra, p. 130.
29 This scheme later collapsed as a result of the sharp fall in demand for wool and its large stock had to be held, at considerable cost, for many years. Thus the claimed paradigm for the Common Fund approach itself showed that such an attempt to control the market could easily send misleading signals to producers and lead to excess and unsaleable reserves overhanging the market and causing large losses to the producers and/or heavy costs to the controlling authority.

Chapter 4

Promoting Australia's Asian Future

Hawke's Commitment to the US Alliance

When Labor returned to office in March 1983 under the Prime Ministership of R.J. Hawke there was a major task of reconciling elements of the Party to the policies which Hawke wished to follow. These elements were diverse and their attitudes did not always coalesce. But they constituted points of attachment which in one way or another could, if not carefully handled, resist some of the shifts which needed to be made to attract a wider constituency to Labor and to overcome the economic and other problems which were holding back Australia's progress. There was still an old guard which had not moved much from its far left days. There were younger activists whose views and ambitions for Labor had been formed in the heady days of the brief Whitlam ascendancy, when to some in the Labor Party (and not only there of course) windows seemed to be opening on a new world exciting for its liberation and various forms of indulgence rather than its opportunities for productive work and responsibility. There was also a continuing revulsion against the attitudes and policies which had engaged Australia in the Viet Nam War, a revulsion which Hawke himself had expressed with force and persistence. There were other elements too in the Party's history and tradition which helped to produce wariness towards the foreign and some of the domestic policies which Hawke wanted to run. But Hawke had a strong base of personal support in the Labor movement. He had spent almost his whole working life in the Trade Union movement, had proved himself as a champion of Labor, and was widely admired and liked by working people. Thus, when he set about widening Labor's appeal and constituency, those within the Party who distrusted that tactic found it hard to rally opposition to him, especially as no alternative offered the same prospect of electoral success. His personal charisma, powerful forensic skills and confidence in managing internal politics of the Party helped him to maintain a strong position in the early years of his ministry.

Hawke like Fraser was convinced that Australia's interests lay with the Western side in the Cold War and that Australia's security required the maintenance and careful tending of the alliance with the United States. In some respects his role model had been John Curtin, another West Australian who, superficially at least, shared some significant life experiences and character traits with Bob Hawke. Hawke admired Curtin[1] and not least for his wartime leadership which had been based on the closest working relationship with MacArthur and the United States[2]. But Hawke had to take into account also that part of the Labor constituency on the left and in the Trade Unions which was ideologically and politically more suspicious than he was of the United States and of its nuclear defence posture, of its 'neo-colonialism' and of its record of supporting undemocratic regimes in the third world. They were also opposed to authoritarian elements in South East Asia including the President of Indonesia, especially in regard to his regime's record in East Timor. There was a link between these views in that the hand of the United States and its intelligence services was seen behind authoritarian regimes and in opposition to 'progressive' movements. Indeed there was still suspicion in some quarters of the role which United States covert operations were thought to have played in undermining the Whitlam government.

With great skill Hawke, Hayden, Evans and others in the government massaged party opinion and took measures which mollified the disarmament and human rights groups who were inclined to oppose the core foreign and defence policies which the government was developing. They did this largely by giving prominence to those issues and participating far more actively than previous Australian governments in the international diplomacy of disarmament in particular. It was necessary *inter alia* to counter the demonization by the left of the arrangements with the United States under which special facilities were operated in central Australia in the context of satellite intelligence gathering. The argument was developed that these were a contribution to peace and disarmament because of the requirement to monitor missile launches etc. A special 'Ambassador for Disarmament' was appointed who prominently took a specifically Australian role in the international forums and also addressed domestic audiences in Australia on the subject and discussed it with Labor Party activists around the country. A series of related initiatives included establishing a Peace Research Institute at the Australian National University and a Disarmament Branch in the Department of Foreign Affairs. Hawke also worked to shore up his position with that part of the Australian public which would have been nervous about the government's policies of strengthening Australia's relations with Asia if they had been seen as reducing the reassuring alliance relationship with the United States. His first overseas visit was to Indonesia, but from the beginning he paid special attention to ensuring that the relationship with the United States was reinforced and preserved as the solid basis of confidence and reassurance on which the government could build its regional and trade policies.

Hawke saw also that he must sharply differentiate the Australian Labor Party government from the New Zealand Labor government which came to office in July 1984 under Prime Minister David Lange. That government banned access to New Zealand ports for all United States nuclear-powered or nuclear-armed naval vessels. In view of the United States policy of neither confirming nor denying whether a ship carried nuclear weapons this was tantamount to denying access to all US Navy vessels. Not surprisingly this was deemed in Washington to be quite inconsistent with the alliance relationship which New Zealand had with the United States under ANZUS (Australia, New Zealand and the United States). And while the United States had no particular need to send its naval ships into New Zealand ports it was concerned at the example which might be set for other western governments which, like New Zealand, had to handle active anti-nuclear and anti-United States elements. Moreover the relevant people in the Administration in

Washington believed the New Zealand action was directly counter to assurances which Lange had given them before he came into office. Lange and his government were detested in Washington for what was seen as deceit and disloyalty. There was some opinion in favour of scrapping the ANZUS Treaty altogether. That was deeply worrying for the Australian side. Although most of those in Washington who talked of abandoning ANZUS said there would have to be a new agreement with Australia alone, it was clear that getting such an agreement through all the US constitutional steps, including the Congressional ones, would be difficult and might well produce something at the end which was less reassuring for Australia than the already rather cautious wording of the ANZUS Treaty. ANZUS was preserved, but on certain conditions affecting New Zealand. Australia was required to ensure that the intelligence and related information which it supplied to New Zealand must not contain United States sourced material. The need for Hawke to distance himself and his government in American eyes from Lange and the New Zealand Labor government was facilitated by the fact that he had no personal liking for Lange and deplored the way the latter had acted in this matter as much as the Americans did[3]. At the same time the government was aware that there were those in Australia who sympathized with the New Zealand position and who would have resented any appearance of Australia joining in punishment of New Zealand. But there were in any case other reasons for seeking to ensure as far as possible that New Zealand was not penalized. It was hoped that opinion in New Zealand would change over time so that the ANZUS alliance could be reinstated and in the meantime it was desirable to encourage the New Zealanders to remain as engaged in joint defence arrangements as their principles and the United States reaction would permit. Hawke did his best in that regard although, according to Bill Hayden, then foreign minister, his efforts at a kind of personal diplomacy in the matter were idiosyncratic and not effective[4].

However that may be it is clear that Hawke managed this issue very successfully. The sentiments which had led the New Zealand Labor Party to adopt the nuclear ship visits policy were also prominent, vocal and committed in the Australian Labor Party where they had real influence. The difference lay in the leadership. 'The Australian Prime Minister and Foreign Minister in particular, forcefully argued the Australian national interest in the alliance within the Labor Party and the electorate at large. The New Zealand Prime Minister was persuaded to another course by expressions of popular support for the policy that he had taken into Government'[5]. For Hawke it was essential to prevent the New Zealand example from infecting his party to the extent of prejudicing the alliance with the United States. His whole world outlook for Australia involved working closely with the United States in multilateral trade liberalization, in Asia-Pacific regionalism and in encouraging the inclusion of a changing China in these constructive endeavours. Moreover all Australian Prime Ministers since at least World War Two have known that visibly close relations with the United States are something which a majority of the Australian electorate finds reassuring and expects its government to foster. Not all have been as comfortable with that knowledge as was Bob Hawke and one or two have come to it only after some time in office, rather than taking it in with them, as did Hawke or, thirteen years later, Howard.

The Hawke government also faced lingering concern in some quarters in Washington about the Australian Labor Party as a result of the difficulties during the Whitlam government. It was feared that the party might still harbour views and policy tendencies seen as inimical to United States interests of the kind which had caused problems between 1972 and 1975, for example with ministers such as Murphy, Connor and Cairns. Such fears were not groundless, but Hawke set about putting them to rest. To establish broad support in Australia for Labor's new foreign policy it was necessary to allay old concerns that Labor was not sound on defence or on the United States alliance, and about pro-Soviet attitudes in the Labor movement. It was soon made clear that the Prime Minister was well accepted in Washington and that he was determined to reinforce the relationship. In seeking regional 'enmeshment' with Asia he would not be going into the water without a life jacket.

Economic Necessity and the Turn to North East Asia

But while the alliance with the United States was seen as essential for Australia's security and as the underpinning of the Hawke government's foreign and defence policies it was difficult to harness it to the government's vision for a solution to Australia's economic future. Certainly the United States had predominant influence in international trade diplomacy and in other areas of great importance to Australia such as the International Monetary Fund and the World Bank (IBRD), the international financial institutions in Washington set up forty years before at Bretton Woods. The United States was also important for Australia as a major investor. But less than 12 percent of Australia's exports went to the United States as against more than 50 percent to East Asia (41.8 per cent to Northeast Asia and 9.3 per cent to ASEAN[6]). Moreover the United States, like Europe, had intractable barriers to major Australian exports making it extremely difficult to increase Australia's market share. It was argued by Australian academic proponents of multilateral free trade and the rapid reduction of Australian protectionism, and also by the United States Administration, that Australia should not become too concerned about the bilateral balance with the United States but should consider the broad pattern of trade in the Pacific region. In that context Australia had a large surplus in trade with Japan, Japan a large surplus in trade with the United States and Australia a large deficit with the United States. The symmetry suggested by this argument had little appeal for those Australian exporting interests which faced severe barriers in the United States. Then the United States Administration decided to fight European export subsidies by introducing a so-called Export Enhancement Program which in effect subsidized United States exports of agricultural commodities to foreign markets, including some of major interest to Australia. Australia's strenuous lobbying in Washington had only limited success and the Reagan Administration insisted that it would be unmoved by any attempt by the Australian side to link these trade concerns to other aspects of the relationship.

There was some similarity between the situation faced by the Hawke government in regard to trade with the United States and that which Fraser had faced with the EEC and fought so long and hard, and relatively unavailingly, to change. In both cases Australia felt aggrieved that, despite close and long-standing relations, it was being excluded from fair and reasonable trading opportunities. In both cases the trade was heavily in favour of the other party, with Australia importing much more from Europe and America than it could sell to those partners. The difference was that Australia had had massive markets in Europe, especially but not only in Britain. Although these had been of diminishing importance it was a savage blow to some industries when they were largely shut down as a result of the protectionist trade policies of the EEC. The industries worst affected were in the agriculture sector which was a cornerstone of the political deals on which the Community was based. Australia had not had that degree of dependence on the United States market but as Europe closed against Australian exports more attention was given to alternatives, including the United States. The sense of grievance was greater against Europe, reflecting both the feeling that Australia had been treated with little consideration in the deals made when Britain entered the Community and the fact that the dislocation to Australia was much more severe than in the case of the Reagan Administration's trade policies. Fraser's sometimes bitter struggle with Europe was different in quality and tone from the trade diplomacy carried forward in Washington under the Hawke government, although that too had its angry episodes. On those occasions the anger was more on the United States side, arising from irritation with Australian persistence and impatience with what was no doubt seen as the importuning of a small country which simply did not have the clout to counter either the Administration's unilateral policy decisions or the strength of the relevant interests in the Congress. Every effort was made to bring Australia's case to the notice of all concerned in Washington, and indeed the justice of that case was acknowledged by many (though not of course by all) and some support was developed in the Congress. But Australia did not have the muscle or the leverage to obtain significant changes in policy in this area. Nor was it prepared to put to the test whatever leverage it did have in terms of the security relationship[7].

Australia's ambivalence in this area was (and indeed remains) essentially rooted in the politics of the issues in both countries. In Australia there was a deep and justifiable resentment, especially of course on the part of the economic interests concerned, with the treatment Australia's trade grievances received at the hands of the Administration and the Congress especially during the latter part of the Reagan presidency. No Australian government could ignore that. The Australian meat industry was more successful than most other Australian industries in protecting and even advancing its interests in the United States and it owed that success as much to the lobbyists it employed[8] as to the unremitting efforts of the official Australian representation. In some areas there was little or nothing effective that the Australian side could achieve on a bilateral basis. In the case of sugar for example it was made clear that the domestic price could not be lowered because the growers in the south Texas constituency of the Agriculture Committee Chairman could not survive on less and the import quota system was not in any visible way related to efficiency or price[9]. Steel, coal and metals encountered major obstacles as well as agriculture. Then the Export Enhancement Program for grains, designed we were told to counter the European export subsidies, threatened to bite into Australian wheat exports to the Middle East. The problem for the government was that it had to be seen to be striving vigorously to counter all this, and indeed to be getting results, without acceding to the demands of trade interests that the security alliance be put into the negotiating equation. We said on Capitol Hill and to the Administration that the trade issue risked undermining the constituency in Australia for the alliance relationship. But that did not carry much weight when it was clear that most Australians were attached to that relationship and the Prime Minister and the Defence Minister (especially) emphasized its importance for Australia. The fact was that the Australian interest was perceived by the government, and especially by Hawke, less in terms of using the defence relationship to exercise leverage on the trade issues and disputes than to *prevent* the trade disputes from spilling over into the alliance relationship and spreading the damage into Australia's key security alliance. This points to the essential difference between the Hawke and Hayden approaches to the relationship with the United States. Hawke saw it as central to Australia's interests and Hayden[10], seeing it as having a qualified importance which had often been distorted and exaggerated by conservative governments in Australia, thought it should be used in a direct way in the trade disputes.

The effect of the reverses in trade with Europe and the United States was to force Australia to look elsewhere. By the time Hawke came to office in 1983 East Asia had already become by far Australia's largest export market. But the implications of that and of Australia's changed circumstances had been addressed only piecemeal and partially. The failure of the Fraser government's efforts with Europe left a sour taste in many Australian mouths but it was clear that the main lesson was that it was necessary to adjust and to make greater efforts elsewhere. Labor's subsequent problems over trade with the United States left the same essential lesson. It would be necessary to continue using Australia's best skills in trade diplomacy in the *multilateral* arena, especially to try to have agriculture brought further into the global trade liberalization regimes, and it would be necessary to intensify efforts to develop existing markets and products and develop new ones in which Australia could successfully compete. The best prospects clearly lay with East Asia where massive economic growth had been proceeding for decades and which had become the principal market for Australia's exports. The disappointments with Europe and America and the recognition that they were not going to provide any significant alternative to trade dependence on East Asia set off a dilemma and a debate about Australia's foreign policy and indeed Australia's future which remains unresolved and perhaps unresolvable. Australia's key security, cultural and family links were with America and Europe. But the Europeans and Americans appeared to be unwilling to provide Australia with the opportunity to earn its living. So it must intensify its turn to East Asia and work out the consequences for its posture in the region and in the world. It was John Howard who said after he became Prime Minister that Australia's emphasis on East Asia did not mean or require turning our back on our long-standing friends (meaning the

United States). But it was Bob Hawke who first put that into practice by doing all he could to preserve and strengthen the relationship with the United States while preparing Australia for much closer engagement with East Asia. Already there were others who were more radical about the implications for Australia and the direction it should take, asserting that Australia must come to terms with the fact that it was a part of Asia, implying a requirement that Australia seek to assimilate to East Asia in many respects and not just economically.

Hawke commissioned a leading economist at the Australian National University, Ross Garnaut, who was probably his most important adviser, to prepare a report on 'The North East Asian Ascendancy'[11] and its relevance for Australia. This extremely influential document laid down the bases of new Australian policies on a wide range of issues on industry protection, immigration, education, regional cooperation and cultural awareness. But most importantly it marshalled a formidable battery of facts, analysis and argument to show that it was essential for Australia's future that it learn to deal effectively across the board with the increasingly prosperous and vigorous nations of North East Asia. Australians needed to learn Asian languages and to escape from the constraints of their own (often provincial) cultural and political ways of looking at the world so that they could engage successfully with the burgeoning East Asian countries.

The Garnaut Report marked a turning point in the shift of Australian policy towards a priority focus on its own geographical region and the opportunities which that offered. Indeed, the central concept of that shift was that Australia's geographical location now held out not threats and reasons for concern about vulnerability but rather immense opportunities. The Garnaut Report, reflecting as it did the thinking of the Prime Minister and the government, set the stage for an unprecedented Australian foreign policy thrust to engage with East Asia. The sense of vulnerability in the face of potential threats from the north, unsurprising in the light of Australia's experience of the Pacific War, was greatly diminished by new defence thinking and by a greater confidence that Australia could by itself handle such threats as might emerge short of assault by a major power. Instead there was the image of East Asia as Australia's opportunity to grow economically, to embark on a new intellectual and political challenge, and to build a new role in the region and the world. The ending of the Cold War added impetus.

The timing was also favourable because it meshed with and provided further rationale for other elements in Hawke's program of reform and change. He had spent more than twenty years in the Australian Trade Union movement and thus had the standing and credibility to introduce overdue changes to open the highly protected Australian economy and make it more competitive. Garnaut, writing in 1989 in the first paragraph of the Introduction to his Report, proclaimed 'This is a time of great opportunity for Australia. It is a time when Australians have a chance to grasp the prosperity, self-confidence and independence in an interdependent world that earlier Australians in expansive times had hoped for their country'[12]. Garnaut referred to the 'beginning of internationalization and liberalization of economic life in recent years' by contrast with 'the first seven decades of the Federation [when] a fearful, defensive Australia built walls to protect itself against the challenge of the outside world and found that it had protected itself against the recognition and utilisation of opportunity'. That is to say, until the Hawke government, Australia had tried to live in what was increasingly a fools' paradise. 'The tide has turned through the 1980s, although we carry still most of the dead weight of a protectionist past'. The program which Garnaut set out to explain in detail in the report was of a piece with the rest of the economic, political and social reform agenda of the Hawke government and would depend on the continued dismantling of the old protectionist structures and practices.

The opportunity Garnaut saw for Australia arose because of several linked developments in East Asia. Firstly the record of growth was unprecedented: 'Never before in human history have economies grown as fast for so long as in North East Asia over the past four decades', and 'As a result, there has been an historic shift in the centre of gravity of economic production and power towards North East Asia'. This would continue with China especially growing rapidly. At the same time the ratio of foreign trade to output in the region was increasing, so that the foreign trade pie was becoming larger not only with rapid growth of the economies but also because the share of foreign trade was increasing within those economies. Australia's share of that trade had been decreasing, as had its share of global trade, and the answer to that was the liberalization and removal of protection which Garnaut strongly advocated. If that could be achieved the outlook for Australia was very promising because of the complementarity of Australia's economy with those of North East Asia already demonstrated by the growth of Australia's exports to the region. This had started with fibres and bulk foods, then minerals for heavy industry, then processed raw materials, then higher quality services and goods. He showed that complementarity in Australian export trade with North East Asia was higher than in any other important trading relationship of Australia or of North East Asia. Various other subsidiary factors supported this scenario: in effect North East Asia was Australia's made-to-measure trade partner and the challenge was to equip Australia to lock into the immense opportunity which its location next to East Asia and its comparative advantages, including its resource endowment, offered.

The thinking embodied in the Garnaut Report had of course been developing for some time. Growing awareness during the 1960s and 1970s of the need for Australia to focus more on East Asia in various fields such as immigration, education and culture not only altered Australia's public perception of Asia, it also prompted the Australian government to develop positive steps towards integration with the region. A policy of 'constructive engagement with Asia' became a fundamental tenet in the foreign policy of all political parties.

As early as 1949, the Australian government began to change its tune on having a discriminatory immigration policy. Minister Holt's decision in 1949 to allow 800 non-European refugees to stay, and Japanese war brides to be admitted, was the first step towards a non-discriminatory immigration policy[13]. By 1973, race as a factor in Australia's immigration policies had been totally eliminated and the 'White Australia' policy had been abolished[14]. With the final dismantling of the 'White Australia' policy immigration from Asia steadily increased including a growing number of skilled immigrants. In the mid-1980s it was estimated that around 200,000 overseas students, almost all from Asia, had graduated in Australian tertiary institutions since World War Two[15].

A further emphasis on skill was recommended by the major enquiry chaired by Stephen FitzGerald in 1988. That Asian Studies Inquiry, 'National Strategy for the Study of Asia in Australia', also drew particular attention to the importance of studying Asian languages and societies in Australian schools and universities. The Fitzgerald Report adopted by the Australian Cabinet in 1989 made recommendations that covered career prospects, education, including visual and performing arts, and the media[16]. It depicted Asian Studies as vital to the national interest of Australia. John Ingleson, introducing his report on *Asia in Australian Higher Education* in 1989, summed up the intimate connection between Asian studies and Australia's national concerns. Ingleson proposed that teaching about Asia and its languages be seen as an aspect of the 'Australianization' (not Asianization) of the curricula in higher education in this country[17]. Ingleson, while basically supportive of what was being done to teach Asian languages, also argued that programs needed to be more proficient and more attractive to students[18].

It was throughout this period and in this dramatically new environment of Asia-Australia relations that the Asian Studies Association of Australia (ASAA) was formed[19]. During the time of the ASAA's operation, the official view that Australia must recognize its geographic location within Asia and the political, social and most particularly economic implications for policy formulation was developed[20]. In the period from the formation of the ASAA up to the late 1990s, Australia's 'Asia' momentum continued to grow with an increase in foreign students studying in Australia and Australians learning about Asia.

The 1980s will probably be recorded as a turning point in the way Australia perceived Northeast Asia. Gareth Evans rightly saw the eighties as characterized by a sense of enthusiasm and opportunity about the future of Australia's relations with Northeast Asia, in trading terms as well as in terms of building up relations of greater depth and texture. As Evans argued, the most eloquent expression of this view has been, and remains, the Garnaut Report on Australia and the Northeast Asian Ascendancy with its wide-ranging checklist of the opportunities which Northeast Asia holds for Australia[21].

Cooperation with Japan in Developing Pacific Cooperation

Moreover there had developed during the Fraser government a strong move to institutionalize cooperation in the Pacific which drew heavily on Australian links with Japan, especially through major mining companies and the Australian National University. This was a large part of the genesis of the Garnaut Report. It was also the genesis of a long and very ambitious effort by Australia to bring into existence an institutional framework which would link the United States on the eastern side of the Pacific Basin with East Asia on the western side, taking in Australia and New Zealand to the south. The principal driving force of this project in Australia was Sir John Crawford at the Australian National University. He focussed that institution strongly on Asia and the Pacific; greatly, it must be said, to the benefit of Australia over time. Crawford fostered governmental and academic links with Japan. He had a close personal association with Dr Saburo Okita who had been for many years in the Japanese Ministry of Foreign Affairs and the Economic Planning Agency. Okita was successively President of the Japan Economic Institute and of the Overseas Economic Cooperation Fund and then served as Minister for Foreign Affairs of Japan. He advised successive governments of Japan on a range of economic and other issues and was an influential figure not only in Japan with a wide range of international contacts. He and Crawford shared a belief in the importance of fostering Pacific cooperation and they worked closely together to promote regional institutional cooperation. Okita had been involved for many years in the development of Japanese policy on Pacific cooperation which was brought to fruition under the government of Prime Minister Masayoshi Ohira with his Pacific Basin Cooperation Concept. Ohira and Malcolm Fraser met in Canberra in January 1980 and, as a result of the agreement they then reached, the Pacific Community Seminar was held at the Australian National University in September 1980. This seminar, chaired by Crawford and Okita, and comprising representatives of government, business and academics, was in effect the founding meeting of the Pacific Economic Cooperation Council (PECC) which Crawford and those associated with him on the Australian side saw as initially performing for the Pacific economies a somewhat similar role to that performed by the OECD (Organization for Economic Cooperation and Development). Ohira and the Japanese had a somewhat different agenda in Pacific cooperation and the PECC, although this was not in conflict with the Crawford concept. The Japanese interest in the project arose largely from the desire to play a larger role in assisting the developing countries of Asia and for some years there had been consideration of ways in which Japan could play a bridging role between the developed countries of the Pacific Rim and the developing countries of Asia[22]. Japan's efforts in this regard were, and continued to be, complicated by suspicion especially in South East Asia that there was an agenda to seek by different means the objectives which had been inherent in the Greater East Asia Co-prosperity Sphere. Ohira himself was more concerned in all this with Japan's position in the Pacific Basin than with Asia and indeed did not originally include the ASEAN countries in the Pacific Concept[23]. The Ministry of Foreign Affairs ensured that they were included but Ohira and Fraser recognized at their January 1980 meeting that ASEAN might not be ready to engage in a full blown Pacific Community and that it would therefore be appropriate to start with the non-governmental Seminar. There was also some way to go in coordinating the Japanese and Australian positions.

This meant that the development of the Pacific Basin project was retained for most of the 1980s largely in the hands of Crawford and his chosen associates. Both the Japanese and Australian sides had expected the Seminar to produce more in the way of intergovernmental involvement but Crawford wanted any such development to be under his control[24]. There were certainly difficult and sensitive issues involved and Sir John Crawford might well have felt that these were best kept in his experienced hands. Certainly he had to a highly developed degree the old Trade official's reservations about the External/Foreign Affairs Department and all its works. In the years that followed PECC had a series of annual meetings and developed into an increasingly elaborate and comprehensive organization. There was a sense that, as the world's economic centre of gravity shifted from the Atlantic to the Pacific, PECC and all its activity was preparing for the future and developing the habits of cooperation and shared interest which would be required if the region were to exercise the sort of influence which had for so long resided with the Atlantic world. But towards the end of the eighties it was not clear what more PECC, as a non-governmental body, could accomplish. PECC's importance lay in increasing awareness and a habit of cooperation in key circles and thus paving the way for APEC, which was the realization of the eventual inter-governmental Pacific Basin organization which Ohira and Fraser had envisaged. And PECC probably did help disarm to some degree the reservations about a Pacific Basin organization which were harboured by ASEAN members. On the Japanese side those ASEAN reservations continued to cause concern on the part of the Ministry of Foreign Affairs and contributed to differences on the Pacific cooperation issue between that Ministry and the Ministry of International Trade and Industry (MITI). The former had had reservations about the intergovernmental Pacific Concept because they thought that it would be resisted by ASEAN which would see it as having the potential to undermine the South East Asian organization. They preferred that Japan concentrate on developing the relationship with ASEAN while leaving the Pacific cooperation project mainly to the private sector. MITI on the other hand was driven in the direction of more institutionalized and effective Pacific Basin cooperation because it was increasingly 'concerned about the development of inward-looking regionalism in the US-Canada Free Trade Agreement, concluded in January 1988, and the EC's move towards a unified market in 1992'[25].

In these reservations and concerns within ASEAN, reflected by Foreign Affairs in Tokyo, probably lay the seeds of an issue which would later cast a shadow over APEC, the inter-governmental organization proposed by Prime Minister Hawke in Seoul in January 1989 which developed strongly up to the East Asian financial crisis in 1997-98. This was the sense that East Asia, the Western side of the Pacific, had interests and a potential for solidarity which it did not share with the Eastern, American, side, and perhaps not with Australia either. In due course this would come to be seen as a real threat to Australian interests and policy on institutional development of Pacific economic cooperation which had focussed on the whole of the Pacific, including the United States. In 1989 the challenge to this in terms of exclusively Asian regionalism was relatively muted and not yet clearly articulated. The Australian approach of including the United States was shared by Japan, unequivocally by MITI and with reservations by Foreign Affairs also. In terms of trade policy Australia wanted to use Pacific cooperation to reduce barriers to trade not only regionally but globally by using the Pacific grouping to produce advances in the GATT framework especially with regard to areas (such as agriculture and textiles) of interest to Pacific countries. This pointed towards a need to have United States participation. Moreover, Americans had been involved in the PECC and other forerunner activities.

Terada[26] describes how since 1986 MITI had been considering ways in which Japan could promote regional economic cooperation at government level with the objective of eschewing the trend of discriminatory regionalism exemplified by North America and Europe and locking in a form of Asia Pacific regionalism which would 'not only be consistent with globalism, but....also aim to promote globalism'. For this ASEAN and the United States would both be needed. Shigeo Muraoka, the principal MITI official concerned, has said 'We hoped that MITI's plan could play a bridging role between regionalism and globalism'[27]. This was very close to Hawke's thinking which was to seek a way of combining the global trade liberalization thrust with the more specific Australian foreign and trade policy which was being articulated in the Garnaut Report and which had a specific regional priority.

The phase of activity which resulted in APEC began in August 1988 with the issuing of a report by a MITI study group. Their report saw a need for 'new forms of regional cooperation' arising from the US-Canada Free Trade Agreement and the EC's move towards a unified market. Drawing attention to expectations that the Asia Pacific region would be 'a locomotive for the development of the world economy' they noted proposals for a US-ASEAN free trade zone, a US-Japan free trade agreement and an Asia Pacific OECD[28]. But the Japanese side was well aware of ASEAN and other sensitivities about Japan proposing a regional intergovernmental organization and Muraoka had discussions with Michael Duffy, the Australian Minister for Trade Negotiations during the Uruguay Round mid-term review in Montreal in December 1988. Muraoka explained Japan's difficulties in the region as a result of the Greater East Asian Co-Prosperity Sphere and said that he hoped that Australia would take the initiative by itself to launch the idea. The Australian view was also 'that it would be better for a small non-threatening country like Australia to launch a new regional initiative, without too many specifics about the nature of proposed cooperation'[29].

As Japan and Australia explored and articulated ideas for an intergovernmental institution in the Pacific there continued to be some uncertainty about ASEAN participation and also about the likely position of the United States. But, despite the differences between Foreign Affairs and MITI and some internal differences in Canberra, momentum was developing. Prime Minister Hawke and other Ministers were receptive to this. The Montreal mid-term review seemed to threaten the Uruguay Round in which the Australian government had been investing such effort. Hawke's attachment to multilateralism and non-discrimination thus seemed threatened and he saw a regional economic institution as a supplementary approach by which he 'wanted now to bring together [the] two fundamental and interrelated themes of a freer international trading environment and Australia's overall foreign economic policy'[30]. At the beginning of 1989 Hawke instructed that a speech be drafted on regional cooperation including a concrete proposal. Before departing on a visit to Seoul later in the month he discussed the proposal with Garnaut. In Seoul he found Korean President Roh Tae Woo enthusiastic and he decided to launch the proposal in a speech there on 31 January 1989. He emphasized that he was not proposing a trading bloc, that a major objective would be to strengthen the GATT, and that he had in mind consultation and the exchange of information. The Hawke proposal for a formal organization led to considerable activity in the region primarily by Japan and Australia with visits to the region by officials of both countries. The reservations in ASEAN took some time and effort to overcome and Indonesia at first opposed the inclusion of the United States. The reaction of the United States to the Hawke speech was one of anger, at least as privately expressed to Australia, and in Japan the Ministry of Foreign Affairs was surprised and disconcerted by the announcement of the proposal in Seoul. It took some time for Japanese interests to be coordinated because the Ministry of Foreign Affairs was solicitous of ASEAN concerns and would not sign on to the proposal until it was sure of ASEAN support. But the following months, up to the middle of 1989 were a period of active consultation and lobbying around the region by Japanese and Australian officials. There were still unresolved issues when APEC held its first meeting, as proposed by Prime Minister Hawke, in Canberra in early November.

The reaction in Washington to Hawke's Seoul speech was sharper than anywhere else. The final form of the Australian proposal was put together only in Seoul but the Japanese side, including Foreign Affairs, had been in close touch with the relevant Australian ministers and officials and what Hawke said was generally in line with MITI thinking, except for Japanese reservations about the Hawke concept of a regional OECD. There had not been anything like that level or intensity of contact with the United States. While both Japanese and Australian thinking appears to have assumed that the United States should be included in any new Pacific or Asia Pacific intergovernmental organization with a primary trade interest it had been by no means clear that the United States itself would welcome such a proposal. Former Secretary of State George Shultz in Jakarta in July 1988 had suggested consideration of 'some kind of Pacific Basin Forum' which could look at transport and communications and some other issues, but apparently excluding trade. James Baker III, now Secretary of State, appeared to envisage United States relations with the region in terms of a 'hub and spokes' analogy in which the United States was the hub. It was also known that some South East Asians (specifically by far the most important one, Indonesia) did not want the United States included and that might have been seen at the time as a reason for not mentioning the United States in the Hawke speech. There was the related consideration also that it had often been seen as an obstacle to a Pacific organization that the levels of development and economic strength were too disparate and it was important not to leave any impression that Hawke had in mind something in which the world's two largest economies, the United States and Japan, might hold all the cards. Moreover, it was concern about United States backsliding from multilateralism and non-discrimination which was one of the drivers of Australian interest in the creation of a regional forum which would have as a major objective the encouragement of the liberalization of global trade.

Australia, and of course Hawke personally, would not have wanted to have unnecessary difficulties with the United States over this matter, especially as it was never Hawke's intention to seek to exclude the United States from APEC (a matter which he makes clear in his memoirs). But Secretary Baker especially was angry and he made that very clear when Foreign Minister Gareth Evans visited Washington in March[31]. The Japanese also spoke firmly to Australian representatives, reinforcing the message about the necessity of including the

United States. Annoyance in Washington persisted for some time but Hawke's visit a couple of months later and closer consultation in the interim settled matters.

The thrust of Australian policy through the 1980s, in cooperation with Japan, was towards the development of institutionalized cooperation in the Pacific Basin. One of Hawke's objectives was to draw China into this framework of cooperation where it would be associated not only with Japan, Korea, the ASEAN countries and Australia, but also with the United States. This was a far-sighted policy, entirely consistent with the argument of the Garnaut Report. Its advantages lay not only in terms of the expectation that the economic networks and habits of cooperation which would develop would familiarize China with the rest of the region, providing benign channels for the ambitions of the world's most populous country which was opening increasingly to foreign trade and investment and experiencing substantial economic growth. The other side of this policy was to help engage the United States with China in mutually beneficial ways as well as to increase the United States' stake in the East Asian region so helping to ensure that it would retain its security role in the Pacific. Other elements of the policy, such as the leverage which APEC might give to the global trade liberalization agenda, also envisaged the engagement of the United States. The exception, as we have seen, was the Australian search for export markets. The foundation of the Garnaut Report and of Hawke's foreign and domestic policies for which it provided the rationale was the need for Australia to develop the capacities and skills to integrate with the burgeoning economies of North East Asia. The selling point was essentially that these were Australia's natural markets and if Australia was to develop and grow it must succeed with North East Asia. The reason for seeking closer engagement in the ways Garnaut set out was essentially economic. Hawke spoke of 'enmeshment' which suggests something more intimate and to some Australians suggested a submerging of some characteristics of Australia as the smaller and supplicant partner. But that was not what he had in mind. The enmeshment of the economy of Australia with the economies of East Asia was a sufficiently formidable task and one about which many Australians would have serious reservations and doubts. It was not part of Hawke's program to enmesh Australia with East Asia in ways which would deliberately diminish the links with the United States. But it began to appear to some students of the situation that Australia would find it difficult to reconcile these two poles in its policy.

Keating Shifts the Policy into Overdrive

As early as 1981 the Australian international relations scholar Nancy Viviani said that Australian foreign policy seemed to be a matter of holding firm with one hand to the United States while reaching out tentatively with the other hand to East Asia. By the time Hawke left office in 1991 the reaching out was far less tentative than it had been a decade earlier during the Fraser government. It was also by then becoming clearer that the attachment to the United States and the West generally could carry the risk of imposing limits on the pace and extent of enmeshment with Asia. East Asia, from China in the north to Indonesia in the south, was experiencing a period of economic growth at a rate and on a scale which were unprecedented. This was generating confidence and intimations of a sense of solidarity in East Asia. In the meantime the Labor government policy of seeking Australia's 'enmeshment' with Asia (to use Hawke's expression) was shifted into a higher gear after Paul Keating succeeded Hawke as Prime Minister in 1991. Keating had no previous record of interest in Asia policy but, as is common with late converts, his commitment and enthusiasm seemed unlimited. He proceeded to travel extensively in the region, made a series of important speeches and cultivated relationships with East Asian leaders, especially President Soeharto of Indonesia and Prime Minister Miyazawa of Japan[32]. Keating's development of Hawke's policy was not so much a change as an intensification. Thus he did not shift away from the emphasis on APEC, indeed he worked harder at it despite the fact that APEC had a wider regional basis and a wider agenda for Australia than engagement with East Asia. APEC took on a new standing in 1993 when it was held in Seattle and added a Leaders' meeting to the agenda. This meant that the heads of government of all the member states would have an additional annual opportunity each year to meet together with the leaders of the most important countries in APEC including the United States, China and Japan and, for some of them, the opportunity to have bilateral private meetings with those leaders. Seattle set the precedent for informal Leaders' meetings, mostly without advisers present and in a relaxed setting.

In his 2000 book *Engagement* Keating dealt at length with APEC. He saw its 'importance and originality...not so much in its function, which was trade and economic cooperation, as in its scope'. It covered the rapidly developing countries of North East Asia, the ASEAN countries, Australia and New Zealand and the two North American economies of the United States and Canada. 'In other words, it was, if not from conception, then shortly afterwards, a trans-Pacific organization, which made it less likely that the United States would turn inwards, economically and politically, to its own hemisphere, as the new North American Free Trade Agreement (NAFTA) gave it the potential to do'[33]. Also 'APEC gave the smaller countries of the Asia-Pacific a say in the nature of the trading arrangements and in its strategic organization'. This argument in favour of APEC thus turns largely on its potential for retaining United States' interest in the Western side of the Pacific. That is a somewhat unexpected projection of the Hawke perspective on APEC which was based mainly on the desire to consolidate and develop the cooperation with East Asia, especially on trade issues. But the difference is probably more apparent than real. Keating goes on to talk of Australia's need to keep the pressure on its neighbours 'to open up their markets further', the need to have a fall-back if the Uruguay Round failed (in which case a 'grouping which included our largest and fastest-growing export markets served the purpose'), and the strategic need to encourage 'an outward-looking United States with a foot in both the Atlantic and Pacific oceans and a healthy triangular relationship between China, Japan and the United States'[34]. Keating decided that APEC could be the vehicle for advancing these Australian interests. But it would need to be beefed up. He decided to raise with President George Bush (who visited Australia two weeks after Keating assumed office) 'the idea of restructuring APEC; of changing it to a more political and powerful organization represented at head-of-government level'. He records that he received a non-committal response from Bush at the time and a subsequent exchange of letters produced 'The basic message...that the United States ought to stand well back from the proposal but that if I could get any interest going with other leaders the United States would be prepared to hear back from me'[35]. Gareth Evans made soundings at the ASEAN meeting and proposed a separate leaders' meeting not in the APEC framework. But Keating said he would have none of that. For him APEC was 'central to the proposal', so 'Gareth set to work on it'. Keating had further discussions with Prime Minister Goh Chok Tong of Singapore and Senior Minister Lee Kuan Yew about the importance of Soeharto in this plan and then in February 1993 Keating 'made the scope of our aims explicit' and public. In the meantime Bill Clinton had replaced George Bush as President of the United States and Keating lost no time in writing to the new President with congratulations and the message 'Have I got an idea for you!'[36]. Mr Keating also continued to promote the proposed restructuring of APEC 'in my selling trips around the region', talking to Prime Minister Miyazawa in Japan, President Kim Young Sam in Korea and the Premier and Vice-Premier of China.

Keating says that it became clear that only Prime Minister Mahathir of Malaysia would have 'any real problems with the proposal', and this was because of his efforts to set up an East Asian Economic Group which would exclude Australia and New Zealand, as well of course as the United States. But Clinton decided to back the idea and issue formal invitations to APEC leaders to meet in Seattle in November following the scheduled ministerial meeting, 'provided there were enough positive responses'. Keating was to play a particular role in seeking Indonesian and Chinese acceptance. Then ASEAN ministers met in Singapore and sought to resolve the problem of Mahathir's separate and competing proposal by accepting the idea of an East Asian Economic Group but only as a caucus within APEC. This transformed the EAEG into EAEC. Keating comments in his book that this was, 'in part, a face-saving device for Malaysia' which is true but only part of the truth because the Mahathir idea also struck a sympathetic chord with many in the East Asian region. Keating then says that the ASEAN device to deal with the EAEG issue 'did not resolve the key question: whether it would weaken APEC by turning it into a more adversarial forum, in which East Asia would range itself against North America'[37]. In fact there was not much danger of that happening as long as APEC fulfilled its purpose of providing advantages to all members and to both sides of the Pacific. It was impossible for ASEAN simply to reject the Mahathir initiative and to place it in APEC in this way was, as Keating acknowledges, 'an obvious improvement'. But his opposition to Mahathir's initiative was deep and active and was to prove costly for Australia in the longer term.

At this time, Keating records, some of the East Asians were asking if Australia would be willing to join the EAEC if that could be arranged. Keating and Evans decided against a positive response. In a cable to Evans which he quotes in the book Keating gave the reasons in simple terms: 'Of its essence, and certainly at this stage, the EAEC is a racially based concept which has the added danger of excluding the United States, the largest customer of most of the EAEC constituency'[38]. It is no doubt true that in Dr Mahathir's mind EAEC was, in part at least, 'a racially based concept' but it was more than that. It appealed to other elements in the rising East Asian consciousness which we shall examine later. But even with regard to the racial element in it, in retrospect it was mistaken for Australia to use this argument as vigorously as we did – or indeed to use it at all – in regional countries in the course of our lobbying against the EAEG and EAEC. If some East Asians were prepared to seek to put us into the EAEC it showed that they at least did not see that forum as 'racially based' and, if we had accepted the invitation and been given a place, that would surely have shown that it was not racially based. It would, incidentally, also have said something very positive in the region about Australia's attitude to race.

In retrospect again, it is unfortunate that Australia did not take up any opportunity that was available to join the EAEC in 1993. Of course that would have had to be handled in such a way as to avoid misunderstanding on the part of the United States. But that would have been possible. For Australia to have been in an East Asian caucus in APEC would have given us more rather than less standing and in no way have reduced the strength of our alliance and other ties with the United States.

As Keating points out Japan, in particular, was 'obviously uncomfortable about being squeezed between Malaysia and Australia'. But we pressed hard in Tokyo for Japan to stand against the Mahathir project at all stages. We used the racial discrimination argument and urged the undesirability of splitting the region (that is the APEC region). We were assured that Japan would take our interests into account and that they saw considerable difficulty in accommodating the Mahathir proposal. But there was another influential strand of policy opinion in the Ministry of Foreign Affairs in Tokyo which supported the Malaysian proposal and believed that that was where Japan's real interests and attachments lay. In retrospect we would have done better to have sought to find a middle way which would have given us the opportunity to be inside the East Asian Forum while still promoting the Pacific Basin cooperation project which had found its apotheosis in APEC[39].

But in 1993 and for the rest of Keating's time as Prime Minister APEC appeared to go from strength to strength and there was little disposition to look to the EAEC as other than a distraction from the main game and little disposition to reflect that it might, in one way or another, become the main game. Keating and Evans, the most formidably energetic foreign policy double act Australia has ever had, with strong and expert bureaucratic support pushed the APEC wagon and related initiatives. The success of the Seattle meeting in upgrading APEC to a Pacific wide Heads of Government forum required that the substance match the standing at future meetings.

Keating persuaded President Soeharto to lead a major initiative for the next APEC annual meeting which was to be held in Bogor, south of Jakarta. This was to be an agreement among all the APEC members that they would make a commitment to introduce open and free trade in the region by specific dates. A great deal of work was done to convince the membership that this was in principle to the benefit of all members and then to accommodate various points of view. The result was the agreement on the introduction of open and free trade in the region under which the developed member countries would shift to zero tariffs by 2010 and the developing members by 2020. This goal was to be achieved in a flexible way with members following individual action plans rather than an identical program. Reports were to be provided annually on progress by each member. It was clear that success or failure of the project would depend on members maintaining commitment to a program which had a very large voluntary element and much scope for variation and hence erosion of mutual trust. But at the time it gave another boost to APEC which, after Bogor, seemed to have developed a major role. The members were at pains to make it clear that what APEC was aiming to do was quite different from other free trade arrangements which reduced tariffs and barriers among themselves on a preferential basis against the rest of the world. APEC was embarking on 'open regionalism' under which the reductions which they extended to each other would be extended on an MFN basis to all other parties. For some members, particularly the United States in view of its problems with Europe, there were concerns about the 'free loader' problem; but these were accommodated against the background of studies which showed that the APEC approach would not be prejudicial to the trading interests of the members and, depending on product coverage (especially whether agriculture was included), would more likely be beneficial. Bogor was a high point for APEC and the forum seemed to have a good prospect of developing increasing importance both regionally and globally as it moved on with a range of other programs on trade facilitation, investment and so on.

Keating's APEC policy was successful in a number of ways. It placed Australia at the centre of the region's multilateral diplomacy and provided an agenda for the Prime Minister to conduct an active personal campaign in East Asia especially which gave him the opportunity to promote various Australian interests and generally to make it known that, under his government, Australia saw East Asia as its primary focus. It was also a key vehicle for promoting the trade liberalization message in East Asia and, up to the time Keating lost office early in 1996, it appeared to be having some success in that regard. His success in achieving the upgrading of APEC to a leaders' forum put it on the map for reasons already explained, and probably ensured that it will continue even if it fails to meet the trade and trade-related policy agenda which is its main rationale. But, as we have seen, the APEC project, which was at the centre of Keating's foreign policy, produced elements of ambiguity, inconsistency and even contradiction.

Ambiguities of Engagement

Keating promoted APEC as a vehicle which would help lock the United States into a Pacific orientation and he strongly resisted an initiative to develop an East Asian vehicle. Thus he placed himself in the line of Australian foreign policy which saw Australia's prime interest as maintaining the engagement of the United States in Australia's region. Yet he also promoted direct links with East Asian countries, continuing Hawke's emphasis and intensifying it. He and his government encouraged Australian business to engage more closely with East Asia[40]. For example, on his first prime ministerial visit to Singapore in 1992, Keating participated in a business seminar on the theme of strategic linkages between Singapore and Australian companies. The meeting was attended by senior business representatives from both sides, including 28 Australian business leaders. The government also promoted the growth of tourism from the region into Australia and pushed Australia as a centre for educational, medical, financial and other services for the region. There was rapid growth in all these areas. At the same time the Australian people were encouraged to see the East Asian region as the area of Australia's prime focus. It was the place where we should naturally look for business, for political and strategic consultation and cooperation and increasingly the region where we should look for cultural linkages and for migrants.

Thus in terms of action and practice Keating focussed on East Asia even though the regional commitment to APEC was in terms of what he and his government referred to as 'the Asia Pacific'. And although he promoted APEC largely in terms of its expected capacity to consolidate the engagement of the United States with East Asia, Keating and Evans were quite prepared to take openly critical positions towards the United States over the disputes with East Asian countries in which the Clinton administration became involved in its first year or so[41]. The impression was indeed created in some quarters in Australia and the United States that the Keating government was aligning itself more with the East Asians than with the United States, that it was seeking to establish its credentials in its own region without feeling constrained by the ties with the United States. Roger Bell, writing in 1997, saw Australia's emphasis on economic interdependence and multilateralism in this period and the 'conspicuously little public comfort' it gave Clinton Administration initiatives in the region as implying 'a recognition of America's declining importance, both regionally and globally'[42]. Certainly the United States had been going through a period of deep self-doubt, largely as a result of the contrast between what had appeared as the rise and rise of Japan and then the other East Asian economies at a time when the United States had been in a period of industrial decline. The work of Paul Kennedy[43] and others had been influential in spreading a doctrine of 'declinism' which saw the United States as in a period of historical decline similar to what had been experienced by all previous great powers. But the Australian policy orientation under Keating was due less to a belief that the United States was in long term decline than a belief that East Asia was in long term growth and that it would continue to grow in importance in the world economy, and in due course in political and strategic terms as well. It seemed inevitable that East Asia would be the greatest external influence on Australia's future and it was that perception that was the main driver of the Keating foreign policy.

Two examples of the Keating government clearly signalling the importance for Australia of major East Asian countries and its willingness to proceed independently of the United States, or contrary to the United States in that context, were the support given to China in the debate in Washington about Most Favored Nation (MFN) treatment and the negotiation of the security treaty with Indonesia. After Tiananmen Square the United States Congress became increasingly resistant to the granting of MFN treatment to China without measurable progress on human rights reform. During the 1992 Presidential campaign Bill Clinton had joined in the criticism of the Bush administration for its alleged leniency to China on this matter. The Australian position was that hectoring the Chinese on human rights and seeking to use the MFN issue as a stick with which to beat them was counter productive, and indeed insulting[44] and Australia lobbied extensively and vigorously in Washington including with the President himself. Keating's appreciation of the importance, dimensions and potential of the Australian relationship with Indonesia grew steadily with his visits to that country and his deepening acquaintance with President Soeharto. They decided to raise the relationship in a formal way to a higher level and had their representatives secretly negotiate an Agreement on Maintaining Security (discussed in Chapter 8). The United States was not consulted or advised during the lengthy negotiation and only informed just before the agreement was signed.

On the face of it there is a discrepancy between the central importance ascribed to the United States in the APEC context, which was itself central to Keating's foreign policy, and the manifest shift towards East Asia in other matters where Keating seemed to want to show that major Asian countries like Indonesia (especially) and China mattered as much to Australia as did the United States. Keating himself offers a possible explanation. This occurs in his book in the context of discussion of Samuel Huntington's[45] assertion that Keating's policy was that Australia should 'defect from the West, redefine itself as an Asian society, and cultivate close ties with its geographical neighbours'. Keating says that 'The last claim is right; the first two are rubbish'[46]. He explains that he wanted to 'sharpen the focus of Australian foreign policy on the region around Australia' where the rewards for effort by Australia would be greatest and where the stakes for Australia are so high 'and because there were powerful cultural and historical forces resisting this transition, I wanted to make our intention abundantly clear'[47]. This suggests some deliberate overstatement and overplaying of the Asia hand in order to make the desired correction of focus against the inertia and entrenched opposition which Keating thought he had to overcome. The real Keating instinct might have been closer to the APEC policy one; that is to say holding on fast with one hand to the United States while reaching out to East Asia with the other. The result, in any case, was one of some ambiguity. 'The region' or 'our region' which was so frequently invoked as of vast importance for Australia was of shifting dimensions and content. During the long period of Australian National University influence on this policy area the expression 'Asia Pacific' took the place of 'Pacific Basin'. Then later it somehow became 'the' Asia Pacific and both Keating and Evans (as well as others) used that label. In an APEC context that meant presumably the region composed of the members of APEC at the time, although Keating was never reconciled to the inclusion of some of the late comers. At other times the context suggested that it meant East Asia plus Australia and New Zealand.

It might not appear that there is much point in a discussion of the invention and usage of this rather odd label. But it is important. That is because Keating assimilated his efforts to get Australians to engage with East Asia to the idea of 'the Asia Pacific'. He also urged on Australia and indeed on the APEC region as a whole the importance of constructing an Asia Pacific community. It is surprising that this extraordinarily ambitious idea achieved even the limited resonance it did. A 'community' stretching from China to Chile and from Canada to Indonesia and including such a large and widely separated mass of countries is not something which has any natural basis. It is too big and too diverse to generate anything which might count as a community spirit or feeling of solidarity. APEC made sense, and still does, as a useful meeting ground and forum for the East Asians and the Americans, with the Australians in the middle speaking up its importance. But it was unlikely ever to rise to the very much more ambitious consummation of a 'community'. One might as well join the calls for world government which have been made unavailingly for so long. The idea of an East Asian community has also been described as ambitious because of the size and diversity of that region. But compared to 'the Asia Pacific' it is much more cohesive and has much more historical and felt affinity. A problem for the 'enmeshment' agenda is that that historical and felt affinity hardly accommodates Australia. That is no doubt part of the reason why Australian policy has placed such heavy emphasis on APEC.

Notes

1. See Hawke, R.J., John Curtin Oration, Creswick, 20 August 2000 where Hawke explains why. The speech starts with the following sentence: 'I tend not to have heroes – but if anyone in Australian political history approaches pedestal status, in my mind it is Curtin'.

2. Hawke's view of the importance of the relationship with the United States and his broad support for the United States as the champion of the Western and anti-communist cause in the Cold War of course had a much wider basis than his attachment to the Curtin role model. It had an intellectual basis in Hawke's own rejection of communism and his own appreciation of the dark side of the Soviet Union's domestic and foreign policies (the latter probably intensified by his recognition that the future of Israel of which he was a strong supporter depended to a degree on the United States), and was fortified by his own links with several influential Americans including the Trade Union leader Lane Kirkland and the Secretary of State George Shultz.

3. It was reported at the time that after a meeting in Port Moresby over breakfast between Hawke and Lange, who was very over weight, the media pressed Hawke for information. A persistent journalist asked 'Mr Hawke what differences emerged between you and Mr Lange?' Hawke replied 'Well, he has a much bigger appetite than I do'. Professor Ross Garnaut, who was the only other person present at this meeting, has since recorded that, afterwards, Hawke wrote to Secretary of State George Shultz expressing his doubts whether Lange would deliver on his undertaking that the NZ Labor Party policy on nuclear ship visits would be modified. Garnaut, R. (2001) 'ANZUS and Australia's Security in Asia' in *The United States-Australia Alliance in an East Asian Context*, Proceedings of a Conference, Defence Publishing Service, Canberra.

4. Hayden, Bill (1996), *Hayden, An Autobiography*, Angus and Robertson, Sydney, pp. 463-4. Hayden cites evidence from a departmental file which he says he discovered later while consulting the file for another purpose. He says that this showed that he and his department were not informed about Hawke's personal efforts to resolve the issue by engaging Lange in some unexplained initiative with the Americans. The

note on the file, he says, makes it clear that the reason for keeping the Minister and Department of Foreign Affairs uninformed was because Hayden himself was suspected of harbouring 'anti-American sentiments'.

5   Garnaut, *op. cit.* p. 9.
6   Garnaut, R. (1989), *Australia and the Northeast Asian Ascendancy* (The Garnaut Report), Commonwealth of Australia, Canberra, Table 3.10, p. 72.
7   There were different views about this within the Australian Government, especially between the Prime Minister and the Foreign Minister with the latter favouring a more holistic handling of the relationship. Secretary of State Shultz was evidently aware of this when he forcefully rejected any suggestion that trade issues be linked to the shared strategic interests and cooperation of the two allies. He said he would refuse to listen to any such suggestions. (The writer was ambassador in Washington at the time.)
8   Clifford and Warnke.
9   Countries with large immigrant communities (and hence votes) for example had an advantage. Thus Ireland had a quota which was filled by buying sugar cheaply on the world market and then selling it at two or three times that price into the US system.
10 See Hayden, *op. cit.* pp. 465-6.
11 Garnaut, *op. cit.* (Note 6 above).
12 *Ibid.*, p. 1.
13 *Australian Immigration Fact Sheet – Key Facts in Immigration*, http://www.immi.gov.au/facts/05policy.html.
14 *Ibid.*
15 King, Rebecca (1997), *Australians studying in Asia: the ASAA 1976-1997*, http://coombs.anu.edu.au/Special Proj/ASAA/King02.html.
16 Milner, Anthony (1999), 'Approaching Asia, and Asian Studies, in Australia', *Asian Studies Review*, Vol. 23, No. 2, p. 196.
17 *Ibid.*, p. 197.
18 Ingleson, John and Nairn, M.E. (1989), *Asia in Australian Higher Education: Report of the Inquiry into the Teaching of Asian Studies and Languages in Higher Education Submitted to the Asian Studies Council*, University of New South Wales Press, Sydney, p. 14.
19 King, *op. cit.*
20 *Ibid.*
21 *Australia and Northeast Asia*, Address by the Minister for Foreign Affairs and Trade, Senator Gareth Evans, to the Committee for Economic Development of Australia (CEDA), Melbourne, 22 March 1990.
22 Terada, T. (2001), 'Directional Leadership in Institution-Building: Japan's Approaches to ASEAN in the Establishment of PECC and APEC', *The Pacific Review*, Vol. 14, No. 2, p. 200.
23 *Ibid.*, pp. 204-5.
24 The author was the Australian Government representative at the Seminar and beforehand was summoned to see Sir John Crawford at the ANU. On that occasion Crawford said he had discussed all the important issues with the Prime Minister (Malcolm Fraser) and had full agreement. The author as an Australian official was to be present only in his private capacity, and if he were to say anything at the Seminar with which Crawford disagreed he, Crawford, as Chairman, would 'immediately rule you out of order'. Recently W.G.T. Miller, who was the government representative at the following PECC meeting, said that he had had the same experience with Crawford prior to that meeting.

25 Terada, *op. cit.* p. 209.
26 *Ibid.*, pp. 208-9.
27 *Ibid.*, p. 209.
28 Terada, T. (1999), *The Genesis of APEC: Australian-Japan Political Initiatives*. Pacific Economic Papers, No. 298, Australia-Japan Research Centre, Australian National University, p. 15.
29 *Ibid.*, p. 17. Terada quotes Andrew Elek who at the time was the DFAT official chiefly involved.
30 Hawke, Robert (1994), *The Hawke Memoirs*, William Heinemann, Melbourne, p. 429.
31 Over a period of four years as Australian ambassador in Washington the writer saw successive Secretaries of State show anger with Australia – both times over trade issues. The meeting and dinner with Baker was the longer and more uncomfortable of the two occasions.
32 For example, in 1994 Keating proclaimed that no country 'is more important to Australia than Indonesia', and in December 1995 negotiated the Australia-Indonesia Agreement on Maintaining Security. In May 1995, Keating signed the 'Joint Declaration on the Australia-Japan Ministerial Committee meetings (May 1991, November 1993, and August 1995). He received a Japanese prime ministerial visit to Australia by Miyazawa (April 1993), and himself made three visits to Japan (September 1992, September 1994, May 1995). There was also a series of other Ministerial exchanges.
33 Keating, Paul (2000), *Engagement: Australia Faces the Asia-Pacific*, Macmillan, Sydney, pp. 76-7.
34 *Ibid.*, p. 80.
35 *Ibid.*, p. 83.
36 *Ibid.*, p. 86.
37 *Ibid.*, p. 89.
38 *Ibid.*, p. 89.
39 The writer was ambassador to Japan at the time.
40 For example, in terms of encouraging Australian firms to invest in Asia, the Development Import Finance Facility (DIFF), including the 1994/5 'Green DIFF' initiative, were established to enable Australian firms to compete in commercial bids for overseas development projects.
41 Bell, Roger, (1997), 'Reassessed: Australia's Relationship with the United States', in J. Cotton and J. Ravenhill (eds), *Seeking Asian Engagement*, Oxford University Press, Melbourne, p. 208.
42 *Ibid.*, p. 208.
43 Kennedy, Paul (1987), *The Rise and Fall of the Great Powers*, Random House, NY.
44 MFN status is of course not a favoured status but rather the norm.
45 Huntington, Samuel P. (1996), *The Clash of Civilizations and the Remaking of World Order*, Simon & Schuster, New York, pp. 151-3.
46 Keating, *op. cit.* p. 245.
47 *Ibid.*, p. 245.

Chapter 5

Commitments and Hesitations

Hesitating to be 'Part of Asia'

Since the demise of the Keating government the lively debate about whether Australia is a part of Asia has largely ceased. This is in part because the Howard government stepped back from the intensity of the Keating engagement policy and made it clear in a variety of ways that, while engagement with East Asia was still an important feature of Australian foreign policy, it did not imply or require modification of other long-standing loyalties and links, or any reduction of emphasis on those loyalties and the attitudes of mind and habits of thought with which they were associated. The fading interest in whether Australia is a part of Asia may also show that proponents of that view became discouraged and saw no prospect of convincing their fellow-citizens of their case. A third and more recent factor may be the rejection of Australia's efforts to win acceptance in the emerging East Asian institutional architecture. And a fourth factor may be the sharp decline in the attraction of East Asia with the ending or interruption of the 'economic miracle' in 1997-98 and then the collapse of the relationship with Indonesia and the exposure for all to see of the death and destruction in East Timor prior to Indonesia's withdrawal in 1999. We shall look in greater detail at these factors in Chapter 7.

Despite the apparent fading of Australian interest it would be surprising if the debate as to whether it is, or should seek to be, part of East Asia were not to surface again in one form or another. It is not plausible to say now, as some do, that it was an essentially empty argument. It did have real substance, if only because of the assertion that Australia is a part of the region. It could not be a part of a region without sharing the label which attached in a primarily geographic sense to all the other members of the region. The nature and extent of the association Australia seeks with emerging East Asian institutional structures remains undefined. As we saw in the last chapter, the main Australian regional policy under the Labor government was directed to 'the Asia Pacific' using APEC as its vehicle. But that never entirely displaced the theme that Australia's efforts were directed to East Asia and to winning acceptance in East Asia. Indeed much of the promotion of the Keating government's Asia Pacific policy switches back and forth between East Asia and 'the Asia Pacific'. Thus in the important book which Gareth Evans and Bruce Grant produced on *Australia's Foreign Relations*[1] the index entry is 'Asia, Australia's Place in, 348-52'. But in the text the heading for the relevant section on pages 348-52 is 'Being an Asia Pacific Nation'. The section starts by explaining that 'the great turn-around in contemporary Australian history is that the region from which we sought in the past to protect ourselves...is now the region which offers Australia the most'. Australia's future lies, 'inevitably, in the Asia Pacific region' and 'This is where we live, must survive strategically and economically, and find a place and role if we are to develop our full potential as a nation'. The next paragraph points out that 'The problem for Australia in fully realising this role does not lie in the "Pacific" so much as in the "Asia" component'. That is because 'it is with the Asian countries in our region that the risks of misunderstanding and non-acceptance are very much higher'. Yet it might be just as much, or more, because Australians have a strong reluctance to agree that Australia is part of Asia, which is not surprising when even the political leadership which was most enthusiastic about engagement with Asia could not bring itself to say explicitly that Australia belongs to the East Asia region.

Certainly it was correct that the risks of 'misunderstanding and non-acceptance are very much higher' for Australia with Asia than with Canada or the United States. The rest of that short section in the Evans and Grant book claimed that the advances which Australia had made in its immigration policy, in multicultural affairs and in other areas where its reputation in Asia is still clouded, have not been fully appreciated there. The authors see human rights as an issue on which Australia is exposed to 'risks of misunderstanding' but argue that Australia should not succumb to cultural relativism for the sake of engagement or enmeshment with Asia. 'To make our views known, quietly and courteously, about values we regard as universal and hold dear, does not entail condescension or interference in internal affairs. The question in all these circumstances – as so often in Asia – is not whether to act, but how to act'. In those few pages Evans and Grant seek to dispose of what is the core problem in Australia's foreign policy. When the book was written that was less apparent than it is now. At that time no doubt it seemed more plausible to deal with the issue of being accepted by East Asia as a member of the neighbourhood as though it were a part of the wider matter of Australia's membership of an Asia Pacific region. But even then it should have been clear that such treatment confused matters. If Australia were to make a real commitment to East Asia, to seek to 'enmesh' with it, then that needed to be approached without hesitation and not under the cloak of shared membership of 'the Asia Pacific'. To do less was to signal hesitation to the region and uncertainty to the Australian public. Especially in retrospect it is clear that making known Australia's different views on human rights and such matters 'quietly and courteously' is not enough to overcome the obstacles to enmeshment and to acceptance of Australia as a member of the East Asian region. The reasons for that lie on both sides; that is both on the Asian side and on the Australian side. Here we look first at the Australian side.

During the second half of the 1980s and up to 1997 it became fashionable in some circles in Australia to assert forcefully that Australia was a part of Asia. It was often said in the sense of issuing a challenge, as a test of 'political correctness', and as the basis for a demand that public policy and public attitudes turn away from much of Australia's past as a prelude to embracing the new agenda of enmeshment with Asia. One influential high point was the publication in 1994 of *Living with Dragons*[2] a book by various hands edited by Greg Sheridan of *The Australian* newspaper. The first chapter, by Sheridan himself, is a striking proclamation of an Australian commitment to Asia in which the author welcomes 'A revolution [which] is sweeping across Australia. The nation is changing fundamentally and irreversibly. The old order is gone, a new order is taking shape with astonishing speed and force'. Sheridan explained that 'I speak of the Asianization of Australian life' and after a discussion of the controversies and changes in Australian immigration policy he hails 'a time of epoch-making historical transformations. I foresee a numerous, honey-coloured people...participating in everything of consequence happening in the region'[3]. Hopefully this vision of the future may still come to pass, but it is clear that the revolution that Sheridan saw as 'sweeping Australia' had not progressed by any means as far as he (and others including the present writer) thought at that time. Nor was it as irreversible as he asserted. Sheridan did not in that chapter directly assert that Australia is part of Asia but that view, or at least the view that it will become part of Asia, is implicit in what he wrote and his views were very much part of the armory of the 'part of Asia' school.

The Keating government, committed as it was to the Asia Pacific model and explicitly rejecting and opposing attempts to form East Asian regional institutional vehicles, never signed off on the view that Australia is a part of Asia. While it was for some time doctrine in the Department of Foreign Affairs and Trade that Australia was part of Asia, and asserted by those responsible that that was the view of Minister Gareth Evans, Evans himself does not appear to have included that assertion in any of his many public speeches over the period. That suggests some degree of uncertainty, but on the other hand Evans clearly did not want to deny the assertion, or have senior officials deny it. The present writer at the time believed the proposition factually wrong, contrary to the sentiments of most Australians, politically servile and unnecessary for the engagement policy. Having been invited to address the National Press Club in Canberra he included some views along those lines and submitted the draft to the press and information office of the Department for clearance. This was given but the Assistant Secretary suggested it would also be prudent to show the draft to the Minister's speech writer. The latter said he thought Senator Evans held the opposite view which he was likely to express publicly and that it would be wise to delete the relevant section. He referred the draft to Bruce Grant who was writing material for Evans. Grant said that the views in the draft were certainly counter to those of Senator Evans and it would obviously not be appropriate for a senior ambassador to be stating views contrary to those of the Minister[4].

There was thus some attempt to establish 'Australia is a part of Asia' as a new orthodoxy and Evans's friend and chief official, the late Peter Wilenski, was especially strident in asserting it. On a visit to Tokyo Wilenski repeatedly used this formula, obviously intending his host, Vice-Minister Owada, and other senior members of the Japanese Foreign Ministry, to be in no doubt that this was the Australian position[5]. But Ministers do not appear to have committed themselves unequivocally to that position as did Wilenski, although Evans attempted unsuccessfully to do so in an indirect way by arguing that Australia is part of the

East Asian Hemisphere. While this is hardly to be disputed in the sense that Australia lies across the same longitudes as much of East Asia it was dismissed at the time as a fudged attempt to insert Australia into the region without saying so outright. Stephen FitzGerald described it as a 'geographical, or cartographical, way of defining Australia in' and said 'cartography is unfortunately not enough'[6].

It is possible that, had there been a general and whole-hearted commitment of the government and leading opinion makers in Australia to the idea that Australia is part of Asia it would have been welcomed, even if cautiously and with reservations, in East Asia. But there was no such commitment and, as we shall see, in the end the Labor government rejected it. Why were Evans and others in the end unwilling to commit themselves publicly to the assertion that Australia is a part of Asia? Probably mainly because they sensed (or knew from private Labor Party polling) that it was seen by most Australians as fundamentally implausible, and by at least a significant minority as repugnant. In that regard the existence of a rather sharp dividing line (the Wallace Line) between Asia and Australia, on one side of which the flora and fauna are Asian and on the other side of which there are quite different Australian forms of vegetation and animal life, was not an influential factor. It was rather that very few Australians felt comfortable with the idea. It seemed to be at odds with the social, cultural and ethnic differences which they observed and which were important to them. It seemed to run counter to that great Australian yardstick, 'common sense'. Those who insisted it was correct tended to overdo things. Presenting advocacy as analysis and prescription as description, there was a tendency to say that it was entirely obvious that Australia was part of Asia, that questioning that assertion was wrong-headed and dangerous, and that the tide of history was making it all too obvious in many ways.

On the other side was considerable scepticism which would not have escaped the notice of the politicians. Moreover, many who were open to the argument that Australia's future lay with Asia, or largely with Asia, did not accept that that must lead on to a requirement to compromise Australia's identity, let alone become 'honey coloured'. That difference was in fact taken up by the politicians too. For Evans especially it seemed important to establish that Australia's different identity did not impugn its claims to enmesh itself with the East Asians and that engagement with East Asia did not threaten Australian identity. He claimed that the great diversity between the countries of East Asia itself 'means that, while we in Australia are manifestly not an Asian people, we are nonetheless culturally and demographically more or less equidistant from all its elements'. As the region develops 'questions of cultural and social identity become less dominant. And, as the region itself changes, Australia's distinctiveness is less striking. So we no longer need be the odd man out in Asia – even if we are destined to be the oddest man in'. This formulation implies that, at some point in the future, Australia will be a part of Asia. In a landmark speech in 1995, entitled 'Australia in East Asia and the Asia Pacific: Beyond the Looking Glass'[7] (which is where he launched his East Asian Hemisphere idea mentioned above), Evans spelled out in more detail his views about the diminishing differences between Australia and the East Asian countries. He starts with a sort of parable in which close inspection shows that the face of a Chinese opera singer and the face of Leonardo's Mona Lisa 'look less and less radically different; more and more they replicate each other, converge'. The same thing is the case if we look closely at the Asia Pacific region and especially at East Asia and an East Asian Hemisphere Australia. In the early 1980s Australians 'began to see ourselves as others had long seen us: politically and militarily dependent on others half a world away; culturally and economically insular; not understanding of, or responsive to, the richness and the opportunity unfolding around us', but now we had 'held that glass to our own region, looked through it, and responded to it And what we have found is more responsive to us, more capable of enriching our experience, and more alike us, than we could have ever previously dreamed'.

Before long it was to become clear not only that Sheridan's welcoming of a perceived revolutionary Asianization of Australian life but also Evans's discovery that East Asia was not very different from Australia were both at least premature. Possibly sensing that, Prime Minister Paul Keating put an end to the 'Australia is a part of Asia' inclinations of Evans and some others in the government. In a major speech[8] in Singapore in January 1996 – shortly before the election which removed him from office – Keating said that Australia was not, and could not become, a part of Asia. It could not be Asian any more than it was European or American or African. It was Australia, a unique country with a diverse multicultural society, occupying a continent. The fact that Australia could only relate to its neighbours as Australians 'should not change this irrevocable commitment – that Australia is and must always be an integral part of the region around us'[9]. This formulation has remained important and is shared by much of the foreign policy establishment five or six years later.

But it is unlikely to be sufficient to meet the policy objectives for which it was designed. The 'irrevocable commitment' is intended to secure acceptance of Australia as an 'integral part of the region around us'. Of course Keating did not on that occasion specify just what region he had in mind. In that Singapore speech as in others he spoke of the 'Asia Pacific' as well as East Asia. But he did imply that he saw Australia as located in the East Asia region when he said 'But Australian governments and the Australian people have recently come to recognise the implications of living in and with the region which Gareth Evans describes as the East Asian hemisphere'. However neither then nor on other occasions did Keating make explicit the proposition that Australia is located in the East Asian region. Sometimes in referring to 'our region' he appeared to have in mind East Asia or South East Asia; but there was generally a balancing reference to our belonging to or our commitment to the 'Asia Pacific'. That in turn sometimes seemed to mean the APEC area, that is including North and parts of Latin America, and sometimes it seemed to mean East Asia plus the South Pacific. The latter interpretation would seem to fit the reference to 'the region around us' mentioned above from the Singapore speech. But his purpose there seems to be to commit Australia to East Asia or anyway the 'East Asian hemisphere'.

A few months later, on 12 June 1996, by which time he was no longer Prime Minister, Mr Keating addressed the Asia-Australia Institute at the University of New South Wales with the title 'Obsession: Australia and the Challenge of Asia'[10]. In that address he discussed what he meant by Australia's region. It derived, he explained, from the two-fold problem 'which confronted us in the early 1990s'. This was firstly the problem of how Australia could 'encourage the institutional changes in this part of the world which were increasingly necessary in the post Cold War environment' and then 'How could we ensure that Australia was part of the conversation'?

The first question, concerning institutional changes, depended on how the region was defined and 'The key issue for us was to ensure that we were dealing with a trans-Pacific region – with the Asia Pacific, not just East Asia'. The reason for that was not to serve United States interests nor because of the comfort Australia might derive from the US presence. Nor did it derive from any hostility to cooperation between the countries on the Western side of the Pacific. 'It was because we were convinced that one of the great dangers to a post-Cold War world was for a new divide to emerge down the Pacific, encouraging the development of a world effectively split into three contending blocs in Europe, the Americas and Asia'. In the subsequent argument of the speech it is clear that a major element in this was a concern about 'a loss of faith in the United States' staying power and commitment to East Asia' if that region were to define itself as separate rather than join with the United States in the trans-Pacific APEC grouping. These considerations may have been persuasive, and indeed they continue to enjoy substantial bipartisan support in Australian politics. But while they address the issue of keeping the United States engaged in the East Asian region, and the issue of balancing China's rapidly growing power, they do not position Australia inside the emerging separate East Asian institutional framework. Indeed they have the opposite effect, modified only by equivocal and ambiguous references to cooperation with 'our neighbourhood' and 'our region' where the context implies that the region referred to is East Asia or South East Asia.

The Keating policy of engagement with a region ('our region') which is not clearly pinned down, sometimes apparently being East Asia and sometimes 'the Asia-Pacific' was still Labor Party policy five years later. In a major address to the Research Institute for Asia and the Pacific[11] on 11 September, 2001, the then Shadow Minister for Foreign Affairs, Laurie Brereton, quoted the Labor Party's platform which stated that 'No more important foreign policy issue faces Australia than advancing our engagement with Asia'. He then said that under a Labor government 'Australia will fully engage with the region: we will be a contributor, a player, and above all, a good neighbour. The Asia-Pacific will not be Labor's only priority – it never has been – but it will unquestionably be our first'. Here it is quite unclear what region is in question, what region is to be engaged with. Is it Asia or is it the APEC region? The promise that, above all, we will be a good neighbour suggests proximity and thus points to the former. Why then is there the old slide from Asia to 'the Asia-Pacific'? In the next paragraph Mr Brereton refers to Labor's proud record of engagement with 'our region' starting with support for Indonesian nationalism and going through to APEC. Again it is APEC which seems to define 'our region'. The Leader of the Labor Party, Mr Beazley, spoke in similar terms. In his Asia Lecture to the Asia-Australia Institute[12] Mr Beazley said that 'Australia needs to broaden and deepen links at all levels in the Asia Pacific, and to secure full participation in significant regional forums and processes'. He then announced that 'Principal among these will be APEC in terms of enhancing our economic engagement with the region, and the ASEAN Regional Forum (ARF) in relation to inclusive region-wide cooperation on security'. Both APEC and the ARF have huge geographical spread in terms of membership. They are no doubt important for East Asia, although APEC's nature and purpose seem to be changing and the ARF has yet to develop significant momentum. But they are both essentially mechanisms for engaging outsiders with the East Asian region. Having put them first in terms of importance and Australian commitment Mr Beazley then mentioned the real litmus tests of Australian acceptance by the region. 'We must also pursue engagement with new and emerging regional forums. While these developments are still in their infancy, the ASEAN + 3 meetings and proposals for new regional institutions, including an Asian Monetary Fund, have potentially profound implications for Australia'.

The problem with these policy formulations is that unless and until there is a clear claim by Australia that it is a member of the East Asian region it cannot expect to be accepted into the new architecture of that region. The key vehicle is ASEAN + 3 which is in effect Dr Mahathir's EAEG in terms of membership, and potentially also in terms of function and purpose. By declining to define itself in, Australia in effect defines itself out. By placing primary emphasis on the vehicles which exist to engage outsiders with the East Asian region and by continuing to defend its old concept of a putative Pacific community, Australia makes itself appear an outsider. And by actually opposing and criticizing the new East Asian projects as it did Australia certainly made any future attempt to gain entry much more problematic[13]. Having later sought entry to the ASEM (Asia-Europe) meetings on the Asian side, and failed, Australia has had to draw back and hope that in time the climate will become more receptive. But of that there has been no sign. In the meantime, under the Howard government, there seems to have been a significant dilution of the commitment to developing Australia as a multicultural society and a significant tendency to seek to emphasize and strengthen the British and earlier Australian features of our society. Thus the 1950s of Mr Howard's youth are represented with nostalgia as a time of superior values to those we now observe.

Foreign Policy with Shallow Roots

As we have seen Paul Keating talked up the Asia engagement policy and devoted much of his own time and energy to developing relationships with East Asian colleagues. He also took suitable opportunities to explain and promote this policy in the Parliament and on public occasions. This was picked up in the media with headlines such as 'Strategies for an Asian Australia', 'Think Asia', 'Can we be Part of Asia', 'PM Points Youth Towards Future in Asia' and 'Keating's Asian Vision'[14]. With an experienced Foreign Minister in Gareth Evans, whose energy possibly even exceeded Keating's own, the government sought to establish Australia as a leading participant in regional diplomacy and especially regional institution-building. They also promoted the growth of tourism from the region into

Australia and pushed Australia as a centre for educational, medical, financial and other services for the region. There was rapid growth in all these areas. At the same time the Australian people were encouraged to see the East Asian region as the area of Australia's prime focus. It was the place where we should naturally look for business, for political and strategic consultation and cooperation and increasingly the region where we should look for cultural linkages and for migrants.

The Keating/Evans policy towards much stronger engagement with Asia seemed to be shifting the country in the direction they favoured. By the end of Keating's term as Prime Minister 61 per cent of Australia's exports were going to East Asia and the country's economy seemed to be locked in to the biggest and most rapid economic growth surge in history. Nearly a million Japanese tourists in a year were coming to Australia and increasing numbers from the other countries of the region. The universities were deriving an increasing proportion of their revenue from Korean, Malaysian, Thai and other East Asian students. Keating and Evans had had considerable apparent success in regional diplomacy and relations with the largest, closest and most problematic of Australia's neighbours, Indonesia, seemed increasingly and reassuringly solid.

There was no striking evidence at the time that the Australian electorate was uncomfortable with the direction or pace of this development. But public opinion polling showed that there were considerable reservations. Milner[15] quotes a poll published in Melbourne's *The Age* in 1993 which showed that only 30 per cent of voters thought of Australia as part of Asia and that young Australians were the 'group most likely to see Australia and Asia as separate'. He illustrates this thinking with quotations from letters to newspapers at the time. Polling on immigration and security issues showed a large gap between public perceptions and official policy even though public attitudes to trade and other economic linkages with Asia seemed to be less sceptical and reserved. This pattern continued in the early years of the Howard government. In the 1998 electoral survey by the Social Science Data Archives (SSDA) at the Australian National University[16], when asked whether Australia's trading future lies with Asia, 54.8 per cent agreed and 15.3 per cent disagreed ('neither' 30 per cent). However 52 per cent saw China as a future threat to Australia's security and 61.9 per cent saw Indonesia as a threat. 88 per cent thought the ANZUS relationship with the United States important for protecting Australia's security and about 80 per cent trusted the United States to come to Australia's defence if threatened by another country. This showed where Australian preferences lay. It showed that, despite the efforts to turn them towards Asia, Australians still felt much more affinity for and trust in the United States than they did for East Asia. Relatively few felt convinced by or comfortable with the idea that Australia is a part of Asia, although they recognized the need to relate closely to East Asia and its importance economically for Australia.

The results of the March 1996 election which returned the Liberal Coalition to power after thirteen years of Labor government were widely interpreted as reflecting in part a popular discomfort with the pace of change and the projected nature of the engagement with East Asia. That interpretation seemed to be supported later by the emergence of a new political party, 'One Nation', which was opposed to Asian immigration. In the last years of the Labor government there were also signs that the extremely energetic Australian regional diplomacy was becoming busier than was welcome to a number of the East Asian governments. This reinforced the Australian public's sense that the Keating government might be flogging something of a dead horse. By far the most acute problem was with the Prime Minister of Malaysia, Dr Mahathir. Keating's reference to Mahathir as 'recalcitrant' upon his failure to attend the 1993 APEC heads of government meeting in Seattle ignited an anti-Australia campaign in Malaysia, and exacerbated claims of cultural insensitivity in Australian foreign policy[17]. While Mahathir finally accepted Keating's expression of 'regret' over the incident and promoted a normalization of relations between the countries, relations between Mahathir and Keating were never smooth. Mahathir's veto of Australian participation in the 1996 Euro-Asia meeting (ASEM) was a particular thorn in the side of Keating's vision of Australia's relationship to the region.

There were other indications that Australia was exceeding the speed limit in a region distinguished by the very deliberate and consensual nature of its diplomacy. For example, the proposal made by Evans at the Ministerial Conference held after the ASEAN Meeting in Jakarta in July 1990 for the establishment of a forum to facilitate a security dialogue between states in the region, along the lines of the Conference on Security and Cooperation in Europe (CSCE) established in Helsinki in 1975, was not well received. ASEAN countries in particular were uncomfortable with the idea of applying the European CSCE model to Asia which they saw as very different with its emphasis on the role of the military (for example in Indonesia) in preserving internal security, and they saw the European neoliberal concern with the institutionalization of rule-bound norms as inappropriate by ASEAN countries. The high water mark of Labor's enmeshment policy was the Agreement on Maintaining Security which Keating negotiated secretly with Soeharto and which was announced in December 1995. This was supported by the Liberals who were to become the government a few months later and did not at the time meet with any significant media or public opposition. On the surface it appeared that the nation had put behind it the old reservations about Asia and the old feeling of separateness and vulnerability. But the government in fact had been moving in advance of public opinion and eventually to the point where public opinion in effect called a halt through the ballot. Keating had been in too much of a hurry.

Moreover, unlike Hawke, he had not sought to reassure the nation that its life belt was kept in place before he plunged it into waters which were still relatively alien to most Australians. Keating never appeared to care much for the United States connection and he was plainly less interested in and comfortable with the British than with the Irish when he visited London, and then Dublin and his ancestral place in Ireland. The Keating government also took sides with Asia over the US in a number of disputes. Of particular note was the debate surrounding the removal of China's MFN status on the basis of human rights violations. Australia was highly critical of the United States stance on this issue, and lobbied the US to change its policy. Albinski notes that 'Australia lobbied industriously on the MFN issue, and generally stressed what it believed to be the unproductivity of aggressively standing over Beijing. It worked in various fora: US-Australian meetings in Canberra at ministerial level; representations through its Washington embassy; through Keating personally with Clinton and before Congress'[18]. Keating's leaning towards Asia at the expense of the United States was perhaps most plainly evidenced by his 1994 decision to back Japan in its trade dispute with the United States over automobiles. On this decision, public opinion definitely lagged behind policy direction. Cotton and Ravenhill note that in the 1996 Australian electoral survey[19]:

> Contrary to Keating's stance on the Japan-United States trade dispute, only 14 per cent of respondents agreed that Australia should side with Japan; 35 per cent either disagreed or strongly disagreed with Australia supporting the Japanese position. Moreover, 55 per cent of respondents agreed with the statement that 'Japanese economic influence is too great in Australia'[20].

Thus there emerged, mostly a good deal later, a range of evidence that the Australian electorate was generally not supportive of the pace and extent of the commitment Keating and Evans were seeking to make on their behalf to East Asia. The constant calls for Australians to commit more and more to 'our region' would no doubt have fallen on stonier ground if the region had been more explicitly defined. There was always that deliberate ambiguity whether it was the whole of the Pacific Basin, the APEC region, East Asia plus Oceania and the South Pacific, or East Asia. Keating inherited a full blown version of the old Crawford commitment to the wider Pacific community. He sought at the same time to graft onto this his 'obsession'[21] with East Asia. He made it clear that he thought the worst thing for Australia's interest would be for the Pacific to be split 'down the middle', with East Asia on one side and the United States on the other. This could produce the most difficult choices for Australia in the future. These were never fully canvassed publicly but it can be assumed that Keating would have thought deeply about them. His policy was to do everything in his power to avoid the need for Australia ever to make that sort of choice. That meant seeking to attach the East Asians as firmly as possible to APEC which would be built into a firm and strong bridge across the Pacific tying East Asia and the United States together economically and in due course in other ways.

Despite the fact that the 1996 election result was thought to be due in part to discomfort in the electorate about Keating's 'obsession' with engagement with East Asia the incoming Coalition government quickly confirmed that the primary focus of its foreign policy would also be East Asia. It had said this during the campaign when it had been met with scorn and derision by Keating and Evans. Indeed throughout the period of Labor government from 1983 to 1996 the engagement policy was accepted at least in principle by the opposition in parliament. But in the election campaign Keating had said that Asian leaders would not take seriously, nor bother to talk seriously, with Messrs Howard and Downer should they become Prime Minister and Foreign Minister of Australia. Gareth Evans argued that 'There is a real danger that Asian leaders will immediately see John Howard for what he is: a man of the past; a man who is not comfortable with Asia; a man the likes of whom simply hasn't strutted our stage for a generation'. In a speech on 27 February, 1996, Evans made a detailed attack on what he described as the Coalition's capacity to carry through their commitment:

> The basic problems are lack of knowledge, understanding and feel for the East Asian Hemisphere as it now is; a disposition to look backwards rather than forwards in approaching the region; a disposition to make statements and strike attitudes which are positively offensive in the region; and some very bad policy decisions already taken which reinforce all the points I have just made. In the coalition leadership, we just haven't seen the hard yards being put into becoming involved with the countries and with the key players of the region that has been characteristic of so many individual ministers in this Labor government[22].

Evans also attacked many expressions of what he called the coalition's 'lack of contemporary perspective' on the region: Howard's several Policy Launch references to Asia Pacific as 'that region' as opposed to 'this' region or 'our' region; Alexander Downer's Policy Launch references to 'turning our faces to the East [not meaning] turning our backs on the West' – which Evans described as 'the view of a man looking out at the world from Stoke Lodge[23] in London, not looking North from Australia'; and Downer's newspaper interview reference to the Australian government being 'obsessed' with Asia at the expense of its ties with Europe and North America. Keating and Evans also criticized the coalition's stance on security arrangements with Asia and their obvious concern to keep the US closely involved in the region:

> Where the government is looking for strategic relationships which give us security in Asia – I emphasise 'in Asia' – John Howard wants security from Asia. He does not want security in Asia; he wants security from Asia. Does he think that the United States will now look to Australia to manage a large economic and political debate in the ASEAN regional forum or in APEC? Do you think the United States wants a pathetic mendicant to walk through the door to the White House saying, 'Here I am. We're so hopeless that we can't defend or protect ourselves. Will you please put your big arm around us?' I know what Bill Clinton would say: 'Oh, God, not another one'. The US wants an ally that can actually stand on its feet, that can think and do things and that can run a debate in a part of the world about economic policy and security policy in which they can see common interests for themselves[24].

This sustained attack, exaggerated though it was, meant that foreign policy for the first six months of the new Liberal coalition government involved Howard and Downer seeking to prove their commitment to East Asia engagement rather than getting on with substantive foreign and trade policy programs. They did this fairly convincingly by attention to Prime Minister Mahathir who was transiting Australia and by public statements. But there was some necessary catch-up because the Liberal-coalition in opposition had not developed a serious critique of the Labor engagement policy and its ideological and intellectual underpinnings. For those who were committed to the engagement policy as it had emerged under the successive Labor governments since 1983 there was a question as to whether or not Howard and his administration would actually maintain a strong commitment to

Asian engagement. That was also an issue that was being examined and indeed contested within the government. The Prime Minister's first visit to Jakarta was interpreted by some of the committed engagement advocates as having been more detached than the Keating commitment. No doubt that was true. But given Mr Howard's conservative cast of mind and attitude and given the almost flamboyant nature of Mr Keating's engagement approach it was inevitable that there would be a perceived difference in emphasis. The new government set about drawing up a Foreign Policy White Paper entitled *In the National Interest* which was published in 1997. In the long discussions and drafting sessions for this document there was strong pressure to ensure the dominance of the engagement with East Asia policy. But the Prime Minister and his personal advisers put limits on that. They ensured that there was balancing emphasis on the importance of the links with the United States and Europe.

Subsequently, various actions on Howard's part – his delay in publicly addressing the Hanson issue, his enhancement of military and consular cooperation with the United states, the cancelling of the DIFF initiative[25] – fuelled the public debate as to whether Howard was as committed to engagement as his policy statements indicated. Later again, with the 'deputy sheriff' issue[26], and under the Bush Administration, support of US policy on National Missile Defence, it appeared that Howard was re-balancing Australian foreign policy in a way which would have the United States rather than East Asia as the primary focus. But it needs to be noted that the world had moved on since 1996. The financial collapse of 1997-98 which struck Thailand, Korea and then Indonesia, and the protracted economic stagnation in Japan which had been the economic dynamo and exemplar of the region, all had taken the glamour and sense of urgency from the Keating vision. Even at its peak that vision, shared in more measured terms by many academics and media commentators, had been well in advance of the comfort zone of a large majority of Australians. By the turn of the century it had ceased to be a prominent topic of attention.

There is an element of unreality about the debate between the two major political forces in Australia on this issue. Labor, the party of Curtin, Evatt, Hawke and Keating on the one hand, and the Liberal/National Coalition, the party of Menzies, Spender, Casey and Howard on the other, have both avoided publicly confronting the issue of Australia's relations with East Asia. Neither embraces an affirmative answer to the question 'Is Australia a part of Asia'? or 'Does Australia belong to East Asia'? Yet both have sought to have Australia included in the embryonic East Asian institutional framework. Both have wanted to engage with East Asia; but both have wanted very much to ensure that that could be done without prejudice to the security, political, cultural and ethnic links which present day Australia has with the United States and Europe.

The style and underlying attitudes of the conservative Howard government is less congenial to the region than was that of Labor. But it is still a matter of commitments and hesitations. Events at the end of the twentieth century have made it likely that the time of decision will be postponed. But the question is still whether Australia will have to face a decision whether it is to be a 'Western' or an 'Eastern' country. Australian policy has been directed to trying to set up institutional and other arrangements which will make it likely that we do not have to face that choice. It may be that the tide of globalization and other developments will make the question irrelevant. But it is probably unavoidable in the long run. That raises another set of questions, of which the most grave is this: will Australia have a choice, or will it be able to contrive a situation where it has a choice, rather than having a resolution of the issue forced on it, regardless of Australians' preferences? As we have come closer to defining the issue to be decided, so we have backed away from deciding to press ahead with the attempt to join East Asia.

Notes

1   Evans, Gareth and Grant, Bruce, (1995) *Australia's Foreign Relations in the World of the 1990s*, Second Edition, Melbourne University Press, Carlton.
2   Greg Sheridan (1994), *Living with Dragons*, Allen and Unwin, St Leonards, p. 3.
3   *Ibid.*, p. 18.
4   The necessary revision was made but the subject came up in the question period after the speech and precipitated a lively discussion. If Australia was not a part of Asia, it was asked, then what *was* it a part of? The answer I gave, which anticipated the view that Paul Keating took a few years later, was that it was not a part of anything – it was Australia, a continent and a nation separate from Asia. This was met with some scepticism on the not unreasonable ground that Australia had only a small population and could not be a region on its own.
5   This may well have had an effect because Mr Owada himself some years later (2001) in a discussion in Sydney quoted it as an argument in support of Australia's inclusion in developing East Asian institutional architecture.
6   FitzGerald, Stephen (1997), *Is Australia an Asian Country?*, Allen & Unwin, St Leonards, p. 9.
7   Fourteenth Asia Lecture, to Asia-Australia Institute, Sydney, 20 March 1995.
8   The Singapore Lecture – *Australia, Asia and the New Regionalism* – Singapore, 17 January 1996.
9   Although in that speech Keating also made, in more explicit terms, the claim Evans had made about the differences being far less than they seemed. The 'core Australian value of "mateship" expresses an ethic of communitarianism and mutual obligation which in other contexts is called "Asian"'.
10 The Asia Lecture at the University of New South Wales, 12 June, 1996.
11 Asia Policy Lecture, Research Institute for Asia and the Pacific, at the University of Sydney.
12 The Hon Kim Beazley, MP, The 23rd Asia Lecture, *Australia in the Asia Pacific. How a Beazley Government Would Revitalise Commitment to the Region*, 6 September, 2001.
13 The Keating attacks on the EAEC project were not as far as I know continued after the Coalition Government took office in 1996.
14 Examples quoted by Milner, Anthony (1997), 'The Rhetoric of Asia', Cotton and Ravenhill (eds) *Seeking Asian Engagement*, Oxford University Press and Australian Institute of International Affairs, Melbourne, p. 34.
15 *Ibid.*, p. 36.
16 Bean, Clive *et al.* (1998), *Australian Election Study* [computer file], Canberra Social Science Data Archives, The Australian National University. Those who

	carried out the original analysis and collection of the data bear no responsibility for the interpretation here.
17	Similar claims had caused the Hawke administration headaches in 1991 when it was claimed that the Australian television series *Embassy* showed Malaysians, particularly Mahathir upon whom one of the characters was believed to be based, in a poor light. *Embassy* sparked a 'buy Australia last' campaign in Malaysia and prompted a suspension of all non-essential cooperative projects with Australia.
18	Albinski, H.S. (1996), 'Responding to Asia-Pacific Human Rights Issues: Implications for Australian-American Relations', *Australian Journal of International Affairs*, Vol. 50, No. 1, pp. 43-58.
19	Jones, Roger; McAllister, Ian; Gow, David (1996), *Australian Elecion Study 1996* [computer file], Canberra: Social Science Data Archives, The Australian National University. Accessed at http://ssda.anu.edu.au/.
20	Cotton and Ravenhill, *op. cit.* p. 12.
21	An expression he used after the 1966 election defeat, accepting Alexander Downer's claim in the campaign that the Keating Government was 'obsessed' with Asia.
22	Evans, Gareth (1996), February 27.
23	*Ibid*. Stoke Lodge is the name of the residence of the Australian High Commissioner in London and Downer's family had occupied it when his father was High Commissioner.
24	Keating, *op. cit.* October 16, 1995.
25	Development Insurance Financing Facility, designed to encourage Australian trade with developing countries.
26	Prime Minister Howard was interviewed by Fred Brenchley for the *Bulletin* and, in the account published by Brenchley in the magazine's issue on 28 September 1999, Howard appeared to have assented to the proposition that Australia would assume the role of deputy sheriff to the United States in its region. After nearly a week Howard indicated that that was not his position.

Chapter 6

Development, Values, Solidarity and Fault Lines

The Japanese Model and the East Asian 'Miracle'

Australia through the 1980s and 1990s made what it deemed an earnest effort to be accepted as a friend and neighbour of East Asia. Although it was a new chapter in terms of intensity and commitment this effort was essentially rooted in the thinking of the Casey era and much of it could have been scripted from his 1958 book *Friends and Neighbours* (mainly written by James Plimsoll[1]). The vast changes which had taken place in East Asia in the intervening years underscored the relevance and prescience of the Casey/Plimsoll view of Australia's situation. In the meantime the European colonial holdings and influence had gone. The United States had been forced to abandon its attempt to prevent the coming to power of the communist party of Vietnam. In most of the rest of East Asia the threat of communism had gone and been replaced by rapid economic development with very active participation in world trade and investment. There was an expectation that this would continue indefinitely and that Japan, the first and most successful East Asian country to modernize its economic system, would lead the way. As Japan became richer and more successful and moved into ever more sophisticated levels of technology others in the region would take up the more labour-intensive and less advanced industries with Japanese investment. So the process would go on, with Japan leading the way and others being drawn along in her wake. This appeared to be what was happening until almost the end of the century.

It is important to understand the nature of that process, the ways it was interpreted in the region and in the West, and the extent to which it contributed to a growing sense of East Asian solidarity. By the time the East Asian currency crisis struck in mid-1997 Japan itself had already been experiencing an increasingly intractable setback for several years after stock market values and real estate prices dropped sharply and financial institutions faced insolvency. So there was at the turn of the century a setback to the surge of confidence and pride which swept East Asia, both North and South, during the great growth years of the eighties and the nineties to 1997. It remains unclear for how long that setback will last, and what changes will be evident in the region when it recovers. But, over the longer term, the East Asian solidarity movement appears likely to continue to put down roots.

The APEC-style vision of a cohesive community of the states around and in the huge and diverse Pacific Basin failed to convince. It was ironic that Australian efforts to promote that idea and at the same time to assert Australia's claims to be considered part of the East Asian region often deployed the argument that the latter region also is very diverse. The diversity of East Asia was seen as emasculating the objection against Australia's claims to fit into the region that, whatever else it was, it was not Asian. The Australian response to that was to ask 'What then *is* "Asian"'? Surely the differences between say the Koreans and the Balinese, or the Singaporeans and the Dayak are no less than the differences between say the Cantonese and Australians. The existing range and degree of diversity among the acknowledged East Asians would not be made significantly greater by the inclusion of Australia. The important thing, anyway, was not difference but shared objectives and commitment. The slogan 'Odd man in', coined by the diplomat Richard Woolcott, gained currency in government speeches on the subject[2]. It is unclear how far this argument from diversity, which could be taken as questioning or even impugning assertions of East Asian solidarity based on shared values and shared experience of Western dominance, helped the Australian cause. Certainly it did nothing to reduce the opposition of the Malaysian Prime Minister, Dr Mahathir, and Japanese reactions were ambivalent, even though majority opinion in the Japanese government favoured the inclusion of Australia in any new East Asian grouping.

This Australian drive for acceptance came at a time when all of East Asia from China in the north to Indonesia in the south, with a few exceptions such as North Korea, Laos and Burma, was experiencing the most sustained and rapid phase of economic growth the world had seen. GDP growth rates of between six per cent and eight per cent had become the norm. Economies had doubled in size and some indeed had then doubled again. Education and public health had greatly improved. There were forecasts, for example by *The Economist* magazine, that five of the ten largest economies early in the twenty-first century would be in Asia and four of those would be in East Asia. The causes of this remarkable success were much discussed and much disputed. Western neo-classical economists who dominated the International Monetary Fund and the World Bank[3] argued that much the most important factor was the way in which the economies of the region had liberalized and opened their markets to international trade and competition. The Japanese and others in East Asia said that the main element in the success was skilful and successful government planning and guidance of the economy in a close working partnership with business. An important group of Western scholars (Johnson, Wade, Amsden etc.) increasingly supported the latter view with detailed empirical research and placed it in the context of economic thought. At the insistence of the Japanese the World Bank carried out a review of the East Asian phenomenon and in 1991 published a report entitled *The East Asian Economic Miracle* which generally took a compromise position, recognizing the importance of strategic direction of the East Asian economies. The publication and the surrounding debate made the 'miracle' even more a focus of world attention and served to increase regional awareness of shared success.

Japan had seen itself as the model and the engine of growth for East Asia, and had indeed been seen by others in that role. In terms of economic advance a metaphor which during the seventies and eighties had wide currency was the flying geese formation as a description of the crucial role which Japan could play in the development of the East Asian region. It was based on the idea that when geese fly in V-shaped formations the leading goose draws those behind it along in its slipstream. As Japan moved into new phases of industrial and post-industrial activity it ceased to be competitive in more labour-intensive and earlier technology production which would be relocated in newly industrializing countries via Japanese direct investment. Japan would support the process with infrastructure and other development aid and technical assistance and training. The process would be emulated serially by the followers in a developmental chain reaction. This was an attractive metaphor in some ways for both Japan and the South East Asian countries. For Japan there was the idea of leadership on a very benign basis. Japan would be doing good by doing well; a leadership in no way imposed but arising from a visible superiority in development level. For the South East Asian countries there was the suggestion of being able to take off and soar into development by hitching to Japan's success with the additional attraction of the cornucopia of Japanese funding based on Japan's booming exports and massive balance of payments surpluses.

More recently this pattern of Japanese economic leadership in the region was criticized on the grounds that it created relationships of dependency in which the level of technology transferred, the management and financial control, and other key aspects of the transplanted or implanted manufacturing often remained as far as possible under the Japanese head offices. Thus was created a high degree of vertical integration between the Japanese main companies and the dependent implants in South East Asia as well as in some cases the extension of *keiretsu*[4] or *keiretsu*-like relationships to the offshore production arrangements where Japanese component suppliers also set up in association with the main transplant. It has been argued that Japanese aid arrangements have supported such extensions of Japanese-controlled production facilities in various ways and that the whole pattern reflects MITI planning which sees Japanese companies as the drivers of industrialization in individual economies in the region and on a regional basis[5]. That line of criticism has also been levied against the Japanese response to the 1997-98 financial crisis in South East Asia, the Miyazawa initiative and the New Miyazawa initiative. Such criticism depicts the Japanese purpose as being to entrench Japanese influence over the regional economies and strengthen Japan's hold over their requirements for capital goods and more advanced products and services. At the same time more advanced Japanese technology would be kept exclusively in Japanese hands and vertical integration pursued with the less advanced and more labour-intensive processes performed in the South East Asian countries.

It needs to be noted that such criticism can sometimes be based on circumstances which can be explained just as well by obvious and rational economic and business theory and practice. In the current era it is clear that part of the comparative advantage of the South East Asian economies is lower labour costs. Equally clear is the fact that that advantage is greater in say Indonesia than in Malaysia, and that it does not exist at all in regard to Singapore. So for Indonesia for example an attraction for foreign investors in general, and not just for Japan, would obviously be the lower wages which are paid to process workers in industries like textiles, clothing and footwear. To reject all vertical integration of the advanced and less-advanced economies is in effect to reject the whole of the flying geese model of regional economic development which not only had considerable influence on thinking about economic development in South East Asia and in Japan but was at least part of the explanation of a good deal of successful practice. It was, moreover, a graphic way of describing how the international market would work under liberalizing conditions. At the other extreme lies the idea that countries can make great leaps forward by making major investments in highly protected technologically advanced industries backed up by specialized higher education and training programs. Indonesia tried the latter course during the Soeharto period under the policies of Dr B.J. Habibie when he was Minister for Research and Technology. Vast off-budget sums were directed into his programs for aircraft manufacture, shipbuilding and so on. It is not possible to make any well informed assessment of the cost-effectiveness of these programs because the costs were in effect concealed. But the results appear quite meagre and it seems likely that on any conventional sort of accounting this whole approach would have to be assessed as a major failure in business terms. There have no doubt been indirect benefits in terms of skills generation and so on but to assess those it would be necessary to know where the engineers and others who were trained in Germany and elsewhere are now working, what has happened to the ancillary supplier businesses and so on. In fact it is doubtful whether Indonesia or indeed governments elsewhere in the region would now see those Habibie programs as good models to follow, even if the resources were still available to do so – which certainly they are not. What the Indonesian and other regional experience seems to suggest is that shifts up the technology scale are more likely to be successful when they grow out of a wider base of preparation in industrial development, education and skills development and when they emerge in an environment where they are required to be competitive in relation to world pricing.

Despite criticisms of Japanese policy and practice in the region, and despite continuing deep resentment towards Japan, especially in Korea, as a result of Japanese imperial and colonial conquest and rule up to 1945, the influence of Japan on East Asian development during the 'miracle' phase was important. From early in the twentieth century Japan was seen as a model by many intellectuals and politically aware people in Asia because Japan had shown it was possible to catch up with and match the major Western powers. Then from the middle of the century for some forty years Japan developed a uniquely successful industrial economy which appeared to surpass in efficiency and flexibility the rest of the industrialized world. Japan's success was seen again as a model for the rest of Asia but in this period there was also great interest in the institutional and policy arrangements and settings which had been used by Japan. There was interest not just in seeking to emulate Japan but more specifically in seeking to adopt where possible particular Japanese methods and arrangements which were believed to have contributed to its success. It is in that second sense that we mostly speak of the 'Japanese Model'. But the other more general sense of Japan as a model for Asia and especially South East Asia has been and continues to be of great importance. It was for example the idea behind Dr Mahathir's 'Look East' policy in Malaysia. It has had a major relevance for the big issue of regional cooperation in East Asia.

Japan's defeat of Russia in 1904-5 was the first occasion in modern times on which an Asian power had defeated a European power. It had a major effect on Asian attitudes even though Japan itself proceeded to behave rather in the pattern of the European colonizing powers. At the beginning of the Pacific War, as Japanese forces swept through South East Asia, they were initially welcomed in most places. This was notably the case in Indonesia where the nationalists were encouraged by the Japanese arrival and early cooperation. Then in the latter part of the twentieth century Japan's economic success gave another fillip to East Asian self esteem, more or less coinciding with the defeat of the United States and its allies including Australia in the Vietnam war. Despite that success of a poor Asian country against the world's greatest power there was an ambivalent reaction in those parts of the region where there was a rooted opposition to communism or where there was some apprehension about Vietnamese intentions. Well before the collapse of the Soviet system and the major shifts in Chinese policy engineered by Deng Xiaoping the alternative of communism had lost its appeal and the Japanese model had triumphed as the exemplar to which East Asian governments and business people looked. Japan gave very important and strong support to the ASEAN countries and indeed continues to do so. ASEAN did not of course owe its existence to Japan but Japan was important for it. Increasingly ASEAN members came to realize that Japan was a key not only to the development of the individual member countries and the cooperation project in South East Asia but also to the wider regionalism which was required if the longer term aims of ASEAN, or at least some of its members, were to be realized. Japan was thus a key to the sense of Asian solidarity which is essentially a twentieth century phenomenon and partly reactive to the power and influence of Europe and the United States.

In East Asia there was a growing sense of confidence and pride in the achievements of the high growth countries. Whereas for more than a century it had been widely thought that the way forward was to copy the leading industrialized Western countries it now began to seem that the East Asian phenomenon, which produced far more rapid growth than during the Industrial Revolution in Europe or America, or in those places at any time since, must have different characteristics rooted in the distinctive cultural assets of the countries concerned. The debate whether to copy European models or to build on distinctively national cultural and institutional bases was as old as Meiji Japan. In its manifestation at the end of the twentieth century it was less a debate than a reassertion of East Asian pride in remarkable achievement following the era of western colonialism and economic domination and then the struggle to establish viable nations since the Second World War. The expectation was that that success would be sustained, that it would make East Asia the new focus and fulcrum of the world economy, and that the region would as a consequence assume a much larger role in the counsels of the world.

Even though Japan's standing suffered from continuing resentment of its imperial and colonizing role up to 1945 when it was defeated by the Western allies, Japan was, especially in economic terms, the exemplar and leader of the East Asian resurgence which produced such remarkable growth and such remarkable expectations up to 1997. To the extent that Japan was the exemplar and the main engine of growth in the region it served further to differentiate the East Asian countries from those of the West. Most of them had been colonies of the West, and all of them had been under Western influence during the European imperium. But in the decades of record economic growth after the middle of the twentieth century Japan, and Japan's version of industrial capitalism, became more influential in most of the region.

While Australia's economy became increasingly linked with that of Japan[6] Australia was not seen, in either of the two senses mentioned above, and neither at home nor in the region, as a part of this Japan-led 'miracle'. There were admirers of the Japanese industrial model in Australia who said that Australia could learn from the Japanese way of doing things; but there was never any question of Australia considering assimilation of major aspects of the Japanese way. Nor of course was there ever any sense in Australia of feeling vicarious pride in the Japanese achievements from the Battle of Tsushima down the years to the triumphant economy of the late nineteen-eighties. But other Asians, and especially East Asians both North and South, might take heart from the fact that the Japanese had shown that Asians could outdo Europeans and Americans.

But the Japanese achievements struck no such chord in Australian hearts and minds. However much they might admire and seek to profit from the Japanese success they could not share the pleasure Asians took in the fact that those who had been the colonial overlords for so long had been surpassed by an Asian power, nor the less publicly displayed satisfaction that an Asian power had shown that 'whites' could be outdone by Asians. Australians were in this context part of the 'other', descendants of the European colonizers who had seen themselves as British and had been prompt to fight in Britain's wars – people who still saw themselves as closer to America and Europe than to Asia.

Asian Values and Expectations of Empowerment

In our context the relevance of the work of Chalmers Johnson, Robert Wade and others was that they made the case that the success of Japan and other East Asian economies was not based primarily on deregulating and opening up to the global market, with government just leaving business to business. Until their work it had been the general belief in the West that development of East Asian economies was a matter of following what was seen as the key to the success of the United States economy and other liberal market economies. Now it appeared that a different account might be more persuasive: that Japan and those which followed in its wake had found a different formula which suited their societies better and was proving very successful. It was not a matter of emulating and catching up with the West but of basing their own formulas for success on Asian values and Asian ways of doing things. It was argued that they had devized ways of guiding industrial, commercial and financial corporate organization and activity in directions largely determined by state policy, and they had been able to do that without stifling initiative and dynamism. The result was claimed to be a formidable mobilization of government and the non-government business sector in the combined task of creating products and conquering global markets.

In a seminal article in *Foreign Affairs*[7] the Japanese journalist and scholar Yoichi Funabashi wrote about 'The Asianisation of Asia' and there was a spate of articles about 'Asian Values'. The most prolific source of the latter became known as the Singapore School following Lee Kwan Yew and led by Kishore Mahbubani and Bilahari Kausikan. The then Deputy Prime Minister of Malaysia wrote an influential book *The Asian Renaissance*[8] in which he also asserted and explored the cultural roots of the 'renaissance'. 'Asian values' included notably those embodied in the received teachings of Confucius, but there were other sources in other places. For example in Indonesia there was always an emphasis on the continuing relevance and sustaining worth of traditional village forms of cooperation and consensual decision making. Accounts of Asian values place emphasis on features believed to be common to all the East Asian countries such as the importance of the family, respect for parents and teachers, emphasis on education, the submergence of individual interest to the needs and interests of the society. The perceived much lower and still declining importance of these in the West was seen as the source of social ills afflicting western countries. An excessive emphasis on individualism in particular was blamed for things such as the drug epidemic in the United States. Asian values, not imitation of the West, were represented as the foundation on which the East Asian Economic Miracle had been built. It was argued that East Asia must avoid replacing Asian values with corrupting western ones in order to ensure the continuance of the development and stability.

The political leaders of East Asian countries routinely argued that those countries should move slowly on political liberalization. The priority must remain the social goals of development, economic security, improved education for all, and so on rather than greater scope for individual rights and expression as in the West. There were assertions that 'Western' democracy was not the appropriate form of democracy for Asian countries, at least not as long as they needed to place emphasis on raising the standard of living of all their people. 'Western' human rights were asserted not to be universal human rights and calls for their observance in the East Asian countries were to be resisted.

Australian scholars were prominent in the critiques of the Asian values thesis. One line of criticism was from historical sociology arguing inter alia that if Asian values were superior to Western values in generating economic development it might be difficult to explain why that modern economic development had got under way much earlier in the West than in Asia. It was also argued that the 'Asian' values which were being so much emphasized were also features of western societies in their developmental phases. But perhaps the most damaging critique was mounted on critical theory lines and pointed to the conclusion that the assertion and promotion of conservative 'Asian values' served to justify the maintenance of authoritarian or 'soft authoritarian' power by existing elites in the East Asian countries, and the maintenance of economic privileges and advantages enjoyed by them or their associates. Australian academics such as Richard Robison and Stephanie Lawson mounted effective attacks on these lines. Robison was a rather trenchant critic of the Asian narrative:

> Proponents of the 'Asian Values' thesis argue that 'East' and 'West' are two discrete systems of social, political and economic organization based on enduring cultural traditions and values that transcend social and economic change. In their view, and in an ironic reversal of the Orientalism of nineteenth-century Europe, it is the 'Eastern' model that is proving to be the most efficient of the species in a Darwinian struggle to dominate the world of industrial capitalism. In contrast, the West is seen to falter in an orgy of democratic and liberal excess, not only losing the economic race but also entering a free-fall into social disintegration[9].

Robison and others argued that in fact 'Asian values' represented various packages of conservative interests in the various countries. They were not at all Asia-specific but were 'important ideological strands in the history of both Asia and the West'. He rejected the whole idea of Asian values and said that there are 'only values that exist in dialectic relationship with real economic and social worlds'.

The Asian values debate involved questioning the universality of human rights and of liberal democracy as practised in the West. Some proponents of Asian values argued that political arrangements in East Asian countries were democratic even if they did not accord with those in the West. There was also questioning of 'Western' versions of human rights, with Asian leaders and their representatives often arguing that economic growth rather than individual rights and freedoms must be the priority goal since it was needed to provide the most fundamental human rights such as food, shelter, education. But economic growth required order and a disciplined society. That in turn meant putting some restrictions on individual freedom and placing the society's interests and requirements above those of the individual. It also meant preserving consensus in political arrangements and policy and thus restricting the freedom of political opposition and criticism. Ardent proponents of Asian values argued that Asian values were superior to those of the West and not just a product of a particular phase of early capitalism. The West, and especially the United States, was represented as decadent, dangerous and in decline – largely because of a surfeit of democracy and individualism. Dr Mahathir Mohamad, Prime Minister of Malaysia, was the leading advocate of this assertive version of the Asian values thesis. He proclaimed that 'Democracies are only beginning to learn that too much freedom is dangerous'[10].

The Asian values thesis looked vulnerable and even suspect in the light of the criticisms to which it was subjected. In particular it was difficult to see that there was anything especially Asian about such values when it could be shown that the same values had been proclaimed in Western societies when the latter were at a similar stage of economic and political development. There were also various arguments against the thesis in the context of cultural relativity and alleged cultural incommensurability. A plausible critique was that 'The kind of politics that deploys cultural myths to advantage is often a carefully and strategically calculated activity designed, above all, to maintain an elite in power by appealing to the most readily available as well as emotive symbols of legitimacy'[11]. But in terms of the politics of Australia's effort to win acceptance by the East Asians it served to underline differences rather than similarities or shared interests. Paul Keating's attempt to argue that Australian values such as 'mateship' were close to the values being asserted as Asian was particularly unconvincing. Some of the features of the United States which East Asian elites abhor and fear as influences which could 'corrupt' their societies and indeed their own children are prominent in Australia too. For many years a major problem for Australian relations with these countries and for Australian diplomacy in the region, especially with Indonesia, was what they saw as the outspoken and uninhibited nature of Australian media reporting and comment. This caused repeated offence and it was always seen as quintessentially 'un-Asian'. Journalists in Singapore or Malaysia, let alone Indonesia, were not permitted to write in such terms, and indeed in the first two of those countries are still not permitted to do so. In the meantime efforts in Australia to develop a more circumspect handling by the media of developments in the region have had an effect so that there is a more careful and less emotive approach to reporting and analysis of East Asian events. But Australia is still seen as un-Asian in the sense of being much more blunt and direct than would be appropriate in East Asian societies.

The Asian values promotion was largely an assertion of East Asian pride against the long wounding it had received directly or indirectly at the hands of the West. The West in this context is the 'other' and Australia is seen as part of it. The most interesting Asian writing on the subject is less concerned with the issues canvassed above about the universal or relative nature of human rights and so on. It is more concerned with the emotional factors which cause Asians to search for 'Asian values'. Thus Kishore Mahbubani writes:

> It is vital for Western minds to understand that the efforts by Asians to rediscover Asian values are not only or even primarily a search for political values. Instead they represent a complex set of motives and aspirations in Asian minds: a desire to reconnect with their historical past after this connection had been ruptured both by colonial rule and the subsequent domination of the globe by a Western *Weltanschauung*; an effort to find the right balance in bringing up their young so that they are open to the new technologically interconnected global universe and yet rooted in and conscious of the cultures of their ancestors...[12]

Mahbubani goes on to speak of Asians seeking 'to define their own personal, social, and national identities in a way that enhances their sense of self-esteem in a world in which their immediate ancestors had subconsciously accepted the fact that they were lesser beings in a Western universe'.

It is these factors which have made the Asian values thesis important and they were linked of course with the pride felt in the 'East Asian Economic Miracle'. No doubt that pride contributed to a certain complacency and a tolerance of abuses and poor governance which was exposed by the financial crisis of 1997-98. But the expectation that East Asia would continue to grow and grow, following the Japanese example virtually without limit, was not limited to East Asia. As already noted that expectation was shared by nearly all observers and commentators in the West too. Nor was it limited to economic development and growth. Chalmers Johnson spoke of the process of 'enrichment' leading to 'empowerment'. The success of ASEAN in shaping and leading East Asia wide consultations and arrangements, in which Europeans and other outsiders eagerly sought participation, appeared to be a harbinger of this. If the world's economic centre of gravity was shifting to East Asia then that region must inevitably attract more political and strategic importance and influence. Its members would have a greater voice in the councils of the world. It would be a distinctive voice, characteristically different from the voice of the West.

The Regional View of Australia

It has been difficult for Australians not familiar with Asia to understand and accept Asian animus against the West. It is not difficult to understand the love-hate relationship which, at least up to the last generation, many Asians felt towards the former colonial powers. That was, for example, manifested in the cachet which attached in certain Indonesian circles to speaking Dutch. Nor is it difficult to understand the frustration and resentment which has often been felt towards the United States as the richest, most successful and most powerful nation on earth which sometimes seemed to make little effort to understand the countries of the region. It has not been only in East Asia that the United States has experienced the problems of power. However none of those factors explain the difficulties which Australia has had at times in East Asia. On the Australian side, the notion that 'Asian values' constituted a dividing line and a barrier between East Asia and Australia was generally treated with scepticism. Indeed it was probably treated with excessive scepticism. While it was not difficult to find weaknesses in the arguments used to support the Asian values thesis the fact remained that there were substantial differences in terms of value priorities between Australia and its neighbours. At a popular level that would be a widely held view in Australia after the highly publicized events of 1998 and 1999 in East Timor and the setback to the regional economies which has given more salience to regulatory failure and 'corruption'. In terms of Australia's diplomacy in the region it is probably better not to seek to pretend such differences do not exist[13]. In practice it is better to acknowledge them if necessary, but avoid public criticism and avoid appearing to 'interfere in the internal affairs' of regional states. But however skilfully Australia conducts its regional diplomacy the values issue will be a constraint on Australia's inclusion in the East Asian institutional development. Certainly Australian values and behaviour *seem* to East Asians different from those in the region itself, and few Australians would disagree.

It is widely believed in Australia that a major reason for the reserve and even resentment manifested towards Australia by many people in the region have been due more than anything else to the 'White Australia' policy and its residue. There is evidence for that belief because editorial writers and others in the media of the East Asian countries still, some thirty years after its last vestiges were abolished, cast that racist immigration policy in Australia's face. In the last years of the twentieth century there was a recrudescence of racist tainted politics in Australia with the launching of the 'One Nation' party by Pauline Hanson. The reaction of the media, and many others, in most of East Asia seemed from an Australian perspective to be quite disproportionate – but none the less distressing for that. Many commentators interpreted 'One Nation' as a major movement and a harbinger of a return to the White Australia policy and simply ignored the fact that the number of votes it attracted was a small proportion (ranging between five per cent and 12 per cent in different elections).

While it is clear that Australia has not yet lived down the resentments in Asia caused by the White Australia policy and the attitudes that accompanied it, it seems unlikely that all those who sounded alarms in East Asia when 'One Nation' came on the scene were as unaware of the real situation as their strident criticisms suggested. There was almost certainly an element of *schadenfreude* in some of the commentary. But if some commentators took pleasure in the discomfort and embarrassment which Australia suffered in the region as a result of this manifestation of minority racist opinion that in itself points to resentment or dislike which Australians have been reluctant until recently to acknowledge. Some of this goes back to the colonial experience, as in the very prominent and perhaps instructive example of Dr Mahathir Mohamad, the Prime Minister of Malaysia. He appears to see Australia as a sort of second-rate[14] colonial remnant of the deeply resented Western dominance, and there is an explicit racist element in his attitude, for example in his statement that Australia could perhaps be accepted as a member of the region when 60 per cent of its population was of Asian origin. There are of course many others in the region who had experience of Australia when it still had a race-based immigration policy but who do not share Dr Mahathir's bitter and scornful attitude. However it would be prudent to recognize that the existence of the policy would not have been forgotten for example by the thousands of Colombo Plan students who lived in Australia at that time, nor by the even larger number of visitors who came either privately or under Australian Government programmes, or for conferences and other events while the White Australia policy was still in operation[15]. Many of those thousands took back privately held but very critical views. In that sense the Colombo Plan and other programmes at the time did not create unalloyed good will as their creators and planners intended. In fact the greatest benefits might have been in the educational effect on the Australian public and its attitudes of having in its midst relatively large numbers of Asian students and others.

From the point of view of some Australians it seemed unfair that the Hanson phenomenon elicited such a storm of protest in East Asia when the evidence of opinion polls and electoral voting was that it was very much a minority phenomenon and, where it had strength, was localized to certain country areas which were unlikely to influence the nation at large. It was easy to point to racist attitudes, political situations and practices in many of the East Asian countries which were much more widespread and entrenched than the One Nation phenomenon in Australia. There was no likelihood of any Asian Australians being subjected to discrimination such as that experienced by people of Korean descent in Japan, let alone pogroms such as those suffered by Chinese Indonesians. Nor was it special pleading when Australians asked why it was apparently quite acceptable for harsh criticisms to be raised in East Asia against any significant manifestation of racism in Australia but unacceptable for Australians to criticize racial discrimination in East Asia. Not many understood that, as seen from East Asia, Australian discrimination against Asians united the whole region in resentment and even outrage against perceived assertions of 'white' superiority with a long background in the collective consciousness, whereas current racial frictions in regional states were 'internal affairs' arising out of the difficulties of nation building in many cases with colonial legacies of imported minorities or, in the case of Indonesia, with borders which included various races and religions. Readiness to criticize Australia was enhanced by the fact that there were always voices in the Australian media and politics which took a high moral line about disturbances along racial or religious divides in the region.

Another exacerbating factor was that, while Australia was not in itself of great significance, Australian voices, if persistent and loud (as they were for example over East Timor) attracted attention more widely in the West and could thus influence opinion in more important places. In fact Australian *governments* have generally had a record of being relatively protective of regional neighbours in such matters. For example when the Netherlands took a strong line against human rights abuses in Indonesia in the 1980s, leading to the replacement of the Intergovernmental Group on Indonesia, the group of aid donors to Indonesia, by a World Bank consortium, Australia sought to ensure a minimum of disruption to the aid flow to Indonesia. It has rather been Australian NGOs (non-governmental organizations) and non-official individuals who have beaten the drums over human rights issues in the region, although government and the major political parties have become more responsive to the pressures brought by NGOs and protest groups. This was notably the case over East Timor where successive Australian governments restricted themselves to private representations to the Indonesian government, while NGOs in Australia accused governments of collusion in genocide etc and protested at the United Nations, organized demonstrations and protests in Australia and elsewhere and generally did all they could to bring the East Timor independence cause to the sympathetic attention of the international community. In the end the Australian government had no choice but to reverse policy on East Timor, largely as a consequence of Indonesian actions there but against a background of steadily rising concern in the Australian community promoted by the campaigns of the East Timor lobby.

Governments in Australia cannot suppress such activity (although Paul Keating tried to marginalize it) and thus inevitably Australia has tended to be something of a thorn in the side of regional states, or at least to those in power in such states. The situation serves to underline the differences between Australia and its neighbours.

It has been the view or assumption of most of those in positions of influence in Australia for many years that time would reduce those differences because the East Asian states would become increasingly liberal in their politics, increasingly prosperous economically and increasingly enmeshed in the international market economy. This would make them more democratic, with more free speech, more active civil societies and more observant of minority and individual rights. The unspoken conclusion was that they would become in these respects more like Australia. The general proposition was actively asserted, as we have seen, by Gareth Evans, and it was, and remains, widely held. It was encouraged by political events in Korea, Thailand and the Philippines and, more equivocally, in Indonesia. That expectation was part of the climate of opinion generated by the 'economic miracle'. In particular it was argued that the rapidly growing middle classes in the increasingly prosperous countries of South East Asia would expect and demand more say in government and that this would generate more openness, wider participation and an accelerating trend to liberal democracy in the region. We may hope that that will remain a realistic model for the longer term, but in the meantime it has been at least postponed by the setback to economic growth in the region. Thus in Indonesia the growth of the middle class has been reversed. More people would have fallen back than would have risen up to modest prosperity in the years since 1998, and to the extent that a growing, more confident and more demanding middle class was seen as the generator of liberal democracy expectations have had to be adjusted. In fact what has happened in Indonesia is rather that the rush into democratic forms following the resignation of Soeharto has created political turmoil the outcome of which is quite uncertain and which no doubt contains possibilities of instability and of retreat from democracy, as well as promising signs[16]. The turmoil has played a part in the exacerbation of Indonesian attitudes towards Australia since 1999 by increasing Indonesian sensitivity to external criticism, real or imagined, and by encouraging appeals to nationalism and xenophobia.

It was a reasonable expectation that increasingly prosperous and open participatory democracies in East Asia would be increasingly compatible with, or accepting of, Australia. But democracies which have not put down roots are likely to be unpredictable in economically adverse times. Perhaps paradoxically, Australia's chances of acceptance by the region seemed to be more favourable when the climate of government there was rather more authoritarian and when Labor was in power in Australia than it did subsequently when the Conservative parties were in power in Australia and popular democracy seemed to be growing stronger in parts of East Asia.

Negotiating Cultural Divisions

We have seen how, under the Keating/Evans foreign policy, Australia tried to minimize and override the cultural differences between Australia and East Asia, especially as perceived from the Asian side. A related policy, primarily in an Australian domestic context, was multiculturalism. This was designed to enhance respect for and acceptance of the cultures, including languages, of migrant and indigenous Australians. It was a rejection of the idea that all Australians should conform closely to the Anglo-Celtic majority model, and in the interest of doing so should largely give up their separate cultures. Most Australians saw some virtue in multiculturalism to the extent that it opposed tendencies to oppression of or discrimination against minorities (which had certainly been present in the past) and to the extent that it ensured that all Australians got a 'fair go' whatever their ethnic or cultural background. But reservations and criticism developed within the majority when they began to perceive the emergence of a multiculturalism 'industry' which appeared to be bent on the reduction of traditional or mainstream Australia to only one of a number of equally valid and equally privileged 'cultures' in Australia. In terms of government policy and programs multiculturalism has become less prominent. As the variety of Australian types and 'cultures' became established and for the most part accepted it also became less necessary, which is not to deny the continued existence of elements of ethnic and cultural prejudice[17]. But to someone who has observed Australian society and attitudes for over seventy years there has been an immense shift away from ethnic and cultural prejudice to the point that Australia seems to suffer less from such prejudice than almost any country in the world. Again, to ensure that judgment is not misunderstood, one needs to add that there is still much ignorance and some rank prejudice. But active discrimination is not common (and not just because it is illegal) and where it occurs it appears usually to be a reaction against some real or rumoured misdemeanours by a particular ethnic or cultural minority[18] – a matter which is itself contentious because minorities argue that there should be no identifying of the ethnic, religious or cultural origin or background in such cases.

Despite this generally benign outlook it is clear that Australians are opposed to receiving substantial numbers of people from countries such as Iraq and Afghanistan arriving in Indonesian vessels unannounced on Australian territory. From the point of view of the government's immigration policy these people are illegal, or at best unauthorized, immigrants while from the point of view of their Australian sympathizers and the United Nations High Commissioner for Refugees they are regarded as asylum seekers. All relevant public opinion polling has shown large majorities in favour of discouraging 'people smuggling' and as far as possible preventing such people from entering Australia. Indeed, even regardless of the mode of their arrival, Australians clearly still have a very cautious attitude to immigration of people from cultures which are felt to be deeply alien. They also have clearly retained much of the concern about foreign intrusions across the enormous coastline and into the empty land which, as we saw in Chapter 1, was a major factor in the Australian outlook on the world almost from the beginning. Australians have made it clear that they expect their government to be in a position to 'control' entry into the country and they are clearly not prepared to cede that control to the United Nations High Commissioner for Refugees or any other international authority, let alone to 'people smugglers' operating through Indonesia.

The Keating government made a major effort to present Australia to East Asia as not just a neighbour but a member of their neighbourhood: enmeshed with them economically, recognizing that its geography committed it to living closely with them and sharing their fortunes for good and ill, and generally throwing in its lot with them. At the same time Keating sought to explain what he was doing to the Australian people while seeking to commit them to the results of his policy. The result was some disjunction between the policy of the government and the commitment of the majority of the people as became clear at the 1996 election and subsequently. For the first year or two of the conservative Howard government which followed Keating, the commitment to engagement with East Asia and in particular the cultivation of the relationship with Indonesia was continued. But it was clear before long that the Prime Minister did not see the East Asia engagement policy in the same terms as Keating. Whereas the latter said with every appearance of conviction that it was the top priority for Australia, which the Howard government White Paper said too, Prime Minister Howard strongly emphasized that it was not to be taken to involve or imply any reduction in Australian ties with the United States or the United Kingdom. It was clear that he wanted no diminution of the traditional and emotional solidarity with the United States and United Kingdom and had none of Keating's sense of driving the development of a sense of solidarity as strong, or indeed stronger because more immediate and closer, with the countries of East Asia.

But while it became increasingly apparent that there was a substantial difference of emphasis and commitment between the Keating government policy and that of Howard they shared the desire to ensure that the United States was kept in play in a broader Asia Pacific context. They wanted to keep the United States committed to East Asia and to avoid any development which might lead East Asia to seek to cast off the security and other links with the United States. Partly for that reason they both sought to minimize cultural and other differences, to emphasize shared interests in liberalizing trade, promoting security and so on. The other reason for minimizing cultural and other differences as between East Asian countries and Australia in particular was of course, as we have seen, to counter allegations that Australia was too different to qualify as a member of East Asia.

The idea that cultures and civilizations might be incompatible or destined to compete for power and influence conflicted with the Australian desire and intention of winning acceptance by East Asia. As we have seen that desire and intention at government level had elements of equivocation and ambiguity. But the idea that Australia might be excluded on grounds of ethnic or cultural incompatibility was anathema. The 'clash of civilizations' theory of Samuel Huntington[19] was regarded as subversive of Australian policy and rejected[20] accordingly. That is understandable given that Australian policy under Labor and, especially initially, under the Coalition after their victory in 1996, was to avoid a situation where Australia had to choose between Asia and the West. APEC was a major manifestation of what was a pervasive policy. Certainly the emphasis varied between individuals and over time. Paul Keating manifestly leaned more to the East Asian side; John Howard manifestly more to the American and British side. Both wanted to position Australia so that it did not have to choose. The idea that the West (and its leading champion the United States) was destined to find itself in fundamental conflict with groups of states clustered around different cultural values on the Asian side was deeply threatening to a long-standing and fundamental objective of Australian policy.

Huntington's general thesis was that the world was moving towards an era where the great divisions would be along the fault-lines between civilizations represented by groups of states sharing core cultural values or common interests which they assert against competing cultural systems. There has been much argument about the location of the fault-lines in the Huntington theory and about the broad alliances and groupings which he arranged into civilizational patterns. But while much of the detail is contestable and some of it unconvincing the basic thesis is a plausible one – that shared and perceived cultural and civilizational roots will be powerful factors in constituting competing power groupings in a multipolar world rather than a universal globalized world based on market capitalism and liberal democracy as practised in the West.

Clearly the Australian situation is an interesting and important test case for this thesis which contains much that is directly relevant to the case of Australia, to the formation and development of Australian foreign policy, and especially to the policy of 'enmeshment' with East Asia. In the first place it bears on the issue whether it will be possible to bridge the Pacific and to maintain the notion of an Asia Pacific Community. It also raises the issue whether Australia itself will be able to engage and 'enmesh' with East Asia without compromising its ties with its Western cultural and ethnic source countries and the United States. Most fundamentally it raises the issue whether Australia will be able to coexist with East Asia without converting itself into an Asian country, the 'part of Asia' argument which we examined in the previous chapter.

Huntington's book would thus have provided sufficient material for Australians to ponder even without the specific discussion of Australian policy which it contained and in which he wrote that Australia had chosen to 'defect from the West, redefine itself as an Asian society, and cultivate close ties with its geographical neighbours'. As we saw in Chapter 4, Paul Keating said that 'The last claim is right; the first two are rubbish'[21]. It will be clear from earlier discussion in this book that Keating had no wish or intention to 'defect from the West'. Apart from his own denial, his APEC strategy and the reasons he gave for his opposition to EAEC make that clear. Moreover he explicitly discarded the view that Australia was a part of Asia. There were, as we have seen, others in or close to the government at the time who took the view that Australia *was*, was destined to be, or should be, a part of Asia. But that was not government policy under Keating. Huntington appears to have been inaccurately advised about the Keating engagement policy resulting in a loose and misleading formulation of Keating's policy intentions and purposes. But that is in a sense incidental. Huntington obviously saw that Australia was in an exposed position in his picture of the new world order because it was a member of the West, culturally and politically, while geographically located alongside (some would say 'in') Asia. If his version of the evolving world order is correct Australia will be confronted with the cruel choices which it has sought to avoid by the foreign, trade and defence policies which it has been pursuing for many years. It is no doubt a recognition of this which has made the book a sensitive issue for Australian politicians.

The strand in Huntington's book which seems most likely to exercise Australian concerns in the foreseeable future is the treatment of Islam as a major factor in the new world order which he projects. Huntington's analysis resonates with powerful currents of thinking in the Islamic world today, rejecting the notion that Muslims are destined to be Westernized. To quote Professor Wang Gungwu on this point: 'It is a good feeling, then, for Muslims to imagine the *umma*, the community of believers, again emerging as a major force in civilisational politics'[22]. Wang Gungwu goes on in the same article to suggest that elements in the Huntington thesis could foreshadow *jihad* in response to efforts by the West to defend its position which may be seen as 'another Western crusade', and he observes that 'Huntington's theory essentially corroborates the classical Islamic worldview'.

For Australians that dangerous 'fault line' between the West and Islam is at its very doorstep – its border with Indonesia. For most of the fluctuating history of the relationship between Australia and Indonesia there was some comfort derived on the Australian side from the fact that a substantial majority of Indonesian Muslims took a relatively relaxed and comfortable attitude towards their religion. In much of Java, where more than half of the Indonesian population live, Islam has been practised in conjunction with older traditional beliefs and residues of Hinduism. But a more observant and demanding Islam has spread in recent years, as is apparent even to casual observation. Thus twenty or thirty years ago in Central Java it was quite unusual to see women wearing head scarves or other Islamic dress. Now it is widespread. Young men have been recruited in Central Java to fight Christians in the Maluku province in eastern Indonesia and even to train and fight with the Taliban forces in Afghanistan. There appears to be considerable Muslim sympathy for the Taliban and even for Osama bin Laden and the al-Qaeda whom some see as defenders of the faith and leaders of a *jihad* against the West which has intruded into Islam's holy land of Saudi Arabia. Of course there remain substantial factors in Indonesia standing in the way of any destabilizing swing to Islamic extremism. Nor is it new for young Muslim men in Java to be organized to engage in killing of people represented as threatening their religion. In the aftermath of the failed coup attempt of 30 September 1965 Muslim youth groups, encouraged by elements of the Indonesian army, led the killing of hundreds of thousands of communists and people who were in one way or another alleged to be implicated in communism. But at that time the West, and Australia, had more fear of Communism than of resurgent Islam which was generally seen as a factor which could be deployed in the Cold War against 'International Communism'. In the aftermath of the terrorist attacks in the United States on 11 September 2001 there is, at least in the West, a far more critical scrutiny of Islam as a global force.

That has been the case also in Australia although there, as in the United States and in Europe, the political establishment and indeed all religious and ethnic groups and other elements of civil society have insisted that the actions and policies they have put in place since 11 September 2001 have been directed against terrorism and in no way against Islam. Nevertheless Indonesian leaders including the President have demonstrated their distaste for the way in which the Australian government aligned itself so closely with the United States action in Afghanistan and committed forces in support. That and other developments at the time exacerbated the climate of the relationship between Indonesia and Australia. That key relationship is the subject of chapter eight. Here we anticipate it in the context of the 'clash of civilizations' theory to note that Islam in Indonesia especially seems increasingly to see Australia as clearly, by its own choice, on the other, Western, side of the Huntingtonian fault line. The climate of opinion in Australia concerning Islam has been adversely affected and the climate of opinion in Indonesia concerning Australia has been adversely affected also.

Australia on the Outside

The 'East Asian Economic Miracle' generated or reinforced perceptions of separateness from the West and of regional solidarity which, though containing elements of myth and despite internal frictions and disputes within the region, seemed to be laying the basis for East Asian institutional cooperation. There was a sense of pride in accomplishment and a belief that that accomplishment was based on Asian values and rooted in Asian cultures and traditions distinct from the West. There was also a view that the West had largely lost its way and was sinking into a restless, rootless, indulgent individualism. That pride, and the satisfaction which had been derived from the Japanese example, of course excluded Australia. Australia could observe with satisfaction because of trade advantages it was reaping and because it believed that the growing prosperity of the region augured well for stability and for democratization which would enhance Australia's compatibility. But Australia was not a part of the East Asian growth phenomenon, did not identify with the values on which it was supposed to be founded, and held on firmly to its historic and security ties with the United States and Europe.

Australian scholars regarded much of the East Asian theorizing about Asian values and their role with scepticism and Australian governments and the Australian foreign policy and trade establishment was opposed to the early attempts to institutionalize East Asian solidarity and cooperation not only because they excluded Australia but because they threatened the Australian priority of developing the institutional links across the whole Pacific, tying the United States and a resurgent East Asia together and including Australia. In the region there continued to be reservations about Australia which derived partly from the White Australia policy even though nearly thirty years had passed since its last elements were abolished. Then, as we have already seen, the emergence of the 'One Nation' political movement attracted far more attention in East Asia than any other development in or concerning Australia. From an Australian perspective the importance attached to this phenomenon seemed disproportionate because it was numerically never a major movement and in the space of a few years declined substantially. But that was to overlook the particular sensitivity in the region to racism from the Western side or from 'whites' who had subjected nearly the whole of the region to colonial or other forms of domination for so long. In the pursuit of acceptance as an insider by East Asia there was an understandable tendency in some quarters to suppress or not recognize some of these obstacles. In other quarters there was a tendency to adopt an excessively self-critical posture.

In fact Australia's historical and formative experiences, outlined in the early chapters of this book, were so different from those of the East Asian nations which it had been aspiring to join that it would have been surprising if there had not been hesitations and reservations on both sides. Huntington's brief treatment of the Australian situation in his major work described above gave an inaccurate version of the Australian problem and dilemma. But he saw that Australia was a key test case of his thesis. From the Australian viewpoint the identification of that dilemma by Huntingon, one of America's most influential and prominent academic analysts of world political trends, should have attracted more attention and more examination than it did. In fact *The Clash of Civilizations* met with disfavour by both government and opposition in Australia partly no doubt because of Huntington's mistaken assertion that Australia was seeking to abscond from the West and join East Asia, thus crossing a major civilizational fault line. The proposition was misconceived in terms of the objectives of Australian governments but dismissal of the claim overlooked the force and substance of Huntington's thesis for which Australia was indeed a relevant test case. Moreover there were some prominent analysts in Australia, such as Stephen FitzGerald of the Asia-Australia Institute and Greg Sheridan of *The Australian* newspaper, whose views seemed to imply something of the kind wrongly attributed by Huntington to Australian government policy.

What Huntington's account points to is the issue whether Australia could win acceptance by East Asia without in effect submerging its ethnic origins and cultural heritage. More specifically that will depend in large part whether Australia can live at peace and on a mutually satisfactory and beneficial basis with a far larger neighbour belonging to a quite different civilizational and cultural tradition. That is probably the key question in Australia's future. While Australia is a smaller middle sized nation and not a major factor in shaping world history, its success or failure in negotiating the issues which will be raised by its juxtaposition to Indonesia will be of wider and possibly exemplary interest.

In the early nineties those conducting Australia's engagement policy and the academic and media supporters of that policy probably under-rated the difficulties and obstacles in the way of bringing it to a successful conclusion. But Keating's conclusion of the Agreement on Maintaining Security (AMS) with Soeharto appeared at the time to be a major achievement in the direction of acceptance and in terms of making a permanent advance in the key relationship with Indonesia. It certainly gave encouragement to all who had been working to those ends. At the end of the century much of that advance and achievement appeared lost. The AMS had been rescinded by Indonesia and there was deep resentment in that country towards Australia. The East Asia institutionalization project had advanced with Australia excluded. The region had suffered a major economic setback and for that and other reasons the Australian interest in pushing on for acceptance was clearly waning. There was a danger that Australia would lose sight of the fundamental national interest in engagement – engagement on terms which would involve Australia's full acceptance by the member countries of East Asia. Not only was Australian interest and enthusiasm waning, there was a clear feeling both in government and in the community that Australia could not continue to push for acceptance when that was being withheld and when there seemed no current prospect of changing matters.

Australian concern about belonging seemed to be in abeyance. Keating had said that Australia was Australia – not Asian, not European or anything other than Australian. Most Australians readily agreed with that, but without considering the implications in terms of future security. The INTERFET involvement of the Australian army in East Timor, and the great success of the 2000 Olympic Games in Sydney gave confidence and pride to the Australian people and that was of course picked up by the politicians. A series of international sporting successes buoyed the public mood. There was no awareness that that sort of success by Australia did nothing to enhance the nation's acceptability in East Asia. In fact Australia's success in such matters underlined its difference from the South East Asians especially. They took no pleasure from Australia's success in international sporting contests in which they themselves had scant success or which were not part of their repertoire. Moreover Australia's resilience in the aftermath of the East Asian financial crisis only contrasted with the failure of Indonesia and the intransigence of Malaysia and placed Australia more firmly outside the community of the ASEAN countries. Australians had little or no feeling for the dynamics of these developments and the effects on perceptions of Australia in the region. Demonstrations against Australia in Jakarta and harsh comments by the Prime Minister of Malaysia and some of his main colleagues reinforced the feeling in Australia that the country was being rejected by its regional neighbours, for reasons which to Australians appeared unfair and unreasonable. Australia had been prompt to come to the assistance of the East Asian countries struck by the financial crisis in 1997-98 and had been outspokenly active on their behalf in Washington with the International Financial Institutions and the United States Treasury. While this was not done in expectation of any gratitude it was disappointing, especially in the case of Indonesia, to find that it did not enhance the neighbourly relationship but rather increased the sense that Australia was on the other side. For example the then President of Indonesia, Abdurrachman Wahid, visited many other countries around the world and repeatedly cancelled or deferred planned visits to Australia because of domestic political opposition to his visiting that country. Eventually he did visit Australia shortly before he was voted out in favour of the National Party leader Megawati Sukarnoputri. The Wahid visit was conducted in a friendly way but with very little serious substance. Its only real significance was that the fact that it took place opened the door for the Australian Prime Minister to pay a reciprocal visit to Indonesia.

By 1995 Australia was closer to East Asia than ever before. But it is now a good deal further removed in terms of fellow feeling, in terms of mutual interest in developing cooperation and institutionalizing such cooperation, and in some cases in terms of economic engagement. It was always the case that the growing links were driven primarily by Australian initiatives and Australian policy. But the problems with Indonesia and the continuing opposition of the Prime Minister of Malaysia and leading associates have considerably raised the bars to Australia's acceptance as well as sapping the Australian interest and will to continue the effort at the previous level. The financial and economic setback has also been unfavourable to the Australian enmeshment project because it has tended to enhance Australia's advantages while regional countries struggled not very effectively with problems which required for their solution major reforms of governance for which the will was lacking. In this area too Australia's cultural differences have become more apparent as the regional countries which had looked to the Japanese model discovered deficiencies which Asian values seemed not well suited to overcome. In general the recent years seem to have carried Australia into something of a retreat from its engagement policy.

Notes

1. Probably Australia's most respected diplomat who was subsequently Ambassador to several major countries, Secretary of the Department of Foreign Affairs, and Governor of Tasmania.
2. See Chapter 5 above, p. 100, for Gareth Evans' version with Australia as 'the oddest man in'.
3. And who also dominated Australian official and mainstream thinking on the issue for most of the period.
4. *Keiretsu* are the families of Japanese companies which are for example grouped around major trading companies and which might comprise steel, shipping and ship-building, engineering, construction, banking, real estate etc firms in mutually supporting relationships with extensive cross-holdings of share capital.
5. This account has been developed in detail in the work of Yamamura, Kozo and Hatch, Walter (1996), *Asia in Japan's Embrace*, Cambridge University Press, Cambridge. They describe the process as 'embraced development'.
6. A seminal trade agreement was signed in 1957 and Japan became the largest customer for Australian coal, iron ore, wool and other commodities. During the 1980s there was also substantial Japanese investment in Australia.
7. Funabashi, Y. (1993), 'The Asianization of Asia', *Foreign Affairs*, Vol. 72, No. 5.
8. Ibrahim, Anwar (1996), *The Asian Renaissance*, Times Books International, Singapore.
9. Robison, Richard (1996), Introduction to special issue *The Pacific Review*, Vol. 9 No. 3.
10. 'No freedom without responsibility', *New Straits Times*, 20 May, 1995, p. 10.
11. Lawson, Stephanie, (1996), 'Political Myths about Asia and the West' in Robison, Richard ed. *Pathways to Asia*, Allen & Unwin, St Leonards, p. 123.
12. Mahbubani, Kishore (1998), 'Can Asians Think?', *The National Interest*, Number 52, pp. 27-35.
13. As was the tendency during the heyday of the 'engagement' policy during the first half of the nineties.
14. Speaking to his UMNO Party Conference in 2001 Dr Mahathir gave a lengthy imitation or parody of Australian pronunciation of English and claimed that Asian immigrants to Australia were not permitted to use their native languages and were forced to adopt a provincial Australian version of English.
15. The writer recalls very clearly Asian journalists visiting Australia in the late 1950s reacting strongly over this. Living in the Philippines between 1967 and 1969 instances of bitter resentment were forced on one's attention.
16. For example the decision by the Parliament that the next Presidential election in 2004 will not be indirect, i.e. by the MPR or People's Consultative Assembly, but by direct popular election.
17. Albeit much reduced. One indication is that at the Federal election in November 2001 support for Pauline Hanson's 'One Nation' party (see above p. 121) was only 4.3 per cent (House of Representatives).

18 For example when police reports in Sydney gave prominence to a series of brutal gang rapes by youths 'of Middle Eastern appearance' (code for Lebanese Moslems) in 2001.
19 Huntington, Samuel (1996), *The Clash of Civilisations and the Remaking of World Order*, Simon & Schuster, New York.
20 At the time when the Coalition Government's foreign policy manifesto *In the National Interest* was being drafted in 1997 the writer put it to Foreign Minister Alexander Downer that there was merit in some of Huntington's arguments. The Minister said that even if that was so he would want to fight against the thesis because it was so contrary to Australia's interests.
21 P. 93 above.
22 Wang, Gungwu, 'A Machiavelli for Our Times', *The National Interest*, No. 46, p. 72.

Chapter 7

Australian Efforts to Qualify

Convergence

Seeking to qualify as a member or perhaps an associate member of the East Asian club, Australian governments and supporters of the 'enmeshment' policy mounted several arguments. We have noted already the argument that Australia was no more different from others in the region than they were from each other. Another argument, directed primarily at the Australian public, has been that Australia has no other anchorage to attach itself to in a world in which regional associations are becoming increasingly important, so that its only recourse is East Asia. There are also arguments to the effect that Australia can make an important contribution to East Asia. But the argument from convergence was of particular importance. It held out the prospect of disarming claims that Australia was too different from the other countries of the region to fit well with them and it offered reassurance to those in Australia who had reservations about throwing in our lot with some countries which were thought to have different standards in regard to human rights, the suppression of minority opinion and so on. Moreover it added a certain sense of inevitability about the appropriateness of Australia engaging with East Asia.

The convergence argument derived largely from the claim that rapid and sustained economic development created spreading wealth and a quickly expanding middle class of entrepreneurs, managers and professionals who would demand a growing voice in policy making thus creating pressure for participatory democracy. There would also be a concomitant development of civil society, of organizations and groups independent of the government. These developments would expand the areas of choice and produce societies that were less traditional and more modern and which would have more in common with Australia[1]. Australia could more easily closely engage with these increasingly similar and rapidly modernizing societies and thus the path to acceptance by the region would be facilitated. At the same time the process of globalization and the rapid expansion of information, including frontier-jumping vehicles such as the Internet, would give impetus to the process of change in the East Asian developing countries and 'modernize' them. As they pressed to expand their exports they would be required increasingly to open their economies and adopt international practices and regulatory frameworks. All this would promote the 'convergence' of those countries and Australia.

Australian scholars found much to criticize in this account. The contention that rapid economic growth entails forms of political liberalization was questioned. There were apparent historical exceptions such as the Soviet Union under the Five

Year plans from 1928 to 1941, or the growth of the German economy during the Nazi period. It was also questionable whether newly emerging Asian middle classes would press for the right to participate in decision making in the way postulated. Might they not rather adopt politically conservative positions of support for the existing more authoritarian structures in order to preserve stability and to defend against the possibility of populist pressure, and pass on to their children, the gains they had made under the existing system? There was scepticism that convergence would occur in ways that would bring Australia and the East Asian countries much closer together as a result of historical and developmental processes already in train, and especially towards suggestions that there was an inevitability about this.

There is now a vast literature on democratization theory and the linkage between economic development and democratization is a contested area. That there is such a linkage has for long been influential for Western and especially United States policy. It has also been influential in Australian policy including especially in regard to East Asia. It has been expected that as the 'dragon' and 'tiger' economies became more prosperous they would shift from autocratic rule of various kinds to elected government institutions and leaderships. That belief was encouraged by developments in Taiwan, South Korea, the Philippines, Thailand and Indonesia. These have been striking changes. The first four of the five countries just mentioned now appear to be established democracies. It will be surprising if they slip back into military or some other autocracy. There is still doubt about the durability of the changes in Indonesia, but an abandonment of the attempt to establish an effective and stable democracy there seems unlikely. In the scholarly debate there is support for the view that the semi-democratic or 'half-way house' model exemplified in the region by Malaysia and Singapore might also be followed by Indonesia[2]. In North East Asia the new democracies of Taiwan and South Korea differ in some ways from Western liberal democracies, just as their economies are different because of the ways in which their state elites engage with capital[3]. But they meet the usual tests for qualifying as democracies.

However it is far from clear that democratization in East Asia will make a big difference to the reservations in the region which stand in the way of acceptance of Australia. So far, in South East Asia, the highest level of acceptance of Australia, and of support for Australia's inclusion, has come from President Soeharto of Indonesia who was swept out of office in 1998 in the name of democracy, and who is now invariably referred to in Western media as a 'despot' or 'dictator'[4]. In some respects Soeharto was a modern figure, especially in his appreciation of the importance of economic development and of raising the standard of living of the population as a whole. He also had a keen grasp of world and regional politics. But in other respects he was essentially a traditional figure, steeped in his Javanese cultural background and roots. In that sense it would be difficult to think of any political leader in the region more different from Australians. The contrast between Soeharto and Whitlam, and Soeharto and Keating, for example, in terms of background, beliefs, cultural interests and so on was extreme. Yet those Australian Prime Ministers developed a close rapport with him and there was mutual respect and indeed liking[5]. Since the primacy of an elected parliament was restored in

Indonesia, with a democratic competition for power between political interests, Australia's relations with Indonesia have deteriorated dramatically and there is little prospect of any early return to the warmth of the Keating era. There is in fact a complex set of connections between these two developments and it is certainly possible that in some cases the development of democratic political institutions in Australia's neighbours will support a convergence of interests, attitudes or values. But it was for many years during the Soeharto period the view of the ruling elite in Indonesia, including the leading military figures, that Indonesia was not 'ready' for democracy and that to throw matters, including the Presidential succession, open to elections would precipitate grave instability and even civil war. While that view is no doubt open to the same sort of scepticism as the elite use of the Asian values argument it had some real plausibility in the context of the time[6]. As we shall see in the next chapter it had particular plausibility in the case of Indonesia in the light of attempts to make constitutional democracy work there in the 1950s.

There were some grounds for thinking that regional reservations about accepting Australia would diminish over time when, under Labor governments, Australia was making a strong and persistent attempt to 'enmesh' with the region. Despite the ambivalence about what constituted 'the region' there was clearly a commitment to engagement with East Asia in every field and there was a recognition of that in East Asia. There were influential figures in the region who encouraged the Australian commitment even if they did not do so publicly with any vigour. On the Australian side Keating's achievement in concluding a security agreement with Soeharto seemed a watershed which in due course would lead on to further institutional links with East Asia, both bilateral and multilateral[7]. But the 1996 election in Australia showed that public support was limited and cautious and then the problems and changes in South East Asia after July 1997 produced a far more challenging environment which saw the interruption and probably the end of the East Asian economic 'miracle'. It would now seem optimistic for a variety of reasons to expect a resumption of the almost region-wide churning out of annual economic growth rates of up to eight per cent. Japan has had a stagnating economy for ten years; by far the largest of the South East Asian states, Indonesia, has been unable to make significant progress to overcoming its grave economic problems; Thailand and Malaysia face difficulties and even Singapore has suffered setbacks. China continues to post high growth rates and it is widely believed that the Chinese economy is on the way to becoming eventually the second largest in the world. But recent policy decisions by both government and the Central Bank have reinforced scepticism about the authenticity of GDP growth figures provided by the Chinese government.

The massive reversal of Australia's burgeoning relationship with Indonesia has also changed attitudes in the region towards Australia and within Australia itself. The efforts of supporters of engagement to make that policy seem attractive to Australians seemed to lose conviction at the end of the 1990s and at the same time within Australia the interest in and drive towards engagement diminished. This was not only a consequence of the reversal of the relationship with Indonesia. It reflected also the entrenched opposition of Dr Mahathir and his associates and a recognition that Malaysia would block all Australian efforts to win acceptance in the emerging institutional framework of the region. Other links and loyalties re-emerged, with encouragement from the Coalition government, and seemed to capture more of the attention and support of many Australians as convergence and engagement appeared to offer less reassurance for Australia's future and less prospect of a secure place in a secure region. In Chapter 10 we shall examine this more closely with a view to assessing the nature and extent of what many observers are seeing as a mutual retreat from engagement.

We have seen that Australian efforts to qualify for membership of what seemed to be an emerging East Asian club were handicapped by ambivalence about what region Australia was seeking to join. No other member or prospective member of the putative East Asian grouping was subject to such strong ties outside the region as Australia – ethnically, historically and culturally. None of the East Asians had the sort of relationship which Australia had with the West. Japan had a security relationship with the United States which was different in quality from Australia's but even more important for Japan's security, at least during the Cold War[8]. But Australia identified with the United States in a way which differentiated the Australian relationship from those of Japan or the Republic of Korea. In a number of ways Prime Minister Howard emphasized the identification with the United States. This was noted around the region and especially after an interview he gave to Fred Brenchley in *The Bulletin*, a weekly magazine. Brenchley's story[9] left the impression that Howard had accepted the term 'deputy sheriff' as a description of Australia's role in the region in association with the United States. Howard later disassociated himself from this description, but only after it had been given wide publicity in the region. It has never been erased from regional perceptions of the Howard Government's foreign policy and has contributed significantly to the discomfort which many feel over that policy. Whether deservedly or not John Howard has established an image in the region as a leader who marches in close step with the United States in the pursuit of its interests and without much careful attention to the views and sensitivities of the regional countries themselves.

Another factor is that Australia still has the Queen of England as its head of state. Australians were not (and still are not) aware of the misunderstanding which that creates in the region. It is widely thought that Australia is still in some significant ways 'under England' and that it is not a fully independent nation. This is probably as great a barrier as the fact that 80 per cent of the Australian population is of Caucasian origin. The ethnic composition of the population is not something which will be much changed in the near term, and which there is in any case no disposition to change at more than a deliberate pace, governed by the need for immigrants and the non-discriminatory policy guideline rather than any decision to change the composition of the population as rapidly as possible. However the constitutional fiction which appears to place Australia 'under' the British Queen could be easily changed by the Australian electorate through amendment of the Constitution in another referendum. The monarchist movement in Australia, in the campaign leading up to the referendum on the issue in 2000, argued that regional countries did not have misconceptions about Australia's independence because the Queen is Head of State, and that anyway Australians should not feel constrained to allow their decision on the issue to be influenced by what foreigners thought. Despite efforts by some on the Republican side it is doubtful whether this aspect had much bearing on the fate of the Republic issue at the referendum which was lost primarily because of the way the question was framed in terms of one particular model for selecting the Head of State. As a result the Republican side was disastrously split over the question whether the Head of State should be popularly elected or chosen by the government of the day as the Governor General is at present[13]. In the aftermath of the referendum it is the view of members of parliament who support the republican cause that it would be damaging to use the argument that retaining the Australian monarchy is an obstacle to acceptance of Australia in the region. The validity of the argument is not questioned, but its effect in the Australian electorate is thought to be negative. They would, it is thought, take the view that the matter is no business of foreigners. Previously the leading Republicans had tended to think that the argument about acceptance in the region would be a telling one with sections of the public. This is one of a number of indications that the commitment to engagement with the region in the Australian community has diminished.

Arguments that convergence had already largely occurred, or that the differences of culture and beliefs between Australia and the countries of East Asia were really much less than was usually thought, also carried little conviction. Gareth Evans, as we saw in the preceding chapter, sought to show that 'the images look less and less radically different; more and more they replicate each other, converge'. But Australians were not convinced any more than were their Asian neighbours. Those Australians who were pressing for more study of Asian languages, history and culture in order to make Australia better equipped to engage with Asia were also uncomfortable with this approach. While it was the reverse of the intention of Evans or others who took that line it could be interpreted as detracting from the need they saw for Australia to change itself in order to be able to fit in better with the region.

Convergence by Australia

Discussion of 'convergence' internationally has generally been concerned with the prospect that modernization of traditional societies in developing countries, the growth of international trade and other exchanges, the rapid expansion of electronic media and especially economic growth and increasing prosperity would drive a demand for democratization and the liberalization of markets. The idea of modernization has been contested especially by conservative interests in the developing countries who have seen much of what has been called modernization as westernization and to be resisted, as we saw in the discussion above on Asian Values. But in general the assumption, either explicit or implicit, has been that the idea of convergence means a shift by developing countries towards a global norm of democratic political institutions and liberal market economies and that is seen as maximizing opportunities for economic growth and improvement in human rights and democratic freedom. That is contested also in the West by opponents of globalization, 'economic rationalism' and the assorted protest movements which disrupted the World Trade Organization meeting in Seattle in 1998 and mounted vociferous demonstrations at various subsequent high level international meetings on trade, finance and development. But the assumption just stated in summary form has been part of mainstream policy thinking in Washington and elsewhere.

It has also been mainstream, or at least very influential, thinking in Australia under both Labor and Coalition governments. But a notable factor in Australian policy thinking has been that, to implement engagement with East Asia, and to produce a convergence that would bring Australia and its neighbours closer together, it was necessary for Australia to do much of the converging. That is to say it was not enough for Australia to await the modernization shift by the South East Asians for example. It was also necessary for Australia to change itself in order to fit better with East Asia. This is not a new idea. We saw in Chapter 4 that, especially from the Whitlam Prime Ministership (1972-5) onwards, there was a series of policy inquiries and changes which were aimed at fitting Australia better to engage with East Asia. Whitlam got rid of the remnants of the White Australia policy and over the following decades immigration from Asia into Australia increased substantially, changing the ethnic mix and feel of Australian cities. Under the Hawke government there was a new emphasis on Asian studies. One of the central figures in this, John Ingleson, introducing the report on *Asia in Australian Higher Education* proposed that teaching about Asia and its languages be seen as an aspect of the *Australianization*, not the *Asianization*, of the curricula of Australian higher education. This was a fertile idea emphasized also by Professor Stephen FitzGerald who chaired the Inquiry into a 'National Strategy for the Study of Asia in Australia' whose report was adopted by the Government in 1989. FitzGerald later developed the idea that it should be part of the Australian identity to have familiarity with Asia and to have the skills and capacities and deeper knowledge which would enable Australians to interact easily and successfully with Asians.

FitzGerald became a persistent and trenchant critic of Australia's reluctance to *adapt* to East Asia, by learning to understand the thinking of the people of the region, to learn their history and to speak their languages, and he came to look on Australian efforts to engage with the region with something approaching despair. In his 1997 book *Is Australia an Asian Country?*[11] FitzGerald wrote of the major changes which had taken place in recognition of the importance of East Asia to Australia but noted the attachment to the concept of the Asia Pacific as a substitute for a direct attachment to East Asia itself. The main problems and obstacles to which he drew attention in the book were the lack of recognition in Australia of what he saw as the *necessity* for Australia to make a far more purposeful and urgent effort to equip itself to live with the East Asian countries and to be accepted by them in the institutional arrangements which he saw emerging in their region.

FitzGerald emphasized the importance for Australia and Australia's future of the Asianization of Asia, the sense 'of being "Asian" in the way that elites in Europe have of being "European"'[12]. He noted that the theory of convergence could be discussed without the element of discomfort involved in the idea of Asianization and he pointed out that 'The dominant ideas of convergence are overwhelmingly Western, as is commonly also the projected end point of the convergence process'[13]. One could thus 'comfortably discuss Asian cultures within the framework of Western convergence, but not so comfortably if the framework is Asianization'. FitzGerald saw convergence for Australia as being more a matter of convergence towards Asia than of Australia's neighbours converging on the West. This is no doubt a simple point but it is one of great importance for the reason just indicated: that acceptance of Australia by East Asia cannot be allowed to depend on change by a modernizing East Asia. It will require active and substantial change in and by Australia to adapt towards East Asia. The pole around which FitzGerald's discussion largely revolves is the idea that Australia can both 'Asianize' *and* maintain its Australian character. At the same time he is often fiercely critical or scornful of what he perceives to be Australian characteristics, attitudes or behaviour which stand in the way of asianizing Australia. In discussing Asian elite impressions of Australia he displays what used to be called the Australian 'cultural cringe' to an extreme degree – but vis-à-vis Asia instead of Europe.

Thus he writes: 'Australia was something of a freak, a Europe-derived culture in a sea of Asian cultures, ruled by a transplanted European people soaking up sun and skin cancer in a climate for which they were never intended. Australia was also a client state, but it strutted in Asia with the airs often attaching to such clients, patronizing and condescending to Asians and discriminating against them racially'. This invites the question whether the Europeans who have lived for some thousands of years around the northern shores of the Mediterranean, or the 'transplanted Europeans' who now live in their many millions in California and Florida for example are also freakish as never having been intended for the climate in which they live[14]. It is true that Australia is one of the survivors of those British colonies which were established as great destinations of Anglo-Celtic emigration. The United States is by far the biggest and already in 1776 broke away from Britain and set out on a course which has made it the world's superpower based on a multicultural society of 250 million people but still having Britain as its closest ally and associate. The others are Canada, whose case is complicated by the French minority, Australia and New Zealand. New Zealand has a population approximately equal to that of Melbourne and its location gives it the comfort of feeling immune from any external threat. Australia is unique. It is still predominantly Anglo-Celtic and its culture is still predominantly European/American, while it is located in 'a sea of Asian cultures'. Other Southern hemisphere British colonies with substantial European settlements, notably South Africa, have not preserved the rule 'by a transplanted European people'. But their cases were different. South Africa and the Rhodesias were in a sea of *African* cultures, and also in a land mass predominantly populated by Africans, whom they exploited economically and repressed politically. The British in South Asia also withdrew when India, Pakistan, and Sri Lanka became independent and British residents of Burma and Malaya went home after those places became independent. Wilsonian ideals of self-determination worked against the British and other European colonies in Asia and then, in the aftermath of the Second World War, and driven by Cold War factors, with demands for egalitarian democracy, those colonies became unsustainable by a Britain exhausted and impoverished by the long war.

Australia is clearly a different case from South Africa, for example, where the empowered European settler population was a minority and was itself divided ethnically and culturally. Australia has nineteen million people, the vast majority of whom are the descendants of European settlers or were themselves born in Europe. It has preserved sovereignty over the whole continent, it has established a political and an economic viability which is not internally unstable or under internal attack. But it *is* a construct of British imperial expansion, and it *is* still a European implant on the other side of the world. And it has not yet come to terms with the fact that its survival may depend on integrating itself more successfully with the Asian countries which stand between it and the equator and then up through North East Asia. The fact that in its modern form it was established as a British colony and that it is still in many ways, including ethnically, a manifestly British offshoot does not in Australian eyes in any way detract from its legitimacy as an independent middle sized nation located off the southern end of East Asia. But in East Asian eyes it is different from all the rest of the region and linked even now with the European empires which colonized the region and exploited it for centuries up to the end of the Pacific War. It appears to many as a residual handful of white people left behind by the retreating tide of European imperialism.

FitzGerald in his book calls for a far more urgent and committed engagement with East Asia by Australia before it is 'too late', at least in terms of Australia's admission to a prospective East Asian Community. But there are passages where he appears to be implying that failure to succeed in the process could mean in some unspecified way the demise of Australia. The last chapter of the book has the title 'Can Australian Society Survive?' He does not appear to be raising again the earlier spectre of Australian society being overwhelmed by far more numerous Asians using force or the threat of force or just the weight of numbers. But nor does he particularly exclude that old fear and he says at one point[15] that 'It is only within [an East Asian] Community that Australia has a chance of preserving its independence...'. That implies that if Australia does not make the necessary adaptations and succeed in joining an East Asian Community it will be taken over by another larger country or other countries in the region.

Two main propositions seem to emerge from his discussion. The first is that Australia must change its education curricula and many other aspects of its public policy, its business and social priorities and its popular attitudes so that it makes itself acceptable to the rising East Asian region. The second proposition is that, urgent and demanding as these changes are, they do not involve the abandonment of the core Australian character and values.

It is the second of these two propositions which is the more problematic. FitzGerald seeks both to energize engagement by showing how dangerous failure will be, in effect by saying Australia would not survive it, and then to balance that by making the goal of successful integration with East Asia appear seductively attractive:

My concern about Australia's performance in the past is balanced by my belief that this can be Australia's future: the lazy country can be a lovely country and the white society can be a honey-coloured society. The prospects for Australia are exciting beyond imagination...this honey-coloured society has a possible future as *the* most attractive society in the world[16].

But 'this will not just happen' and one of the requirements is that 'We have to be Australian and not European'. The retention of the core Australian values, and indeed their enhancement in the twenty-first century, is however a matter of definition. We saw how Professors Ingleson and FitzGerald spoke of the introduction of much more Asian content into the Australian educational curriculum as the 'Australianization' of that curriculum. FitzGerald uses the same meaning shift to argue that the transfer of Australian cultural and other links from Europe to Asia is to make the country more Australian. He also argues that 'Australia is already the most outward-looking of all the countries of the region, and potentially the most "Asian"'.

The problem with this is that it is hard to see how all these arguments and assertions can be reconciled except on the assumption that the ideal Australia would be much more 'Asian' than the actual Australia is now or is likely to become in the foreseeable future unless it is forcibly changed by some form of conquest. Australians show little disposition to take on the 'Asian' characteristics which are said to be essential to their survival, even if that is presented as somehow contributing to making them more 'Australian'. The study of Asian languages has actually slipped back in recent years and the Asian studies departments in the Universities have lost staff and other resources. On the other hand FitzGerald's account of Australians' attitudes, misconceptions and inadequacies in regard to Asia seems exaggeratedly critical. There is certainly much to criticize but the situation is not as grotesquely bad as he claims. It is rather that there is not sufficient focus on and interest in East Asia by Australians to generate a dynamic of the kind required to support a policy thrust such as that which Paul Keating sought to implement. There is still a strong resource in terms of academic specialists, but it is not growing, and few politicians have a strong interest. The number of Australian finance and business people with relevant knowledge or experience is growing. In the wider community there are some lesser known aficionados such as the surfers who go year after year to Lombok, Nias and other less travelled places in Indonesia and who have had to learn how to live in harmony with local people.

But for most Australians the interest in East Asia is at best episodic and there is not much of that sense which Keating sought to develop of Australia being part of a region or neighbourhood. It has to be said that Australians generally do not feel any great sense of community or shared interests with, say, Indonesians even though that country is geographically close. The context of life for Indonesians and Australians is very different. Very few Australians indeed have any sense that they should alter their attitudes, interests etc. to fit in better with Indonesians. Rather, as a result of East Timor and other well-publicized events, Australian attitudes towards Indonesia have become more distant than they were in 1996 when they reacted against the Keating engagement policy. Nor is there any prospect that developments on the Indonesian side will change that. In her address on Army Day on 30 December, 2001, President Megawati Sukarnoputri reportedly told the Army that they were needed to act 'without any doubts' against separatists 'to protect our beloved nation and motherland from breaking up' while respecting the law[17]. The outlook for West Papua, which is scrutinized in the Australian media, is thus for continued suppression by the military with the predictable reactions of the human rights lobby in Australia.

FitzGerald's book is open to criticism on a number of grounds. But its great importance is that it raises the issue which has hardly been raised in Australia since the Pacific War. Does Australia have a long-term future as a predominantly white, small country with an overwhelmingly European cultural inheritance and strong continuing links to America and Europe, anchored at the southern end of East Asia? To anyone who thinks that is a real question, perhaps the most important question facing Australia, it is mystifying that it receives so little attention. A certain stridency on the part of someone who has spent most of a working life in this area is understandable.

A Busy Middle Power

It was also the intention and expectation of Keating and Evans that Australia's credentials would be enhanced by extremely active regional diplomacy. Evans developed a doctrine of the role of the middle power which could work effectively for the general good of the international system and in its own interest by deploying a high level of expertise which others would value and by forming coalitions. The leading example of the latter, coalition-forming, initiative was the formation and effective deployment of the Cairns Group, an association of middle and smaller GATT members concerned to ensure that trade in agriculture was not excluded from the Uruguay Round of trade negotiations as it had been from previous trade negotiation rounds. The Group first met in the city of Cairns at Australian invitation and subsequently played an important role in the Uruguay Round and beyond. It has always been claimed as an Australian initiative, and indeed it was Australia that took the lead and then devoted a major diplomatic effort to it, and it is something which Australian trade diplomacy has handled very well indeed. But there is some doubt whether the idea was of Australian origin[18].

There were several Australian middle power initiatives that were the products of Evans' drive and flair, exploiting his own skills and those of teams of able officials from the Department of Foreign Affairs and other Australian agencies. In terms of the East Asian region the most important were the long, arduous and taxing work to secure a settlement in Cambodia in which Evans worked particularly closely with the then Indonesian Minister for Foreign Affairs, Ali Alatas, an experienced career diplomat, and the work which led to the formation of the ASEAN Regional Forum, ARF, which was set up to provide a regional body for the discussion of security issues and to develop confidence building and other cooperative measures.

There is no doubt that this activity gave Australia a higher profile in the region and brought it into closer contact with the diplomatic and policy processes of the East Asian countries. The intention and hope was that Australia would acquire the status of a colleague with helpful and friendly motives and a range of useful skills and assets which could be deployed to the advantage of the region generally and particular members of it. Besides the positive aspects the very active foreign policy pursued by Australia especially after Keating became Prime Minister also produced some negative effects. Others in the region began to feel that the activism and capabilities of the Australians were too much in evidence, that the Australians were taking a more prominent role than the Asian regional members, and that it would be more fitting if they were to adopt a somewhat lower profile. This is not surprising to anyone familiar with South East Asian attitudes. It is reminiscent of the Australian incomprehension of the fact that their superiority in international sporting competition does nothing to endear them to their regional neighbours. Indeed the reverse is often the case: they would be rather better liked in the region if they were not so much more successful than their neighbours. Nevertheless there is no doubt that Australian relations with Indonesia in particular, guided by the increasingly close Soeharto/Keating relationship, reached a level of cooperation which had not previously been achieved.

The two tests of Australia's standing with the East Asians were whether they could be persuaded to overcome Mahathir's opposition to Australia's participation in the second (London) meeting of ASEM and whether they would do all they could to ensure the success of Australia's campaign to secure election to the Security Council in 1996. These efforts were both well under way when Labor lost the 1996 election. The incoming Howard government pursued the previous government's policies on both issues, the Security Council campaign only after assurances from the Australian ambassador at the United Nations that the prospects were good. On both issues Australia was rebuffed. The ASEM failure was not a surprise. Mahathir was not to be shifted by the sort of diplomatic persuasion which appears to have been used by Australia's supporters and they were not prepared to risk damage to the enterprise by subjecting him to heavier pressure. The Security Council defeat at the hands of Portugal was painful. It was a heavy defeat and some of Australia's regional associates were believed to have voted against her. The government had not been well advised but it is difficult to assess support in such matters. Although lack of support in Africa and Latin America was more costly it was a real disappointment that East Asian support seemed to have been patchy.

These disappointments had an effect on the Howard government's attitudes and policies. While they maintained the Labor government's position that the highest priority of Australia's foreign policy was the relationship with East Asia they reduced expectations and sought to avoid alienating that body of opinion in Australia which did not favour 'enmeshment' with Asia. The Prime Minister declined to enter into public controversy about the racist statements of Pauline Hanson, including her maiden speech in the House of Representatives. It was left to others, mainly on the Opposition side, to express the repugnance which many Australians felt for her opinions.

On the other hand the Howard government continued to seek to follow a pragmatic policy towards engagement with Asia, based on strengthening bilateral relationships rather than ambitious initiatives designed to demonstrate Australia's regional credentials and capacities. When the East Asian Financial Crisis struck with the collapse of the Thai Baht in July 1997 the Australian government moved promptly to support the IMF rescue operation for Thailand. They were similarly helpful in the cases of Korea and Indonesia. They had reservations about some aspects of the IMF packages imposing conditions requiring major reforms of institutions and practices in the target countries and they expressed these in Washington. Their public comments were sympathetic, supportive and practical. The financial crisis and its aftermath seemed likely to affect Australia severely given the importance of the region in Australia's foreign trade and investment. But the Australian economy proved surprisingly resilient. Exporters found other markets and the reductions in some export products were made up for by increased exports of other goods and services. The rate of GDP growth increased and there was a sense that the extent of the country's dependence on East Asia had been exaggerated. East Asia might not be the only option. The region's growth had at least temporarily collapsed and seemed unlikely in the foreseeable future to retrieve the tremendous dynamism of the previous twenty years. It was also strikingly evident that the region seemed not to be in a position to help itself. Japan made the largest financial contributions to the rescue operations, but an earlier proposal by Vice Minister for Finance Sakakibara to establish an East Asian monetary fund had been still born largely because of American opposition. ASEAN was nowhere to be seen in relation to the financial crisis. Nor was APEC. There was little or no consultation between the affected countries. It was in Washington that the planning and policy making was done and from Washington that the consultation and coordination were managed.

For Australia the challenges and problems of gaining acceptance by the Asian members of the region and of qualifying for membership of any East Asian cooperative arrangement suddenly seemed less urgent. But the crisis stimulated the East Asian institutional process and the Australian government had to respond.

Efforts to Qualify under Howard

While the period since the early setbacks experienced by the Howard government has witnessed a diminishing level of urgency in Australian policy circles regarding deeper cooperation and involvement with East Asia, an opposite trend in respect of East Asian integration is clearly discernible in many regional capitals. In recent years a number of multilateral institutional developments, bilateral agreements, formal and informal officials' meetings and leaders' statements have indicated a growing impetus around East Asia towards institutional development of what might be called the East Asia solidarity project. These developments have not gone unnoticed in academic circles, and have generated a growing literature charting progress and seeking to discern the character, composition and purpose of a future East Asian grouping. The Australian government has of course followed this closely, but the possible implications of the trend, and of Australia's exclusion from it, do not appear to be the subject of sustained debate in foreign policy circles in Canberra. Indeed what public debate there has been on this issue has been driven by a small number of journalists and academics, while the government shows signs of disenchantment with both the multilateral focus of the engagement policy it has hitherto pursued, and the East Asian states who have barred Australia's entry into regional forums such as the Asia-Europe Meetings (ASEM) and ASEAN + 3.

As we have already seen, broad issues of identity have sometimes made it difficult for Australia to craft a successful Asia-focused foreign policy, and more recently they have led to the nascent but identifiable move among East Asian states towards a form of community excluding non-Asian members. Recent developments in the area of East Asian institution-building are casting these elements in a sharper light. The move towards greater institutionalization of relations among East Asian states is not the only aspect of the recent growth of communal sentiment in the region. But it may be seen as a tangible manifestation of an increasingly influential sense of shared 'Asianness' in East Asia, whose foundations are in shared memories of European imperialism, of Western patronizing, and more recently of the victory over the United States in Vietnam and the heady years of rapid economic growth when the world appeared to be their oyster. All this has been shaped and channelled toward institution-building by the shared hardships of the financial crisis. Large powerful structures are unlikely to emerge in the near future. But as the prospect of their emergence in the coming years increases the possible costs of exclusion, Australia should be working to secure membership in due course. At present, Australia's exclusion from East Asian multilateral entities such as ASEAN + 3, which brings together the ASEAN states and their Northeast Asian counterparts, and the ASEM process, which involves these same states, minus Laos, Cambodia and Myanmar, in multi-layered dialogue with EU member states, is a compelling example of the challenges which the growth of East Asian solidarity pose for Australia. The failure of efforts to meet those challenges appears to have impacted significantly on the East Asia policy of the Howard government, and the story needs to be told.

Stephen FitzGerald's assessment of the importance of the first ASEM, held in Bangkok in 1996, and of Australia's exclusion from it by the Asian participants, is characteristically strident:

> ...when the world looks back on 1996 from 2026 this will probably be seen as the point at which the definition of an 'Asian community' really began. Australia was not present at this meeting on either side...the message is one of the utmost gravity for this country. Europe was not an option for it. Asia was not open to it[19].

In apocalyptic terms FitzGerald goes on to outline a future in which Australia is potentially relegated to 'colonial status', in which our independence is threatened, and in which defining features of Australian society are extinguished. While this view of Australia's exclusion appears somewhat overwrought, there can be no doubt that ASEM1 marked a significant milestone in the development of a shared consciousness among the participants on the Asian side. The importance of a mutual sense of achievement and progress among East Asian states was remarked upon in Chapter Six, and is reflected in the Asian participants' attitudes towards ASEM:

> For the Asians, the political symbolism of having sixteen European leaders journey to Bangkok was in and of itself important. It was to be a symbol of Asia's new status on the world stage, and Europe's recognition of that status[20].

The 1996 meeting arose from an idea advanced by the Prime Minister of Singapore, Goh Chok Tong. It was aired among ASEAN nations for the first time in October 1994, and the Prime Minister and his Foreign Ministry worked assiduously throughout 1995 to gain acceptance for the proposal around Asia. A fear in East Asia that the world trading system was splitting into regional blocs, centred around the EU, NAFTA and APEC, as well as a general recognition that Asia-Europe relations were the weak link in the triangle of ties between Asia, Europe and the US, led to the concept being accepted in Asia and Europe with notable alacrity. The 1996 meeting was held at summit level, and resounded with the atmospherics normally associated with such occasions. Summit meetings have since been held in London in 1998 and Seoul in 2000. ASEM4 is scheduled for Copenhagen in 2002. Significantly however, the ASEM process, which remains a series of meetings rather than an institutionalized structure, has grown to include a variety of lower-level ministers' meetings, bringing together foreign affairs, economics, finance and other representatives of the participating states. It is unnecessary to detail the evolution of this process, or to review the growing literature it has generated. Its significance for our purposes lies in the opportunity it has given the Asian participants to cooperate on agendas for the various meetings, to discuss issues of mutual concern, and more profoundly, to conceive of themselves as members of a coherent and defined East Asian region, and to deal with an external actor (the EU) as such. These are issues to which we will return shortly.

The growth of the ASEM process has been paralleled by the proposal, acceptance and rapid development of the ASEAN + 3 concept. ASEAN + 3 links the ten ASEAN nations with the powerful Northeast Asian nations of Japan, China and South Korea, allowing participants further opportunities to discuss issues of importance to East Asia, and to forge a deeper sense of common interest and identity. The first ASEAN + 3 summit meeting took place at Malaysia's suggestion in Kuala Lumpur in 1997, as an adjunct to the ASEAN summit meeting marking the thirtieth anniversary of the Association. The successful Malaysian proposal followed a similar idea advanced by Goh Chok Tong at the 1995 ASEAN summit in Bangkok, the difference being that the Malaysian proposal met with a positive response from Japan[21]. ASEAN + 3 summit meetings have since been held in 1998 (Hanoi), 1999 (Manila), 2000 (Singapore) and 2001 (Brunei). A significant feature of the rapid evolution of the ASEAN + 3 concept has been the enthusiasm shown for it by the powerful economies of Northeast Asia. At the 1999 Manila summit, Premier Zhu Rongji of China hailed a 'growing momentum of co-operation' among East Asian nations, and emphasized that 'China cannot develop without

East Asia'[22]. At the same meeting, President Kim Dae-Jung of South Korea expressed the hope that ASEAN + 3 could 'nurture East Asia into a single community of co-operation'[23]. Japan's contributions to the process, particularly its financial agenda, have been considerable, including the provision of technical support through the ASEAN Secretariat for the monitoring of short-term capital flows, and heavy involvement in currency swaps made under the Chiang Mai initiative, concluded by ASEAN + 3 finance ministers in 2000[24].

The focus of ASEAN + 3 activities thus far has been primarily on financial and monetary issues, reflecting the seminal influence of the Asian financial crisis in its establishment. The Chiang Mai initiative is its most significant tangible achievement to date. This may seem a small return, since this agreement itself builds on a range of pre-existing regional currency swap and repurchase arrangements, including an intra-ASEAN swap facility established in 1977. However, such a view ignores the reality that

> ...the web of relations between [ASEAN + 3] members has grown quickly since...1997. Not only heads of government, but also finance, economics and foreign ministers, central bank governors and senior government officials in some domains have meanwhile started meeting regularly[25].

Commentators in Australia and elsewhere have viewed the growing array of linkages between ASEAN + 3 economies as evidence that a monetary union or even a common currency for East Asia has become a 'possible policy goal'[26]. Indeed Philippine President Joseph Estrada raised these possibilities in his address as host of the 1999 Manila summit[27]. Richard Higgott sees the Chiang Mai initiative as 'the beginning of a new era of regionalism' in East Asia[28]. According to Paul Kelly, ASEAN + 3 represents 'the centrepiece of the new East Asian regionalism'[29], while for Anthony Milner, ASEAN + 3 portends the emergence of a strident 'new East Asianism'[30]. Milner makes the further point that ASEAN + 3 has not restricted its focus merely to financial technicalities, but has also discussed the need to reduce tensions in the South China Sea. An East Asian Vision Group has also been established, with a brief to 'explore ways to expand co-operation in all sectors and at all levels among the countries of East Asia'[31]. Furthermore, at the 1999 Manila summit, ASEAN + 3 leaders released a 'Joint Statement on East Asia Co-operation', in which they pledged, *inter alia*, 'to intensify [East Asian] co-ordination and co-operation in international and regional forums such as the UN, WTO, APEC, ASEM and the ARF'[32]. It is clear that this is a solidarity project with momentum on its side.

In considering why regionalism is gaining ground in East Asia, the profound effects of the Asian financial crisis of 1997-99 represent an obvious starting point. In the words of one Japanese commentator, the crisis 'reawakened the countries of the region to the reality of their economic interdependence and to the need for a new form of co-operation'[33]. Closely linked to this was a strong feeling that because the region was incapable of cooperating effectively it was left at the mercy of Western agents: first the managed funds of various kinds and then the international financial institutions. This produced resentment in many East Asian policy circles towards the Washington based actors, principally the International Monetary Fund which they saw as dominated by the United States Treasury. It was noted earlier that the most well-established East Asian and Asia-Pacific institutions, ASEAN and APEC, found themselves unable to formulate an effective response to the crisis, or to settle upon a coordinated strategy for minimizing its impact. As a result, the crisis played a crucial role in convincing East Asian governments of the need for an institution capable of better representing their mutual interests on the world stage.

An insightful analysis of the role of the crisis in the rapid progress made by ASEAN + 3, and in creating at least a perception that ASEAN and APEC face serious challenges to their relevance in East Asia is offered by Douglas Webber. He argues that:

> The crisis has...fostered East Asian co-operation because it has greatly strengthened not only perceptions of economic interdependence between Southeast and Northeast Asian states, but also, owing to the way in which it was managed by the IMF, resentment against the United States and its (at least perceived) domination of international monetary and financial affairs[34].

Webber points out that the crisis, which was precipitated by the collapse of the Thai baht but which spread as far north as South Korea, 'has greatly strengthened perceptions of mutual economic interdependence and vulnerability' across East Asia, and cites Singapore Prime Minister Goh Chok Tong to support this view:

> You cannot talk about Northeast Asia and Southeast Asia. What happens in Southeast Asia will have an impact on Northeast Asia. The financial crisis which engulfed ASEAN economies in 1997 later spread to South Korea, whose economic slowdown partly caused...investment flows into Southeast Asia to contract. So now we are thinking in terms of evolving an East Asian community...[35].

The resentment against the IFIs and the United States not only reflected the regional chagrin at its loss of face and the distaste felt in being dependent on these outsiders, but also the fact that the Fund's terms were seen as unnecessarily harsh, especially in the case of Indonesia. Moreover the minimal role played by the US in contributing to the IMF rescue packages for Thailand and, later, Indonesia, 'gave the region the impression' of a 'lack of interest in the Asian financial crisis issue in the United States'[36], a factor recognized by US Defence Secretary William Cohen in July 1998: 'the American people have not fully appreciated the depth and significance of the Asian crisis'[37].

Tsutomo Kikuchi's analysis of the establishment of the ASEAN + 3 framework places particular emphasis on the conspicuous role of Japan in pushing for an Asian Monetary Fund designed to alleviate regional financial problems. Kikuchi records that the AMF was conceived by officials in Japan's Ministry of Finance as a 'safety valve' for the countries of East Asia 'to cope with the overwhelming power of international capital'. Japan presented it as an institution that would in principle be implemented in conjunction with the IMF, but that 'would be likely to change its internal rules and principles in line with changing political and economic conditions'[38]. Its nucleus would be $US10 billion provided by the Japanese government. Both Kikuchi and Terada[39] note the strong positive reaction to this proposal among East Asian countries, and the concomitant frustration they felt at the vocal opposition of the US to it. Indeed Japan was pressed by Asian governments to persevere with the AMF idea even after US and IMF opposition saw it lapse[40]. In stark contrast to the willingness of Japan to use its economic power to assist its fellow East Asian nations, the reluctance of the US to support a proposal which might derogate from IMF supremacy in policy and prescriptive terms saw it cast as an obstructionist external power. Terada contrasts this lukewarm response with the $44 billion contributed by Japan to the rescue of Thailand, Indonesia and South Korea, making the point that nations affected by the crisis realized they could turn to one of their own for leadership and assistance, rather than a non-East Asian power. A tangible consequence of this realization was growing enthusiasm for an East Asian organization that would bring Japan and the Northeast Asian countries together with those of ASEAN.

A concept which assists greatly in accounting for the role of ASEM and ASEAN + 3 in the development of an atmosphere of community in East Asia is that of 'acclimation'. Takashi Terada deploys this idea to quantify the consequences of the steadily expanding array of meetings, conferences, consultations and cooperative linkages which have characterized relations among East Asian states over the last decade. He argues that these contacts represent a process whereby countries in East Asia have, over time, become acclimatized to the concept of seeing themselves as parts of a discrete region, within defined boundaries and sharing strong mutual interests. This process has begun to culminate in an increasingly enthusiastic acceptance of a common East Asian identity among the participants. Terada sees Malaysia's 1990 proposal of an East Asian Economic Group, comprising only East Asian states, as a crucial forerunner of later, more successful manifestations of regionalism in East Asia. He writes that the EAEC 'introduced the concept of East Asia, integrating Northeast Asia and Southeast Asia into one regional unity', and cites former Philippine Foreign Minister Domingo Siazon: 'EAEC...provided the initial rationale for the establishment of an East Asian grouping'[41]. In Terada's view the EAEC proposal met a lukewarm reception among prospective participants because of a lack of shared interests among them in a regional economic group which excluded the US However, the later success of ASEAN + 3, comprising exclusively East Asian states, followed a period of acclimation to the East Asian concept in which the inauguration of ASEM was significant, which was accelerated by the Asian crisis, and which created a perception that US involvement was not an essential precondition in the creation of an effective East Asian grouping.

Such a process of acclimation provides an instructive counterpoint to the idea that a process of cultural convergence between East Asia and Australia would intervene to assist Australia's pursuit of the engagement project. As noted in Chapter 6, this idea proved particularly seductive to Australian policy makers during the Keating/Evans era, as it held out the prospect that Australia could achieve deep and lasting engagement with its very different neighbours because these differences would gradually diminish. However, if a process of acclimation has indeed been taking place, in which East Asian states are becoming accustomed to seeing themselves as sharing a unique East Asian identity, this effectively portends the frustration of any Australian ambition to become part of a future (or current) East Asian grouping. The constructivist approach to international relations theory on which Terada's argument is based holds that 'the emergence of a sense of community among countries in a region is an important component in promoting regional co-operation'. On this view, 'the creation of a regional identity within the community can strengthen shared beliefs and consensus...and consolidate the solidarity essential for increasing the understanding of cultural and social differences in their regions'[42]. ASEM and ASEAN + 3 can be seen as significant components in such a process. That suggests that Australia's original exclusion from both will become deeper as the habits and 'acclimation' of the years of meetings and cooperation build up. Australia's cultural differences with its neighbours would increasingly appear too manifest, and its identification with the US and Europe too close, to be reconciled with the forces driving East Asian regionalism. The process of acclimation has already acted to reinforce the participants' perceptions of excluded states, such as Australia and the US as outsiders, and to reinforce the demarcation between Australia and East Asia. The rationale for Australia's exclusion was stated succinctly by a delegate at the 2000 ASEAN + 3 summit in Singapore: 'Australia wants to be the Americans in ASEAN. That cannot be accepted'[43].

The foregoing analysis has attempted to provide a sense of the regional mood by focussing on developments in East Asia. We turn our attention now to Australia's efforts to qualify for the nascent East Asian grouping represented by ASEM and ASEAN + 3. Why has Australia's campaign to secure a meaningful role in the community and identity-building process thus far been unsuccessful? Regional developments only partially explain why this has been so. The following section aims to trace Australia's efforts to become involved in the ASEM and ASEAN + 3 groupings. These efforts have not been high profile, but rather have amounted to the 'quiet diplomatic battle' alluded to by one journalist[44]. Nonetheless they have been considerable, and the Howard government's disappointment at the rebuffs it has received has been palpable. An analysis of these episodes reveals that this disappointment has significantly influenced official attitudes towards Australia's role and place in East Asia, and that the government's current attitudes, outwardly at least, are far colder now than those discernible early in its tenure. A clear manifestation of this is the sense of negativity which appears recently to have pervaded official Australian thinking about the prospects, and even the desirability, of inclusion in an East Asian grouping. Malaysia has been a persistent and influential critic of Australia's attempts to seek deeper involvement in the region, and the consensus-based model of cooperation used by ASEAN states has meant that Malaysia's opposition has been sufficient to frustrate Australia's advances. However, Dr Mahathir has not been alone and it seems likely that for the foreseeable future Indonesia will also be in opposition. We shall see that one discouraging consequence of Australia's failures has been that Australia's differences from its neighbours and the barriers which continue to block the path towards meaningful engagement with East Asia have been accentuated and reinforced.

The election of a Coalition government in 1996 was accompanied by a degree of speculation over the future directions of Australia's engagement policy. The claim of Higgott and Nossal that the new government 'was clearly not as committed to Labor's bravura "new" world'[45] was representative of an expectation that under Howard and Foreign Minister Downer the relative weight accorded Asia in Australia's foreign policy calculations might diminish. Such commentators noted the caveat attached to engagement by Downer that 'a policy of "Asia First" does not mean "Asia Only"'[46], and the Coalition's 'renewed emphasis on rekindling relations with Europe and North America'[47]. Despite this conjecture it is clear that the Coalition did not in its early years abandon its predecessor's conviction that Asia was the key to Australia's future economic wellbeing. Upon taking office Downer stated unambiguously that the Coalition would be 'building on, not tearing down, the previous government's work'[48] with respect to Asian economic engagement. Likewise Howard talked of 'a fundamental continuity between my government's objectives and those of my predecessors'[49] in terms of regional economic relations. Notwithstanding its misguided predictions regarding uninterrupted medium-term growth in East Asia, the government's 1997 foreign and trade policy White Paper confirms the abiding focus of Australian policy on the region:

> ...as the industrialising economies of East Asia continue their high growth rates the primacy of the Asia Pacific in Australian...policy will become even more evident[50].

That those economies have not continued their high growth rates has no doubt been one factor in the cooling off of the Howard government's attachment to the engagement policy.

But the new government certainly recognized, and resolved to take advantage of, the opportunities for Australian commerce and investment which Asia's geographic proximity and economic dynamism presented. However, it is equally clear that its commitment to continuity in the conduct of the engagement policy did not extend to the cultural re-orientation seen by their predecessors as crucial to Australia's regional future. Howard's desire to disassociate the Coalition from this aspect of the Keating government's attitude to regional relations is evident in his declaration that '[w]e do not have to turn ourselves into something we are not in order to be confident of our place in the region'. In a statement presaging his government's willingness to claim the virtues of Australia's 'national characteristics' he asserted that '[w]e do not have to pass tests set by others'. Howard further distanced himself from Labor's rhetoric by emphasizing 'the government's strongly held view that "there is no requirement on Australia to choose between its history and its geography"'[51]. Indeed this statement has become something of a mantra for the Prime Minister. There can be no doubt that Howard himself felt strongly that the idea of convergence was neither accurate nor desirable, and spoke against the alteration of the national identity on a deeply personal level:

I am not one of those people who believes that Australia suffers from an identity crisis. I believe that the Australian identity is so distinct and our shared values so robust and so many of our past achievements such a legitimate source of pride, that we don't need endless navel gazing[52].

But despite such statements the government in its first term pursued the multilateral Asian policy goals inherited from Keating. While demonstrating a willingness to emphasize rather than minimize the social and cultural differences between Australia and East Asia, the government nonetheless made clear its desire to be included in the region's emerging institutional architecture. It made a considerable investment of energy and diplomatic capital in attempting to gain admission to ASEM, on the Asian side, in time to attend the second ASEM summit meeting in London in late 1998. Indications are that the Keating government had pursued the issue of ASEM membership, but as a bonus rather than a core goal. Greg Sheridan, attributed to Keating the 'fatuous' suggestion that 'ASEM membership is not important'. Keating is said to have made this remark 'presumably because he was so obsessed about [APEC], and because he knew his own bad relationship with Malaysia meant we would not get invited anyway'[53]. In Parliament Alexander Downer sought to highlight a difference between this attitude and the ambitions of his own government: 'It was your failure to get Australia into ASEM at the beginning, your negligence on this issue, which has led us to have to take up the task'[54].

Downer's efforts did not go unnoticed in East Asia, with several regional governments commenting on them in the first half of 1997. Most significant among these was Japan, a vocal and consistent supporter of Australian membership, and of deeper Australian involvement in Asian affairs generally. Japanese Prime Minister Hashimoto is said to have 'bluntly cut short' Dr Mahathir when the latter questioned Japan's support for Australia in respect of ASEM[55]. There has been speculation that Japan's position is merely a by-product of its broader geopolitical goal of containing China using its close ties with Australia, New Zealand and the US[56]. But this is an inadequate explanation. For more than forty years Japan has cultivated the relationship with Australia for a mixture of economic and political reasons, and Australia has cultivated the relationship with its main export market even more assiduously. It is a complex and complementary relationship which does not lend itself to facile oversimplification. Despite the essential asymmetry of the relationship, Japanese support for Australian efforts to win acceptance in East Asia reflected their bilateral and wider interests at the time. That support was seen by the Australian side as particularly important given Japan's place as the dominant economy in the region and the leader in a number of other ways. Moreover it secured support elsewhere, the Philippines' government stating that 'we respect the view of the Prime Minister of Japan', and that it was 'also our view'[57].

Singapore's support was also said to be steady, although there seems to have been evidence of some divergence between levels of support in public and what was said in private to other regional representatives. Public statements such as that of Foreign Minister Jayakumar stressing that 'we have felt right from the beginning Australia...could be playing a useful role in ASEM, and we've been quite candid that we are supportive'[58] were certainly helpful. The Thai government was also supportive[59]. An indication that East Asian states appreciated the significance the Howard government attached to the ASEM issue was their occasional willingness to make their support conditional on Australia's behaviour. Citing an advisor to Prime Minister Hashimoto, one report asserts that 'Japan's continued backing of Australia would depend on how effectively Canberra dealt with...sensitive Asian issues'. Significantly, the advisor himself stresses that Japanese support 'is conditional on Australia showing that it wants to be a part of Asia'[60]. A fear also existed among senior Australian officials that China might 'imply a linkage' between Australia's ASEM membership and any adverse stance it might take on human rights issues in China, such that support may be withdrawn[61].

However, such recognition of the significance of ASEM to Australia was insufficient to permit Australia entry. Malaysia consistently opposed Australian membership, and due to the consensus-based decision-making process used by ASEAN, a single objection by a member state would ensure failure. Despite pressure from those East Asian nations supporting Australia's cause, and indications on the European side, notably Britain, that Australia should join, Malaysia, with the later support of Indonesia, successfully delayed a decision on membership, initially until the 1998 summit meeting, and then, apparently, indefinitely. One explanation offered by Malaysia was a belief that ASEM should consolidate before considering expansion, but that 'when the time comes' Australia's chances were positive[62]. Downer, having little choice, appeared to accept this, saying that Malaysia would be 'happy for Australia in the fullness of time to participate, but the question is going to be when'[63]. But more revealing comments have been made by Dr Mahathir, who said at the 1998 summit that 'it's a little bit difficult for us to think of Australia as an Asian country', and that India and Pakistan should be given priority in respect of membership[64]. While Malaysia's veto was accepted with apparent equanimity, the Australian government was furious that, despite repeated assurances of support, Indonesia backed Malaysia's stance at the summit. Downer indicated he was 'personally hurt' by Indonesia's reversal, in view of strenuous efforts being undertaken at the time on Indonesia's behalf to soften the IMF's demands for reform in response to that country's financial and economic crises[65]. The Prime Minister's disappointment was also clear, Howard stressing that Australia had been 'very understanding of Indonesia in recent months – very, very understanding'[66].

Australia's exclusion is made more noteworthy by the fact that expanded membership has been a subject of active debate, and degree of contention, in ASEM since its inception. Australia, New Zealand, India and Pakistan have been seeking inclusion on the Asian side since the inaugural ASEM meeting in 1996. Burma's entry into ASEAN, which raised the prospect of its automatic participation in ASEM, caused considerable concern among European participants, askance at the prospect of sharing dialogue with Burma's repressive junta[67]. Burma was eventually denied ASEM membership. At the Bangkok summit Dr Mahathir urged Australia's permanent exclusion from the ASEM process, on the grounds that to permit it entry would be akin to 'admitting Arabs to the EU'[68]. At an ASEM Foreign Ministers' meeting in 1997, at which Australian membership could have been secured, Malaysia refused to remove its veto, succeeding in deferring a decision until the 1998 summit[69]. At that summit, Malaysia again, now with Indonesian support, ensured the membership issue would be deferred until the Seoul summit in 2000[70], by which time, as we shall see, Australia's own enthusiasm appeared to have waned. The Chairman's Statement for the Seoul meeting omits any mention of discussions over membership[71]. That the objections of Malaysia and its supporters to Australian membership are not based on the matters of finance and economics which ASEM was primarily created to discuss cannot be doubted. Drawing on official discussion papers produced in the lead-up to the first ASEM summit, one analyst concludes that 'for Asia, the most important consideration...was to include economies which had contributed to the region's prosperity and growth'[72]. As the Asian participants began to confront the financial crisis, ASEM leaders emphasized the significance of members cooperating to minimize and alleviate its impact, at a time when Australia was showing surprising economic resilience, was contributing to IMF rescue packages, and in the Indonesian case, lobbying the IMF for remedial measures which took greater account of that country's unique difficulties.

For Australia, ASEAN + 3 represents a different circumstance to ASEM. Malaysia's similarly frigid response to the prospect of Australia involving itself more deeply in this nascent grouping has been of greater concern. Unlike in ASEM, Australia has not explicitly sought inclusion in ASEAN + 3 by way of a formal application, although there can be no doubt it would accept any invitation to join with alacrity. The special 30-year anniversary summit of ASEAN in Kuala Lumpur in 1997 also served as the first summit meeting of what is now termed ASEAN + 3, and, pointedly, Malaysia did not invite Australia. This was seen as a rebuff in Canberra, and by Japan as a sign that 'Australia's position in Asia was weakening'[73]. Australia had been present at the 10-year anniversary summit in 1977. As ASEAN + 3 gained momentum, any reserve within the Howard government regarding membership evaporated[74], and the government made a number of statements unambiguously acknowledging the grouping's importance. In July Downer praised ASEAN + 3 as an 'enormously positive step forward', and stated that 'if we were invited to participate in it, we'd be happy to do so'[75]. In August Dr Ashton Calvert, Secretary of Mr Downer's department, told the National Press Club that the government 'recognized the potential significance of the forum', and echoed precisely the Minister's words on the desirability of membership[76]. Writing immediately prior to the 2001 election, Mr Downer remained positive concerning the benefits of membership, although now his enthusiasm was qualified: 'We remain a very interested observer of the ASEAN + 3 grouping – and we continue to hope that we might play an active role in the group's work in the future, should its members so desire and Australia's own interests so dictate'[77]. Notwithstanding these overtures, the varying degrees of vitriol emanating from senior levels of the Malaysian government regarding Australia's regional aspirations have made it clear the latter would not pass ASEAN's test of consensus for inclusion in ASEAN + 3.

Mahathir has accused the Howard government of arrogance, and 'behaving as if it is there to teach us how to run our country', as well as declaring that Howard would not be 'welcome in Asia'[78]. He has even engaged in an unflattering parody of the Australian accent for the benefit of an audience of his UMNO party members[79]. The repeated broadsides have accompanied more substantial political manoeuvring aimed at restricting Australia's role in East Asia, and come in spite of the considerable diplomatic effort invested by the Howard government in improving the bilateral relationship; indeed Howard has gone so far as to declare that 'it is very important that we understand that Australia does have a special relationship with Malaysia'[80]. However, these special qualities have not prevented Mahathir from persistently citing the fundamental social, cultural and even racial differences which he thinks separate Australia from East Asia as reasons why its voice should not be heard in East Asian councils. It is noteworthy that none of Mahathir's attacks on Australia's regional aspirations have impugned Australia's economic credentials, or have sought to downplay the economic role it plays in East Asia. Even during the most tense moments between Australia and Malaysia, Mahathir has not, at least during the Howard government's term, made any suggestion that Malaysia should review the economic, trade, financial or educational links with Australia, and nor has it suggested that other East Asian countries should do so. At the level of bare economics, Australia's standing in East Asia is sound. The perceived points of difference which, in the eyes of Mahathir and those who share his views, militate against deeper Australian inclusion, appear to be far more profound.

In a way, Australia's economic standing in the region is vindication of the East Asia policy pursued by the Howard government, and the style in which it has been pursued. Speaking in Beijing in July 2000, Mr Downer made an ungainly attempt to deconstruct the notion of East Asian regionalism by identifying two variants: the cultural, 'built on common ties of history, of mutual cultural identity [and] emotional links'; and the practical, 'where countries which are bound by geography find practical ways of working together to achieve their mutual objectives'. Mr Downer's point was that Australia is only able to attain, and thus only interested in, practical regionalism. This formulation is instructive. 'Practical regionalism' is a phrase which captures perfectly the essence of the Howard government's approach to East Asia. It has been an approach focussed unwaveringly on the tangible realities of Australia's economic and security relationships with the nations of East Asia, and how these realities can be changed to ameliorate Australia's position. Of course a clear focus on advancing Australia's interests cannot be faulted. The natural predisposition of the Prime Minister and his Foreign Minister to eschew pursuit of the grand designs of which Keating and Evans dreamt was reinforced by a desire to distinguish the new government's East Asia policy from that of its predecessor. Certainly Downer, at least early in his tenure, resented the perception that he remained in Evans' shadow on the East Asian stage. Accordingly, the Howard government has articulated its regional agenda using a language of pragmatism, regularly employing terms such as 'clear-minded' and 'practical' to describe its approach. It has sought outcomes which it could touch, and advances it could measure in statistics; and a fair judge would say that on this level it has done well. In particular its performance in keeping the economy buoyant in the face of a crisis which affected many of Australia's major export markets was laudable, and the government revelled in the praise it received, from home and abroad.

But a close look at Australia's efforts to gain a meaningful role in East Asian institutions demonstrates that it is in the area of what Downer called cultural regionalism that the grounds for the rejection of Australia's overtures are to be found. Malaysia's opposition is revealing in this regard. No-one would argue that any Australian government should accede slavishly to the demands made by Dr Mahathir, or any leader like him; or that Australia should, or needs to, discard values and practices which give its society cohesion and strength. It is also debatable how widely Dr Mahathir's views find resonance among the vastly heterogenous group of East Asian nations for which he frequently presumes to speak[81]. But they have been and are criticisms which Australia has found unanswerable. Where Labor attempted to minimize the perception of difference between Australia and East Asia through the postulation of convergence, the Howard government has been comfortable in portraying Australia as in effect permanently and irreparably separate from East Asia. An image of Australia as merely a practical contributor to regional affairs was more suited to its philosophical leanings. However, the decisions concerning the formation and evolution of groups such as ASEM and ASEAN + 3 have not been made solely on pragmatic grounds. These cannot be characterized entirely as manifestations of 'practical regionalism'. They signify the convergence of East Asian nations, and, to a minimal extent, East Asian cultures; but they are converging among themselves, and the absence of Australia (and New Zealand and the US) is conspicuous. It is an absence which should confirm the sceptics' view of the Keating/Evans version of convergence. It should also confirm the relevance of that version of convergence which says that Australia must do most of the converging. It is that version which the Howard government, supported by most of the Australian electorate, appears to have rejected.

The arguments advanced by Malaysia to justify its opposition to an Australian role have commonly been dismissed in the Australian press as gratuitous and reactionary. However, they form a narrative of Australia's exclusion from the early stages of the East Asian solidarity process, and it is difficult to draw from this experience positive inferences concerning Australia's future participation. Convergence appears dead. The dialogue between Australia and Malaysia over Australia's regional role has been one in which neither side has sought to minimize the manifest differences which separate them. Rather, the Howard government has argued that shared interests of the type which Downer claimed foster practical regionalism can and should be the basis for Australia's inclusion in nascent East Asian institutions. Thus far, it is an argument which has failed. The East Asian solidarity project remains at a relatively early stage, although we have seen the rapid advances it has made. We have also seen that questions concerning Australia's role have not been decided by considerations at the level at which Australia has sought to pursue its relationships with the states of East Asia. But the consequences of exclusion have not yet clearly emerged. There are signs that the rebuffs have induced a policy change in Canberra. Over the past year the government has increased its efforts at the bilateral level, with a free trade agreement with Singapore under negotiation. More strikingly, a similar arrangement with the US is being pushed. This idea appeals to many in the present government, who value it as much for the strength it may add to what has long been Australia's only true 'special relationship' as for the economic benefits it would provide for Australia. The suggestion has been made that on this issue the government may be partially motivated by its exclusion from East Asian arrangements, Paul Kelly arguing that the Howard government must 'run a foreign policy that works, which means Australia can't keep knocking on a closed East Asian door if the US door is swinging open'[82]. If the interest in a free trade deal with the US does presage a halt, temporary or otherwise, to the Howard government's efforts to gain entry to East Asian institutions, it is a venture whose end displays an unfortunate symmetry. It is a further compelling demonstration that this government, like each of its predecessors, has yet to reconcile Australia's history with its geography, and that in fact, they remain in conflict. Rather than face the most fundamental challenges which the engagement project has posed for it, rather than seize the challenge presented by the need for convergence, Australia, like the countries of East Asia, continues to seek sanctuary with those with whom it has always felt its sense of greatest affinity.

While the further development of the embryonic institutional proposals under discussion in East Asia is uncertain it does seem quite unlikely that they will come to nothing. The engagement of both China and Japan in those discussions with the rest of the region and with ASEAN in particular is potentially momentous. There is a recognition that the region needs to reduce its dependence on the United States market and to develop arrangements to grow trade and investment within the East Asian region. Although the region has still not overcome the effects of the 1997-98 crisis, and although the hyper-growth years seem unlikely to come again, there is a recognition of the enormous potential of the region. The performance of China, exaggerated though it may be in that country's official statistics, is a source of dynamism and on such a scale that it has the potential to drive the region's growth into the future if it is opened to the rest in free trade and related arrangements. Foreign investors have thus far responded positively to WTO entry. So Australia will have an important interest in participating in these regional developments. There is disagreement in Australia about how important that will be. Some are sceptical about the outlook for East Asian cooperation and about the potential benefits of membership for Australia. Others think that Australia will be invited in due course to participate because of the assets and capacities that Australia can bring to the regional table. We shall examine these issues further in Chapter 10.

But it seems unlikely that Australia will be welcomed into regional institutional networks if there is continued opposition by Indonesia and Malaysia with equivocation by others. Indonesia is as always probably the key player and it is not well understood in Australia how that relationship has fluctuated over more than fifty years, nor how great a continuing effort it will require on the Australian side if it is to be productive and mutually supportive. We turn to that in Chapter 8.

Notes

1. For example the Government's *Defence Review 2000 – Our Future Defence Force*, p. 12, argued that the shift to more democratic arrangements in Indonesia offered the chance not only to base the relationship on 'shared strategic interests in the stability of our region', but also on a 'closer convergence of civic values' inherent in democracies.
2. See two articles by William F. Case: (1996), 'Political Myths about Asia and the West; Can the "Halfway House" Stand? Semidemocracy and Elite Theory in Three Southeast Asian Countries', *Comparative Politics*, Vol. 28, No. 4, pp. 437-64; and (2000), 'Revisiting Elites, Transitions and founding Elections: An Unexpected Caller from Indonesia', *Democratization*, Vol. 7, No. 4, pp. 51-80.
3. Jayasuriya, Kanishka (1994), 'Political Economy of Democratization in East Asia', *Asian Perspective*, Vol. 18, No. 2, Fall-Winter 1994, pp. 141-80.
4. Labels which obscure his considerable achievement and the extent to which for most of his time in office he sought to attend to the concerns of the people.
5. The differences between Sukarno and Menzies in terms of culture and background were just as large but perhaps more important factors in their uneasy relationship were differences of ideology and personality.
6. While it served the interests of the military leaders who were at the top of the tree it was a view which they were ready to defend in discussion and which they gave every appearance of genuinely believing. (Based on many conversations with such figures as Admiral Sudomo, General Panggabean, and General Sudharmono.) And it was largely accepted by the Australian political leadership of the time.
7. That was the view of this writer. See *The Weekend Australian*, 16-17 December, 1995, p. 22.
8. American and Japanese rhetoric on state occasions greatly exaggerated the similarities between the two societies and distorted the nature of the Japanese political process and thinking.
9. *The Bulletin*, 28 September 1999.
10. Formally the Queen is the Head of State and the Governor General her representative and it is she who appoints the Governor General. But in practice the Prime Minister decides who will be Governor General and the Queen endorses that choice. And in practice the Governor General exercises the functions of the office of Head of State.
11. FitzGerald, Stephen (1997), *Is Australia an Asian Country?*, Allen & Unwin, St Leonards.
12. *Ibid.*, p. 39.
13. *Ibid.*, p. 40.
14. See review article 'Orientalists of the South?' by Rawdon Dalrymple in *The Times Literary Supplement*, p. 12, October 3, 1997.
15. FitzGerald, *op. cit.* p. 177.
16. *Ibid.*, p. 179.
17. *The Sydney Morning Herald*, 31 December, 2001, p. 8; Associated Press report.
18. Clayton Yeutter, the United States' Senior Trade Representative, told the writer that he and Richard Lyng who was Secretary for Agriculture, had conceived the idea and very privately inserted it into Australian ministerial thinking.
19. FitzGerald, Stephen (1997), 'Home Alone', *The Sydney Morning Herald*, 3 May 1997.
20. Yeo Lay Hwee, (2000), 'ASEM: Looking Back, Looking Forward', *Contemporary Southeast Asia*, Vol. 22, No. 1.

21 The development of ASEAN + 3 is chronicled in considerable detail in Terada, T., (2001), 'Constructing the East Asian Concept and Growing Regional Identity: From EAEC to ASEAN + 3', conference paper, Singapore.
22 Address at the Third ASEAN + 3 Informal Summit, Manila, 28 November 1999.
23 Address at the Third ASEAN + 3 Informal Summit, Manila, 28 November 1999.
24 Hamilton-Hart, N. (2001), 'Regionalism and Reform: States and Regional Co-operation in Asia', draft conference paper, San Francisco, September, pp. 6-7.
25 Webber, D. (2001), 'Two funerals and a wedding? The ups and downs of regionalism in East Asia and the Asia-Pacific after the Asian crisis', *Pacific Review*, 14 (3), p. 340.
26 Castellano, M. (2000), 'East Asian monetary union: more than just talk?', *JEI Report*, no. 12A, 24 March, cited in Webber, *ibid.*, p. 341.
27 Kelly, Paul (2000), 'United States of East Asia', *Weekend Australian*, 29-30 April.
28 Heribert, Dieter and Higgott, Richard (2000), 'East Asia looks to its own resources', *Financial Times*, 16 May.
29 Kelly, Paul (2000), 'Downer finally sees benefits of Asia regionalism', *The Australian*, 9 August.
30 Milner, Anthony (2000), 'Neighbours must be our priority', *The Sydney Morning Herald*, 1 August.
31 ASEAN Secretariat, Press Release, 'External Relations', undated. Accessed at www.aseansec.org.
32 ASEAN Secretariat, Press Release, 'External Relations', undated. Accessed at www.aseansec.org.
33 Kikuchi, T. (2002), 'East Asian Regionalism: A Look at the "ASEAN Plus Three" Framework', *Japan Review of International Affairs*, Vol. 15, No. 1, p. 23.
34 Webber, D., *op. cit.* p. 342.
35 *Straits Times*, 'ASEAN to push free trade plan as part of recovery', 29 November 1999, cited in Webber, *ibid.*, pp. 357-8.
36 Terada, T. (2001), 'Constructing East Asian Concept and Growing Regional Identity: from EAEC to ASEAN + 3', paper presented for 'Asian Values and Japan's Options' conference, National University of Singapore, 5-6 October, 2001, p. 12.
37 *The Australian*, 31 July, 1998, cited in Terada, T., *ibid.*, p 12.
38 Kikuchi, T., *op. cit.* p. 29.
39 Terada, T., *op. cit.* p. 13
40 Luz Baguioro, (1999), 'ASEAN wants Japan to make currency fund permanent', *Straits Times*, 27 November
41 Terada, T., *op. cit.* p. 4.
42 Terada, T., *op. cit.* p. 2.
43 *The Sydney Morning Herald*, 'Asians wary of bloc with Australia', 24 November 2000.
44 Stott, Diane (1998), 'Britain backs Australia for forum', *The Sydney Morning Herald*, 10 March.
45 Higgott, R.A. and Nossal K.R. (1997), 'The International Politics of Liminality: Relocating Australia in the Asia Pacific', *Australian Journal of Political Science*, Vol. 32, No. 2, p. 178.
46 *Ibid.*
47 Ungerer, C. (1997), 'Australia and the World: A Seminar Report', *Australian Journal of International Affairs*, Vol. 51, No. 2, p. 256. This renewed emphasis was given clear expression by the attention given to the 1996 AUSMIN talks with the United States.

48   Downer, Alexander (1996), *Australia and Asia: Taking the Long View*. Address to the Foreign Correspondents' Association, Sydney, 11 April.
49   Howard, John (1996), Address at the opening of the R.G. Casey Building, Canberra. 29 November.
50   Department of Foreign Affairs and Trade, *In the National Interest*, 1997. Accessed at www.dfat.gov.au/ini/ch2.html.
51   All references are from John Howard (1996), *op. cit.*
52   Howard, John (1997), Fifth Annual Sir Edward 'Weary' Dunlop *Asialink* Lecture. Melbourne, 11 November.
53   Sheridan, Greg (1997), 'Our absence in Asia is becoming conspicuous', *The Australian*, 19 February.
54   *Commonwealth Parliamentary Debates*, 3 September 1997.
55   Skelton, Russell and Hewett, Jennifer (1997), 'Hashimoto the man to welcome us into Asia', *The Sydney Morning Herald*, 28 April.
56   *The Sydney Morning Herald*, 'Asia, as seen by Japan', 5 May 1997.
57   Baker, Mark (1997), 'Australia backed on ASEM membership', *The Sydney Morning Herald*, 2 May.
58   *Ibid.*
59   Sheridan, Greg (1997), 'Thailand our regional link', *The Australian*, 26 February.
60   Skelton, Russell (1997), 'Fix race row or we may abandon you', *The Sydney Morning Herald*, 11 June.
61   Skehan, Craig (1997), 'China warns Howard: don't meddle', *The Sydney Morning Herald*, 11 March.
62   Baker, Mark (1997), 'Malaysia blocks Australia in forum', *The Sydney Morning Herald*, 15 February.
63   Baker, Mark (1997), 'Our role in power group blocked', *The Sydney Morning Herald*, 29 July.
64   *The Age*, 'Australia left on the sidelines', 6 April 1998.
65   Barker, Geoffrey (1998), 'Canberra, Jakarta in falling-out', *Australian Financial Review*, 17 April.
66   *The Sydney Morning Herald*, 'Indonesia's ASEM snub disappoints Howard', 18 April 1998.
67   Baker, Mark (1997), 'Burma question a threat to closer East-West ties', *The Sydney Morning Herald*, 21 January.
68   Stott, Diane (1998), *op. cit.*
69   Baker, Mark (1997), 'Malaysia blocks Australia in forum', *The Sydney Morning Herald*, 15 February.
70   The Chairman's Statement for the 1998 meeting notes only an agreement that 'discussions should continue on the timing and modalities concerning expansion of membership'. Accessed at www.aseansec.org/world.
71   Accessed at www.mofa.go.jp/policy/economy/asem/asem3/statement.html.
72   Yeo Lay Hwee (2000), *op. cit.*
73   Skelton, Russell (1997), 'Japan fights for our role in Asia', *The Sydney Morning Herald*, 23 April 1997.
74   Paul Kelly suggests that Downer's initial reaction to the grouping was dismissive: 'Downer finally sees benefits of Asia regionalism', *Australian*, 9 August 2000. The author sees only dubious strength in Kelly's argument on this point.
75   Kelly, Paul (2000), 'Downer finally sees benefits of Asia regionalism', *The Australian*, 9 August.
76   Calvert, Ashton (2000), *Australia's Foreign and Trade Policy Agenda*, address to the National Press Club, Canberra, 3 August.

77 Downer, A. (2001), Australian Foreign Policy – a Liberal Perspective', *Australian Journal of International Affairs*, Vol. 55, No. 3, p. 338.
78 Lague, David (2000), 'PM hits back at "unwelcome in Asia" slur', *The Sydney Morning Herald*, 18 May.
79 *The Sydney Morning Herald*, 'Mahathir's old joke', 29 June 2001.
80 Henderson, Gerard (1998), 'Special ties, the Australian way', *The Sydney Morning Herald*, 24 November.
81 One who believes they are widely held is Greg Sheridan, 'Stay away, arrogant Howard: Mahathir', *Australian*, 6 July 2000.
82 Kelly, Paul (2000), 'Two-ring circus', *The Australian*, 9-10 December.

Chapter 8

Dealing with Indonesia

The 'Litmus Test'

Australian attitudes and policy towards Indonesia have exemplified, more than any other bilateral relationship, many of the issues and problems discussed in previous chapters. At times Indonesia has seemed to offer an opportunity for Australia to bridge the gap with East Asia. At other times it has seemed to stand in the way. Despite major difficulties since 1998 the opportunity is still there if responsible Australians are prepared to make some of the shifts discussed in the last chapter. Indonesia is in a process of massive change, but the past is inescapable and indeed in some ways is pressing more heavily on the present than at any time in the last fifty years. We cannot usefully look to the future of Australian policy towards and relations with the region without a closer examination of the evolution and present state of the relationship with Indonesia.

Indonesia has posed a special challenge and test for Australia's regional relations in the post-war world. Huge in terms of population, extent and resources, and lying across Australia's lines of communication, it was seen as both deeply foreign and very adjacent. Dealing with Indonesia has been the most difficult test of Australian foreign policy for more than fifty years. Its importance, and the difficult issues which it has posed for Australian policy, have placed it at the centre of Australian efforts to establish a close engagement with East Asia. It has always been clear that if Australia had a troubled relationship with Indonesia, when other members of the region did not, it would be much harder to make progress with Australia's engagement policy; and a good relationship with Indonesia, including Indonesian support for acceptance of Australia, would facilitate that policy. Over several decades, through good times and bad, Australia dealt on the whole pragmatically and patiently with the problems and opportunities presented by the relationship with Indonesia. The attempt to make a great leap forward with the relationship during the Prime Ministership of Paul Keating, and the subsequent events in Indonesia itself, appear to have left a residue of scepticism about the relationship in Australia. In some quarters in Indonesia there is resentment and even bitterness which could take a long time to dissipate altogether and could cause further difficulty in the event of a nationalistic political leadership coming to power in Indonesia.

The experience with East Timor has given encouragement to those in Australia who believe that Australia should actively assist the independence movement in Irian Jaya (or West Papua), a course which would be likely to do profound damage to the relationship. There is little knowledge or understanding of the story of the relationship with Indonesia, except for the issue of East Timor on which highly partisan accounts have mostly dominated. But that story is central not only to deciding how Australia should approach Indonesia now and in the future but also to Australia's attempts to engage more closely with East Asia as a whole. A major part of the reason for that is the influence on Australian attitudes and Australian public policy of Australia's Western heritage and culture. Human rights and related issues have a strong resonance in the Australian community. In this regard Australia is a very Western country and this complicates its relationship with a country like Indonesia. The East Timor case, which will be examined in the next chapter, is the most striking example impacting on the relationship with Indonesia. There had been a growing awareness in the Australian community that human rights abuses of various kinds were widespread in New Order (Soeharto's term for his regime) Indonesia and this boiled over into outright revulsion with the well-publicised events after the plebiscite in East Timor. Obviously it is more difficult to promote engagement when the electorate's dominant feeling is one of alienation.

Australia and Indonesian Independence

Up to the time of the Pacific War Australia had become used to dealing when necessary with the Dutch administration in what was then called the Netherlands East Indies, or NEI. At the beginning of the war allied strategy was to be coordinated by a grouping known as ABDA, an acronym for American, British, Dutch and Australian. But the Netherlands quickly fell under German occupation and resistance to the Japanese invasion of the NEI was even less effective than that of the British and Australians in Malaya and Singapore. The Japanese had no difficulty in overrunning the Netherlands empire in the Indonesian archipelago, including Ambon at the eastern end, near New Guinea and Australia, where the Australian defending force was quickly overwhelmed.

At the end of the war, after the Japanese surrender, British troops were inserted to hold the position until the Dutch could return and directly reassert their sovereignty. This brought the British forces into conflict with the Indonesian independence movement. Some Australian units were initially involved in those operations. But Australian government policy shifted to support for the Indonesian Republican movement, and opposition to the reimposition of Dutch colonial rule, with the exception that the Australians did not want the Dutch-administered western half of the island of New Guinea included in a new independent Indonesia.

By the time Japan surrendered Curtin had died and J.B. Chifley had succeeded him as leader of the Labor Party and Prime Minister. Curtin had not fully shared the view of the world, and of Australia's place in it, of Dr H.V. Evatt the Minister for External Affairs and, had he survived, Evatt's foreign policy might have been more constrained. But, under the new Prime Minister, Chifley, Evatt had a rather free hand to pursue his belief that Australia could play a major role in asserting the rights and influence of small and medium powers and of countries which were emerging from colonial status into independence and membership of the United Nations. In terms of the ending of colonialism he was closer to elements in mainstream United States tradition and thinking; while at odds with Great Britain. But his high octane activism at the United Nations was regarded with reserve by some in the United States Administration especially as difficulties emerged with the Soviet Union. The case of Indonesia, however, fitted fairly well with the Evatt approach and the Chifley/Evatt government, at least from mid-1947, made the clear choice to support the Indonesian Republic against the Dutch policy of reasserting their colonial suzerainty. But this had not been a spontaneous and immediate policy development. On the conservative side in Australian politics there were strong voices in favour of supporting the continuation of Dutch rule in the NEI, and the Dutch in Australia 'did everything in their power to nurture fears of race wars and Communist aggression from Indonesia'[1]. The Labor government through 1946 and into 1947 took a position of qualified support for the Indonesian freedom movement. They were sympathetic but had 'some wariness about the use Indonesians might make of freedom and how well they might handle their serious post-war difficulties'[2]. They thought the Indonesians would need Dutch administrative skills and support so they favoured substantial self-government without the ending of Dutch sovereignty.

The Indonesian independence movement had divided its resources during the Japanese occupation. Sukarno and Hatta worked with the Japanese while Sjahrir and Sukarni led two underground groups. With the Japanese in retreat and heading for defeat in the Pacific they called Sukarno and Hatta to their regional headquarters at Dalat in Vietnam to receive a promise of independence. On return the two leaders found that Sjahrir and his group had concluded that the time had come to rise up against the Japanese. The disagreement between Sukarno and Hatta on the one hand, who looked to a peaceful transfer of power by the Japanese, and Sjahrir and his forces who wanted to seize power, was resolved by an extraordinary series of events. On 16 August 1945 students sympathetic with the underground movement kidnapped Sukarno and Hatta only to find that the day before the Emperor of Japan had surrendered. This meant that the Japanese no longer had any authority to pass power to the independence movement. It was decided to take the initiative and on the morning of 17 August, at Sukarno's house in Jakarta, the Republic of Indonesia was proclaimed. Sukarno was named president, Hatta vice-President and Sjahrir prime minister. The Republican government was able to take over administration in most centres from the Japanese and when the British and Australian troops arrived on 20 September the Republic appeared to be in control with the support of the people. The British used Japanese troops to push the Republican forces out of Bandung and other places and, with Indian troops, fought a bitter battle for Surabaya in East Java. The Dutch built up their forces and a difficult period for the Republic ensued with fighting against the Dutch and the suppression of an internal coup attempt by communists led by Tan Malaka in mid-1946. Political manoeuvring with the Dutch saw the leadership achieve qualified recognition of the Republic in November 1946, envisaging a form of union with the Netherlands in 1949. But this (Linggadjati) agreement broke down and the Dutch, now with a large army in the country[3], strengthened their position in Java and Sumatra.

The fighting within Indonesia and the publicity given to the first Dutch 'police action' in July 1947, which was seen as a refusal by the Dutch to exercise reasonable flexibility over the terms of the Linggadjati agreement, had a major effect on Australian, and some other international, opinion, increasing sympathy for the Republican cause. When Australia and India brought the issue to the Security Council of the United Nations on 30 July 1947 the atmosphere was largely supportive, and Australia recommended a series of measures including withdrawal of troops and arbitration. This was modified on the proposal of the United States and then adopted. With Australia continuing to work with India and China on this issue the Council a few weeks later ensured its continuing involvement by offering its good offices in helping to resolve issues by providing a committee of three members of the Council to assist the parties. Two of the members were to be nominated by the disputants. The Netherlands nominated Belgium and Indonesia nominated Australia. Australia and Belgium nominated the United States as the third member[4].

Evatt was a strong supporter of the Indonesian independence movement. But his agenda was also wider. He saw Australia, and himself personally, as leading the upsurge of the newly independent nations, bursting the yoke of colonialism and western dominance, and thus creating in the United Nations a strong voice for freedom and equity as against the old forces of colonial oppression and of great power dominance. For a while, as we have seen, Evatt achieved something like this and was elected to the Presidency of the General Assembly of the United Nations on the basis of that approval and support. The active role in support of Indonesia which Evatt conducted, and the parts played by Mr Justice Kirby and then by the diplomat T.K. Critchley on the Good Offices Commission became part of the history of Indonesia's successful struggle for independence. This constituted a capital store of good will towards Australia in Indonesia which was very helpful in the years ahead and through some difficult times.

The post-war struggle for independence and for the establishment of a unified Republic, both at home and in the United Nations, against the Dutch and also against domestic opposition, is still seen as an heroic phase in the nation's history. The ideals and principles of Indonesian nationalism were established in adversity and struggle and even in parts of the archipelago where there was resistance to a Jakarta-based unified Republic that is seen as a time when Indonesians generally were motivated by principle and acted with a generosity and bravery which were not always sustained in later decades. That Australia played a helpful and sympathetic role at that time got the relationship off to a very strong start. In the circumstances it is not surprising that there has been a tendency for Australian commentators and politicians to draw attention to that fact. That has naturally been the case especially on the Labor Party side seeking, usually implicitly, to claim the inheritance of attention to and support of the relationship with Indonesia. They have tended not only to draw attention to Australia's role under Evatt in the United Nations in support of Indonesia but also to the fact that Australian unionized dock workers and others, affiliated with the Labor Party, banned the loading of Dutch supplies and munitions in Australian ports at the time. Thus Gareth Evans and Bruce Grant write that 'Most Australians opposed Dutch colonialism and sympathised with Indonesia's struggle for independence'[5]. But Australian feelings about the newly emerging neighbouring state were not as unambiguously supportive as such later commentators have suggested. Gallup polls on the subject in Australia in 1945, 1947 and 1949 all showed a majority in favour of Dutch control of Java (which was the part of the archipelago primarily in the news because it was where most of the fighting between the Dutch and the Republicans was taking place). Many of those asked had no opinion ('Not followed Java news') or were undecided and there was a significant minority in favour of joint control. If the percentage with no knowledge/opinion were added to those undecided it would constitute a substantially larger proportion (42 per cent) than the percentage in support of the Dutch (on 28 per cent the largest in the Gallup categorization). But the percentage in favour of Dutch control actually increased between 1947 and 1949[6]. There were also strong voices, in the Opposition in the Federal Parliament and in the media, which had major reservations about the Evatt-led policy. It was represented as Communist-backed and even inspired (the Australian waterside workers were under Communist leadership). In March 1946 the Government policy of practical toleration of the bans on Dutch shipping and of leaning towards the Indonesian Republicans produced attacks in Parliament by the Opposition. Menzies referred to the security value to Australia of the Dutch presence in Indonesia and noted that Sukarno had collaborated with the Japanese during the war. By undermining Dutch rule in Indonesia the government was in effect 'contributing to a doctrine which would justify the expulsion of all colonial powers in South and South-East Asia – a dreadful prospect for Australia'[7].

Despite the fact that there were major reservations in the Australian community about the emergence of a very large new independent Asian nation on their doorstep, it is clear in retrospect that the leadership of the Labor government, and Evatt in particular, had a keener sense of the historical shift which was taking place in Indonesia and other parts of the region than did Menzies and some of his influential colleagues or a large part of public and press opinion. There is also an important point in the claim which Evans and Grant, and others, make. In those early years there was a fellow-feeling between the Indonesian Republican leadership and Australian representatives, such as Kirby and Critchley which was the forerunner of the sort of engagement which others on the Australian side later sought to sustain and develop. The Colombo Plan and other programs developed some wider underpinning. That engagement reached its peak so far at the end of 1995, was disrupted by the events leading to the separation of East Timor from Indonesia, and has yet to recover.

It is not to detract from the value and importance of Australia's early and enlightened support of Indonesia to observe that there were from the outset reasons why the relationship would not be sustained at that level. One which soon emerged was the dispute over the future of the Western half of New Guinea which was part of the Netherlands East Indies, and regarded by the new Indonesia as part of its inheritance, but claimed by the Dutch to require separate treatment. A more general and increasingly divisive factor lay in global political developments in which Indonesia and Australia became caught up on different sides. We have already noticed that Australia's own importance and salience in the United Nations was bound to decline relatively as a range of new members joined the organization and a new era of post-war world politics got under way. Those new members included some which were much larger than Australia, Indonesia itself being one such. They developed a new agenda which diverged substantially from that of the Western powers, which were increasingly drawn into a struggle for power and influence with the Soviet Union and its satellites. Australia, after Labor lost office in 1949 to the conservative coalition led by R.G. Menzies of the Liberal Party, engaged increasingly closely with the United States and its Western associates. These divergent trends affected the Australia-Indonesia relationship directly, because Sukarno, the first President of Indonesia, was deeply committed to the anti-colonialist cause and had always been influenced by the Marxist view of history and of economic development. Like some other leaders of the newly independent countries he sought to reinterpret elements of Marxism and other western-derived thought and practice in terms of traditional Indonesian (primarily Javanese) thought. The synthesis which Sukarno and his political associates called 'Marhaenism'[8] was certainly very remote indeed from anything which could engage the sympathetic interest of a man like Menzies, who had spent his life as a highly successful barrister very much in the British tradition and then as a politician again in the British tradition. He saw the Commonwealth, with the British monarch at its head, as the most important element in world politics for Australia. Sukarno saw himself as one of the leaders of a new wave of change, representing the exploited and oppressed former colonial countries rising up in independence with confidence, newly released energies and with vast populations to assert themselves in the councils of the world. Menzies must have seemed as foreign to Sukarno as Sukarno to Menzies and we have seen that the latter saw Indonesian success against the Dutch as presaging a calamitous ending of Western colonialism in Australia's region. Nevertheless Menzies made the effort to develop an understanding with Indonesia. One of the first acts of his government on taking office was to extend recognition to Indonesia. The Minister for External Affairs, Spender, visited Jakarta in January 1950 and he and his successors as foreign ministers in Menzies' governments, Casey and Barwick, all tried in their different ways to preserve a cooperative and friendly relationship with Indonesia. Menzies himself visited Indonesia in 1959, and although it could hardly have been a comfortable experience (by then problems had become more intractable) the civilities were observed and Sukarno gave renewed assurances about not using force over West Irian.

Dealing with Sukarno

The exclusion of West New Guinea from the former NEI territory transferred to Indonesia by the Dutch did not initially disturb the cordial relationship which had been created between Australia and Indonesia. But, given the determination of Sukarno, and indeed all political elements in Indonesia, to prevent that territory being excluded from the rest of the former NEI and withheld from Indonesia, any opponent of transfer of the territory to Indonesia was bound to encounter some strong feelings. Given Australian reservations about the inclusion of West New Guinea in the new South East Asian state, it was inevitable that this issue would cause difficulties in the relationship. As Sir Alan Watt pointed out, that was in no way a function of which Australian political party or parties were in government. 'If the Australian Labor Party had remained in office during the period when the unresolved dispute over West New Guinea became a serious current problem, Australia's relations with Indonesia would have suffered, just as they did under the Liberal-Country Party government; for the Labor Party at no time endorsed the Indonesian claim to West New Guinea – indeed, when in opposition it was often critical of the Menzies Government for not being sufficiently tough and decisive on this issue'[9]. Casey and Spender, in their different ways both tried to prevent the issue from causing damage to the relationship. Casey tried to keep it in the background, in 'cold storage', while firmly stating the legal and other reasons why Australia did not support Indonesia's claim. He followed Spender too in asserting Australia's 'vital and legitimate interest in the future of Dutch New Guinea' and its 'right to a voice in any discussions which would change its present status'[10].

In the following years Indonesia waged a diplomatic campaign in the United Nations and with other Afro-Asian nations to obtain support for the transfer (or as they put it, the return) of West New Guinea to Indonesia. In 1954 and subsequent years at Indonesia's request the West New Guinea (or as Indonesia called it the West Irian issue) was placed on the agenda of the United Nations General Assembly. In that year and later Australia opposed the Indonesian case in the United Nations and supported the Dutch. Indonesia was unable to obtain the two-thirds majority it needed in the General Assembly but, partly because of Sukarno's relentless and effective demagogic skills, this served to increase the pressure within Indonesia to achieve the desired result. In the meantime, Australia and the Netherlands cooperated in areas such as health, agriculture, education and social development, and improving transport and communications between the two halves of the island[11]. The issue was caught up in Indonesia's increasingly turbulent domestic politics and also in the shift of her foreign policy towards China and the development of 'unity and solidarity among leaders of the ex-colonial world'[12]. The latter objective was advanced strongly by the Afro-Asian Conference held at Bandung, south of Jakarta, in 1955, the final communique of which reflected strong support for Indonesia's position on West Irian. Especially during the Prime Ministership of Ali Sastroamidjojo the shift towards a more active Indonesian foreign policy which was more at variance with Western views and interests, and towards closer relations with China, placed more distance between the Indonesian and Australian governments. At the same time the size and influence of the Indonesian Communist Party (PKI) was growing from 100,000 in 1952 to perhaps one million members in 1956[13]. The Army had settled internal differences and greatly strengthened its political influence. But constitutional democracy was not working effectively in Indonesia either in terms of delivering effective government or in terms of unifying the country. Early in 1958 rebellions erupted in Sumatra and Sulawesi which severely challenged the central authority of the Republic but also engaged foreign interests. In Australia, concerned about the possibility of the Western half of New Guinea falling under Indonesian control and about apparent increases in communist strength within Indonesia and Indonesian links with communist countries, there was sympathy for the rebels. But the latter, who were given covert assistance by the United States, were overcome within a few months by the Government's forces.

This was a turning point in the diplomacy affecting the West Irian issue because it produced a shift of United States and other Western policy. Washington sent a new ambassador, Howard P. Jones, to Jakarta who emerged as an uncritical supporter of Sukarno over the seven years of his tenure of the post. The United States announced an arms sale to Indonesia and shortly afterwards Britain followed suit, reversing an earlier decision not to sell military aircraft to Indonesia and eliciting protest from the Netherlands and 'regrets' from Australia[14]. The following year the Indonesian foreign minister, Subandrio, visited Australia at the invitation of the Australian government. He and Casey issued a joint statement which, as Watt says, 'caused much controversy'. The controversy arose over interpretations of an 'explanation from Australian Ministers' contained in the statement which was read by some as a weakening of Australia's stand on the Dutch New Guinea issue and both a concession to Indonesia and an 'invitation to Indonesia to mount pressure on the Dutch'[15]. The 'explanation by Australian Ministers [was] that it followed from their position of respect for agreements on the rights of sovereignty that if any agreement were reached between the Netherlands and Indonesia as parties principal, arrived at by peaceful processes and in accordance with internationally accepted principles, Australia would not oppose such an agreement'[16]. When later that year Menzies visited Indonesia, Sukarno repeated the assurance Subandrio had given about not using force[17]. 1960 saw intensified activity by Indonesia and an accelerated program for Papuan self-government by the conservative Dutch government which had come to office the previous year. The Dutch also reinforced their military strength and arrested Indonesian armed groups. Faced now with the prospect of the Dutch moving the territory to self-government and having failed to secure their objective through the United Nations, the Indonesians decided to seek extensive military aid from the Soviet Union and to confront the Netherlands.

Through this period Australian policy had been characterized by an apparent lack of decisiveness. The Dutch had made it clear that they would welcome a joint Dutch-Australian program to bring the two halves of the island together to self-government. There was discussion about a Melanesian Federation. But the Australian government was not ready to move on self-government for Papua and New Guinea, or anyway could not make up its mind. At the same time the Australian Prime Minister asserted his government's position on the issue in unchanged and uncompromising terms. Australia declined Indonesian overtures to adopt a neutral position in the dispute between Indonesia and the Netherlands. Menzies also visited the new United States President, J.F. Kennedy and pressed the case for resisting Sukarno and for leaving the Dutch to bring the territory to self-government. Kennedy was non-committal in response and Menzies believed he had made an impression on the President's thinking on the matter. But a year or so into the Kennedy Administration it emerged that they had decided that the main priority should be to keep Sukarno from leading Indonesia into an ever closer embrace with the Soviet Union and the Indonesian Communist Party (PKI). Moreover, Kennedy had been unimpressed by the way the Dutch Foreign Minister lectured him on the issue. By late 1961 the United States was looking for a formula for settling the issue essentially on Indonesia's terms. This was made public at the United Nations in November in the form of a proposal that the Indonesians should be allowed access to the territory to campaign in favour of union with the Republic. The Indonesians stepped up pressure and the Dutch responded, sinking two Indonesian torpedo boats. There was a great deal of warlike posturing on the Indonesian side and a series of parachute landings. In June 1962 the Australian Defence Minister, Athol Townley, visited Indonesia where he was reported as having 'displayed an understanding of Indonesia's rights with regard to West Irian'[18]. This drew criticism in Australia as did the agreement which shortly followed between the Indonesian and Dutch sides on 15 August 1962. Brokered by the American nominee Ellsworth Bunker the Treaty signed by the two parties effectively ensured that Indonesian aims would be met. The rights of self-determination for the indigenous people were supposed to be guaranteed by the provision for an 'act of free choice' to be held under UN auspices before 1969. But in the meantime the Indonesians moved in and were able to ensure that the act of free choice was no more than a stage-managed ceremony which had nothing to do with any genuine ascertainment of the wishes of the indigenous people, leaving aside the question whether any such meaningful ascertainment would have been possible in the time allowed.

There was unhappiness in Australia about the way this issue was resolved, with Indonesia in effect getting its way by the threat, and indeed the use, of force and by diplomatic bluster; and there was some apprehension about how Indonesian occupancy of the western half of the island would affect Australian interests in the longer term. But there was recognition too that, once the United States had decided that it would not back the Netherlands and that its broader interests lay in brokering a settlement which would satisfy the aspirations of the largest country in south-east Asia, there was nothing Australia could do except make the best of things and try to ensure that its relations with Indonesia were not prejudiced. Indeed that had in effect been Australia's policy for some years. Although Menzies and his successive Ministers for External Affairs stuck to opposition to the Indonesian case until a late hour, and although they worked within the Commonwealth and the United Nations in that sense, they avoided being drawn into commitments to the Dutch which would put them out on a limb, and they made sure they kept open the doors to Indonesia and persisted in assuring Indonesia of their goodwill and friendship. While this policy came in for much criticism in Australia it had the merits that it enabled Australia to argue a case which appeared to be sound in law and was at least partly grounded in a desire to protect the interests of the indigenous people. Moreover the course they followed avoided putting the national interest seriously at risk and preserved the relationship with Indonesia. At the end of the chapter on 'West New Guinea' in *Friends and Neighbours* Casey wrote already in 1958 of his regret that this had been 'repeatedly brought forward for international discussion. Australia recognises Dutch sovereignty. At the same time we do not see why this should affect our friendly relations with Indonesia'. Subsequently, Casey himself,

Barwick and their successors made considerable efforts to preserve those friendly relations. Between them, and with the help of a number of skilful and dedicated Australian diplomats, they had a fair measure of success in steering Australia through a difficult passage. It is true, as has often been observed, that Casey's policy of putting the West Irian issue into 'cold storage' in the relationship was not entirely realistic. But it probably worked at least in terms of preserving as much as possible of the relationship with Indonesia while presenting the minimum target to critical opinion in Australia, including those whose preferred policies would have led Australia into sharp and damaging confrontation with Indonesia. It was thus much better than either of the alternatives: joining the Dutch in some extensive campaign (which would have had military implications) to stop the Indonesians; or abandoning the Dutch and the long-standing (but decreasingly persuasive) considerations about Australian security and switching policy to accept the Indonesian demands. In any case, as we have seen, once the United States came down on the Indonesian side there was no longer any realistic policy for Australia but to accommodate. For those who believed the outcome was nevertheless a poor one, and they included Menzies himself, that was small comfort[19].

The West Irian issue is of particular interest in the context of a study of Australia's relations and policies towards Indonesia. It remains a major point at issue between those in Australia who attach high importance to preserving and developing the state to state relationship and those who argue that Australian policy has pursued that objective at the expense of principle and humanitarian considerations. With the increasing activity and salience of the autonomy or independence movement in the territory it is also being argued by some supporters that Australia, because it did not go to the brink or beyond over the issue, was complicit in the Indonesian 'seizure' of West Papua. Finally, the disappointing Indonesian performance there over some thirty-five years has added to disillusionment on the Australian side about the prospects for close and friendly relations. No doubt that performance has fallen short of the Indonesian undertakings and also of some Australian expectations. From time to time Australia has made representations privately to Indonesia on policy or developments in Irian Jaya; but it is doubtful if those representations had much effect.

Sukarno's nationalist and regional ambitions were not diminished by the success of the Irian Jaya campaign and he embarked on efforts to frustrate the plan to unite the former British possessions in peninsular Malaya, Singapore and Borneo into a new Federation of Malaysia. The Indonesian announcement of confrontation of Malaysia came after a period of diplomatic negotiations between Indonesia, the Philippines and Malaya. Their heads of government met in Tokyo on 31 May and 1 June, 1963 and their foreign ministers in Manila from 7 to 11 June. These consultations produced concessions to Indonesian demands including the postponement of the date for announcing the formation of Malaysia and for the Secretary-General of the United Nations to 'ascertain prior to the establishment of the Federation of Malaysia the wishes of the people of Sabah (North Borneo) and Sarawak' and 'much of the language of the agreement reflected Sukarno's views on "new emerging forces", use of bases by "big powers" and primary responsibility of the signatory powers for the security of the so-called "Maphilindo" area'[20]. Australia sought to play a calming role at this point with Barwick praising the 'spirit of conciliation and responsible statesmanship' of the three leaders and then seeking to 'compose the differences' which emerged between Indonesia and Britain over the former's demands for access and privileges of Indonesian observers of the ascertainment process[21]. In the end Sukarno rejected the report of the representative of the Secretary-General of the United Nations that 'there is no doubt about the wishes of a sizeable majority of the people of these territories to join in the Federation of Malaysia'[22]. The creation of Malaysia proceeded on 16 September 1963 and Sukarno repeated his intention to 'crush' Malaysia. On 25 September Prime Minister Menzies promised that Australia would 'add our military assistance to the efforts of Malaysia and the United Kingdom in the defence of Malaysia's territorial integrity and political independence' in the event of armed invasion or subversive activity 'supported or directed or inspired from outside Malaysia'. As Watt emphasizes this declaration was made only after long and persistent, if largely quiet, efforts by Australia to help calm the situation. Such efforts were directed not least to those in London who would have preferred to give a short and muscular answer to Sukarno. Indonesia proceeded with military infiltration and other measures in pursuit of its policy to 'crush Malaysia' and in the process there were limited engagements between Indonesian and Australian forces in the border areas in Borneo and elsewhere. Australia refrained from publicizing these and throughout sought to maintain a calm and restrained public front towards Indonesia and its policy. Australia also sought to exercise a restraining influence on rising British impatience with Sukarno and thus avoid any step which would place reconciliation and compromise out of reach or permanently damage the relationship with Australia[23]. Sukarno himself appears also to have been reluctant to see the dispute do deep damage to the Indonesia/Australia relationship. The late K.C.O. Shann, who was Australian ambassador in Jakarta at the time, recounted that, after receiving a highly classified message reporting an engagement between Australian and Indonesian patrols in which casualties had been inflicted, he paid his respects to President Sukarno at a ceremonial occasion. Sukarno tapped Shann lightly with his baton and said 'we have to put a stop to this'. But in such circumstances the relationship was of course fragile and Australians were unlikely to be indifferent to the burning of the British Embassy in Jakarta and other increasing manifestations of the radicalization of Indonesian policy as well as what appeared to be Sukarno's continuing shift towards what he declared to be a communist-based axis in East Asia and the growth in size and influence of the Indonesian Communist Party.

The Kennedy policy of tolerating and humouring Sukarno which had been parallelled by Australia (albeit for largely different reasons) appeared to have failed to achieve its objective of keeping Indonesia at least neutral in the Cold War and on the path of economic development. Under Sukarno's nationalist and populist policies the economy had suffered severely and Indonesians were poorer than they had been a decade earlier. The foreign policy of Sukarno and Subandrio had also estranged Indonesia from the United States and other Western countries, including Australia, although Australia had managed to retain significant benign elements in an ambivalent relationship. Sukarno and others in the Indonesian leadership placed Australia in the company of the old and declining world forces, as distinct from the new emerging forces of which they saw Indonesia as one of the leaders. But it was appreciated that Australia took Indonesia seriously and sought seriously to understand it. Moreover Australia, for all its relative smallness in terms of population and power, worked hard in Jakarta and other places in Indonesia at maintaining contacts and was well informed.

Dealing with the 'New Order' and its Aftermath

During 1965 the domestic political situation became increasingly tense with Sukarno appearing to lean more and more towards the PKI and its leadership. The armed forces were divided with the Air Force substantially communist-influenced (partly because their equipment and training had been largely Soviet supplied) and the Army divided but still predominantly anti-communist and holding a balance against the PKI and the radicalizing trend. On the night of 30 September an attempt was made on the life of General Nasution, the Minister for Defence and Chief of Staff of the Armed Forces. Nasution escaped but six other generals were killed in their homes or kidnapped and taken to the village of Lubang Buaya in the area of the Halim Air Force base. Those who were not killed in their homes appear to have then been murdered at Lubang Buaya by members of PKI youth and related group members who were assembled there, and their bodies thrown down a well. The following morning the plotters took over the Radio Republic Indonesia central studios and the Office of the State Telecommunications. They announced that their 30 September movement had acted to prevent a coup by an alleged Council of Generals who had been plotting to move against the Government. Early in the afternoon they announced the establishment of a Revolutionary Council of 45 persons led by Lieutenant-Colonel Untung. Major-General Soeharto, Commander of the Strategic Army Command (Kostrad) in Jakarta, in the meantime was informed of these developments and of the confusion caused by the killing of key elements of the Army leadership and other events of the previous night, including the fact that President Sukarno was at Halim Air base which was under the control of the Revolutionary Council. Soeharto set about neutralizing the army units which had sided with the Untung group and succeeded over the next days in asserting control.

The outcome of these dramatic events was that Soeharto consolidated his position, Sukarno was compromised and marginalized, the PKI was deemed responsible for the attempt to seize the organs of the state, and a huge purge was put under way with Moslem organizations working with the protection or sanction of the army to get rid of the communist party and its network of affiliated and satellite organisations. On 11 March 1966 Sukarno signed a letter handing the powers of the presidency to Soeharto and what became known as the New Order in Indonesia began.

Soeharto and his associates took over a ruined state as a consequence of gross mismanagement under Sukarno. The economy was in collapse with what export income there was in the hands of local military commanders outside Java. With virtually no earnings of foreign currency, and with the capacity to raise foreign loans having long since been choked off by a huge backlog of unpaid interest and capital, their imports had almost ceased. With no replacement parts or maintenance imported machinery and capital goods ran down and most ceased to operate. The infrastructure of Jakarta and other major cities was in such disrepair that traffic could hardly negotiate the streets and utilities worked only sporadically. There were desperate shortages and poverty especially in rural Java. In this dire situation Soeharto and his associates turned to a group of mostly American-educated economists whom they had met at the Army staff and command college where the academics were part-time lecturers while being professors at the University of Indonesia and other leading schools. There was considerable relief as it became increasingly clear in Washington and not least in Canberra that there was a possibility that this new regime which seemed to be firmly in control rejected the nostrums of Sukarnoism and his anti-western policies, and intended to put in place economic measures which might enable the restoration of Indonesia's economy. With strong backing from the United States, the International Monetary Fund organized a meeting in Tokyo of representatives of a small group of countries which were interested in assisting at this point. Australia was invited and, after some uncertainty in the bureaucracy, accepted on the decisive direction of the Minister for External Affairs, Paul Hasluck. This meeting, in which the new Indonesian economic team including Professors Widjojo, Ali Wardhana and Emil Salim participated, was followed by a second meeting in Tokyo with some additional members[24]. The German banker Dr Hermann Abs was commissioned to produce a report on the major issue of the massive Indonesian indebtedness which had been incurred during the Sukarno period and a scheme was devised to enable foreign aid in kind to generate income for the central government and at the same time begin alleviating critical shortages. It was in due course resolved to set up a formal Aid Consortium for Indonesia and Australia was sounded out about taking the chair of the new Inter-Governmental Group on Indonesia (IGGI). The Australian response was in the negative and the Netherlands assumed chairmanship of the IGGI when it was set up, a step which had difficult and unhappy consequences much later – consequences which would very likely have befallen Australia had we taken on the chairmanship[25].

In the early years of the Soeharto presidency Australia developed a wide-ranging aid program as well as seeking to develop trade and investment. Efforts were also made to develop defence contacts, the high point in that regard being the Sabre project which required a major commitment of funds and personnel. The Indonesian Air Force (AURI) had been equipped with Soviet aircraft acquired during the Sukarno period and these were visible parked at air fields all over the country. But parts and maintenance had dried up and almost all were unserviceable. AURI itself had been purged and was demoralized because of its involvement in the 30 September movement and the subsequent repercussions. Those left had virtually nothing to fly. At the beginning of the 1970s the Australian Air Force was to be re-equipped with Dassault Mirage fighters as its front line aircraft, replacing the F86 Sabres which had been in service for some twenty years, but which had been well maintained and were of roughly the same generation as many of the MiGs which the AURI had been using. It was decided to offer the Sabres to Indonesia as a way of putting AURI on the road to recovery. This involved the restoration and upgrading of the Iswahjudi air base in Java and extensive training of AURI personnel as well as the stationing of Australian maintenance and other technical people at Iswahjudi. This all required almost as much a process of education and adjustment for the Australian side as it did for the Indonesian. In terms of cross-cultural adaptation it probably required more from the Australians since it was they who were required to make most of the adaptation[26]. A beginning was also made with contacts between the Intelligence organizations of the two countries with talks between the respective heads in Jakarta. Prime Ministers Gorton and MacMahon visited Indonesia and Soeharto visited Australia in February 1972. After the change of government in Australia Prime Minister Whitlam took a close interest in the relationship with Indonesia and had a meeting with Soeharto at Wonosobo which had important implications for the issue of East Timor. Those discussions were continued during an 'unofficial working visit' which Soeharto made to meet Whitlam in Townsville, Queensland, in April 1975.

The Indonesian invasion of East Timor and the consequences for the relationship will be dealt with in the following chapter. The Fraser government in Australia sought to keep things going despite anger on the Indonesian side and discomfort on the Australian side, and on the whole that worked. The Indonesian military, and especially General L.B. Moerdani who had been in charge of the East Timor operation, were resentful and suspicious of Australia and made this clear in various ways including obstructions to the defence cooperation program and, under military influence, the Information Ministry placed vexatious restrictions on access by Australian media representatives. But the technocrats maintained other programs, and business, or at any rate frequent contact, between the respective foreign ministries continued. By the early 1980s some cordiality began to return including at the Presidential level and by the time Labor under R.J. Hawke won office in 1983 it was possible for the new Prime Minister to make a well publicized and generally positive visit to Indonesia. Increasingly both sides showed that they wanted to move on, although as always the initiative was left almost entirely to the Australian side. In 1986 *The Sydney Morning Herald* published an expose of the Soeharto family's expanding interests in Indonesian finance and business which caused great offence. In the atmosphere which by then characterized the Indonesian scene the slight to the President and his immediate circle was taken up by all those – and they were of course many – whose interests were dependent on their allegiance or at least their conformity. There was not a great deal of scope for dissent in publicly visible or audible discourse in Indonesia by 1986; nor did it increase in the following years. There was undoubtedly discontent at the way in which the Soeharto family and the President's cronies were taking advantage of their favoured position to extract rent in a range of ways, some quite crude and amounting to little more than standover tactics. But for the vast bulk of the Indonesian population things continued to get better through the 1980s and 90s. Economic growth was strong and the benefits were spread widely despite the greed of those at the top. Across the country this was quite visible to the traveller over the years in terms of the standard of dwellings, vehicle numbers, dress, numbers and types of businesses and the goods in even small shops. Exports and imports soared. Government programs in education, health and agricultural improvement spread and produced real improvements.

There were sufficient instances of bitter resentment of grave injustice, such as the virtual seizure of peasants' land for private development by those with power and influence, including those who had access to the power and influence of the Soeharto family. But resentment was generally bottled up because resistance or public protest tended to be met with forceful and sometimes brutal repression. Despite this, it was the opinion of most observers that Indonesians overall were favourably disposed to the New Order which was delivering a better life to most of them and appeared to be leading the country towards a more prosperous and influential future.

This was the situation when Paul Keating took the Leadership of the Labor Party from Hawke and became Prime Minister in 1991. Keating inherited a foreign policy which had engaged Australia strongly with East Asia and, in Prime Minister Hawke's expressive term, sought to 'enmesh' Australia with that region. Regular talks at senior official and ministerial level were arranged and an Australia-Indonesia Institute was established to encourage and promote cultural and other projects. Also during the Hawke period there had been close cooperation in efforts to reach a settlement of the Cambodia issue and to agree bilaterally on a regime for the so-called Timor Gap. But Keating from 1992 raised the intensity, commitment and urgency of the relationship and placed Indonesia at the centre of his regional agenda. To that end he made a series of visits to Indonesia to consult with President Soeharto and took every opportunity to meet with the President at various international meetings attended by both of them. It was clear that Keating developed a close rapport with Soeharto and, especially at the Bogor summit meeting of APEC (Asia Pacific Economic Cooperation), worked particularly closely with him. Keating also made it clear in Australia that he saw Australia's interests as lying in close engagement with Indonesia in all fields and he expressed his impatience with the activists and protesters who, as he saw it, placed their perception of the interests of the East Timorese before the interests of Australia. He made it plain that he saw that issue as something on which history had turned the page. The summit of Keating's Indonesia diplomacy was the negotiation of the Agreement on Maintaining Security between the two countries at the end of 1995. This agreement was negotiated in secret, with the Australian negotiators being the former Chief of the Defence Force, General Peter Gration, and Allen Gyngell, Keating's foreign affairs adviser. When the Agreement was announced it appeared to be quite well received in Australia. The Opposition in Parliament supported it in substance as did most commentators in the media. But there were complaints about the secrecy of the negotiation. Early reactions possibly gave an inaccurate idea of the public reception of the agreement. In retrospect it is clear that it came as a real surprise, with nothing to prepare public opinion for such a radical step towards a country which had generally previously been thought of as much as a potential threat as a likely friend, and as a result it took some time to digest. The heavy defeat of the Keating government in the election in early 1996, although attributable to a number of factors, was probably a better guide to the public reaction than the rather muted immediate responses at the time of the agreement's announcement.

Keating's policy towards Indonesia and his close association with President Soeharto were in some respects reminiscent of Whitlam's similar cultivation of Soeharto twenty years earlier. But otherwise they were different from the mainstream of Australian policy towards Indonesia since independence. The consistent elements of that policy, pursued by successive governments, were to recognize the importance, present and especially prospectively, of Indonesia for Australia; to seek to limit and reduce differences and problems wherever possible, and where not possible (as with West Irian or confrontation of Malaysia) to isolate and try to compose those differences or in the end to live with an unwanted outcome; to seek to develop as wide a range as possible of shared contacts and interests as a foundation for building a growing relationship into the future. Keating went further than that, especially with the Agreement on Maintaining Security. His actions and his statements signalled a more intimate association, an Australian decision to throw in its lot with Indonesia in a more committed and unreserved way than ever before. There were and still are good reasons for doing that if and when it is feasible, and Keating's effort had much to recommend it. But the timing and urgency of his push to elevate the ties with Indonesia to a new level made it dependent on the continuation of political stability and of the central elements of the Soeharto outlook and policy mix. That was to bank on there being in due course a smooth transition from Soeharto to a new President and political establishment which would essentially share his outlook. As it turned out this was a higher risk strategy than could reasonably have been predicted at the time and it fell with the Soeharto presidency and the subsequent disasters over East Timor.

Gareth Evans[27] has claimed that it was only during his term as Foreign minister and the parallel appointment of Ali Alatas as Indonesian Foreign Minister in Jakarta that attention turned from the 'relationship' to its content and 'a mutual desire to build up the relationship, layer by layer, across a wide range of activities, including defence, culture and commerce'. Evans and Grant argue that Australia built up 'more substantial links in South-East Asia with Singapore and Malaysia', economically focussed 'overwhelmingly on Japan' and after 1972 directed enthusiasm towards establishing a substantial political and economic relationship with the People's Republic of China. They summarize all this with the observation that 'The relations that we went out of our way to cultivate in Asia always seemed to be with other countries' rather than Indonesia – until Evans arrived to correct the balance. This highly tendentious account ignores many years of effort some of which has been outlined in this chapter. And it is bizarre to criticize previous Australian policy for concentrating on developing economic relations with Japan, on its way to becoming the second largest economy in the world, rather than on Indonesia, whose economy Sukarno was proceeding to destroy. Throughout the most difficult years considerable effort was devoted to maintaining links with Indonesia, including economic links, and after the transfer of power to Soeharto Australia, as we have seen, was among the first small group of countries to join the initial efforts to help revive the economy. While Whitlam certainly devoted considerable effort to the opening to China that did not prevent him seeking to develop a close relationship with Soeharto and Indonesia. Indeed he was subsequently much criticized, including from within his own party, for allegedly having gone too far in that regard. In the 1995 edition of their book Evans and Grant conclude the section on Indonesia[28] with the claim that 'The days when the bilateral relationship was characterized, at best, by non-specific good-will and expressions of "good neighbourly relations" are now over. The last six years have been a period of rapid expansion as both Australia and Indonesia came to realise that they share an ever-expanding range of fundamental interests...The value of the ballast that has been laid down in recent times is that it should prevent any single problem in the relationship from assuming too much importance, as has occurred in the past...The situation today is very different.'

One can applaud Evans's intentions in all this while regretting and rejecting his denigration of all the work which had gone into the relationship over the four preceding decades. To imagine that nothing had been done to put 'ballast' into the relationship until he came along is pure hubris. He would have done better to have studied the history of the relationship in a more detached way and to have presented his own useful efforts in a more realistic light. He said that 'only a very large storm would seriously disturb' the relationship which he had made 'so much more substantial'. Unfortunately it was not long before such a storm blew up, Soeharto was swept away, the East Timor issue which Evans thought he had transformed in the relationship exploded, Alatas and many others in Indonesia savagely criticized Australia, and the relationship fell into a worse state than at any time since at least 1965. Evans's hyperactivity, precipitate judgments and over-confidence are warnings of the pitfalls in Australia's dealings with its neighbours, and especially with Indonesia.

The conservative coalition government under the Liberal Party leader, John Howard, has followed a much more muted course with Indonesia than did Keating. In early 1998 when the regional financial crisis struck Indonesia the Australian Reserve Bank urged the International Financial Institutions in Washington to act promptly to support the rupiah and the Indonesian financial system without imposing stringent conditions. The Foreign Minister, Alexander Downer, made follow-up representations in Washington, but it is unclear to what extent the Prime Minister and the Treasurer shared this concern. In any case the Fund, in concert with the US Treasury, continued a struggle with Soeharto and his advisers in an effort to leverage extensive change in Indonesian policies. While there was no doubt such changes were desirable the result was confusion and delay with consequential collapses of the value of the rupiah and of the viability of Indonesian entities which held dollar-denominated foreign borrowings. The situation went from bad to worse and led in May to the riots which forced Soeharto out of office, an outcome for which it was no secret there had been a desire in some influential quarters in Washington[29]. The East Timor issue dominated the relationship from 1999 and continues to cast a long shadow in both countries. But that has not been the only factor in the erosion in public support in Australia for close engagement with Indonesia and for putting more and more 'ballast' into the relationship. It is regrettable but hardly surprising that ordinary Australians, seeing nightly on their television screens scenes of violence and terror in East Timor, often involving men in Indonesian uniforms, should have reacted quite adversely in 1999. But subsequently they were exposed to extensive media reporting of a catalogue of awful events over many months including, for example, the horrors in Maluku and especially Ambon (an island relatively well known in Australia) where the Indonesian armed forces (TNI) appeared to defy the President's instructions to prevent the transport and arming of thousands of members of the so-called Islamic Jihad, recruited and trained in Java with the mission of attacking Christians. The image projected from Indonesia was a largely negative one, including violent demonstrations against Australia, stridently critical statements about Australia by Indonesian political leaders such as the Minister of Defence and repeated postponements of a visit to Australia by President Abdurrachman Wahid who eventually did make a lame duck visit shortly before his removal from office. His successor has made some progress in extending the authority of the government and in implementing reform measures agreed with the International Financial Institutions. A start has been made and hopefully it can be sustained. In the meantime much, including the judicial system, remains as bad as in the Soeharto period. It has been recognized that much of this is inevitable in a shift from an authoritarian system to a much more open and active democracy; but the violence and the elements of hostility towards Australia have created a much more reserved attitude in Australia towards Indonesia.

It is not surprising that, in those circumstances, a rather conservative Australian government, which in any case never had the commitment to the relationship with Indonesia which the Keating government had, should have decided that it was time for Australia to take a lower profile in Indonesia. Indeed that was in line with a good deal of the longer course of Australian policy towards Indonesia since the late 1940s which mostly sought to handle the relationship pragmatically, taking reverses when they came up as far as possible quietly and patiently while pressing ahead with initiatives which could be made acceptable to Indonesian governments at the time. The Keating period can be seen as to some degree an aberration both because it was more ambitious and because it was higher risk, depending as it did on the continuation in power if not of Soeharto personally then of a government with essentially the same orientation. Prime Minister Howard's dealings with President Habibie over East Timor were a departure too, and had far more dramatic and immediate consequences than he had expected or intended, and we shall examine that in the following chapter. In his book *Engagement* in 2000 Keating has discussed in detail his handling of the relationship with Indonesia and his relationship with Soeharto.

Paul Keating's own explanation and defence of the basis for his policy towards Indonesia in *Engagement* could in large part, with allowances for differences in times and circumstances, have been written by more than one earlier Australian Foreign Minister or Prime Minister. What was different about Keating was his intensity and urgency. But his intentions were sensibly in line with Australian long-term policy and interests and he certainly made impressive progress. He saw in a clear-minded way, which was not at all obscured or distorted by ideology, that

Soeharto and the New Order had made an enormous contribution to the economic development of Indonesia and to the advancement of the material and social welfare of its people. He leaves the impression that he had some sympathy with the view Soeharto put to him soon after he had been forced from office that 'he had believed the only way for Indonesia to get to prosperity was through security. Now people wanted to get to prosperity through democracy'[30]. Soeharto said Indonesia's growth and stability had been hampered as a result. Keating saw that Soeharto had delayed too long the demand in Indonesia for political change and evolution, especially from the expanding and better-educated middle class, and that he should have been able to 'bring himself to change a harsh and unworkable policy in East Timor'. But Keating's overall estimate of Soeharto's achievement is clearly positive: 'The record may be flawed but it is very substantial'. He specifically rejects the accusation that Soeharto was driven by greed. He enabled or at least permitted his family to make too much money. But 'Nation-building was really his mission in life'. Keating's judgement in these matters is a useful corrective to the current popular view in Australia and elsewhere that Soeharto was merely a predatory dictator and Keating is surely right that in the course of time the historical record will be brought back to a better balance.

The question remains whether Keating attempted to go too far, too fast with Soeharto. He recognizes the criticism that he 'over-personalized' the relationship with Indonesia, 'placing too much weight on my own relations with the President' but says that he knew that neither he nor Soeharto would be around for ever and 'no relationship between states can rely on evanescent personal contacts'[31]. His purpose was to use the relationship to seek 'structural changes' that would outlast both of them. As noted above that was a high risk endeavour because in the event of the overthrow of Soeharto's New Order such structural changes could be exposed to criticism or rejection by a new regime with different priorities and objectives. Was it worth the risk? Keating regards the Agreement on Maintaining Security as the most important 'structural' achievement in the relationship, and indeed it was seen on both sides as a watershed development when it was announced at the end of 1995. If it had survived and developed it might indeed have provided the basis for a shift of the relationship between the two countries to another level. Keating blames his successor as Prime Minister, John Howard, for the abrogation of the agreement during the East Timor crisis by President Habibie because at that time Howard said publicly that the agreement was 'irrelevant'. Keating believes that Howard should have challenged the Indonesian decision, meaning presumably that he should have asked Habibie to think again or to delay implementation of any step to end the agreement until the two sides could meet and discuss in a calmer atmosphere. While agreeing with Keating that it is regrettable that Howard described the agreement as irrelevant it is hard to imagine anything he could then have said that would have caused the Indonesian side, smarting from the unexpected outcome of the plebiscite in East Timor and resentment of international criticism, to reverse or delay the decision.

Keating's argument later that, in effect, his effort to build structural changes in the relationship was worth the risks involved has a good deal of plausibility. Certainly the financial crisis which was the undoing of the New Order and

Soeharto's nemesis was not anticipated. Right up to the eve of the crisis the IMF and the World Bank were praising Indonesia's macroeconomic management. Predictions by the IMF, which were widely publicized, had it that Indonesia would be one of the world's main economies early in the twenty-first century. In a very short time the outlook changed radically so that early in the year 2001 the political and economic outlook for Indonesia was reported as very grave with many predicting that the Republic would fall apart. Now it seems clear that a less adventurous policy would have been more prudent. Keating's argument at the time, that he had to move quickly because he knew that if he lost the election in early 1996 Howard and the conservatives would not pursue the same sort of active agenda towards Indonesia, was also plausible as a prediction of Howard's approach and policy. But of course it is now more difficult to sustain the argument that that was a sufficient reason for putting matters on fast forward and trusting that those who came after Soeharto, or unforeseen events, would not undo what Keating had hurried to put in place. In the light of what has happened it will be some time at least before it would be useful to seek to persuade the Australian public that their future requires them to establish a close and fraternal relationship with Indonesia. But decades of experience with Indonesia underline the importance and usefulness of the more modest objective of always extending sympathetic understanding for Indonesia's difficulties and for showing a readiness to be supportive and helpful. Above all it is essential for Australia to show respect for Indonesia and that is something which is sometimes absent now. There is now impatience on the part of some in and around government towards arguments that Australia must take pains to ensure that Australian policy and Australian attitudes towards Indonesia be seen to reflect respect and goodwill.

From the viewpoint of many Indonesians, Australia departed from that objective and policy in 1998 and 1999 with regard to the East Timor issue. It seemed likely that the relationship would be impaled on that issue for a long time, although Howard and his Foreign Minister, Alexander Downer, pronounced that the ending of Indonesian rule in East Timor would remove the major irritant in the relationship. Probably both views have some substance. There will for a very long time be resentment in some quarters in Indonesia. On the other hand there is an awareness that Australia has a useful voice, including notably in Washington, that Australia can thus be helpful indirectly as well as directly, and that Indonesia needs all the help it can get. The East Timor issue has left its mark also on Australian attitudes. There is a widespread feeling that responsible ministers and officials over many years closed their eyes to the abuses perpetrated by the Indonesian army under Soeharto's policy in the interests of seeking closer engagement with Indonesia. The very active lobby for East Timor independence had a growing and eventually decisive effect on Australian attitudes and policy. Their argument was that Australian policy from Whitlam on amounted to a shameful betrayal of the East Timor people who had fought unselfishly and loyally with the Australians against the Japanese. It is becoming better understood in Indonesia that no Australian government in 1999 could have stood by and done nothing in the light of the dreadful events in East Timor. The success of the Australian intervention had its positive side in Indonesia also. But what was perceived there as 'triumphalism' and self-congratulation by the Australian Prime Minister and others exacerbated Indonesian resentments. The next chapter examines the background and implications of these East Timor issues which have played so critical a part in Australia's relationship with Indonesia.

Outlook

It is almost inconceivable that Australia could win acceptance in a developing East Asian institutional framework without at least the acquiescence, and probably not without the active support, of Indonesia. That was achieved between Soeharto and Keating during the last years of the former's Presidency. But as we have seen it was transitory, and for two reasons. Firstly, President Soeharto was overthrown and the immediate aftermath created circumstances in which his successors could not have maintained the closeness of the 1995 relation with Australia even had they wanted to do so. Secondly, Australians turned against the sort of engagement with Indonesia which Keating had sought. Indonesia's reputation and standing in Australia have clearly gone down as the negative side of Soeharto's legacy and subsequent political and economic problems have been exposed.

For more than fifty years Australia has been devoting much of its diplomatic and other foreign policy efforts to the relationship with Indonesia. A sufficient reason for that would have been that Indonesia is a huge country lying right next to Australia, and different from Australia in challenging respects. But there have always been other reasons as well, involving Indonesia's place in the world and in the region. With the emergence of a nascent East Asian regionalism that second category of reasons becomes ever more important. However it does so at a time when the outlook seems less favourable and the opportunities seem to have diminished. There are more people in each country who have links with the other, more Indonesian students and more Australian tourists for example. But the great period of Indonesian scholarship in Australia and by Australians seems to have passed. The problem created by the refugee flow from Iraq, Iran and Afghanistan through Indonesia has generated an apparent opportunity for major cooperation between the two neighbours. But there is no sense of warmth or reaching out for a deeper engagement of interests and perspectives. Indeed on both sides there is a much more careful approach. That is more marked on the Australian side because of the contrast with the rhetoric of the Keating era.

The possibility of Indonesia and Australia reaching that deeper engagement of interests and perspectives seems as remote as ever it has. The way that affects perceptions of Australia's readiness for acceptance into an East Asian community can be illustrated by looking back on recent events. As we shall see in the next chapter, a significant body of opinion in Australia had long been preoccupied by the East Timor issue. No doubt there have been individuals in other East Asian countries who have closely followed Indonesia's difficulties in East Timor and other parts of the archipelago. But in no other country in the region has there been such critical and open attention as in Australia. There was no explosion of outrage anywhere else in the region such as there was in Australia at the events in East

Timor following the plebiscite in 1999. No other country in the region showed any desire to intervene in the matter until Australia forced the issue and others joined in under pressure, in order to make the Australian-led INTERFET less offensive to Indonesian sensibilities. There has never been a time when Australia has seemed more different, or more in contrast to the core ASEAN commitment of non-interference in the internal affairs of other regional members.

Notes

1 Levi, Werner (1958), *Australia's Outlook on Asia*, Angus and Robertson, Sydney, p. 180.
2 *Ibid.*
3 According to Herbert Feith, by July 1947 the Dutch had 150,000 soldiers in Indonesia. (See *The Decline of Constitutional Democracy in Indonesia*, Cornell University Press, Ithaca, 1962, p. 10.)
4 In January 1949 this was converted into a Good Offices Commission to assist the parties in implementing a further Council Resolution.
5 Evans, Gareth and Grant, Bruce (1995), *Australia's Foreign Relations in the World of the 1990s*, Melbourne University Press, Carlton, second edition, p. 199.
6 The Gallup poll results for the three polls (1945, 1947 and 1949) are set out in detail along with some useful comment on pp. 537-9 of Meaney, Neville (1985), *Australia and the World*, Longman Cheshire, Melbourne.
7 Albinski, H.S. (1959), *Australia's Search for Regional Security in South-East Asia*, PhD Thesis, University of Minnesota, p. 226. The same work, drawing on *Commonwealth Parliamentary Debates HR*, Vol. 186, March 6, 1946, p. 18, notes that (on the same day in the House) Prime Minister 'Chifley confessed that there was "a good deal of truth" in the charge that the Indonesians were ill prepared for self-government, but added that the old order could not be expected to obtain in post-war Indonesia as the Dutch yielded to irresistible nationalist demands, it is not realistic to offer succour to a policy of nationalist suppression'.
8 Marhaenism was the official ideology of Sukarno's party, the PNI. It was collectivist, nationalist, asserted democratic rights but opposed individualism and western liberalism.
9 Watt, Alan (1967), *The Evolution of Australian Foreign Policy 1938-1965*, Cambridge University Press, Cambridge, pp. 249-50.
10 Casey, R.G. (1958), *Friends and Neighbours* (Student Edition), Michigan State University Press, East Lansing, p. 140.
11 *Ibid.* and Watt, *op. cit.*
12 Feith, *op. cit.* p. 392.
13 *Ibid.*, p. 407.
14 Grant, Bruce (1964), *Indonesia*, Melbourne University Press, p. 158.
15 Watt, *op. cit.* p. 254.
16 *Ibid.*
17 Although Indonesia had already in previous years made what Feith called 'a series of experiments with infiltration into Irian' and in late October 1954 put 48 infantrymen ashore on the south coast (Feith, *op. cit.* p. 391); and both the President and Foreign Minister in 1957 had made ominous statements about what Indonesia might do if the United Nations persisted in failing to take up the issue in a substantive way.

18	Grant, *op. cit.* p. 162. Grant recounts that Townley lost his baggage and appeared at a Siliwangi Division training camp in Indonesian army clothing which added to Australian criticisms of the visit.
19	Some years later, reflecting on how the concept of 'colonialism' had been captured by the Asian and African countries with the support and encouragement of the Soviet Union Menzies referred to 'Dutch New Guinea' as an Indonesian colony. '...Nor was it rational for Sukarno of Indonesia to have invoked the passion against colonialism in order to support his claim to convert Dutch New Guinea into an Indonesian colony'. Menzies, R.G. (1967), *Afternoon Light: Some Memories of Men and Events*, Cassell, Melbourne, p. 232.
20	Watt, *op. cit.* pp. 264-5.
21	*Ibid.*
22	*Ibid.*
23	Source is a former Foreign Affairs officer who was in the relevant senior position at the time in the Department in Canberra. According to him the British raised the possibility of bombing targets in Indonesia precipitating some urgent consideration on the Australian side.
24	The writer and Harold Heinrich of the Australian Treasury were the Australian representatives at these meetings.
25	Dutch unhappiness with and protests against human rights abuses in Indonesia led to increasing friction to the point where the Soeharto Government declined to accept further Dutch aid or to sit under Dutch chairmanship. The IGGI was then transformed into a World Bank consultative group (such as operate for a number of aid recipient countries).
26	At one point during the rehabilitation of Iswahjudi it was estimated that a very large quantity of gravel for concrete would need to be obtained at substantial cost. The Australian Embassy reported to the Defence Department in Canberra that it was aware that AURI itself operated commercial gravel businesses in the area so that it might be appropriate to require them to provide the gravel for upgrading their own air base. A very firm cabled reply signed 'Tange' (then Secretary of the Defence Department) came back insisting that the original instructions be followed. The writer's recollection is that the reason given was the need to ensure that Iswahjudi, which was to be used by Australian pilots during the handover and training period, be completed to the requisite standard.
27	See Evans and Grant, *op. cit.* pp. 200-201.
28	P. 204.
29	See Dalrymple, F.R. (1998), 'Indonesia and the IMF: The Evolving Consequences of a Reforming Mission', *Australian Journal of International Affairs*, Vol. 52, No. 3.
30	Keating, P.J. (2000), *Engagement, Australia faces the Asia-Pacific*, Pan MacMillan, Sydney, p. 153.
31	*Ibid.*, p. 134.

Chapter 9

East Timor and the Watershed in Policy

A Special Australian Responsibility?

East Timor emerged as a major issue in Australian relations with Indonesia in 1975 and from then on has continued to trouble the relationship. Successive governments sought to discount it or remove it from the agenda, and Gareth Evans thought that that had largely been achieved with the Timor Gap Treaty, a cleverly contrived arrangement for setting the boundaries for exploration and exploitation of the oil and gas resources under the sea between East Timor and Australia. In the euphoria of the flowering of the Keating/Soeharto friendship East Timor appeared to be pushed further into the background. Keating spoke of the East Timor independence cause with some irritation and made it clear that he was not going to let Australia's relationship with a neighbouring country of more than 200 million people be made dependent on developments in a very small territory of a few hundred thousand, or by agitation about such developments. But the East Timor issue still simmered. Internationally Indonesia was unable to shake it off in the United Nations, in Washington or in Europe, and indeed in all those places in later years it attracted increasing attention. Nor were they able completely to suppress armed resistance in the territory itself. In Australia for some years it was a cause sustained largely by three or four Labor Party politicians, a former Australian Consul in Dili and a handful of others. Gradually it became a focus for a larger number of human rights activists and for increasing anti-Indonesian agitation and propaganda. In later years it provided much of the basis for criticism of Australian politicians and officials who were said to have advocated and carried out a policy of 'appeasement' of Indonesia involving acceptance of gross human rights and other violations by the Soeharto government and the Indonesian military. Much of that criticism was motivated and influenced by the campaign to force Indonesia to disgorge East Timor. It sought to shame Australia into reversing its long-standing policy of accepting the Indonesian incorporation of the territory. It had a cumulative effect in terms of troubling the conscience of a wide range of Australians in the media, the universities and the law and generated a ready response from many students. And it resulted in Australia being in the vanguard of increasing international scrutiny and criticism of the Indonesian performance in East Timor.

In 1998 and 1999 there was a series of changes in Australian policy which led, partly deliberately and partly driven inexorably by a chain of events, to a reversal of direction which has placed in question the previous nurturing of the relationship with Indonesia and possibly made it more than ever hostage to the future of East Timor. Those events, and the role Australia played in them, have been critical to saving East Timor from even greater loss of life and destruction, as well as to the emergence of East Timor as an independent entity. Within Australia there is, at a popular level, pride in what Australia achieved with INTERFET. But those who see all Australian policy on East Timor over the last twenty five years as betrayal and deceit still insist that 'East Timor is Australia's greatest foreign policy disaster of the last quarter of a century'[1]. While others might think themselves fortunate to have no worse a disaster than this with which to lament the quality of their governments' policies over a quarter of a century, it is certainly the case that East Timor has cost Australia dear over that period. That can be assessed in terms of our relationship with Indonesia, in terms of our acceptance in the East Asia region, and in terms of the expense and possible vexation we shall have to bear in the future in support of an independent East Timor.

So the East Timor issue has great importance in Australian foreign policy. It not only overhangs the Australia-Indonesia relationship, it is also central to the issue of whether Australian moral attitudes are compatible with acceptance in the Asian region. It thus casts light on the obstacles to Australia's engagement with East Asia as a whole by underlining the continuing differences between Australia and the countries of that region – not just differences of values but differences of expression and behaviour.

This chapter examines the emergence of East Timor as a critical issue for Australia and explores the policy problems it raised.

A vocal and effective group of activists have claimed that Australia betrayed the people of East Timor, or sacrificed them to Australia's concern not to prejudice the relationship with Indonesia. This was based on the assertion that Australia had a moral debt to the East Timorese arising from events in 1942 during the Pacific war, that Prime Minister Whitlam in 1974 and 1975 effectively acquiesced in the Indonesian seizure of East Timor and thus removed the potential inhibition of Australian opposition either in terms of leading international disapproval or in terms of some form of direct intervention, and that subsequent Australian governments until 1999 continued to decline to support the claims of the East Timorese independence movement against the Indonesian occupation. The vehemence and effectiveness of this as an appeal to Australian opinion was partly due to the assertion that Australia owed a major debt of honour and blood to the East Timorese people for the way in which, it was claimed, they supported Australian forces against the Japanese in Portuguese (East) Timor in 1942, suffering greatly in the process from deaths in action and retaliations of various kinds by the Japanese against the population. This wartime experience has been proffered as establishing a continuing Australian responsibility to the East Timorese, and a responsibility on which Australia for many years shamefully turned its back[2]. It has also been part of the case of the East Timorese activists in

Australia that the Japanese would not have invaded East Timor in early 1942 if Australian and Dutch forces had not entered the Portuguese colony first.

There is certainly substance in both these points but neither is as unambiguous as has sometimes been made to appear. Nor is the issue of Australian responsibility as simple and clear as it has often been represented. It is necessary to examine the grounds for what a recent official Australian account describes as the perception of guilt, for many Australians, arising from the 'belief that a people close to Australia's doorstep have had their wartime kindness and suffering on Australia's behalf repaid by betrayal'[3].

Over three decades critics of Australian policy towards East Timor have cited these events of 1942 as constituting a moral obligation on Australia to support and assist the East Timorese. Thus James Dunn, in his book *Timor: A People Betrayed*[4], refers to the Allied landing as having been made 'in disregard of the protests of Governor Ferreira de Carvalho, who insisted that their "protection" was unnecessary'. Dunn goes on to say that 'the Allied decision to intrude into East Timor and thus jeopardise its neutrality was based largely on speculation, and not hard evidence that the Japanese intended to invade and use the territory as a base for operations against Australia'. He refers to exchanges on the subject between Tokyo and Berlin and their reluctance to provoke the government in Lisbon by breaching the neutrality of Portuguese Timor. He argues that if the Allies had not intruded into the territory the Timorese 'would thus have been spared the devastating consequences of the military operations and the occupation'. A succinct version of the argument was given in *The Australian* on 13 June, 1997, by that newspaper's national affairs editor, Mike Steketee, in an article criticizing the government's reluctance to admit more East Timorese asylum seekers to stay as refugees in Australia. Steketee claimed that there was only 'one credible reason' for the government's position and that was 'good relations with Indonesia, which is less than keen on the idea of Australia allowing people to stay because, under the grounds for establishing refugee status, they have a well-founded fear of persecution in Timor'. In support of his argument that Australia had a moral obligation to these people Steketee claimed there was 'a debt that stretches back another three decades when, in a little known chapter of World War II history, Australian troops invaded East Timor, drawing the Japanese into a theatre of the war they otherwise might never have entered'. Steketee argues that East Timor would not have been exposed to Japanese invasion at all if Australian and Dutch troops had not moved into the colony ten days after Pearl Harbor. He and others have quoted a figure of 'at least 40,000' for the number of East Timorese who then died during the war; '8.5 per cent of the population in the 1930 census', although presumably not all of these died as the result of Japanese action.

It is no doubt true that, as Dunn says, the Australian reading of Japanese intentions was 'based largely on speculation', but it was not uninformed or baseless speculation. The security of East Timor 'had been an Australian preoccupation since Federation'[5] and early in 1941 'the Australian War Cabinet became increasingly concerned with the possibility of a Japanese attack on Portuguese Timor'. In view of increasing Japanese penetration an official of the Department of Civil Aviation, David Ross, was stationed in Dili with the dual role of assisting the regular Qantas flights between Singapore and Sydney which overnighted at Dili and to report secretly on political and economic developments. Among many other tasks Ross reported on the increasing number of Japanese flights and resident Japanese airline employees, and in due course the arrival of a Japanese Consul. In these months before the Pearl Harbor attack there was not only increasing nervousness on the Australian side about Japanese intentions, there was some evidence of increasing Japanese interest and activity in East Timor.

For years the Japanese sought to prepare for their conquest of South East Asia by various forms of penetration including a network of trading companies and often unprofitable commercial ventures throughout the region including in East Timor. In 1938 one of these companies obtained a controlling interest in SAPT, the government-owned agricultural company in East Timor. They also began a Japanese shipping service with ships 'clearly captained and crewed by Japanese naval personnel'[6] and then the shipping company (Nanyo Kohatsu) acted as agent for Dai Nippon Airways which in 1940 and 1941 made a series of flights on the route Kobe-Palau-Dili. The four-engined Japanese seaplanes used 'were in fact naval reconnaissance planes crewed by Japanese Naval Air Service personnel'[7]. Peter Hastings writes that

> In August and September of 1941, the Australian Government was much concerned to obtain agreement with Holland and Britain for the despatch of an Allied force to Portuguese Timor if there was (a) a German invasion or occupation of Portugal, (b) war with Japan without an invasion or occupation of Portugal, or (c) occupation of Timor by Japan irrespective of invasion or occupation of Portugal. The United Kingdom Government accepted the thrust of the argument but urged consultations with Portugal. These duly took place and on December 13 the Dominions Secretary informed Canberra that Portugal had agreed to the suggestion and had also 'agreed instruct Governor either to invite assistance or acquiesce in its being furnished'. On December 16 Canberra asked London to make sure that Portugal fully understood and agreed to the proposed plans. On the same day London cabled a draft of the statement which would be made to Holland and Portugal. On December 17, with British agreement, the 2/2 Australian Independent Coy together with Dutch troops landed near Dili where the Australian and Dutch commanders called on the Portuguese Governor and explained the situation[8].

But the Governor said he needed to consult Lisbon and it became clear that the Portuguese government was not agreeing with the move. There followed an angry message from Prime Minister Curtin to the Dominions Secretary[9] which 'amounted to a charge of British double dealing'[10]. The British had not wanted to draw attention to their role in the plan and had apparently not explained it frankly in Lisbon. Just as the Germans and Japanese had wanted to avoid antagonizing the Portuguese so too did the British. In their reply to Curtin the British expressed concern about 'the consequences to the general strategy of the war...if an amicable solution of the Portuguese Timor problem is not secured'. They feared that the Portuguese might break off relations with the United Kingdom and thus 'precipitate Axis penetration of the Iberian Peninsula'. That would make Gibraltar unusable as a base and would deny the Azores to the British. These were obviously huge consequences for the war at sea and for Allied communications and supply, though it is unlikely that the danger of such a reaction by the Portuguese would have lost anything in the telling in the British cable to Curtin. For their part the Portuguese announced that they were sending a force of 700 men to East Timor from Angola, when the Australian and Dutch forces were expected to withdraw and the Portuguese force would take over the defence of the territory. But when the Portuguese force was approaching Sumatra it was told by the Japanese that it would not be permitted to proceed and the Portuguese had little choice but to abandon the project. In thus preventing the Portuguese from asserting their authority and control in the colony the Japanese could also be said to have violated Portuguese neutrality, to have closed off the possibility of the removal of the allied forces and the restoration of the Portuguese control, and to have demonstrated their own intentions.

Whatever the consequences of the Australian move into East Timor it was seen at the time as a prudent measure taken, as the government thought, with the acquiescence of the Portuguese authorities and in line with the allied policy which proposed such a move in any one of three situations, the second of which had now occurred with the Japanese entry into the war. It needs to be remembered, too, that by the time the Dutch and Australian force was put into East Timor the Japanese had already embarked on their southwards thrust and for Curtin and his colleagues the situation was becoming daily more ominous. In the result the Australians were unable to do more than create a costly diversion for the Japanese in East Timor, but if it caused the Japanese to put 20,000 troops there that presumably meant 20,000 fewer in some other theatre further east. So what the Australians did seems reasonable and defensible in the circumstances of the time. But if they had not gone into East Timor would the Japanese have kept out too, respecting Portuguese neutrality? Was the Australian action responsible in this sense for the disasters and suffering which befell the people of Portuguese Timor during the Pacific war under Japanese occupation?

While it is not possible to say whether or how Japanese policy towards Portuguese Timor might have developed as the war proceeded it does appear that, at the outset, their intention was not to invade the colony. A recently published book[11] by Waseda University Professor Kenichi Goto shows that, in planning the advance into Dutch Timor, the Japanese army had placed Portuguese Timor outside the operation. The reasons mirrored those of the British already mentioned in their dealings with Portugal over Timor. The Japanese were concerned about the effects on the Axis' interests if the Portuguese were alienated and turned to the Allied powers. Germany had requested Japan not to violate Portuguese neutrality because of the possibility of the Portuguese offering the Azores to the Allies as a base. Secondly, Portugal, though a small country in Europe, had importance in the international political scene including with countries in the sphere of influence of the United States such as Brazil which had large numbers of Japanese people. Lisbon also had significance as an intelligence 'window to the West' like Bern and Stockholm. The sending of Australian-Dutch forces into the Portuguese colony on 17 December 1941, Goto records, was something that Japan could not ignore and brought about 'an important turning point in Japanese policy towards this territory'. The Portuguese had not done anything to hinder the allied forces and had not prevented them from interning Japanese residents and the Japanese Consul in what was a neutral country. There appears to have been some argument between those who saw the Allied incursion into Portuguese Timor and the Portuguese failure to prevent or even resist it as a sufficient pretext for Japan to regard its neutrality as no longer constituting an obstacle to Japanese action, and those who continued to attach weight to the factors already mentioned which had until then caused the Japanese to exclude Portuguese Timor from their plans. Thus Foreign Minister Shigenori Tojo argued firmly that diplomatic relations with neutral Portugal should still be given priority and that any move by Japan to advance on the Allied forces in Portuguese Timor should be preceded by a warning to Portugal so that it would not be represented as an invasion. Moto Sugiyama, Chief of the General Staff, objected that such a warning would endanger the Japanese landing which should be kept strictly secret. The Chief of the Naval Staff, Shushin Nagano, enthusiastically supported the army plans which accorded with the Navy's aim to mount operations against Australia.

On 23 January 1942 the arguments of the military were accepted and Imperial Headquarters decided that there would be no advance warning of the operation to the Portuguese. However another difficult issue now arose: what should be the policy after the objectives of the operation had been achieved and the Allied forces neutralized? Prime Minister and Minister for War Tojo argued that, when their objectives had been achieved and if Portuguese neutrality was guaranteed, the Imperial Army should withdraw from the territory. But the Navy took a different view, with Nagano demanding that the Portuguese territory be occupied for the longer term as a 'base of anti-Australian operations'. Goto in his book recounts that Nagano argued that what was happening in Portuguese Timor was a 'violation of Japan's justifiable actions' in the region and moreover Japanese people were imprisoned in that territory. He expressed extreme doubt whether Portugal had the strength to repulse allied pressure and the capacity to maintain security (in the absence of a Japanese occupying force). 'Heated argument' developed in the upper echelons of the government and military regarding this issue, continuing from the end of January through the beginning of February 1942. In the event the Japanese force had few problems in their initial landing but then had considerable difficulty with the Australians who went into the hills and fought a guerilla campaign for about a year.

The question whether the Japanese would have gone into Portuguese Timor had the Allies not done so can probably be answered in the negative if it is taken to refer to the time period of the developments just recounted. But given the strength of opinion in senior military and naval circles in Japan there would very likely have been demands on the Portuguese before long to permit facilities for Japanese military aircraft and so on. Moreover the porous border between West and East Timor might well have drawn the Japanese in from occupied Dutch Timor. Professor Goto in the book cited above describes the difficult course of Japan's relations with Portugal over the Timor territory after the insertion of the large Japanese force. Officially Japan respected Portugal's sovereignty but in reality they decided to ignore it or where necessary severely limit it[12] and this became the major point of argument between Portugal and Japan during the war. Then, after the Allies did reach an agreement with Portugal for use of the Azores, the arguments for restraint on the Japanese side would have anyway fallen away or been much less influential. Moreover, if the allies had observed Portuguese neutrality in Timor in the early months of the war, for how long would they have continued to do so with the Japanese bombing Darwin and with the war on Australia's doorstep? It seems unlikely that the war would have continued for long before one side or the other, or both, would have made some use of the Eastern end of the island. It is not hard to see why Macau was not drawn into the war, but it is more difficult to imagine that the Pacific war could have happened without spilling over into East Timor. That is not to argue that Australia did not carry away from the war some moral responsibility to try to ensure a decent future for the people of the territory. But it suggests that it is excessive to present the matter as though Australia had the predominant responsibility, or as though Australia should have placed this responsibility above other responsibilities and requirements of policy in its own and other interests. Portugal was the sovereign power in the territory, negligent for hundreds of years and thus responsible for its desperately backward state, and it was Japan which started the war and smashed its way down to the threshold of Australia.

The other issue on which the responsibility and betrayal cases have been constructed is the 'unstinting help' (Keating) or 'selfless support' (Dunn) which Timorese people extended to Australian soldiers who fought the Japanese in the hills until they were evacuated in early 1943. It is clear from the records of Australian soldiers involved that, especially in the early stages, there was indeed such help and support. That has been shared ground by most of those on both sides of the argument about Australian support for the Timorese independence struggle against the Indonesians and Australian policy in that regard. But again the picture is not a clear and unambiguous one as such descriptions as 'unstinting help' or 'selfless support' would suggest. Those descriptions belong in the realm of wartime mythic images rather than reality. They are a partial reflection of the reality.

Most of the Australian 'Sparrow Force' consisted of the Tasmanian Second/Fortieth Battalion which was in Dutch (West) Timor. After the Japanese landed on 19 December they defeated and captured the Second/Fortieth Battalion by overwhelming numbers in an encircling movement. Some of the Australians and Dutch soldiers who had evaded Japanese and hostile Timorese got away to the East where they joined up with about 160 Australian commandos of the Second/Second Independent Company who had arrived with the Dutch near Dili on 17 December and then withdrew after the Japanese in much greater strength forced the small Allied force out of the town and surrounding areas. This Second/Second force began guerilla operations in February 1942 which they continued until September, when they were mostly replaced by the Second/Fourth Independent Company. They were effective and caused a large number of enemy casualties. This was the more remarkable because until April they had no radio communications with Australia and were under great pressure. David Ross, the Consul, who had remained in Dili, was sent into the hills by the Japanese commander to contact the Australians and demand their surrender. To his surprise he found them in good spirits and still an organized fighting force. They refused surrender and Ross was sent again in late June and again they refused; but this time Ross did not return to Dili because by then the Second/Second had established a radio link and he was able to arrange evacuation by the Australian navy. Certainly in the early months of the operations of the small Australian Second/Second force the Timorese who assisted them did indeed perform in the way suggested by the 'selfless support' image. Partly this was due to the help of officers of the Portuguese colonial administration[13]. The Australian official war history, referring to the situation in late May of 1942, presents a picture of the Second/Second as 'a picturesque band, tattered, bearded, each man accompanied by one or more loyal natives (creados) to assist and serve him personally'[14]. There can be no doubt about the importance of the role played by these *creados* or of the extent to which the effectiveness and indeed survival of the Australians depended on them. They carried the commandos' heavier gear so ambushes and escapes could be more effective; they guided commandos both on marches and during close escapes, occasionally dying themselves to save the Australian, and stayed with their 'master' for every moment until his evacuation or death. In a number of personal accounts members of the Second/Second – Archie Campbell[15], Sir Bernard Callinan[16] and C.B. Doig[17] – provide testament to the importance of these Timorese.

But a couple of months later the mood of the native Timorese was changing. There was a lull in Japanese activity in July as they received and absorbed reinforcements for an offensive in August. Sir Bernard Callinan, commander of the Australian force, writes that at this time 'reports were coming in of native treachery, ambush positions given away to the [Japanese], and refusal of food and assistance'[18]. (This refers to the East Timorese; all accounts agree that the West Timorese were hostile all along). Callinan reported that at this time the Japanese began the tactic of telling the native East Timorese that Australians were devils and offering 100 patacca (eight Pounds) on the head of each Australian[19]. The August offensive saw the Japanese enlisting native Timorese who were required to move ahead of the Japanese flushing out ambushes, resulting in much higher casualties among the Timorese than the Japanese. The Australian official history explains the shift in Timorese attitudes to the Australians in terms of their assessment of the latter's prospects: 'the locals reasoning that surely, this time, the end had come for the Australians and no sensible man would side with the losers'[20]. That some Timorese remained loyal to the Australians until the end suggests that the inevitability of Japanese victory over the Australians was not the only factor present and that differences of religion, tribe, region and exposure to the Japanese were probably also relevant. Inter-Timorese fighting fomented by the Japanese reduced the food supply and made the locals more reluctant to provide sustenance for the Australians. By October the Australians were fighting hostile bands of Timorese. By November, when the Second/Second had been mostly relieved by the Second/Fourth, it was clear that Australian defeat was only a matter of time[21].

The Australian Defence Association, in a submission to the Senate Foreign Affairs, Defence and Trade Committee Inquiry into East Timor in 1999 presented the following analysis:

Much has been made of an alleged Australian obligation to the Timorese because of their support for the Australian commandos against the Japanese occupation force. This has become an Australian myth, much more so than a Timorese one. No one can deny that, for some months in 1942, the small Australian force did enjoy substantial intelligence and logistical support from the Timorese. But this was encouraged by Portuguese colonial officials who were quickly marginalised by the Japanese. The occupation government consciously set out to exacerbate the existing divisions in Timorese society to destroy the support for the Australians. As the histories make clear, the Australians withdrew the commandos early in 1943 for a number of reasons but one critical one was that they no longer enjoyed local support. Indeed, by fostering civil war, the Timorese managed to inflict most of the casualties of the time on themselves. It is also a matter of historical record that every Allied intelligence party infiltrated into Timor until the end of the war was routinely betrayed to the Japanese. So much for an Australian obligation[22].

This account reflects some of the information which has been disregarded by the East Timor activists in Australia. But it is unsympathetic to the Timorese, for example by referring to the East Timorese 'fostering a civil war'. Tribal fighting had been endemic for hundreds of years and the Portuguese had been able to rule the colony for so long because they pursued a divide and rule policy, arming and using neighbouring rulers and tribes against those who caused serious problems. The Japanese followed much the same course. None of this alters the fact that *creados* gave indispensable support to the Australians and many of them died or suffered as a result, as did their families. Clearly there was more East Timorese blood shed and more damage to their livelihood in 1942 at least than if the Australians had never been there at all. It is also clear, and understandable, that at a certain point in 1942 the tide turned and the environment began to be hostile for the Australians. By August the native Timorese had transferred their fear from the Portuguese to the Japanese and, with the exception of the declining number of *creados* who remained attached to the Australians, and a small number of other supporters, the Timorese were cowed and enlisted by the Japanese. It needs to be remembered too that these were people with perhaps a five per cent literacy rate and no education who would have had little conception of any difference in doctrine or cause between the two sides. Australian personal accounts tell of unbridled Japanese brutality against natives and the families of natives suspected of hiding information. It is understandable that support for the Australians dried up.

Again on this issue it seems an exaggeration in the light of what happened to assert that Australia has a more or less unlimited moral obligation to the people of East Timor because of the help given by the *creados* and some others to some 150 Australian soldiers over much of the period of twelve months during which they were active, and because of the suffering those people and their families continued to endure at the hands of the Japanese after the Australians had left. The events of 1942 did establish an obligation which we now can recognize more easily than would have been the case for Australians at that time. But there has over the years been plenty of legitimate room for disagreement as to how that could best be discharged.

1975

In 1943 the British reached an agreement with Portugal about use of the Azores and in that context Dr Evatt as Minister for External Affairs agreed to a special assurance to the Portuguese government that Australia had no designs on Timor after the war[23]. Later there was some argument between Spender for the Opposition and Evatt about this undertaking and some discussion about the possibility of including Timor in the Australian Naval Station. But after the war Australia soon lost active interest in the territory.

With the emergence into independence as Indonesia of the Netherlands East Indies, and Australia's role in that historic development, there was a new focus which displaced the lingering wartime strategic interest in Portuguese Timor. And the Portuguese for their part were more than content to return to the old somnolent colonial ways with little or no outside intrusion into their remote possession. It is worth noting that Australia's championing of Indonesia's independence was conducted by the Chifley Labor government in which the Minister for External Affairs was H.V. Evatt who was in some ways a precursor of E.G. Whitlam and Gareth Evans in his intellectual eminence in the law and the way he carried that over into foreign policy making. At that time leaders of the conservative side of Australian politics expressed apprehension and reservations about the ending of Dutch rule in what was to become Indonesia. Both Menzies and Spender made speeches to that effect. So the Indonesian cause and focus came to be seen by some influential figures on the Labor side of politics as a particularly Labor contribution to the shaping of Australia's foreign policy and place in the region. When Whitlam became Prime Minister in 1972 he had already visited Indonesia several times and was better informed and prepared on that subject than any of his predecessors. He was, as he later wrote, 'determined to restore the trusting relations with Indonesia which Australia had established in the later 1940s'[24]. He visited Indonesia in February 1973 and had further meetings with President Soeharto in Wonosobo in Java in 1974 and in Townsville in 1975. Whitlam related strongly to Soeharto (and continued to do so long after the seizure of East Timor) whom he admired and trusted. It was inevitable that he saw the developments of 1974 and 1975 in East Timor very much with an understanding of the problems which they constituted for the Indonesian leader.

Whitlam had come into office in 1972 determined to make major changes to Australian foreign policy and to the way Australia conducted itself in the region and the world. An aspect of that was a desire to establish independent and stronger relations with the region, and especially with China and Indonesia. He also made a much greater effort to understand the point of view of those countries than any of his recent predecessors. At the same time, in regard to Indonesia and the East Timor issue, he was influenced by strong feelings about the way in which the Menzies Government had handled the issue of Dutch New Guinea, when Australia, insisting on self-determination, had been left, along with the Dutch, as virtually the last obstacles to the Indonesian claims, bypassed by the United States and all of Asia. Moreover, as the published documents show, Whitlam and his advisers saw East Timor as part of 'the Indonesian world' and a territory which, in its post-colonial phase, belonged with the rest of that Indonesian world. It now seems to many Australians that this was a mistake because a large majority of the East Timorese in the end, nearly a quarter of a century later, rejected incorporation in the Indonesian world. But if it was a mistake it was an understandable one. In 1975 there was what seemed a possible recent precedent in the Portuguese colony of Goa which had been seized by India and then settled into that huge country without much difficulty. And the formerly Dutch, western half of the island of Timor, which had many connections with East Timor, had become part of Indonesia when the country was established. Moreover East Timor was known as one of the most backward and neglected colonial backwaters in the world. Literacy was under five per cent, there was little infrastructure, the economy was very undeveloped and indices in such areas as public health were all among the lowest in the world. There had been no development of political opinion among the rural people who made up most of the population. The small articulate section of the population were mixed race men like Ramos Horta, the Carrascalaos and others who had been educated in Portugal or Macau. Against this background of policy, precedent and geography it would have been surprising if Whitam had not formed a preference for East Timor to join Indonesia and then argued that that was natural and proper.

The Army coup in Portugal in April 1974 brought a commitment to decolonization with extensive repercussions in Africa. Also in East Timor political parties were promptly formed and a period of manoeuvring between them began. This has been frequently recounted and need not be repeated here. The point of importance in our context is that the Indonesian government appears not to have had any prior ambition or intention to take over Portuguese Timor. Had there been any such intention there would have been little to stop them earlier following the example of India with Goa, a course which would presumably have been welcomed by many countries and accepted by virtually all. However, with the radical changes in Lisbon following the coup, the Indonesians quickly became concerned by the fragility of Portuguese influence and commitment and the consequent exposure to the risk of a communist-influenced mini-state within the Indonesian archipelago. It was not territorial expansionism so much as apprehension about what might develop in East Timor, and the problems that might create for Indonesia and his New Order, that led Soeharto, after some hesitation, to agree to Indonesian intervention. Close military and intelligence advisers, especially Ali Murtopo, who had been deeply involved in the elimination of the PKI (Communist Party of Indonesia) and its affiliates from the Indonesian body politic after the crisis of 30 September 1965, urged the President to sanction Indonesian action to ensure that with the departure of the Portuguese colonial administration East Timor would come under Indonesian control, by one means or another. Soeharto was initially cautious, apparently concerned primarily with Indonesia's reputation and the desire to avoid appearing expansionist with what that might imply for relations with others in the region whom he had taken pains to reassure after the adventurism of the Sukarno period.

But only a couple of months after the coup in Portugal the possibility of Indonesia initiating covert action to bring about integration was being discussed and by July the Australian Department of Foreign Affairs and the Australian

Embassy in Jakarta were in consultation about the implications of such a step. Harry Tjan, adviser to Ali Murtopo, had spoken to an official of the Embassy about a plan to develop by special operations support in East Timor for integration with Indonesia. In this plan a role was envisaged for Australia in 'neutralizing' unfavourable opinion in third countries, reassuring Papua New Guinea, and smoothing the way in the United Nations. Tjan appears to have felt encouraged in making this approach by a discussion he had had with the late Peter Wilenski[25], then Principal Secretary to Prime Minister Whitlam. The response to this from the Department of Foreign Affairs in Canberra[26] was that 'Australia could not afford to be associated with an Indonesian covert operation because of the risk of exposure, if for no other reason. Any hint of Australian involvement or even acquiescence would be damaging to the government's reputation overseas, to its domestic credibility and to the confidence in us of small countries, especially PNG'. Therefore 'we should not encourage the Indonesians in any way to talk to us along those lines'. The Department's disposition at that time (July 1974) was to counsel 'patience all round', continued emphasis on self-determination, preservation of the option of 'an independent Portuguese (sic) East Timor'. Ambassador Furlonger in Jakarta at the end of July wrote another Top Secret letter[27] to G.B. Feakes, Head of the relevant division in Canberra, in which he discussed the line which should be taken with President Soeharto by Prime Minister Whitlam on his forthcoming visit. Furlonger said he thought that 'the very least Soeharto would expect from us would be to share his judgement that it would be in the interests of the region – not only Indonesia – if Portuguese Timor were to become part of Indonesia'. Furlonger proposed that the Prime Minister should say he shared that assessment and then 'qualify it by saying that, in the modern world, self-determination cannot be ignored, and that there could be problems in bringing about union. This could in turn open up the question of independence and other options'.

This might have been seen as a good tactical approach for the Prime Minister to take without prejudice to the emphasis Feakes had placed on self-determination and on the independence option. But it also implicitly put the stronger emphasis on the proposition that absorption of East Timor by Indonesia would be in the interests of the region, including Australia. This became the dilemma for Australian policy on the issue, exacerbated by the way in which the Indonesians now placed increasing pressure on Australia to shift from the patient, wait and see policy to one of greater commitment to what was emerging as the dominant Indonesian objective – absorption of East Timor. The brief[28] prepared for Whitlam for his visit to Indonesia in September 1974 drew heavily on what Harry Tjan, the key Indonesian adviser, had told the Embassy and then the Department of Foreign Affairs when he visited Canberra on Soeharto's instructions to sound out the ground before Whitlam's visit. Tjan had said that Portuguese Timor had become an urgent issue for Indonesia, partly because there was suspicion that Australia might be embarking on a policy which would in one way or another obstruct the Indonesian objective and partly because of a growing conviction that the Portuguese were on the point of abandoning Timor to the independence party. The Department's brief went on to suggest a number of points which the Prime

Minister might make to Soeharto including that 'we are committed to decolonization in Portuguese Timor on the basis of valid self-determination'.

It is difficult to be sure to what extent Tjan, and other key Indonesian interlocutors, were seeking to explore the extent of Australian and other international opposition to the proposals they were putting to the President and to what extent they were seeking to draw the Australians into a position where they would be more or less complicit in a rapidly maturing Indonesian project to seize East Timor. But the official documentary record shows that there was uneasiness about the latter possibility. What it also clearly confirms is Whitlam's preference for integration of East Timor with Indonesia and the way in which that cast some ambiguity on the other plank of his East Timor policy – the emphasis on self-determination and the warning to Soeharto that an Indonesian seizure of the territory would damage Indonesia's standing in Australian public opinion. The Australian record of the Whitlam/Soeharto meeting at Wonosobo on 6 September 1974 contains the following paragraph:

> The Prime Minister noted that, for the domestic audience in Australia, incorporation into Indonesia should appear to be a natural process arising from the wishes of the people. He recalled adverse public opinion towards Indonesia which had arisen almost twelve years ago...in relation to Irian Barat. There was suspicion of Indonesia and its methods in effecting the return of the province. The Prime Minister said that he personally had expressed himself in favour of the return of Irian Barat to Indonesia...Indonesia should be aware, however, of the effects on public opinion in Australia of incorporation of the province into Indonesia against the wishes of the people[29].

Later the same month, back in Canberra on 24 September, Richard Woolcott who was shortly to succeed Furlonger in Jakarta, recorded for the Secretary of Foreign Affairs 'that the Prime Minister put his views on this subject frankly [in discussion with Woolcott and Feakes the previous night] in the following way: "I am in favour of incorporation but obeisance has to be made to self determination. I want it incorporated but I do not want this done in a way which will create argument in Australia which would make people more critical of Indonesia"'[30].

This ambiguity has been interpreted by the critics of Whitlam's approach to the issue as virtually consigning self-determination to fig leaf status and as constituting part of a pattern of Australian 'diplomatic deceits'[31]. Whitlam no doubt believed he was doing the best he could, in the context of a policy of seeking to establish Australia as an accepted member of the region, to get the best outcome for all concerned including the people of East Timor. And it is incorrect to assert that the Indonesians were not told that Australia expected them to ensure that there was a defensible process of ascertainment of opinion in Portuguese Timor. Thus in July 1975 the Embassy was instructed, with the authority of the Minister for Foreign Affairs, in the following terms:

> reiterate to Tjan and other relevant Indonesians that, if Indonesia acts as Tjan forecasts, she will precipitate serious problems in relations with Australia. The Australian Government could not condone the use of force in any form[32].

The embassy assured the department that Tjan spoke with authority about Indonesian plans and policy on East Timor, that the Embassy had told him and others of 'our worries and our fears' about the effects on the relationship with Australia, and that Tjan had acknowledged that Australia would be 'their greatest problem'. The implication was that it was a problem Indonesia could live with. In the meantime, according to the embassy, other key embassies in Jakarta were treating Timor almost as a taboo subject – the ASEAN states, the United States, the Netherlands and the British: 'They know what is inevitable, and they attach a higher importance to their long term interests in Indonesia'. The embassy thought Australia was 'getting more and more active and increasingly involved as a party principal' which risked 'trapping ourselves in a corner'[33]. There might have been something of a problem for the Indonesians to interpret the Australian position in the light of the signals they were getting. But the emphasis at the Prime Ministerial level was certainly on incorporation.

While self-determination is a right enshrined in the UN Charter and elsewhere it is at least unclear whether in 1974/75 it had any particular resonance in East Timor. Fretilin seems to have had no intention of holding any ascertainment of popular opinion on the future of the territory, as indicated by the communique they issued with UDT in January 1975 and by what Ramos Horta said in Canberra the previous month to the effect that 'he saw no need for an election or plebiscite: Fretilin's goal of independence was supported by the people and that was that'[34]. That was the pattern followed in Portugal's African colonies. In August 1975, after prolonged manoeuvring, covert Indonesian intervention, and fighting between the Timorese factions, Mr Whitlam made a statement in the House of Representatives in which he said:

> It is a matter of record that none of the three major political groups in the territory has shown any genuine willingness to work with the others. Each demands that it alone be recognised as the sole legitimate nationalist group. None seems prepared to test its claims to lead the country through any conventional form of democratic process[35].

Subsequent critics have sometimes assumed that self-determination would inevitably have produced independence under Fretilin but that is by no means clear. Much would have depended on the extent to which parties were supported from outside, and it seems implausible to suggest that in early 1975 East Timor was swept by nationalist fervour, even though that was no doubt observable in the Fretilin elite leadership in Dili[36].

The real issue is rather the policy of favouring incorporation of East Timor in Indonesia. Was it morally defensible and was it in the interests of Australia and the other parties concerned? Whitlam and advisers like Woolcott thought the answer to both these questions was affirmative, and it is not hard to see why. In the first place, as stated above, they looked at the matter in the context of Australia's desire to establish itself as a member of the region. Secondly, although to a lesser degree than the Indonesians, they thought there was substance in the concern that a separate East Timor could be an unpredictable source of instability either by attracting interference by outside big powers (the stated main Indonesian worry) or by lapsing into internal strife, a condition to which it was certainly prone. Thirdly, they thought that if East Timor passed to Indonesia the Indonesians would make a major effort to treat the new province well and to integrate it as smoothly as possible into the national fabric. It is on this third matter that Australian policy foundered.

On 6 December, 1975, having just been informed by the office of the Indonesian Defence Minister that Indonesia was about to launch an invasion of East Timor, Woolcott, now ambassador in Jakarta, cabled Canberra and the incoming Fraser government. He argued that Fretilin and UDI (not Australia) should bear much of the responsibility for what was happening. Fretilin 'should have sought an accommodation with its large and powerful neighbour in the first place and those who discouraged it from this course in the early days ultimately did the party a disservice' and it was 'the folly of the UDI which triggered off the present situation'[37]. He painted in stark terms the choice for Australia of 'our relations with Indonesia and integration [of East Timor] on the one hand and, alternatively, support for Fretilin and moral objections to Indonesia's means on the other'. In terms which have been much discussed over the years since the cable was leaked Woolcott described this as 'a choice between a pragmatic and realistic acceptance of what is going to happen and our longer term national interest, on the one hand, and on the other, a moral and principled stand about the means to the accepted end which might ease our national conscience but which is unlikely to have an effect on what actually happens and which would erode our relations with Indonesia. It is really a choice between a pragmatic realistic position and a principled but ineffective posture'[38].

In the light of subsequent events Woolcott's formulation has been exposed to the charge that the course he recommended was 'Neither principled not pragmatic'[39]. It has also frequently been reviled as simply *un*principled and stigmatized as 'a shabby act of appeasement' (Maley), 'betrayal' (Dunn *et al.*), 'deception' (Tiffen *et al.*) and so on. But the real weakness of this and other related communications was that the choice was not as stark as he described it. Governments seldom make decisions on the basis of principle alone and when they do the result is often dreadful. On the other hand, assertions that some course is only realistic and pragmatic usually need to be deconstructed to establish what is at issue. The question is whether, in 1975 in the case of East Timor, it would have been possible to devise and carry out a policy which did not commit Australia irrevocably to either side of the argument and left the government in a position where it could calmly and patiently urge all parties to hasten slowly towards a resolution of the issue without Australia being drawn into a hazardous role and without destroying the relationship with Indonesia. That was clearly what Foreign Affairs was hoping to do earlier in 1974 when Feakes was discussing such a policy with Willesee and with the Embassy. It would have needed superior judgment and greater resolution to carry through with Tjan and others skilfully exploiting the anxieties and probing the weaknesses on the Australian side. But it would have been better in the long run than plumping for the Indonesian case even after the invasion. As indicated above the problem with the course that was taken was not that it was immoral or unprincipled but that it left Australia's credibility and the respectability of the policy dependent on the Indonesian behaviour in East Timor.

As Woolcott himself observed 'As it turned out neither independence under Fretilin nor integration could be achieved without the use of force'[40]. We cannot know whether Fretilin would have been able to preserve the apparent calm in the territory which existed briefly between the defeat of the main UDT forces and the Indonesian invasion or whether there would anyway have followed years of civil war or internecine fighting in the hills and forests. But it seems unlikely that Fretilin and a continued low level resistance by UDT and other opposed elements would have resulted in such massive loss of life as did the Indonesian occupation under General Moerdani and his successors. As it was, given the policy Australia followed and the Indonesian invasion, everything depended on Indonesia either achieving a quick and complete military resolution or soon establishing a settlement with the indigenous leadership on terms which gave them confidence that they could expect a good place and decent treatment for East Timor in the Republic of Indonesia. It needed to be made clear from the beginning that there was to be an honourable place for the people, their culture and language and with a respected Timorese as Governor, with a good measure of autonomy. Things might well then have settled down. According to Woolcott, the Indonesian commander, General Moerdani, gave him a strong personal assurance that Indonesia would treat the East Timorese people well and would seek to ensure their welfare and progress in Indonesia[41]. But General Moerdani and the Army were in effect allowed to run the territory for years and, even though every effort was made to conceal what was happening, it gradually became clear that the principal means of pacification and control were the brutal use of force, destruction of crops and villages and relentless attempts at search and destroy using aircraft as well as ground forces.

Australian government policy under successive governments continued to seek to build on the promising foundations of the relationship which Prime Minister Whitlam had established with President Soeharto. The objective was to develop a broader base for the relationship and a network of shared interests. It was hoped and indeed expected that over time the problem of East Timor would fade into the background of this wider, stronger relationship as the Indonesians gradually established an acceptable regime in East Timor and as the East Timorese accommodated to their membership in the Indonesian Republic. It was thought that the best way to promote this was to intensify the contact and exchange of views between the two governments, their representatives and their armed forces. It is possible to see this motive at work in the reports of Ambassador Woolcott's discussions with Indonesian interlocutors reproduced in the DFAT Documents volume. On a number of occasions he is at pains to emphasize that the Indonesian interlocutor is speaking 'frankly' or that the discussion was 'very frank'. Such protestations are worrying to the professional ear. Why was it necessary to make them? Was it to reassure Canberra that the Indonesian side was not baiting a trap or just responding with formulae which were designed to fob Australian off while, if possible, putting the enquirer on the wrong foot? In any case the Indonesians were notably uncommunicative and unhelpful to the Australian side over a number of years on the subject of East Timor after 1975. The Australian side had rather more knowledge of what was happening than what has been published in the DFAT Documents volume because of their intelligence reporting which of course has not been published. But, at least in the early eighties[42], that did not give a very full picture of what was happening in East Timor. Critics have tended to make much of the failure of Australian government to bring Indonesia to account on the basis of Australian intelligence information, especially in the period between the cross border incursions at Balibo and elsewhere and the full scale invasion. But it is not realistically or reasonably to be expected that an Australian government should have accused the Indonesians of lying on the basis of information we had acquired by secret and unacknowledged means.

After the occupation there were of course regular attempts to access Indonesian thinking on East Timor and Indonesian interlocutors often provided information. No doubt there was a good deal of obfuscation and plain lying on the Indonesian side about what was happening inside the territory, but there were also occasional more reliable responses on the progress of the military campaign and other matters. However the Indonesian authorities refused to permit any Australian aid projects in East Timor, for years insisting that any such aid should be channelled through the (Indonesian) Red Cross. Moerdani let it be known that he harboured suspicions that Australia was spying and giving covert assistance to East Timorese by aircraft and submarines and it was said by other Indonesians working with him on East Timor that he attributed the confusion of the rather botched Indonesian invasion partly to Australian advance information which had allegedly been given to Fretilin[43]. After an initial period of appraisal and reserve by the Fraser government it and its successors took the view that the Indonesian seizure of East Timor was irreversible and that it was therefore in the best interests of all concerned, including the East Timorese, to work quietly to establish Indonesian confidence in the Australian desire to help develop the territory and to see it become a peaceful province drawing on the social and development programs then increasingly being deployed across the archipelago. Specific aspects of policy followed from that, including the controversial efforts over the years (long obstructed by General Moerdani) to develop cooperation and defence assistance with the Indonesian armed forces.

Until probably 1998 the priority of Australian policy was to build and cement stronger relations with Indonesia across the widest possible range of activities and interests. This was not seen as being in conflict with seeking a good outcome for the East Timorese within Indonesia but as contributing to that objective because it would give Australia more leverage with the Indonesian government and military. Given the reservations on the Indonesian side, especially on the part of Moerdani and the military, about Australian interest in East Timor, instructions to the Embassy to make enquiries and representations about the situation meant an approach from a weak position which required polite persistence and avoidance of confrontation even when one knew that what one was being told was untrue. Inevitably there were those in Australia who naively looked for a key to early access to the real information and thinking of those who were running the show on the Indonesian side. As a result certain claims to have influence with General Moerdani because of past association were given quite unwarranted credence. For all the Australian efforts over the years there was little sign of any improvement in the Indonesian handling of the situation in East Timor. We thought that matters were improving during the nineteen eighties but the Santa Cruz incident seemed to signify that they were as bad as ever[44]. The Indonesian enquiry afterwards was claimed by Evans as a step forward because it put military officers and personnel in effect on trial; but their sentences were light and far less severe than the sentences on some of the Timorese civilians involved in the procession to the Santa Cruz cemetery.

By 1995 there was increasing speculation that Soeharto was preparing to settle the East Timor problem on the basis of an agreement with Portugal which would open the way for a United Nations sponsored plebiscite on the future of the territory. But asked directly about this by one[45] of a group of senior Australian editors and journalists who met with him the President said he would not agree to East Timor separating from Indonesia. By that time the East Timor issue had achieved a much higher profile than it had had since 1975. But even so it was not prominent on the world map of trouble spots.

In the meantime the policy of successive Australian governments appeared to have achieved its objectives. There is no doubt that the relationship between the two countries had become closer and stronger despite the East Timor issue. But for most of the East Timorese things had not improved. For the Indonesian army it was a matter of the same policy of exploitation and suppression. They controlled the export of sandalwood and coffee as they had since the seizure of the territory. And they profited greatly from the monopoly which their joint trading company had on most imports. Part of the capital accrued from these operations was invested in the casino on Christmas Island, an Australian possession. It is not clear what view the Australian government took of that, or to what extent there was interest in it – a matter which has attracted surprisingly little attention by the Australian media.

Although it was clear that powerful interests in the Army would resist a negotiated withdrawal from East Timor there was a growing number of younger officers who argued that the cost, in terms of Indonesia's international reputation, and in terms of the disproportionate allocation of resources to East Timor, of continuing to hold down a disaffected population was no longer worth while. Although in Soeharto's last years there were negotiations with Portugal and the United Nations, and persistent rumours that the President himself was looking for a way out, it is quite unlikely that Soeharto would have agreed to any resolution which involved East Timor ceasing to be a Province of the Republic of Indonesia. The main hope was that he would agree to an autonomy arrangement which would place the province unambiguously under civilian jurisdiction and withdraw the military control which had been and continued to be the central problem. But if Soeharto was moving towards such a solution he moved too slowly, and he ran out of time. A complicating factor for him might have been that his son-in-law, General Prabowo, was deeply involved in all aspects of the military control of East Timor.

In assessing Australian policy on this issue from 1974 to 1996 it is now often suggested that the course of events in East Timor would have been different if Australia had not supported the incorporation of the territory in Indonesia. But it is

not clear that a different position by the Whitlam government and its successors would have made much difference, or indeed any difference, to what happened. What if Whitlam had reversed the order of priorities and said that:
i. The key thing for Australia was for Portuguese Timor to have the opportunity to determine its own future and
ii. if they then decided to accept an Indonesian invitation to join the Republic that would be welcomed by Australia?

In the light of what we know of Indonesian thinking about the unfolding situation during 1975 it is unlikely that such a stand by the Australian Prime Minister would have made a difference to what happened. As it was, the Indonesians were told that the use of force would cause a strong reaction in Australia and that clearly did not deter them. If Australian policy were to have had any chance of preventing an Indonesian seizure of East Timor in the circumstances which gradually developed through 1975 it would have had to be firmly, actively and openly opposed to what the Indonesians were preparing to do. It would have been necessary at a minimum to seek to mobilize international support for opposing Indonesian seizure of East Timor. However none of Indonesia's other neighbours would have participated and it is unlikely that many, or even any, other members of the then IGGI, the aid group for Indonesia, would have done so. The United States was aware of Indonesian planning and did not object, and later urged the Fraser government not to make any problems for the Indonesians.

Thus it seems unlikely that any Australian diplomatic measures would have prevented the Indonesians from moving ahead with the invasion once they had decided not to permit a Fretilin-dominated independent East Timor to arise in the Indonesian archipelago. The critics of the Whitlam policy do not assert that Australia should have launched a military campaign to assist Fretilin and seek to prevent the Indonesians from invading or from consolidating the invasion. Australia would have had a capacity to make the Indonesian invasion at and around Dili very problematic. But it might not have had either the will or the capacity to maintain a long campaign on the ground in East Timor resisting Indonesian incursions across the land border and by sea. Would the Australian people have supported what would in effect have been war with Indonesia over East Timor? Clearly not.

1999

As discussed in the last chapter, the Agreement on Maintaining Security at the end of 1995 was the high point of the Keating policy of building the Australian relationship with Indonesia. Changes in both countries then affected the relationship. A conservative Coalition government under John Howard replaced Keating's Labor Party government in early 1996 and the financial crisis which struck Indonesia the following year led in May 1998 to Soeharto's replacement by the Vice-President, Dr Habibie. Howard's approach to Indonesia was more measured than Keating's and his agenda did not include the sort of engagement which Keating had developed with Soeharto. But the tentative moves which had been under way in Soeharto's last years as President to find a solution to the East Timor problem accelerated under Habibie. The negotiations with Portugal and the United Nations by Foreign Minister Alatas, who had stayed on after Soeharto's resignation, gained momentum and Habibie offered a measure of autonomy for the territory. Howard saw an opportunity for Australia to give encouragement to a process which might remove at last the 'pebble in the shoe' of the Indonesia/Australia relationship. He had several discussions with Habibie on the matter in which he urged the new President to withdraw military, increase autonomy, permit more international involvement and take other steps to promote an agreement.

After his government was re-elected in October 1998 Howard decided to send a letter to Habibie setting out in detail what the Australian government saw as the best way ahead. The core of the letter was a proposal for an extended period of autonomy during which Indonesia would 'focus on winning acceptance for your offer [of autonomy within Indonesia] from the East Timorese themselves' with an eventual act of self-determination. The model Howard drew on and described in the letter was the Matignon Accords in New Caledonia which 'have enabled a compromise political solution to be implemented while deferring a referendum on the final status of New Caledonia for many years'. In Australia this letter has been strongly criticized by those who have always seen Australian policy on this issue in terms of 'betrayal', 'deceit' and so on. And there has been much argument about the effect it had on Habibie and on the outcome for East Timor. It was in fact a moderate and cautious document, carefully drafted to praise the President's statesmanship in offering autonomy ('a bold and clear-sighted step that has opened a window of opportunity'), to emphasize the advantages of resolving the issue which would 'make a substantial difference to Indonesia's standing in the world', and to show a practical means of achieving an acceptable outcome gradually over a period of years in circumstances which would take the heat off Indonesia.

It is also striking how similar the proposal is to what the Department of Foreign Affairs was proposing twenty three years earlier under the Whitlam government and which was in effect amended by Whitlam and his most influential advisers (Wilenski and Woolcott) to place the emphasis not on a gradual process but on the importance of seeing East Timor incorporated in Indonesia. Now Howard was proposing something very like what Foreign Affairs had proposed then, with the balance restored or even tilted somewhat towards the other requirement of self-determination. In the December letter Howard said that he wanted to emphasize that Australia's support for Indonesia's sovereignty was unchanged. It had been a longstanding Australian position that the interests of Australia, Indonesia and East Timor were best served by East Timor remaining part of Indonesia. That was part of the original Whitlam position. But the Howard letter then brought back into play the other leg of the Whitlam position which had been in effect submerged by the Indonesian action in 1975 and the Australian reaction to it. He urged Habibie to enter into negotiations with the East Timorese and talk directly to their leaders, such as the two Bishops and Xanana Gusmao. The letter reportedly also said that the East Timorese were now increasingly committed to having an act of self-determination.

Habibie apparently reacted angrily to this, and not only Habibie. So did Alatas. The reason for anger on the Indonesian side was that Australia was changing its approach to the whole issue and telling Indonesia that the long-standing Australian commitment to Indonesian sovereignty over East Timor was now in question and to be tested at some time in the future – five or ten years perhaps – against acceptance by the local population. In the meantime that local population would obviously make increasing demands on the Indonesian budget and could also seek to hold Indonesia up to the court of international opinion on human rights and other aspects of administration of the province. Why should Indonesia, which saw itself as having spent a disproportionate share of its budget and the lives of thousands of its soldiers on seeking to incorporate East Timor, leave itself open to further costs for perhaps another decade in the possibly empty hope that the East Timorese would decide in the end to stay with Indonesia? Habibie decided that it would be better to resolve matters promptly and let the East Timorese have a plebiscite as soon as possible on whether to stay in Indonesia with autonomy status or leave altogether. This was not the reaction the Australian side had expected and they have been criticized for not having anticipated it. William Maley writes 'While Australia had not explicitly called for a ballot, Habibie's unpredictability should have made policymakers ready for anything' and he likens Habibie to 'the idiot son' who sells a family heirloom to a 'huckster' (presumably Howard) while the family is away from home[46]. Maley's point is that the Australian side should not have treated Habibie as a rational actor or rational individual. But given the Indonesian experience with the issue, and the calculations Habibie had to make at a time when he was facing an election, his decision to hold a plebiscite promptly was not irrational. It can be criticized as dangerous for the East Timorese and as placing Australia in a difficult position, but that does not show that it was irrational from Habibie's or Indonesia's point of view even though it was no doubt mistaken from the point of view of the Indonesian military at least in that it produced a different outcome from the one they had expected.

The Indonesian military meanwhile were arming and training local militias in East Timor and violence was increasing and spreading. Howard and Downer and their advisers have been trenchantly criticized for not being more active in calling for international intervention to curb what the Indonesian military were doing. The public record lends support to that sort of charge, containing as it does statements by Downer and Defence Minister Moore expressing confidence in the intention of the Indonesian military leadership to control the militias and otherwise act in a responsible way. But it is likely that this was done with the intention of promoting a more responsible policy on the part of the military leadership in Indonesia. The commander, General Wiranto, had probably told the Australians what they wanted to hear and then avoided any confrontation with his officers responsible for what was happening (the extent of his own complicity is unclear). The Australians knew that Habibie and the military would not permit a foreign peacekeeping force under United Nations or any other auspices at that stage and may have thought that increasing the heat on Wiranto and the leadership would only make matters worse. At their meeting in Bali on 27 April 1999 Habibie had refused Howard's proposal that international peacekeeping forces be put in place[47].

Another criticism of Howard's letter and the policy it reflected has been that, when Habibie responded by saying Indonesia would bring on a plebiscite soon instead of waiting five or ten years, the Australians should have said publicly and internationally that that was not what they had in mind and demanded that Indonesia follow the Matignon Accords pattern as suggested in the letter. But that was not a real option. In the first place, it was soon clear that the East Timorese leaders did not seek any postponement. And if Howard had sought to persuade Habibie to postpone the plebiscite he would have been exposed to ruthless criticism from the East Timor lobby and possibly his political opponents in Australia. It would have been argued that he was again seeking to take away the right of self-determination from the East Timorese. If Habibie had backed off his decision to have an early plebiscite Howard would have been blamed. As it was he was blamed by some for the destruction and carnage which the Indonesian military and their surrogates, the East Timorese militias, wrought in the territory after the overwhelming rejection of the autonomy-within-Indonesia option in favour of independence from Indonesia. The Howard government has been blamed for that not just because it is alleged that the December letter to Habibie pushed the latter over the edge into deciding to have the plebiscite, but also because it is alleged that the Australian government did not favour the insertion of an international peacekeeping force before the plebiscite or immediately thereafter. Leaked documents indicated that the Secretary of Foreign Affairs and another senior officer in Washington in February 1999 argued to Stanley Roth, Assistant Secretary of State for Asian and Pacific Affairs, that an offer of a UN peacekeeping force at that time would remove the incentive for the sorting out of both internal East Timorese differences and East Timorese/Indonesian differences. Rodney Tiffen, in his book *Diplomatic Deceits*[48], describes this as 'obscenely optimistic'. Two months later in Bali Howard tried to get Habibie to agree to UN peacekeepers and was refused. Whatever the precise reasons for the position taken in February with the State Department there was no possibility that the Indonesians would agree to the insertion of foreign forces before the plebiscite and it was only with great difficulty that they were persuaded to permit it after the carnage that followed the plebiscite in September.

Emotional accounts such as Tiffen's fail to mention the fact that it was Howard who mobilized the international peacekeeping effort after the plebiscite. If it had not been for Australia and the leading role it took there would have been no such effort; no INTERFET, or at least not until much too late and on a much smaller scale. Australia was the only country which had prepared itself to mount a peacekeeping operation in East Timor. Troops had been stationed in the northern base areas and supplies built up. A fast twin-hulled transport vessel was chartered and other advance arrangements made. But Howard made clear that Australia would not move into East Timor without Indonesian agreement to international peacekeepers. To do so would in effect be an act of war. It was essential to mobilize international support and participation and, in close consultation with the UN Secretary-General, approaches were made to regional countries, the United States and others. The Indonesian government was persuaded to agree to an international peacekeeping operation and on 15 September the Security Council resolved to establish INTERFET. It was led by an Australian commander and the majority of the troops were Australian. In addition Australia provided the logistics for much of the rest of the force. It was an operation which would not have happened without Australia and the success of which was due to Australian professional competence. Nor could it have been carried out as expeditiously as it was without key United States logistic, communications and intelligence support. The United States involvement was also important in helping to ensure that the operation was essentially unopposed. For Australia, the price of this in terms of the relationship with Indonesia was high because the Indonesians immediately revoked the Agreement on Maintaining Security which had been the crowning achievement of Keating's diplomacy. But what Australia did at this critical point prevented further loss of life in East Timor at the hands of the militias and further massive removal of East Timorese people to West Timor and other parts of the Indonesian archipelago. At no earlier point in the history of East Timor could Australia have had a direct and decisive influence on the fate of the people. On this occasion when Australia was able to have such an influence it acted decisively to stop what would have been certain massive further carnage, destruction and dislocation.

Nor do those who see Australia's involvement in East Timor only in terms of betrayal, appeasement, deceit and so on mention the large financial cost of the INTERFET exercise to Australia and the prospective financial burden Australia has now assumed for an independent East Timor, even though the East Timorese leaders have shown appreciation for this.

Argument about the Howard letter will no doubt long continue. Was it the critical factor in Habibie's decision to hold the plebiscite with the independence option? Possibly yes. Should it have been preceded by or made conditional on an Indonesian agreement on the stationing of a UN peacekeeping force? This was refused by Indonesia and the answer to the question about conditionality by the East Timorese leadership is clearly no. Would it have been better for the East Timorese if Howard had not sent the letter? Clearly a majority would answer no, despite the huge cost to East Timor of what followed in terms of destruction, loss of life and dislocation of people.

Prime Minister Howard's foreign affairs adviser[49] later likened the chain of events deciding the outcome for East Timor, from the assumption of the presidency by Habibie to the insertion of INTERFET, as rather like the chain of events which led to the outbreak of the First World War. Much of what happened was not, and probably could not have been, anticipated. Actions and developments in some cases had unforeseen consequences. Yet the course of events in retrospect appeared inevitable.

Subsequently of course the Howard government sought to put the best face on the consequences which these events would have for the relationship between Australia and Indonesia. Howard brushed aside the Indonesian renunciation of the Agreement on Maintaining Security and Downer made several statements to the effect that the troublesome issue in the relationship all these years was now out of the way. After Habibie was replaced as President by Abdurrahman Wahid there were further expressions of optimism from the Australian side. It was well known that Habibie had deeply resented the Australian role in the loss of East Timor.

General Feisal Tanjung, who had been Minister for Political and Security Affairs in Habibie's government published an autobiography in which he recorded that when UN Secretary-General Kofi Annan pressed Habibie hard to stop the rampage by the militias after 30 August 1999 the President had reacted angrily and had told Annan that Indonesia would take 'any risk including war', if Australian troops aboard warships lying off East Timor landed in the territory^{50}. It was hoped that Wahid, who had considerable connections with Australia, would take a less inflexible view. Speaking on Channel Nine television in Australia on 31 October Prime Minister Howard said 'I respect the fact that Indonesia feels a degree of tension and there's a degree of sensitivity, but the repair process has begun and it is moving well'^{51}. He indicated that he expected things would change for the better in the relationship under the new President.

At first President Wahid spoke out strongly against Australia but gradually appeared to moderate his position and then indicated that he would visit Australia. That visit was scheduled and then postponed several times and it became clear that he was under extreme pressure from the then Vice President and her party PDI-P as well as other political and military elements including the so-called New Order (Soeharto) interests not to undertake a reconciliation visit to Australia, and that his own position was not strong enough to resist that pressure. His eventual visit shortly before his downfall at least opened the way for Howard to make a return visit, which he did after Wahid had been replaced as President by Megawati Sukarnoputri. Alexander Downer and a new Indonesian Foreign Minister, Hasan Wirayudah, have taken steps on refugee issues and other matters which hopefully foreshadow a wider practical working relationship between the two governments. But there is no prospect that Australia will enter on another period of something like the neighbourly comradeship which was developing up to the mid-1990s. The East Timor issue showed in the most striking and dramatic way how different Australia is, not only from Indonesia, but from all the countries of East Asia. None of them would have done what Australia did, and none of them was comfortable with what Australia did. Those who participated in INTERFET did so in an effort to provide some comfort to Indonesia, not to support Australia.

Notes

1 Tiffen, Rodney (2001), *Diplomatic Deceits*, University of New South Wales Press, Sydney, p. 1.
2 This has been in increasingly unbridled terms by the critics of Australian policy. Thus William Maley, writing in *Australian Journal of International Affairs*, Vol. 54. No. 2, July 2000, claims that popular sentiment was of 'a craven betrayal of people who had assisted Australian soldiers at great personal cost during the Second World War'.
3 Department of Foreign Affairs and Trade (2000), *Australia and the Indonesian Incorporation of Portuguese Timor 1974-1976*, Documents on Australian Foreign Policy, Melbourne University Press, Carlton, p. 1.
4 Dunn, James (1966), *Timor: A People Betrayed*, ABC Books, Sydney, Chapter Two 'The Historical Background'.

5   Hastings, Peter (1975), 'The Timor Problem III – Some Australian Attitudes, 1941-1950', *Australian Outlook*, Vol. 29, No. 3, reprinted in J. Cotton (ed.), *East Timor and Australia: A.I.I.A. Contributions to the Policy Debate*, Australian Defence Studies Centre, Canberra, 1999.
6   Hastings, Peter (1975), 'The Timor Problem II – Some Australian Attitudes, 1903-1941', *Australian Outlook*, Vol. 29, No. 2, reprinted in Cotton (ed.) *ibid.*, p. 34.
7   *Ibid.*, p. 34.
8   Hastings, 'The Timor Problem III – Some Australian Attitudes, 1941-50', *op. cit.* in Cotton, *ibid.*, p. 44.
9   Text is in Hastings, *ibid.*, p 44.
10 *Ibid.*, p. 45.
11 Goto Kenichi (1999), *A History of International Relations Surrounding East Timor, 1900-1945* (in Japanese), Misuzu Shobo, Tokyo.
12 *Ibid.*, pp. 165-6.
13 See Appendix II 'Timor' of McCarthy, Dudley, *Australia in the War of 1939-1945 Series One – Army, Vol. 5 South-West Pacific Area – First Year: Kokoda to Wau*, where special mention is made of Senhor Antonio Policarpe de Sousa Santos in charge of Fronteira Province who provided supplies and ensured support of local natives. Other personal narratives expand on a picture of considerable assistance by Portuguese officials, often at great personal risk to the Portuguese involved.
14 *Ibid.*, p. 605.
15 Campbell, A. (1995), *The Double Reds of Timor*, John Burridge Military Antiques, Swanbourne.
16 Callinan, B. (1984), *Independent Company: the Australian Army in Portuguese Timor 1941-43*, Heinemann, Melbourne.
17 Doig, C.D. (1986), *The History of the Second Independent Company*, C. Doig, Perth.
18 Callinan, *op. cit.* p. 144.
19 *Ibid.*, p. 104.
20 McCarthy, *op. cit.* p. 608.
21 In the Official History McCarthy draws an instructive parallel with the Boer War; *ibid.*, p. 624.
22 Australian Defence Association (1989), *Submission to the Senate Foreign Affairs, Defence and Trade Committee Inquiry into East Timor*. In his book *Silent Feet: The History of 'Z' Special Operations 1942-1945*, McCrae, Melbourne, 1993, G.B. Courtney gives detail of Allied intelligence missions sent into Timor from mid-1943 which shows a variety of causes for failure of the following: Lagarto, Cobra, Adder, Sunbaker, Sunable, Suncob and Sunlag. Only Lagarto is shown as 'betrayed by Timorese' while Sunable is shown as 'some killed, some captured with strong Timorese involvement'. Two of the others were killed or captured because of Japanese signals intercepts, one because of plane crash, and two were assisted by Timorese.
23 See Hastings, 'The Timor Problem III', in Cotton, *op. cit.* pp. 47-8.
24 Whitlam, E.G. (1979), 'Australia, Indonesia and Europe's Empires', in Cotton *op. cit.* p. 140.
25 Department of Foreign Affairs and Trade, *op. cit.* Document No. 12, letter from Furlonger to Feakes, 3 July 1974.
26 *Ibid.*, Document no. 16.
27 *Ibid.*, Document no. 17.
28 *Ibid.*, Document no. 24, paragraph 9(c).
29 *Ibid.*, Document no. 26.
30 *Ibid.*, Document no. 37.

31   Tiffen, *op. cit.* p. 18.
32   Department of Foreign Affairs and Trade, *op. cit.* Document no. 155.
33   *Ibid.*, Document no. 156.
34   *Ibid.*, Document no. 79.
35   *Ibid.*, Document no. 191.
36   Tiffen, *op. cit.* p. 17.
37   Department of Foreign Affairs and Trade, *op. cit.* Document no. 359.
38   *Ibid.*
39   Tiffen, *op. cit.* Chapter 2.
40   Department of Foreign Affairs and Trade, *op. cit.* Document no. 365.
41   Writer's conversation with Richard Woolcott.
42   When the writer was ambassador in Jakarta (1981-85).
43   Whether Moerdani himself believed these stories or whether they were produced with a view to putting his Australian interlocutors on the defensive is another matter. Certainly he had an interest in doing the latter because of the persistence of the enquiries and his reluctance to give answers which would reveal the true state of affairs.
44   The writer was at that time in Tokyo and received phone calls from Indonesia stating that the death toll was far higher than had been published and promising a video cassette which arrived shortly afterwards. I spoke then to Foreign Minister Evans telling him I had been informed that I believed that those killed numbered more than 200 and that the overall total might be a good deal higher because the information was that many more had been taken away in trucks and had not returned. Senator Evans said that there was a range of information but the important thing was that the Indonesians were assuring us that they would carry out a proper enquiry into the military action and punish those responsible. This was the first time they had agreed to such a step and it was important to ensure that they followed through as he had been assured that they would.
45   Ian MacIntosh of the ABC. The group was sent to Indonesia by the Australia/Indonesia Institute and led by Richard Woolcott who was then President of the Institute.
46   Maley, William (2000), 'Australia and the East Timor Crisis', *Australian Journal of International Affairs*, Vol. 54, No. 2, p. 156.
47   Downer, Alexander (1999), Speech to Asian Studies Association of Australia, Brisbane, 29 October, *Australia, Indonesia and East Timor – Moving Forward.*
48   Tiffen, *op. cit.* p. 86.
49   In a conversation with the writer.
50   *The Straits Times*, Nov 1, 1999, Habibie 'threatened to go to war with Australia'.
51   *Ibid.*

Chapter 10

Opportunities and Constraints

Conservation and Adaptation

Post-1788 Australia is a creature of the age of European colonization. It was the remotest of the great European settlements, and the most determined to preserve its inherited racial and cultural character. As we saw in the early chapters these two factors were linked by the sense of vulnerability. Whether the sense of vulnerability is still influential in the Australian mind is currently a contested topic. If it is, it would appear to be in a different form from the powerful concerns of the early nineteenth century or the fears as the Japanese approached in 1942[1]. In any case, in the early years of the twenty-first century, Australia's roots and its inheritance are still very visible in its ethnic complexion, its political, legal and other institutions, in its culture and in many aspects of people's lives.

The British inheritance still in some respects affects the attitude of other regional countries to Australia. Lee Kuan Yew in a television interview a couple of years ago said that the East Asian countries would continue to develop useful links with Australia but 'we could never regard you as *family*'. That sense of Australia as part of the *other*, which we explored in previous chapters, will be an obstacle to Australian efforts to join in the growing institutional links between the countries of East Asia as long as Australia remains a predominantly Anglo-Celtic nation, mainly European in race and culture. Later in this chapter we shall assess whether that will be an insuperable obstacle.

If, one way or another, the obstacle cannot be overcome, that is likely to be to Australia's cost. But Australians remain to be convinced that it is a major issue for them. Certainly there is little sign of any disposition to make major accommodations in order to try to assimilate to East Asia. Many would see it as anyway inevitable that Australia will fail the test if it turns out that the only way of winning acceptance is to bring in non-Europeans in such numbers as to make Australia a predominantly Asian country in the foreseeable future. No one in Australia now regards that as a realistic prospect and even the objective of a fully multi-ethnic, multicultural Australia has been pushed off the policy agenda, at least for the present. It may well be that Australia's population will eventually be 'honey-coloured' (FitzGerald, Sheridan), but it will not happen soon – unless in the unlikely event that the present population is overwhelmed by force.

Nor is there any disposition to make substantial changes to Australians' way of life and predominant culture in order to adopt a sort of cultural protective colouring. There are many aspects of Australian life and institutions deriving from our British heritage which no one would want to compromise. They have worked well and are the foundation stones of a strong polity and society. Most Australians see these things as strengths and assets that should not be compromised or abandoned. Nor is there reason to believe that most of those aspects of our inheritance are in themselves obstacles to acceptance by East Asia, except perhaps when they are celebrated in ways which sound to the neighbours like assertions of British superiority. But taken together, and with the regionally unique ethnic character of the population, they give Australia the appearance to many people in the region of a British white outpost – a last residue of the European colonial era. Moreover, some Australians have clung to anachronistic elements of the British heritage, especially the British monarchy, which have unnecessarily exaggerated or prolonged that image of Australia in the region. During the 1980s and early 1990s there was an increasing weight of influential opinion calling for the ending of the monarchy by minimal changes to the constitution. But with a monarchist Prime Minister from early 1996 that mood met with increasing resistance. The resistance which Mr Howard encouraged and exploited was stronger than the reform fatigue 20 years earlier after the reforming and in some ways radical Whitlam Ministry which, inter alia, abolished the similar anachronism of British imperial honours (knighthoods and other awards in such orders as that of the British Empire) and introduced an Australian system of honours. The ending of the similarly anachronistic institution of the British Privy Council being the highest court to which appeals could be made, and which therefore could overrule the High Court in Australia, required a series of Federal and State Acts of Parliament. These were passed over a period of nearly 20 years from 1968, with the process being completed with the Australia Acts, both State and Federal, in the 1980s which terminated the right of appeal to the Privy Council from State Courts in matters governed by State law. The monarchy remains the last stubborn remnant of the constitutional subordination of Australia to Britain.

Under the Howard government there has also been an apparent erosion of support for multiculturalism and for immigration of non-European peoples. In some quarters this has been described erroneously as a return to the White Australia Policy, but it has nothing to do with colour prejudice. Australia seems to have rid itself of that, if not yet of some other forms of corrosive social prejudice. After the Second World War Australia was driven to open its doors to a large number of non-British European immigrants, partly as insurance for its White Australia policy. It was clear in the aftermath of the war that Australia needed a larger population than the seven million who then inhabited the continent. This was so on both economic and security grounds. The White Australia Policy was still firmly in place but the potential supply of British immigrants fell far short of what the government believed the country needed to develop necessary infrastructure, and to continue the process, begun during the war, of moving beyond the pastoral economy which had been its mainstay for so long. An assisted immigration programme, combining British with large numbers of people from war-ravaged Europe, was the obvious way of achieving a rapid increase without abandoning the White Australia Policy. Although that discriminatory policy was eventually abolished in the 1960s and 1970s, and although people from Asia now make up 40 per cent, the largest component of the ongoing immigration into Australia, there is still wariness about accepting large numbers of immigrants from some non-European source countries. Indeed, as the debate over the small numbers of asylum seekers from Iraq, Iran and Afghanistan attempting unauthorized entry during 2001 showed, there is quite strong community opposition to the entry of people from cultural backgrounds deemed to be more or less incompatible with that of Australia.

For some fifty years there was a growing trend in Australian foreign and other external policy to place more emphasis on Asia and particularly on East Asia, meaning those countries from China in the north to Indonesia in the south. Australian governments, business people, academics and media analysts and commentators increasingly shared the view that the country's economic, strategic and political future would be inescapably intertwined with that of its geographic region. That awareness and focus grew with the independence of former European colonies in the region and then more rapidly as a series of East Asian countries experienced the most rapid sustained economic growth the world had yet seen and, in most cases, a commensurate growth in confidence. For the first time there emerged a sense of East Asian solidarity and community. The prospect of an eventual East Asian economic bloc, which would exclude the United States and Australia, caused concern in both Washington and Canberra, and the United States made its opposition to this thinking quite clear. Australia lobbied in the East Asian capitals in favour of retaining and intensifying the focus on the Pacific Basin or so-called Asia Pacific Economic Cooperation (APEC) which included both the United States and Australia and against the narrower East Asian project which would leave Australia and its ally and protector, the United States, on the outside.

For a while the opposition of the United States and Australia, along with doubts held by Japan, prevented the advance of the East Asia project. But persistence on the part of the Prime Minister of Malaysia and other supporters, and the desire of the members of the European Union to have an institutional link with East Asia which would to some degree compensate for their exclusion from the APEC, resulted in 1996 in the holding of the first Asia-Europe Meeting or ASEM. As we saw in Chapter 7, Australia sought participation in this on the East Asian side, but was refused, despite support by Japan. The collapse of the so-called East Asian miracle with the financial crisis of 1997-98 and the subsequent problems in the region at first seemed likely to set the cooperation project back too. But it has probably served as a stimulus and there are now few who doubt that institutionalized cooperation will gradually develop in the region.

The Australian drive to engage with East Asia as the region of greatest importance to Australia reached its peak during the Prime Ministership of Paul Keating which was replaced by a conservative coalition government under John Howard in early 1996. But even under the Keating Labor government it was not unequivocally asserted that Australia belonged in the East Asian region. At first the Howard government sought to continue a similar, primary, focus on East Asia but gradually the commitment diminished with a reassertion of older ties and loyalties.

There are several developments that appear to have contributed to this, apart from the conservative and anglophile orientation of the Prime Minister and a group of associates. Keating's defeat in 1996 was widely expected, but it emerged from private and other polling that one of the reasons for it was popular reservations about the speed and intensity of his engagement policy culminating in the security agreement between Australia and Indonesia. Asked whether that agreement meant that Australians could trust Indonesia never to be a military threat, nearly sixty per cent of respondents strongly disagreed or disagreed with the statement and fewer than ten per cent agreed or agreed strongly[2]. As we saw in the last two chapters the relationship with Indonesia, which had been the centrepiece of Keating's foreign policy, fell apart after the demise of Soeharto and the cataclysmic end of Indonesian misrule in East Timor. That changed one of the main bases on which Australian foreign policy had rested for many years. The outlook for Indonesia became so fragile, and the outlook for Australia's relations with Indonesia so uncertain, that it was no longer plausible to hold up policy towards Indonesia as demonstrating the success of Australia's engagement policy with the region. Indeed the Liberals saw it as demonstrating the opposite case – that Keating's policy had been out of touch. For his part Keating argued that his policy had been correct, that Australia's future depended on its continuance, and that it had been overturned by egregious errors on the part of the Howard government. But clearly public opinion in Australia was with the Prime Minister. A further factor was that Australia's initiative in securing international intervention in East Timor and Australian leadership of INTERFET created a new surge of Australian confidence in the role the government appeared to be asserting as a champion of democracy and human rights in the region and as a guardian of security in association with the United States. This represented something of a shift from the Keating/Evans foreign and defence policy. That policy had sought to develop close relations with regional countries more or less regardless of ideology or system of government, although it was always assumed that the region as a whole was moving towards greater democracy and better observation of human rights and that Australian 'quiet diplomacy' was helping in that direction. The Howard government's assertion of Australia's new and more active regional role in security affairs, and in the promotion of human rights, democratization, and good governance, also reinforced the sense of Australia's difference from its Asian neighbours. None of them, including Japan, the United States' major ally in the region, would have seen itself in such a role.

As discussed in Chapter 9, there had been increasing discomfort in Australia about the role that successive governments, starting with that of Whitlam, had played (or declined to play) in the Indonesian misrule in East Timor. The criticism of Keating that he became too close to Soeharto, and too ready to overlook abuses of human rights by the Indonesian military and other authorities, began to weigh on public opinion. There was thus a cathartic element to the reversal of Australian policy on East Timor in 1998-99. As we saw, that reversal proceeded much further and more quickly than the Australian government had intended or expected. But the government afterwards was quick to say that the freeing of East Timor from Indonesian rule removed the 'stone from the shoe' of relations between Australia and Indonesia. While it was not explicit, the point here was that the removal of the East Timor issue would permit a more steady condition less subject to upsets by the protest lobbies and their increasing effect on public opinion in Australia.

Soeharto had declined every invitation to visit Australia from the time of the takeover of East Timor until his resignation because of the protest demonstrations which would have been mounted. Such demonstrations in Australia would perforce have been reciprocated, perhaps in magnified form, in Indonesia, and any benefits of a visit nullified. But the argument which Downer put forward after INTERFET that this would remove the main irritant to the relationship and in effect usher in a new era was flawed. The Australian policy reversal and the subsequent intervention left deep scars, especially on the Indonesian military, which will have an influential role in the Indonesian political establishment for the foreseeable future and it also offended nationalists like the present President, Megawati Sukarnoputri. Some Indonesians recognize that the Australian role did indeed help Indonesia relieve itself of a damaging and insoluble problem. But they are in a minority. The most direct response on the Indonesian side was abrogation of the Agreement on Maintaining Security which had been the crowning achievement of Keating's Indonesian diplomacy. But it was clear that on the Australian side too, and for the foreseeable future, there would be no public tolerance for a defence relationship which involved cooperation with the Indonesian armed forces.

Keating had sought close defence relations with Indonesia and other neighbours on the basis of defence *with* those neighbours rather than defence *against* them. The putative threat envisaged in the 'defence with' approach was not openly mentioned but in Soeharto's mind it was certainly China. On the Australian side the motivation was rather that a collegiate relationship in the defence area would enhance Australia's security by promoting the development of trust and mutual support. It would also be an important element in seeking acceptance of Australia by the region. As we saw in Chapter 8 this was no new idea on the Australian side. It went back at least to the Sabre project of the early days of the Soeharto regime. But it caused considerable and continuing uneasiness in the Australian human rights community which saw the Indonesian army as an unsuitable associate for Australia, partly because of its role in East Timor and partly because of its record of suppression of opposition to the New Order generally in Indonesia. Expressions of that uneasiness did not much hamper Keating's policy at the time, but one of the effects of the East Timor events of 1999 and the INTERFET intervention was to reinforce the opposition in Australia to defence cooperation with Indonesia and to generate respect for the Australian army.

In addition to the effects of the Indonesian and East Timor dimensions of change in the context of Australia's policies was the ending, or at least substantial interruption, of the East Asian economic development phenomenon. The world's second largest economy, Japan, which had widely been seen as the model for the emerging economies of the region, and which had promoted the view that its model was different from that of the United States and more appropriate to Asian values, had been in stagnation since 1990. Korea and South East Asia were seriously affected and would have to make major institutional and policy changes before they could resume strong growth. Talk of East Asia becoming the new dynamo of the world economy in the first twenty years of the twenty-first century ceased. Initially it was thought that the crisis and stalling in East Asia would impact severely on the Australian economy because some 60 per cent of its exports went to that region. But the Australian economy proved surprisingly resilient, taking advantage of a fall in the exchange rate to find markets elsewhere and actually logging substantial increases in exports through the following years. By 2002 Australia had the highest GNP growth rate of all the OECD (industrialized) countries. Thus another of the foundations of the engagement policy was called into question. It had been widely accepted, and had been bipartisan policy, that Australia's economic future depended on increasing economic integration with East Asia. Now it seemed that Australia had acquired the competitive edge and range of skills and products to manage pretty well by painting on a global canvas and with less dependence on East Asia.

Reaction

The shift of Howard government policy on East Asia was in part a reaction to indications of feeling in the electorate, which fit with those of the Prime Minister himself, partly a reaction to the developments in Indonesia, East Timor and elsewhere in the region mentioned above, and partly a reaction to the apparent spurning of Australia's efforts to win acceptance in the emerging East Asian solidarity and institutional structure. As we saw in previous chapters the attempt to assimilate Australia to East Asia lacked sufficient sustaining support in the Australian community. In its full-blown form it was based on unconvincing arguments and did violence to the sense of Australian identity of most Australians. The backlash in the form of Pauline Hanson's One Nation party appeared to be tolerated by John Howard and some others in his government. There were even suggestions on the conservative side that Hanson's maiden speech in the Parliament was a welcome exercise of free speech and a timely defiance of 'political correctness'. This led to an impression in the region that the Prime Minister and his associates supported the Hanson agenda. While that was an exaggeration it would be true to say that his views on relevant matters lay somewhere between those of Keating, Evans and those who shared their position, on the one hand, and those of Hanson and her supporters, on the other hand. As was made clear in the 1997 White Paper, Howard's government wanted to continue the development of mutually beneficial links with East Asian countries. But they did not want to do that in ways that might detract from the British inheritance or the alliance relationship with and loyalty towards the United States. Howard was also seen, whether correctly or not, in Australia and in the region, as the guarantor of the predominance of the Anglo-Celtic element in the population. Moreover the government reacted strongly to suggestions that attachment to the British monarchy or outspoken support of United States foreign policies might stand in the way of East Asian acceptance of Australia. They took very firmly the position that turning towards Asia did not require turning Australia's back (as they put it) on its traditional friends. They made it clear that they were not prepared to contemplate any diminution of the commitment to the US alliance or the ties with Britain in order to win acceptance by East Asia. In this they appear to have been in tune with widespread popular feeling in Australia. Shortly before the federal election on 10 November 2001 an influential Labor Party figure (who became Opposition spokesman on foreign affairs after the election) said in answer to a question at a public meeting that it would only damage the republican cause to use the argument that continued attachment to the British monarchy was detrimental to Australia's standing in East Asia[3]. This was because Australians did not believe it was anyone's business but their own whom they chose to have as Head of State, and they did not intend to be influenced by foreigners.

There is a certain artificiality to much of the discussion about the basic issues for Australian policy that are involved here. At the extremes the strident arguments between Paul Keating and others on the one hand and conservative Howard supporters on the other tend to overlook some obdurate facts. Mr Keating has been arguing for years that the Howard government has reversed the previous government's policy of developing the key relationship with Indonesia, and before the November 2001 election Laurie Brereton, then Labor spokesman on foreign affairs, and others on the Labor side, said that if Labor were returned to office they would immediately move to re-establish the closeness of that relationship. But this was an empty claim because to do so would have been impossible in the aftermath of East Timor and other developments. It is arguable that the Howard government could have done more to reduce the irritants in the relationship. At least the rhetoric could have been more emollient and taken more account of Indonesian sensibilities[4]. But there was not much scope for enhancing the closeness and warmth of the relationship when the Australian Embassy in Jakarta was experiencing violent demonstrations and the whole atmosphere was very tense. Moreover, Australian opinion was outraged by what happened in East Timor in 1999 after the plebiscite. The television networks carried extensive coverage showing, night after night, Indonesian-backed militias and men in Indonesian uniforms burning and killing. Much of East Timor was rendered a wasteland. Many people were killed and horrific scenes were shown on television and in the newspapers. The coverage in Australia was more extensive than anywhere else because it was all taking place so close to Australia – just a short flight from Darwin. The impact on Australian opinion can be assumed to have been greater than elsewhere, if only because of the greater exposure and the background of more than twenty years of agitation by the East Timor lobby in Australia. In other parts of East Asia the coverage was limited, especially in the ASEAN countries where there was no doubt reluctance to depict the troubles of the senior partner in the Association – in line with the usual ASEAN rule of non-interference in the internal affairs of other members and of solidarity in the face of outside criticism or scrutiny. In addition some of the other partners might have been constrained by other factors including sympathy with the Indonesians on the part of elements of their own military.

Thus, given Australia's leading role in the East Timor intervention, there was no possibility of avoiding adverse impact on the relationship both on the Indonesian side and in terms of Australian opinion. A widespread view in Indonesia was that Australia, despite all the protestations of friendship and of the desire to cement strong ties, had suddenly switched its position and led the way in Indonesia's humiliation before the court of international opinion. A widespread view in

Australia was that the Indonesian military had shown itself cruel and brutal and that Indonesia had utterly failed in the responsibility it had seized for itself with its military occupation of East Timor in 1975. The Australian view was complicated by the Whitlam acquiescence in 1975 and thereafter in the Indonesian occupation. As discussed in the previous chapter there was a sense that Australia had a strong obligation to the East Timorese to relieve them, even belatedly, of what was represented in Australia as a dreadful burden for which Australia was partly responsible. But it would be a distortion to suggest that the Howard government just jettisoned the Indonesia relationship in response to Australian public opinion. It has been argued[5] that the Australian government suppressed, or at least did not share fully with its US ally, its knowledge that the Indonesian army was building up the militias that were to cause such havoc in the immediate aftermath of the plebiscite. Certainly it appears that the government hoped to the last, and indeed beyond the last, that the Indonesian government would be able to control the situation and would do so in accordance with the agreements reached at the United Nations. Critics in Australia such as Laurie Brereton, then the Labor spokesman on Foreign Affairs, and various media commentators and East Timorese supporters attacked what they saw as the government's failure to condemn the Indonesian government or demand that it bring under control what the Australian government was calling 'rogue elements' in the military in East Timor. Far from precipitating the collapse of the relationship the government sought to preserve it.

In any case, the notion that the tortuous legacy of Australian involvement (and non-involvement) in Indonesia's disastrous colonial episode in East Timor could be simply disposed of and the relationship returned to the former closeness was clearly an illusion. There will be a residue of resentment towards Australia in some Indonesian quarters for a long time. And in Australia there will be a reserve and wariness towards Indonesia for a long time. It is difficult to imagine many ordinary Australians feeling enthusiastic about politicians' undertakings to restore the relationship to its Keating condition even if that were possible. After the November 2001 election in Australia there were signs, for example at the APEC Shanghai Summit, that at the President/Prime Minister level relations were distinctly cool. But the agreement of the two foreign ministers to co-host an international conference on people smuggling and the visit by Prime Minister Howard to Jakarta in February 2002 suggest that business-like relations are again possible at least in principle. And, out of the limelight, contacts continue and indeed grow. Thousands of Indonesian students are in Australian institutions. Australian tourists continue to visit Bali and other venues. Trade is growing. Both governments seem now prepared to re-engage in some of the business of neighbourly discussions on issues of real mutual concern. Despite the continuing resentment and dislike of Australia in some Indonesian quarters, engendered largely by the East Timor involvement and fanned from time to time for internal political reasons, there is reason to expect that a new equilibrium will be gradually established. But the Howard visit of February 2002 involved episodes which left a very sour taste in the mouths of the Australian government. Howard was snubbed by the Speaker of the MPR (the Consultative Assembly and highest representative body) Amien Rais, and by Akbar Tanjung, Speaker of the DPR or Parliament, both of whom cancelled at short notice scheduled meetings with the Australian Prime Minister. They were responding to the vociferous views of some parliamentarians who were strongly opposed to the Howard visit. It was falsely alleged that Australia was encouraging the Papuan separatists, the OPM, and the Acehnese separatists, the GAM, and that the agenda of the Howard government was to secure the break up of Indonesia. Australians generally do not understand that truth or falsity in such matters is in a sense irrelevant in Indonesia. People have no way of knowing the truth. Accusations or allegations of this sort are made to demonstrate attitudes, resentments and so on which may have quite different sources, or indeed no source at all other than the deep pockets of some interest which can deploy the crowds which are for rent.

When the relationship does settle down it will not be the sort of relationship which a couple of generations of Australian academics, diplomats and business people envisaged, let alone the sort of relationship which Keating envisaged. Rather the aim on the Australian side will be the 'realistic and practical' relationship and policy which the Howard government has always contrasted with what they saw as the exaggerations and excessive ambitions of the Keating engagement policy. There will for example be no more talk of a 'special relationship'. Nor is it likely soon to be the sort of bilateral relationship which will lead Indonesia again to support Australian inclusion in East Asian institutional networks, as Soeharto did.

The sense in which the political argument about these issues in Australia has been artificial is that, given the course of events, and the effect of those events on attitudes in Australia, Indonesia and the East Asia region more generally, there is no way that the relationship with Indonesia, or indeed with other states in the region, could have been unaffected. The political antagonism of charge and counter charge in Australia has shed little light on the matters said to be at issue. Nor *could* it shed much light so long as each side claimed that it had the answer to setting the relationship to rights again. That was not within the reach of either party. In the campaign for the election on 10 November 2001 neither side produced grounds for much confidence that it would make the best of a difficult situation. There is however one issue where it is possible to point to real and basic choices for Australian policy. But here again public opinion probably keeps current policy pretty firmly in the conservative mould. The issue in question is the one first raised in the Howard/Downer contention that turning towards East Asia did not require turning away from the United States or the United Kingdom. That issue has been challenged in the specific context of Australian policy towards China by a number of scholars and commentators[6], and it has been pursued with passionate conviction and persistence by former Prime Minister Malcolm Fraser[7]. Mr Fraser has made it clear that he thinks that Australia's interests in the future will lie much more with China and the rest of East Asia than with the United States. He has no confidence that the United States will make realistic and sensible accommodations to the growing power and influence of China and its region and no confidence that the United States would in the future come to Australia's support under the ANZUS Treaty. At the Australian National University Stuart Harris has for years argued that at some point Australia is likely to have to face a choice between standing alongside the United States in opposition to China and preserving the substance of the relationship with China which it has been cultivating since 1972. With China's growing economic strength and power projection capability it can be argued that the relationship could well be Australia's most important in East Asia before many more years have passed. Even at current levels Australia's relationship with China is one of its most important. China is Australia's fifth largest export market (but still only about one-third the size of exports to Japan and substantially smaller than exports to the United States) and it has already important reach and influence into the South China Sea and South East Asia. Its importance for Australia, both in absolute terms and relative to others, seems likely to continue to grow. Focus on the relationship seems therefore to meet the test of 'practical and realistic' which is the Howard government benchmark. Given the strains on the China-United States relationship and the tough line taken by many Republicans in the United States it was not unreasonable to question how the intensifying of the Australian defence and regional strategic relationship with the United States was to be advanced without prejudice to the relationship with China. Both the Bush camp and the Chinese government seemed at some pains to make it clear to the Australian side that this could involve uncomfortable choices.

Concern about possible demands by the United States for Australian support in the event of another crisis in the Taiwan Strait was stimulated by remarks attributed to senior associates of George W. Bush before the Presidential election in 2000. Richard Armitage, then an important member of the Bush team, told Australian participants in an annual meeting organized by the businessman Phillip Scanlan, that Australia would be expected to stand by the United States with force involvement should conflict develop over Taiwan. His remarks were interpreted as meaning that the ANZUS alliance would be on the line. The following year when Armitage visited as Deputy Secretary of State he confirmed in an interview on the ABC 'Lateline' program that he had spoken of expectations that Australia would be prepared to be involved in the 'dirty, hard and dangerous' work if it came to that over Taiwan[8].

The issue of Australia's regional role as an associate of the United States has also been raised in wider terms in relation to the so-called 'Deputy Sheriff' description of Howard's policy in the region and to the 'Howard Doctrine'. In these cases statements by the Prime Minister were interpreted (or misinterpreted) as casting Australia in the role of junior associate of the United States in maintaining the security and stability of the region. Interpreted in that light they caused considerable offence especially in Malaysia and Thailand, and in the perception of many in the region showed that Australia did not see itself as 'one of us'. The 'Deputy Sheriff' label especially became enough of an issue for the Prime Minister to make a statement in response to an arranged question in Parliament. It had arisen from an exclusive interview and article by the journalist Fred Brenchley in *The Bulletin* magazine on 28 September 1999. After a storm of criticism in the region and domestically, Howard asserted that he had not taken the position attributed to him by Brenchley and said 'the government does not see Australia as playing the role of a deputy for the United States, or indeed any other country in the region'. The United States' regional involvement was vital to Australia's security but he did not see the United States in the role of a regional policeman. The indications from the Bush camp of their tough interpretation of the obligations the alliance imposed on Australia, specifically in the context of Australia's policies in the region, prompted concerns in Australia about the very potential problem whose existence the government denied – that turning towards Asia involved some degree of turning away from the United States. But when the Prime Minister gave the impression that Australia was now the close associate of the United States in bringing light and peace to East Asia the reaction in the region was unequivocally negative. It served to make Australia more alien in its own part of the world.

The plausibility of the 'Deputy Sheriff' and Howard Doctrine interpretation of his policy approach to the region was enhanced by the emphasis which the Howard government had given to restoring the relationship with the United States after its alleged neglect by the Keating government. John Howard did not succeed in getting American 'boots on the ground' in East Timor, but it scarcely mattered because of the importance of the other support he obtained from Washington. Indeed the Australian success with INTERFET would probably not have been possible without United States support, especially the weight of their insistence that Indonesia not interfere. The rhetoric of the Howard government has been far more committed and conveyed much more solidarity in regard to the United States than to the East Asian region or any of its members. Moreover it has become a special project of the Prime Minister and some of his closest advisers to conclude a Free Trade Agreement with the United States, a goal that would not have seemed within the bounds of possibility in previous times. Indeed most observers with experience in this area regard the attempt with scepticism.

Professor Garnaut and others who have from the beginning unequivocally placed primary importance on the economic and other relationships with East Asia have expressed reservations about the campaign to get a Free Trade Agreement with the United States partly because they believe that it will be seen in East Asia as a decision by Australia to turn away from engagement with East Asia.

The 'Howard Doctrine' has always been a term of convenience used mostly by critics and it has not committed Mr Howard himself in any very specific terms. But much of the same meaning was captured by the claim that there was no tension between Australia's ethnic and cultural origins and its geographic location, and that claim was made strongly and openly by the government. As we have seen in previous chapters Gareth Evans and others spent much time and effort on seeking to explain away or on devising ways of overcoming what was seen as a major obstacle to Australia's engagement with East Asia. This was the incompatibility between Australia's 'history' and its 'geography'. It was the basis of the 'odd man in' debate and the subject of much writing such as Stephen FitzGerald's book *Is Australia an Asian Country?*. Just as the Howard government denied that emphasizing the relationship with East Asia meant turning away from the United States so, from the beginning, Howard denied what had become conventional wisdom and said that there was no incompatibility between Australia's history and its geography. He rejected the interpretation of Australia's circumstances as 'the scene of an often acute tension between the largely European (indeed predominantly British) political and cultural heritage of non-indigenous

Australians, and the "Asian" location of the settler colonial society they collectively dominated'. And 'from the moment it entered office the Howard government began claiming something quite different, and claiming it in a progressively more robust form'[9].

This is a core difference between the Keating/Evans foreign policy and that of Howard. But it is more than that. It involves rejection of a long tradition of Australian foreign policy thinking and development that saw a need for Australia to adapt in order to find a way of fitting safely and productively with the emerging region of East Asia. In effect the Howard doctrine is that there is no need for adaptation or compromise by Australia. Keating rejected the idea that Australia was or should seek to become an Asian nation. It could and should be just Australia, but it should make great efforts to understand and be acceptable to the countries of the region. Its differences with them had largely been exaggerated (or could be explained away). His personal experience with East Asian leaders, and particularly with Soeharto and Miyazawa, no doubt reinforced his confidence in this approach. He and Evans thought Australia could make itself very useful in many ways to the regional neighbours and in so doing would make itself acceptable to those who doubted. Evans wrestled much more with explanations. Keating appears to have thought such expedients as the 'East Asian Hemisphere' a bit of a joke. But they shared a view that Australia needed to work hard to win acceptance; that there were obstacles to overcome and that it was enormously important to make the effort to overcome them.

The Howard approach, as it has emerged since 1997 after the publication of the White Paper, seems radically different. It places Australia as a country of predominantly European ethnic character and history, proudly British inheritance, and of Western orientation, unapologetically in or next to East Asia.

On that account there is no need for Australia to seek to change or adapt, nor to abate its connections to those more distant countries with which it shares closer ethnic, political, cultural and ideological characteristics than any it has with East Asia. On that account it should pursue good relations with the countries of East Asia, with whom it has many shared interests including very important economic interests. But it should do this in a practical and realistic way, not seeking to make unnatural changes to its own character, nor claiming similarities which are not recognized by others. It should be proud of its history, of making a nation from the smallest and most unpromising beginnings far from its mother country, of fighting for good causes in two world wars and subsequently, of making substantial contributions to the development of the region. In Howard and his associates we hear echoes of Parkes and others who followed, including Hancock and Menzies. It is a recognizable version of much that is strong in the Australian story. But it reflects a reserve, indeed sometimes a harsh antagonism, towards the sort of enthusiasm that inspired many Australian scholars and diplomats to build relationships with East Asia and especially South East Asia. The last politician in high office in government in Australia who shared that enthusiasm and whose work reflected it was Tim Fischer, Leader of the National Party and Deputy Prime Minister in the first Howard government. Since Fischer left the government it has been very noticeable that the mood has changed.

But it is true, as the government claims, that much is being done to develop links with the East Asian countries. That is indeed a major part of Australia's current foreign policy. However two major questions need answering. What is being done to build the awareness of the Australian people that these are the countries which will largely determine Australia's future and which therefore need to be studied and understood? What is being done to overcome the increased sense in the region that Australia has lost interest in joining in, that Australia is too different ever to be accepted and that that is the view also of the Australians?

As for the first question the answer seems to be that the Australian people will be left to decide for themselves. They are thought to have shown clearly that they were not persuaded by the Keating engagement push. While many of the academic community supported it, and some were indeed an important part of its substance, they are not much regarded by the conservatives now in power. Those who seek to make the case for engagement are now often treated with a degree of scorn by the government's supporters in conservative institutions and the media. That is especially so since the divisive disagreements about the treatment of 'asylum seekers' from Iraq, Iran and Afghanistan who were brought by 'people smugglers' through Indonesia to Australian waters or Australian territory.

The second question runs into two sorts of answer. In terms of public debate the government argues that it has in fact achieved great advances in the substance and fabric of Australia's relationship with the region. Indeed there has, as we have noted, been continuing growth in trade and student numbers. Measurable things of that sort can be adduced to make a sort of case. The case on the other side is much harder to substantiate because the evidence is anecdotal[10] and does not come through to many people in Australia. Thus those who have heard East Asian reactions to the present government's policy stance towards the region, and who make public reference to those reactions, are now derided as 'intelligentsia' who only 'preach' and who allegedly criticize without regard to the government's achievements. The government's most strident defenders include former apologists for the white supremacist regime in South Africa and people who opposed the 1980s Asian immigration into Australia. The new 'positive and realistic' line seems to be confidently built on a belief that it is backed by public opinion which sees no need for Australia to compromise, which is robustly attached to Australia's mainly British inheritance, and which feels no particular affinity for the East Asian countries and peoples who are its neighbours.

Making a Virtue of Necessity

The Howard government has wisely sought to avoid any expressions of impatience or even disappointment at the unwillingness of the East Asian regional countries to accept Australia into their developing institutional network. As noted earlier foreign minister Downer produced a kind of rationalization on the basis of a distinction between cultural and practical similarities and relations. The latter, he argued, could flourish despite differences in the former. Subsequently there has been increasing emphasis on the 'realistic' nature of the relationship which is being developed[11], both towards Indonesia and towards the region generally. That is to be welcomed in the sense that no-one favours a policy based on *un*realistic premises (and there were some such elements in the Keating/Evans policy). But there is no doubt that there is resentment in the government that Australian overtures during their first term fell on stony ground. That resentment and disappointment might increase if the policy of realism includes a realistic long-term adaptation to life outside the East Asian grouping. In that event it will eventually emerge that there are costs involved in being left outside trade, financial and other groupings. But not surprisingly there is an unwillingness to continue to court·rejection at the hands of Indonesia and Malaysia and to risk something close to humiliation[12]. There is moreover a view that it is not appropriate that Australia continue to court Indonesia while influential parts of that country's establishment treat Australia with indifference and worse. This rests on the unstated view that Australia is a far more successful and, in world terms, a more influential state, than Indonesia, despite the huge and increasing[13] difference in population size[14]. From an Indonesian perspective this is painful indeed, especially because the country is in such genuine difficulties of its own making. Leading Indonesians have always said that it must be in Australia's long term interests to cultivate friendship with Indonesia because sooner or later Indonesia would be a major power rather than a struggling developing country. It appeared in the decades between 1966 and 1996 that Indonesia was moving steadily in that direction. Despite vicissitudes in the relationship from time to time responsible Australian ministers and officials always regarded that progress as very important for Australia's interests because failure or fragmentation of Indonesia would have unpredictable but probably very damaging consequences for Australia.

In that regard Australian policy should remain in principle broadly on track, and indeed there is no reason to think that there has been any change in underlying policy. Alexander Downer said at the beginning of 2002:

> With Indonesia we are developing a positive and realistic relationship based on permanent, institutionalised ties and senior political visits. Our ties with Indonesia will be different to those of the past, and deservedly so. Indonesia is a different country as it moves down the path to a modern, inclusive, decentralised democracy. Australia will continue its active support for Indonesia's efforts to implement necessary reforms[15].

It could be argued that, after the heady days of Keating's diplomacy with Soeharto, it was in any case time to take stock and proceed more deliberately. But, as we have already noted, *whoever* had been in government after 10 November 2001, it would have been manifestly impossible to return to that previous phase. As we saw above, both on the Indonesian side and on the Australian side there was no stomach for that. The best Australia can hope for now, and probably for years to come, is what Downer calls 'a positive and realistic relationship', which is to say a relationship which is correct and hopefully of mutual benefit but constrained by some reserve. Such a relationship will leave Australia on the outside, not 'family' in the sense in which Malaysia or Thailand or even Myanmar are family, but part of the West, the *other*.

There is another subtle change in the relationship. During the Soeharto period when Indonesia's GNP per capita was rising steadily, even though its distribution was open to criticism, Australian policy makers tended to heed the Indonesian reminders that with continuing economic and social advancement the world's fourth biggest country would in due course be a major power. That prospect carried the implication that Australia should show respect, and adopt a helpful stance during the period of Indonesia's period of modernization and development from the ranks of the very poor. The time would come when Indonesia would emerge as a much more important and influential country on both the world and the regional scene and it would be in Australia's interests to have its huge neighbour's goodwill built up from support during the hard times of development. This argument was actually put by important New Order figures and its resonance was present in the Australian policy thinking of the times at least to the extent that it was thought to be far more in Australian interests to be on side with Indonesia than off side, given the expectation that Indonesia's influence and power would only increase over time. There was always an element of scepticism or at least doubt in some Australian quarters about how Indonesia would turn out in the end. But the weight of policy thinking was for the most part clearly that there was a likelihood that, in time, Indonesia would be influential and powerful and that it was therefore in Australia's interests to tie its giant neighbour to Australia with strong and mutually beneficial links of various kinds. It was especially important that Australia develop as much expertise and as much supporting awareness in the Australian public as possible. This thinking seems to have dropped out of the policy mix in Canberra. Indonesia's emergence as a major economic, political and military power is seen now as much further off than had been thought as recently as 1996. Australia is seen as having emerged as a significantly more important effective power. Australia needs to seek to develop a 'positive and realistic' relationship with Indonesia, but it does not need to 'kow tow' (as one highly relevant Minister has said privately).

In the meantime it is of course sensible to put the best face possible on the situation and hope that either it will not work to Australia's disadvantage or that it will change over time. But that is not to say that the work of making Australians more effectively aware of the region and more capable of dealing with it and feeling at home in it should be seen as less important than during the active 'Engagement Policy'. Because of the legacy of the White Australia policy in the folk memory of the region it is clear that there will be great sensitivity in the region to issues affecting race in Australia. The increasingly negative attitudes to Australia in the region have much to do with impressions that the country has turned away from the multiculturalism at home and efforts to accommodate to the neighbours abroad which were evident during the eighties and early nineties. It is not to be expected that the present Foreign Minister would agree with such observations. He claims that Australia is now well placed in the region: 'Australia has a lot to offer our region. Our strengths are recognised and respected'[16]. Those strengths, he said, are not measured in trade statistics alone as proof of which he cited the Australian leadership of the East Timor intervention 'with our regional neighbours front and centre'. But the regional neighbours were not there because of respect for Australia's leadership; rather despite that leadership. They were there because they wanted to preserve some element of protective cover over Indonesia's perceived embarrassment.

All this smacks of making a virtue of necessity. There is no prospect of Australia being admitted to the emerging institutional structures of the region when that is opposed by Malaysia and now Indonesia. There may be cases where such opposition will not be forthcoming, but in the politically significant cases such as ASEM and ASEAN + 3 it will be adamant as long as Mahathir is there and indeed as long as Australia is unable to convince its neighbours that it better understands their outlook and until it offers what they would see as a more comfortable collegiate involvement than at present. There is now little support in the region for Australia's inclusion. Formerly Japan appeared in support, despite opposition in parts of the bureaucracy. But now that opposition is in the majority and Australia is unlikely to be able to count on effective Japanese support. In these circumstances, and at least for the time being, there is little point in pushing the matter. As noted earlier, to do so would be to court further discouraging and even humiliating rebuff. It is thus not surprising if there are now political attractions in representing Australia as building practical ties in increasing trade and as asserting a leadership role in security and the promotion of human rights and democracy. That may appeal to an Australian constituency. But it will do nothing to promote Australian understanding of the region and it will do nothing to enhance Australia's chances of eventually being accepted into an East Asian club.

It may be that the more sceptical climate since the financial crisis has led to a major writing down of East Asian prospects and an assessment, especially with Indonesia in mind, that the region's importance will not increase significantly in the near future. In particular it may be assessed now that the prospects for ASEAN + 3 and perhaps an EAEC are no longer bright. Or it may be thought that Australia will be able to continue managing well without belonging to them, that any advantages would not outweigh the possible costs of membership including overcoming resistance in Australia itself on the part of those who do not want to see the country come more under Asian influence, as they would see it. Perhaps most likely is a sense that we cannot be sure how all this will turn out, but that there is little useful Australia can do about it and so the best course is to put it on one side and get on with the positives like trade. That would be understandable but it would not account for the 'Howard Doctrine' aspects, nor for the manifest effort to link more closely with the United States including in economic terms. Those elements make the present Australian stance appear as a sharper turn away from East Asia than perhaps it is, and certainly sharper than is prudent in Australia's long term interest.

The shift in policy also raises questions about Australia's longer term standing with the United States. It used to be the case that Australia's strong position in its own region, the depth of its knowledge and deployed information resources of various kinds, and its access in the region's capitals were regarded as assets valued by the United States in the context of the relationship with Australia. If those assets are allowed to wither perhaps the relationship with Australia will seem less valuable to Administrations in Washington.

Australia and East Asia

In previous chapters we have explored the factors on the Australian side which have affected attitudes to the region, including through the shift in policy under the Howard government. We have also looked at the attitudes on the side of the regional countries towards acceptance of closer and more institutionalized links to include Australia. The prospect that Australia may be left outside the cooperative arrangements of the region of which it is geographically part seems not to cause particular concern to either the government or the wider public. As suggested above the government's apparent insouciance may be partly due to putting the best face on an outlook that does cause some concern. But outside the government too there are few voices raised to express such concern. There is virtually no discussion or analysis of what it might cost Australia to be left out. How would it be disadvantaged? The Ministers for Foreign Affairs and Trade have announced that a new White Paper will be prepared to replace that of 1997. It will presumably address some of these questions. The indications are that it will shift the foundations laid down in the 1997 White Paper and especially those which were inherited from the Labor governments of Hawke and Keating. A Howard government is always likely to place more emphasis on the sustaining influence he sees the United States and British connections having on the Australian identity and, in one way or another, to emphasize Australia's cultural and institutional independence of East Asia. In short it is likely that the new White Paper will in some respects be a reactionary document.

The questions noted above about the consequences for Australia of being left out of East Asian regional arrangements are virtually unanswerable except in very general and speculative terms. For example, the consequences of being left out of an ASEAN + 3 Free Trade Area would depend very much on the terms of such an FTA and especially on whatever tariffs or other barriers it kept against non-members. It would depend too on what if any Australian bilateral arrangements with members remained in place and on what arrangements (for example with the United States and/or NAFTA) which Australia had been able to make in place of membership of an East Asia FTA. It would of course depend on the growth of the East Asian economies and the growth of their participation in world trade, their openness. Whatever answers are essayed to these questions the likelihood is that there would be costs in terms of export opportunities, in merchandise trade and also over time in services and investment. Transnational companies would be less likely to put regional headquarters in an Australia which was not part of a regional economic and financial architecture. There would be less business travel between the region and Australia and fewer exchanges between universities, professional bodies and so on. But perhaps tourism and the foreign students market might not be much affected.

An even more imponderable factor is the extent to which Australia could feel isolated and vulnerable. If regional groupings are to be increasingly important, following the lead of the European Union, and if the East Asian Economic Group comes to fruition, Australia will surely want to be included in the latter. The attempt to strike an FTA with the United States suggests that the Australian government has in mind linking with the North American FTA and eventually with a Free Trade Area of the Americas. But that seems an unnatural direction to take and unlikely to be consummated. A far more natural and appropriate outcome for Australia would be to win acceptance in the emerging East Asian grouping. The problem with the latter, as we have seen, is the obstacles that at present exist both on the East Asian side and in terms of Australian attitudes and then also the costs which might be demanded in terms of Australian adaptations.

So Australia drifts, looking with some puzzlement at sour reactions in the region, and showing no disposition to hasten an ethnic and cultural blending with East Asia. Most Australians support the government's rejection of boat people claiming to seek asylum from bad conditions in Iraq, Iran and Afghanistan. Yet it is not the case that this is some sort of reversion to the White Australia policy. It is not a matter of colour now, but of culture, a concern that these people will not fit in and that there will be trouble and friction as a result. There is, for example, no similar opposition to the entry of Chinese people from around the region. The opposition to even quite small numbers of illegal immigrants from the countries mentioned above presumably betrays some lack of confidence in Australia's capacity for tolerance and civic generosity. But it is different from the vulnerability which we surveyed in earlier chapters of this book. A few thousand Afghan asylum seekers are unlikely to threaten the security and welfare of the Australian nation. But Australians are sensitive on the 'border security' issue and wary of precedents.

But Australians now appear to have little concern for vulnerability in the old sense. In February 2002 they observed the 50th anniversary of the fall of Singapore to Japan and the surrender of most of the Eighth Division and some other elements of the Australian Army. The speeches of politicians and others and the media comment for the most part commemorated the bravery and suffering of the Australian forces, but there were references to the long-running argument whether the Australians had been let down by bad British planning and generalship in the defensive campaign on the Malay peninsula and on Singapore itself. There was also reference to the British publicity given to the desertion of Australian troops at the end and to cases of rank bad behaviour by some of those deserters. But it was clear that no-one wanted to probe too deeply into all this while the veterans were still living, mostly in their eighties, and on that day mourning their fallen comrades. There was little or no discussion of the nature and causes of the worst defeat in the history of British arms or of the part played in that by the Australians. But most strikingly there was no reflection of the fact that the smaller invading force of Japanese troops had fought with greater skill, determination and effectiveness than the substantially larger force of British, Indian and Australian troops who were the defenders. Before the war Australians had taken a racist view that Asian troops could not equal Australian soldiers. But in Malaya and Singapore and then in a series of other engagements the Japanese overwhelmed Australian defenders. The latter were heavily outnumbered in such outposts as Timor and Ambon, but there was not the determined resistance which the Japanese themselves demonstrated later in the war when they were on the defensive.

Indeed the time is rapidly approaching when it will be important for Australians to assess objectively, indeed critically, the role and performance of their armed forces in World War II and subsequently. This would involve not only the armed forces *per se* but policy and performance in defence purchasing and production. We saw in Chapter 2 that work which has been done so far shows an uneven performance in World War II, from the top of the government through to those on the battlefields. Australians did very well in some areas and at some times; less well at others. The defeats they suffered were often a consequence of planning and circumstances over which they had no control. In Greece and Crete, for example, they appear to have been sent into unwinnable situations where they did well without air cover and against weight of numbers. It is hard now to justify the decision to agree with the British demand that they be made available for this task; but there were reasons for doing so and the episode deserves a careful review. The Malaya and Singapore disaster is in a class of its own in terms of magnitude, in terms of the multiple failures of preparation, assessment of the enemy, planning, leadership and performance. It alone should serve as a warning to Australia never again to be lulled into a sense of superiority and complacency. There were of course Australians in responsible positions in the years beforehand who were not so lulled. They sought to persuade government not to rely on the British strategy based on Singapore and the navy for protection against Japan. But there was not much disposition to argue with anodyne responses from London, and little disposition to make realistic assessments of Japanese strength, particularly in military and naval aviation.

Even where Australia was successful, as eventually in the long campaign down the Kokoda Track and back again, and other bitter fighting in New Guinea and later in the Solomons and elsewhere it required substantial superiority of Australian numbers against an enemy which was often suffering from being at the end of inadequate or severed supply lines. In the air the attacks on the mainland, that is to say mainly Darwin, exposed the truly lamentable state of the Australian air defences. Later with modern equipment the RAAF did far better, but it was handicapped by divided and flawed leadership and of course many of Australia's trained air crew fought through the war in the British RAF. The Navy's record, in terms of ship wins and losses, was not impressive. It sank an Italian light cruiser early in the war and a German merchant raider. Later it sank a submarine and shared in sinking another. But 'it lost three of its biggest and newest cruisers, three destroyers, two sloops and a corvette to enemy action and a destroyer grounded in Timor'[17]. These figures give no sense of the courage and tenacity shown by Australian naval personnel throughout the war in a wide range of roles. But that is hardly relevant to our purpose here which is just to point out that Australia's actual experience of warfare seems almost startlingly at variance with some public attitudes in Australia. A compound of pride in what is assumed to be Australian superiority to others when it comes to fighting and a lack of concern about Australia's capacity to defend itself effectively in the event of threats arising in or through the region to its west and north could be put in perspective by greater familiarity with the time when Australia's vulnerability was shown up.

If East Asia does continue to move along the path of regional institution-building and over time extends that to the security area, *prima facie* Australia would be less vulnerable and safer inside such a regional institutional framework than outside it. It may well be a long time before such a framework comes into existence, but if and when it does access would be unlikely to be granted easily to a neighbouring country which had not participated already in a regional framework which had been long growing in other areas. That is to say there is a case in defence and security terms as well as economic terms for Australia to continue to pursue admission to an East Asian grouping. The basis for the idea of a *family* is no doubt partly imagined. But that does not make it less powerful. And in fact it is especially the partly imagined elements which work against Australia.

It needs to be borne in mind that, in addition to the need to adapt in various ways (which as we have seen could be deemed unacceptable by Australians), there is the possibility that demands could be made on Australia by other members. It seems unlikely at present that an East Asian Grouping would be able to develop the degree of freedom of movement, work and so on which has been achieved by the European Union. In fact, as things now stand, to be subject to that sort of pressure would be even more unwelcome to some of the East Asian states than it would be to Australia. Even now Malaysia is in the process of expelling thousands of unauthorized Indonesian residents. Japan would have to undergo radical changes to overcome the deeply-rooted racial solidarity which prevents it admitting more than a handful of special immigrants. The same goes for Korea. But Australia's perceived emptiness, and the fact that Australia is seen as different, even as a sort of discrepancy and a legacy of white European imperialism, could generate demands which would not be directed towards others in the same way. Australia stands out as an easy target in this context and others might even find it convenient to fall in with pressure on Australia to divert it from themselves. That raises the issue of Australia's small population as a factor contributing to vulnerability. We shall not attempt here to review that issue in detail. The point is rather that, whereas Australians at one time felt themselves to be highly vulnerable because of the relative smallness of the population, now they seem indifferent to that and discuss the population issue in terms of the purported limitations of the continent to sustain a significant population or in terms of the economic consequences of the aging population. But in relative terms Australia's population of nineteen million is *smaller* than was the seven million population at the time of the Second World War. There are now eleven Indonesians for every Australian. The population of Indonesia increased by 19 per cent during the decade of the 1990s, as did that of India. The population of the Philippines increased more rapidly. All across the region with the exception of China, Japan and the city-state of Singapore populations are rising quite rapidly. Not all of these countries are experiencing over-crowding although there is increasing pressure on resources and severe poverty in some parts of Indonesia near to Australia. In Java there is severe population pressure. Nor is it argued that there is any sign of people wanting to shift in large numbers from South East Asia to Australia. But across the region and beyond Australia is seen as a largely empty land, certainly a very under-populated one.

To some degree this reflects an unawareness that Australia is the driest of the continents and that most of it is arid or semi-arid. But Australians make too much of that. Water is grossly wasted and misused in Australia. Precisely because it is scarce its price should be high to ensure it is used efficiently. Australia should not be subsidizing massive use of water for irrigated, water-intensive crops. Australia makes large export income from cotton for example. But at what cost in terms of degradation? Some environmentalists have argued that the population is already much too large and should be reduced to, say, eleven million (a figure mentioned by Dr Tim Flannery, a prominent commentator on these matters). They argue that the degradation of the environment is a consequence of the demands made on it by the size of the population. But that assumes that public policy including taxing and pricing policy cannot control and reduce those demands and that environmental management cannot constrain the effects of human use of the natural environment. No doubt great damage has been done to the Australian environment since European settlement. But to the extent that the main agent for this has been agriculture and introduced animals the number of people involved has been small. Only a small proportion of the population is now engaged in agriculture, sheep and cattle, and there are constant complaints that once thriving rural towns are dying as people desert the 'bush' to go to the cities. A larger population need not, and very likely would not, result in an increase in pressure on the land in the most vulnerable areas. Nor need it result in greater demands on the river systems which are being depleted for crops which need not, and perhaps should not, be grown on a large scale in Australia.

There are large areas in Australia which appear to outsiders to be hospitable but empty. It seems unlikely that Australia will be able to escape growing attention in this context. At some point there could well be calls on the basis of equity for an opening of the country to more settlers from overcrowded places. Of course that would do nothing significant to relieve the population pressures elsewhere but that argument is unlikely to carry weight. Nor would the likelihood that new settlers will prefer life in the cities and, one way or another, make their way to the growing large conurbations on the East Coast. Whether Australia would be better or worse placed to meet such challenges from inside an East Asian Group is hard to say. But Australia would be more likely to qualify for acceptance if its population were growing more robustly and if there was a more rapidly growing regional component in that population. At present few in Australia are likely to see that as an argument for population increase. Whether or not Australia can succeed in consummating the engagement policy the sensible course would be to increase the population at a steady rate, including with immigrants from the region, so that Australia's population grows to a point at which it will not appear disproportionately small by contrast to those around it. At least a doubling of the present population would be a reasonable long term goal by that test. But as things now stand there is little prospect of an increase of that order. Since 1945 the population has increased by 170 per cent. But the rate of increase that involved would be quite unacceptable now. The task now is to convince Australians that a moderate rate of increase is needed to avoid the risk of being marginalized and losing control over their future.

With about twice the present population Australia might generate a gross national income approaching US$1 trillion at present values. This would give it a much larger weight in the regional and global economic and trading environments, even allowing for the fact that the size of at least some of the other regional countries would grow significantly at the same time. What needs to be avoided is a *decline* in Australia's relative position such that it falls behind in economic weight and in its relative defence capabilities. It is essential in Australia's national interest that it have highly capable intelligence capacities, a capacity to control its immediate strategic environment by air and sea, and a capacity to insert ground forces in emergency situations. These are requirements not only in terms of the defence of continental Australia but also if it is to continue to be able to sustain its end of the alliance with the United States. With a population and economy in the order of size mentioned above it would be difficult to overlook an Australian wish to participate as a full member in an East Asian Group, assuming reasonable compatibility requirements.

That is the future towards which Australia should be aiming and for which it should be preparing. It should be preparing in terms of public debate and argument, in terms of public policy including substantially increased immigration, in terms of its diplomacy in the region and in terms of a resumption of the emphasis on Asian languages and studies in the universities to maintain and develop the capacities to relate to the region and interpret it with understanding and expertise. But there is little sign that that will happen soon. Australia still seems to be reacting against the earlier attempts to engage much more closely with East Asia, and to be drifting rather aimlessly with only a firm commitment to the United States alliance and leadership as the main determinant of policy.

Notes

1. The current sense of vulnerability, as shown by the public support for the Howard Government's 'border security' policies especially relating to people from Iraq, Afghanistan etc arriving without authorization in boats organized by 'people smugglers', is different from the fears of invasion which have surfaced in the past, most recently and acutely in 1942. The present concerns may be closer in nature to one aspect which Parkes and others exploited around the end of the 19th century in that they reflect concern that such people are too radically different in culture to assimilate to the majority. What seems to be different now is absence of the earlier race-based fear that non-white people would dilute or displace the Anglo-Celtic majority. There is also popular support for the argument that Australia should preserve the right to decide who is allowed to come in.
2. Jones, Roger, McAllister, Ian, Gow, David (1996), *Australian Election Study, 1996* [computer file]. Canberra: Social Science Data Archives, The Australian National University. Those who carried out the original analysis and collection of the data bear no responsibility for the further analysis or interpretation of them.
3. This was Kevin Rudd, a former Foreign Affairs officer with considerable experience in the region. It was clear that he was reflecting Labor policy, probably based on their opinion polling.
4. In particular the treatment of the highly professional work and success of the Australian Defence Force in INTERFET which at times sounded like the sort of congratulations extended to successful national sporting teams.

5   See for example Leaver, Richard (2001), 'The Meanings, Origins and Implications of "the Howard Doctrine"', *The Pacific Review*, Vol. 14, No. 1, pp. 15-34. This issue is examined in more detail by Tiffen, Rodney (2001), *Diplomatic Deceits*, UNSW Press, Sydney, Chapter 6.

6   See especially Harris, Stuart (1998), *Will China Divide Australia and the United States?* The Australian Centre for American Studies, Sydney.

7   Fraser has written several times on the subject on the Opinion page of *The Australian* and has spoken on both public and private platforms about it. He has made it clear that he considers it a critical issue for Australia's future.

8   Transcript of interview with Tony Jones on 17 August 2001 at http//www.abc.net.au/lateline/s348556.html.

9   Leaver (2001), *op. cit.*

10   With occasional exceptions, notably an ill-tempered article by Jusuf Wanandi in the *Jakarta Post* on 15 November 2001, which was then also carried in *The Australian* and *The Straits Times*. Australians appear to have felt it best not to respond.

11   See for example Downer's article on the *Opinion* page of *The Australian* on 4 January, 2002, under the heading 'Growing Intimacy with Asia'.

12   While for obvious reasons details cannot be given there is anecdotal evidence of dismissal in Government circles of what is seen as 'going cap in hand to the Indonesians'.

13   Since the end of the New Order, and largely for budgetary reasons, the family planning program which had become one of the Soeharto era success stories has lost impetus. For the whole of the 1990s decade the increase in the Indonesian population was 19 per cent which was the same as India's. China's increase was 11 per cent. (Source: US Census Bureau as reported by State Department information service 7 February, 2002.)

14   See for example an interesting article on p. 10 of *The Australian Financial Review Weekend* for 28 December 2001 by Rowan Callick: 'Fresh faces to drive debate in region'. Callick quotes with approval 'the brilliant young writer on regional business strategies, Michael Backman' as saying 'If ever there was a country that punches under its weight on the world stage it is not Australia but Indonesia' (presumably a reference to Gareth Evans's call for Australia to 'punch above its weight'). If that is to be the approach to the 'new discussion about Australia's future role in Asia', which Callick describes, it will lead to further disappointment. A sure way for Australia to alienate Indonesia is to presume to be taking the lead.

15   Downer (2002), *op. cit.* ('Growing Intimacy with Asia').

16   Downer, *ibid.*

17   Robertson, John (1984), *Australia Goes to War*, Doubleday, Sydney, p. 214.

Bibliography

Albinski, Henry (1959), *Australia's Search for Regional Security in South-East Asia*, PhD Thesis, University of Minnesota.

Albinski, Henry (1977), *Australian External Policy Under Labor*, University of Queensland Press, St. Lucia.

Albinski, H.S. (1996), 'Responding to Asia-Pacific Human Rights Issues: Implications for Australian-American Relations', *Australian Journal of International Affairs*, Vol. 50(1), pp. 43-58.

Asian Studies Council (Australia) (1989), *A National Strategy for the Study of Asia in Australia*, Australian Government Printing Service, Canberra.

Australian Defence Association (1999), Submission to the Senate Foreign Affairs, Defence and Trade Committee Inquiry into East Timor.

Beazley, K. (2001), 'Australia in the Asia Pacific. How a Beazley Government Would Revitalise Commitment to the Region', The Twenty-Third Asia Lecture, Asia-Australia Institute, Sydney, 6 September.

Bell, C. (1988), *Dependent Ally, A Study in Australian Foreign Policy*, Oxford University Press, Melbourne.

Bell, R. (1997), 'Reassessed: Australia's Relationship with the United States', in J. Cotton and J. Ravenhill (eds), *Seeking Asian Engagement: Australia in World Affairs 1991-1995*, Oxford University Press, Melbourne, pp. 207-29.

Callinan, B. (1984), *Independent Company: The Australian Army in Portuguese Timor 1941-43*, Heinemann, Melbourne.

Calvert, A. (2000), 'Australia's Foreign and Trade Policy Agenda', address to the National Press Club, Canberra, 3 August.

Campbell, A. (1995), *The Double Reds of Timor*, John Burridge Military Antiques, Swanbourne.

Case, William (1996), 'Can the "Halfway House" Stand? Semidemocracy and Elite Theory in Three Southeast Asian Countries', *Comparative Politics*, Vol. 28(4), pp. 437-64.

Case, William (2000), 'Revisiting Elites, Transitions and Founding Elections: An Unexpected Caller from Indonesia, *Democratization*, Vol. 7(4), pp. 51-80.

Casey, R.G. (1958), *Friends and Neighbors*, Michigan State University Press, East Lansing; (1954) Cheshire, Melbourne.

Charlton, P. (1983), *The Unnecessary War: Island Campaigns of the South-West Pacific 1944-45*, Macmillan, Melbourne.

Coates, John (1999), *Bravery Above Blunder: The Ninth Australian Division at Finschhafen, Sattelberg and Sio*, Oxford University Press, Melbourne.

Coates, John (2001), *The Australian Centenary History of Defence, Vol. II: An Atlas of Australia's Wars*, Oxford University Press, Melbourne.

Committee on Australia's Relations with the Third World (1979), *Australia and the Third World*, Australian Government Printing Service, Canberra.

Commonwealth of Australia (2000), *Defence Review 2000 – Our Future Defence Force*, Australian Government Printing Service, Canberra.

Cotton, J. (1999) (ed), *East Timor and Australia: A.I.I.A. Contributions to the Policy Debate*, Australian Defence Studies Centre, Canberra.

Courtney, G.B. (1993), *Silent Feet: The History of 'Z' Special Operations 1942-1945*, McCrae, Melbourne.
Dalrymple, R. (1998), 'Indonesia and the IMF: The Evolving Consequences of a Reforming Mission', *Australian Journal of International Affairs*, Vol. 52(3), pp. 233-39.
Day, D. (1993), *Menzies and Churchill at War*, Oxford University Press, Melbourne.
Department of Foreign Affairs and Trade (1997), *In the National Interest*, Australian Government Printing Service, Canberra.
Department of Foreign Affairs and Trade (2000), *Australia and the Indonesian Incorporation of Portuguese Timor 1974-1976*, Department of Foreign Affairs and Trade in association with Melbourne University Press, Melbourne.
Doig, C.D. (1986), *The History of the Second Independent Company*, C. Doig, Perth.
Downer, Alexander (1996), 'Australia and Asia: Taking the Long View', address to the Foreign Correspondent's Association, Sydney, 11 April.
Downer, Alexander (1999), 'Australia, Indonesia and East Timor – Moving Forward', Speech to Asian Studies Association of Australia, Brisbane, 29 October.
Downer, Alexander (2001), 'Australian Foreign Policy – a Liberal Perspective', *Australian Journal of International Affairs*, Vol. 55(3), pp. 337-41.
Dunn, J. (1996), *Timor: A People Betrayed*, ABC Books, Sydney.
Edwards, P.G. (1983), *Prime Ministers & Diplomats: The Making of Australian Foreign Policy 1901-1949*, Oxford University Press in assoc. with the Australian Institute of International Affairs, Melbourne
Eggleston, F. (1947), 'Foreign Policy' in C.H. Grattan (ed), *Australia*, University of California Press, Berkeley, pp. 135-50.
Elphick, P. (1995), *Singapore: the Pregnable Fortress. A Study in Deception, Discord and Desertion*, Hodder and Stoughton, London.
Evans, Gareth (1990), 'Australia and Northeast Asia', address to the Committee for Economic Development of Australia (CEDA), Melbourne, 22 March.
Evans, Gareth (1995), 'Australia in East Asia and the Asia-Pacific: Beyond the Looking-Glass', the Fourteenth Asia Lecture, Asia-Australia Institute, Sydney, 20 March.
Evans, Gareth and Grant, B. (1995), *Australia's Foreign Relations in the World of the 1990s*, 2nd ed, Melbourne University Press, Carlton.
Farrell, B. (1999), 'Controversies Surrounding the Surrender of Singapore, February 1942', in M.H. Murfett et al. (eds), *Between Two Oceans, A Military History of Singapore From First Settlement to Final British Withdrawal*, Oxford University Press, Oxford, pp. 341-64.
FitzGerald, S. (1997), *Is Australia an Asian Country?*, Allen and Unwin, St. Leonards.
Feith, H. (1962), *The Decline of Constitutional Democracy in Indonesia*, Cornell University Press, Ithaca.
Funabashi, Y. (1993), 'The Asianization of Asia', *Foreign Affairs*, Vol. 72(5), pp. 75-86.
Garnaut, Ross (1989), *Australia and the Northeast Asian Ascendancy*, Australian Government Printing Service, Canberra.
Garnaut, Ross (2001), *The United States-Australia Alliance in an East Asian Context; Conference Proceedings, 29-30 June, 2001*, Defence Publishing Services, Canberra, Chapter 4.
Goto, Kenichi (1999), *A History of International Relations Surrounding East Timor, 1900-1945*, Misuzu Shobo, Tokyo (in Japanese).
Grant, Bruce (1964), *Indonesia*, Melbourne University Press, p. 158.
Hancock, W.K. (1945), *Australia*, Ernest Benn Ltd, London.
Harris, S. (1998), *Will China Divide Australia and the United States?*, Australian Centre for American Studies, Sydney.
Hasluck, P. (1948), *Workshop of Security*, Cheshire, Melbourne.

Hastings, Peter (1975a), 'The Timor Problem II – Some Australian Attitudes, 1903-1941, *Australian Outlook*, Vol. 29(2), pp. 180-96. Reprinted in Cotton, J. (1999) (ed.), *East Timor and Australia: A.I.I.A. Contributions to the Policy Debate*, Australian Defence Studies Centre, Canberra, pp. 23-40.

Hastings, Peter (1975b), 'The Timor Problem III – Some Australian Attitudes, 1941-1950' *Australian Outlook*, Vol. 29(3), pp. 323-34. Reprinted in Cotton, J. (1999) (ed.), *East Timor and Australia: A.I.I.A. Contributions to the Policy Debate*, Australian Defence Studies Centre, Canberra, pp. 41-53.

Hawke, Robert (1994), *The Hawke Memoirs*, William Heinemann, Melbourne.

Hawke, Robert (2000), *John Curtin Oration*, Creswick, 20 August.

Hayden, B. (1996), *Hayden, An Autobiography*, Angus and Robertson, Sydney.

Higgott, R.A. and Nossal, K.R. (1997), 'The International Politics of Liminality: Relocating Australia in the Asia Pacific', *Australian Journal of Political Science*, Vol. 32(2), pp. 169-85.

Horne, D. (1964), *The Lucky Country*, Penguin, Melbourne.

Horner, D.M. (1978), *Crisis of Command*, Australian National University Press, Canberra.

Horner, D.M. (1982), *High Command – Australia and Allied Strategy 1939-1945* George Allen & Unwin, St. Leonards.

Howard, John (1996), Address at the opening of the R.G. Casey Building, Canberra, 29 November.

Howard, John (1997), Fifth Annual Sir Edward 'Weary' Dunlop Asialink Lecture, Melbourne, 11 November.

Huntington, S. (1996), *The Clash of Civilizations and the Remaking of World Order*, Simon & Schuster, New York.

Hwee, Y.L. (2000), 'ASEM: Looking Back, Looking Forward', *Contemporary Southeast Asia*, Vol. 22(1), pp. 113-44.

Ibrahim, A. (1996), *The Asian Renaissance*, Times Books International, Singapore.

Ingleson, J. and Nairn, M.E. (1989), *Asia in Australian Higher Education: Report of the Inquiry into the Teaching of Asian Studies and Languages in Higher Education Submitted to the Asian Studies Council*, University of New South Wales Press, Sydney.

Jayasuria, L. and Kee, P. (1999), *The Asianisation of Australia? Some Facts About the Myths*, Melbourne University Press, Melbourne.

Keating, Paul (1996), 'Australia, Asia and the New Regionalism', The Singapore Lecture, Singapore, 17 January.

Keating, Paul (2000), *Engagement, Australia Faces the Asia-Pacific*, Macmillan, Sydney.

Kikuchi, T. (2002), 'East Asian Regionalism: A Look at the "ASEAN Plus Three" Framework', *Japan Review of International Affairs*, Vol. 16(1), pp. 23-45.

King, R. (1997), *Australians studying in Asia: the ASAA 1976-1997*, accessed at http://coombs.anu.edu.au/Special Proj/ASAA/King02.html.

Lawson, S. (1996), 'Political Myths about Asia and the West' in Robison, R. (ed.) *Pathways to Asia*, Allen and Unwin, St. Leonards, pp. 108-130.

Leaver, R. (2001), 'The Meanings, Origins and Implications of "the Howard Doctrine"', *The Pacific Review*, Vol. 14(1), pp. 15-34.

Levi, Werner (1947), *American Australian Relations*, University of Minnesota Press, Minneapolis.

Levi, Werner (1958), *Australia's Outlook on Asia*, Angus and Robertson, Sydney.

McCarthy, D. (1959), *Australia in the War of 1939-1945, Series One, Army, Vol. 5: South-West Pacific Area – First Year: Kokoda to Wau*, Australian War Memorial, Canberra.

Mahbubani, K. (1998), Can Asians Think? *The National Interest*, No. 52, Summer, pp. 27-36.

Maley, W. (2000), 'Australia and the East Timor Crisis: Some Critical Comments', *Australian Journal of International Affairs*, Vol. 54(2), pp. 151-61.
Meaney, N. (1985), *Australia and the World: A Documentary History from the 1870s to the 1970s*, Longman Cheshire, Melbourne.
Menzies, R. (1967), *Afternoon Light: Some Memories of Men and Events*, Cassell, Melbourne.
Millar, T.B. (1978), *Australia in Peace and War: External Relations 1788-1977*, Australian National University Press, Canberra.
Milner, Anthony (1997), 'The Rhetoric of Asia', in Cotton, J. and Ravenhill, J. (eds), *Seeking Asian Engagement: Australia in World Affairs 1991-1995*, Oxford University Press and Australian Institute of International Affairs, Melbourne.
Milner, Anthony (1999), 'Approaching Asia, and Asian Studies, in Australia', *Asian Studies Review*, Vol. 23(2), pp. 193-203.
Renouf, Alan (1979), *The Frightened Country*, Macmillan, Melbourne.
Renouf, Alan (1986), *Malcolm Fraser and Australian Foreign Policy*, Australian Professional Publications, Sydney.
Robertson, J. (1984), *Australia Goes to War 1939-1945*, Doubleday, Sydney.
Robison, R. (1996), 'Introduction', *The Pacific Review*, Vol. 9(3), pp. 305-08.
Sheridan, G. (1994), *Living with Dragons*, Allen and Unwin, St. Leonards.
Spender, P. (1967), *Exercises in Diplomacy: the ANZUS Treaty and the Colombo Plan*, Sydney University Press, Sydney.
Terada, Takashi (1999), *The Genesis of APEC: Australian-Japan Political Initiatives*, Pacific Economic Papers, No. 298, Australia-Japan Research Centre, Australian National University, Canberra.
Terada, Takashi (2001a), 'Directional Leadership in Institution-Building: Japan's Approaches to ASEAN in the Establishment of PECC and APEC', *The Pacific Review*, Vol. 14(2), pp. 195-220.
Terada, Takashi (2001b), 'Constructing the East Asian Concept and Growing Regional Identity: From EAEC to ASEAN − 3', conference paper, Singapore, October.
Tiffen, R. (2001), *Diplomatic Deceits*, University of New South Wales Press, Sydney.
Ungerer, C. (1997), 'Australia and the World: A Seminar Report', *Australian Journal of International Affairs*, Vol. 51(2), pp. 255-61.
Walker, D. (1999), *Anxious Nation: Australia and the Rise of Asia 1850-1939*, University of Queensland Press, St. Lucia.
Wang Gungwu (1996/97), 'A Machiavelli for Our Times', *The National Interest*, No. 46, Winter, pp. 69-73.
Waters, C.W.P. (1994), 'Anglo-Australian Conflict over the Cold War: H.V. Evatt as President of the UN General Assembly, 1948-49', *The Journal of Imperial and Commonwealth History*, Vol. 22(2), pp. 294-331.
Watt, A. (1967), *The Evolution of Australian Foreign Policy 1938-1965*, Cambridge University Press, London.
Webber, D. (2001), 'Two Funerals and a Wedding? The Ups and Downs of Regionalism in East Asia and the Asia-Pacific after the Asian Crisis', *Pacific Review*, Vol. 14(3), pp. 339-72.
Whitlam, E.G. (1979) 'Australia, Indonesia and Europe's Empires' in J. Cotton (ed.), *East Timor and Australia: A.I.I.A. Contributions to the Policy Debate*, Australian Defence Studies Centre, Canberra, pp. 137-48.
Yamamura, K and Hatch, W. (1996), *Asia in Japan's Embrace: Building a Regional Production Alliance*, Cambridge University Press, Cambridge.

Index

acclimation 149–50
Afghanistan 127
Agreement on Maintaining Security 105, 129, 176, 180, 207, 215
Alatas, Ali 142, 177
Anglo-Japanese alliance 10
anti-communism 22–7
Anzac Day 36
ANZUS Treaty 22–3, 64, 69, 75–6, 220–221
APEC (Asia Pacific Economic Cooperation)
  and Asian financial crisis 144
  commitment to 'open regionalism' 90–92
  origins 85–6
  role in Australian foreign policy 85–91, 93–4, 213
  US and 86–7, 88–9, 102
appeasement 16, 35
Armitage, Richard 220
ASEAN 66, 83–5, 89–90, 105, 144
ASEAN + 3 concept 103, 146–50, 154
ASEAN Regional Forum 103, 142
ASEM (Asia-Europe meetings) 103, 105, 143, 145–6, 152–6
Asia
  animus against West 119–20
  Australia as part of 2, 93, 97–103, 108
  fear of 5–6, 8
  see also 'engagement with Asia'
Asia Pacific
  Australia's identification with 2, 93–4, 97–8, 101–3, 213
  see also APEC
Asian financial crisis 130, 144, 147–8, 215–16
Asian immigration 8–9, 81
Asian Monetary Fund 148–9
Asian studies 82, 138, 141
'Asian values' debate 116–20, 128
asylum seekers 124, 213, 228
Australia-Japan Trade Agreement 62

Australian identity
  as distinctive 100–101, 152
  effect of World War I 33
  as 'part of Asia' 2, 93, 97–103, 108
  sense of Britishness 1, 18, 25, 32–6, 53–4
Australian Labor Party
  and Indonesian independence 165–6
  regional engagement policy 102
Australian nationalism 33–4, 36

Baker, James 86
Barwick, Garfield 172
Beazley, Kim 102–3
Bennett, Major-General Gordon 40–41
Blamey, General Thomas 42–4, 45, 46, 56
blocs 102, 146, 213
'border security' 4–5
Brereton, Laurie 102
British Commonwealth 12–13, 56–8, 62–3, 66, 69
British nationality 34
Britishness see Australian identity
Bruce, S.M. 35
Burton, John 26

Cairns Group 142
Cambodia 142
Casey, R.G. 17, 25, 34, 111, 168–71
Chifley, J.B. 55
China
  Australia's relations with 27, 63, 65, 68
  future importance 219–20
  MFN status 92–3, 105
  as perceived threat 8–9
Churchill, W.S. 17, 35–6, 39–40
'clash of civilizations' thesis 126, 128–9
  Australia as test case 126, 129
Colombo Plan 121
Common Agricultural Policy 70
Common Fund 70–71

communism 24–7
Connor, R.F.X. 67
convergence (of interests, values)
  by Australia 156, 212
    resistance to 211–13, 216, 221–2
  by East Asia 100–101, 122–3, 133–4,
    137–8, 149–50, 156
Crawford, Sir John 82–3
Curtin Government
  relations with Churchill 39–40, 55
  turns to US 19, 42, 46
Curtin, John 17–18, 19, 39–40, 48, 183–9
  dependence on MacArthur 19, 42–4,
    46, 57–8
  reasserts British connection 47, 56–8

Darwin 17–18
Deakin, Alfred 10–11, 54
democratization 134
disarmament 75
domino theory 26–7
Downer, Alexander 106–7, 151, 224

East Asia
  Australia viewed as outsider 112, 116,
    119–23, 128–31, 135–7, 153,
    220–221
  Australia's cultural compatibility with
    18, 100–101, 119, 120–123, 125–
    6, 129–31, 221–3
  Australia's engagement with (*see*
    'engagement with Asia')
  Australia's pursuit of insider status
    103, 108, 111–12, 125, 150–7
    rejection of 89–90, 103, 104, 145–6,
    150–7, 213, 223, 225–7, 230
  as 'economic miracle' 111–16, 125
  institution-building 89–90, 144–50,
    213
  Japan's economic leadership 112–16
  sense of solidarity and pride 111, 115,
    119–20, 128, 145–6
  see also Asian financial crisis; 'Asian
    values' debate
East Asian Economic Group/Caucus
  (EAEG/EAEC) 89–90, 103, 149
East Timor
  Australian policy 122, 185–6, 217
    1999 policy reversal 203–8, 214–15,
    217–18
  incorporation into Indonesia 186,
    194–203
  and sense of moral debt 186–93
  independence plebiscite 204–7
  peacekeeping intervention 205–8
  in World War II 186–91
  see also Portuguese Timor
'engagement with Asia'
  foundations 21–2, 25, 60–62, 111, 166
  Hawke and Keating Governments 2,
    79–82, 87–94, 98–102, 103–6
  Howard Government 106–9
  obstacles 211–12, 221, 222–3
  through cultural convergence 138–42
  waning commitment 3, 135–7, 141,
    144, 150–151, 213–16, 222–3,
    225–6
European Economic Community (EEC)
  70, 78
Evans, Gareth 82, 86, 89, 92, 97–8, 99–
  101, 103–4, 106–7, 137, 166, 177–
  8, 202, 222
Evatt, H.V. 20–21, 45, 47–8, 55–6, 58–
  60, 163–5, 194
Export Enhancement Program (US) 77,
  79

Fadden, Arthur 23
Feakes, G.B. 196, 199
Fischer, Tim 222
Fitzgerald, Stephen 82, 100, 129, 138–
  42, 221
foreign and security policy, Australia
  anti-Communist orientation 22–7
  Australia's independence in 32, 33–4,
    39–40, 47–8, 49–50, 54, 55, 58–
    60, 63–7, 71–2, 92
  as busy middle power 142–4
  continental integrity 7, 12, 22
  dependence
    on Britain 12–13, 16–19, 38–41, 54,
    56–8, 61
    on US 10–11, 12, 19–20, 22, 42, 49,
    61, 63
  diplomatic representation 34
  East Asia *versus* Asia Pacific
    commitment 2, 93–4, 97–8
  'history' *versus* 'geography' dilemma
    12, 79, 108–9, 125–6, 142, 151,
    157

see also East Timor: Australian policy;
    'engagement with Asia';
    Indonesia: Australian policy;
    names of specific Australian
    governments
France, as threat 5
Fraser Government 67–72, 78, 82
Fraser, Malcolm 28–9, 219
Fretilin 198–200, 203
Friends and Neighbours (Casey) 25,
    111, 170
Funabashi, Yoichi 117

Gallipoli 36–7
Garnaut Report 80–81, 87
Goh Chok Tong 146, 148
Gorton, John 63
Grant, Bruce 87–98, 99
Great Britain
    Australia's attachment to 32–6
    Australia's security dependence on
        12–13, 16–19, 38–41, 54, 56–8
    Singapore strategy 40–41
    treaties with Japan 9
Guam doctrine 27

Habibie, B.J. 203–7
Hancock, W.K. 12, 33
Hanson, Pauline see One Nation party
Harries Report 69–70
Harris, Stuart 219
Hasluck, Paul 59
Hawke, R.J.
    APEC proposal 85–7
    foreign policy outlook 74–7, 79–80
Hawke Government
    Asia Pacific regional policy 85–7
    commitment to US alliance 74–7
    engagement with East Asia 79–82
    trade diplomacy with US 77–9
Hayden, Bill 79
Holt, Harold 63, 81
'Howard Doctrine' 220–222, 226
Howard Government
    commitment to US 5, 125, 136, 220–221
    East Asia focus 106–9, 125, 143–4, 151–7, 213–14, 216–17, 220–226
    East Timor policy 203–8
    foreign policy 107–8, 216, 220–223
    'practical regionalism' 155–6
    regional rebuffs 143, 145–6, 150–157
    relations with Indonesia 178, 180–181, 214–15, 217–19
    Security Council defeat 143
Howard, John
    on Australia's identity 152
    'deputy sheriff' speech 136
Hughes, W.M. 11–14, 20–21, 59
human rights 117, 122
Huntington, Samuel 2, 93, 125–6, 128–9

immigration policy
    illegal immigrants 4–5, 124, 213
    postwar program 55, 212
Indian Ocean demilitarization 68–9
Indonesia
    Australian public opinion towards 4, 166, 178–9, 217–18
    Australia's policy towards
        defence and security cooperation 93, 105, 129, 135, 176, 180, 207, 215
        East Timor question 122, 185–6, 195–203, 203–8, 214–15, 217–18
    Independence struggle 163–6
    Malaysian confrontation 171–2
    during Soeharto regime 173–83, 214, 225
    West Irian issue 168–71
    economy 114
    human rights abuses 122
    Islam in 127
    political instability 123
    resentment of Australia 127–8, 153–4, 181–2, 207–8, 218–19
    see also East Timor; Soeharto
Ingleson, John 82, 138
INTERFET (International Force-East Timor) 205–8
International Monetary Fund 149, 174, 181
invasion fear 5–8, 15, 17, 19–20, 22
Islam 126–7

Japan
    and Asian Monetary Fund 148–9
    Australia's ambivalence towards 9–10, 16
    Australia's fear of 9–11, 13–21, 22, 24
    Australia's trade with 62

Index

close relations with Australia 152–3
invasion of Portuguese Timor 187–91
Pacific War 19–22, 39–41, 43–4, 47
and regional economic cooperation 82–7
as regional economic model 112–16, 148–9
trade dispute with US 106
treaties with Britain 9
'Japanese Model' 114–16

Kausikan, Bilahari 117
Keating, Paul
  on Australia's identity 101, 126
  on engagement with Asia 87–91
  rapport with Soeharto 93, 105, 143, 176, 178–80
  regional diplomacy 103, 105, 176
Keating Government
  APEC policy 87–91, 106, 126
  disputes with US 105–6
  East Asia policy orientation 87–94, 103–6, 105–9, 124–6, 213–14, 222
  opposition to East Asian Economic Group 89–90
Kennedy, J.F. 169–70
Kissinger, Henry 63
Korean War 22–3

Lange, David 75
Latham, J.G. 14–15
Lawson, Stephanie 118
Lee Kuan Yew 66, 211
Levi, Werner 6
Lloyd George, David 35
Lyons Government 14–16

MacArthur, General Douglas 19–20, 42–7, 56
Mahathir Mohamad 89–90, 105, 118, 121, 135, 143, 154–5, 156, 226
Mahbubani, Kishore 117, 119
Malaysia 105, 135, 146, 150, 153–4, 156, 171–2
Manila Treaty 23
McEwen, John 60
McMahon Government 27, 63
Meaney, Neville 54
Menzies, R.G. 61, 167
  tensions with Churchill 35–6, 38

Menzies Governments
  anti-communism 24–7
  dealings with Indonesia 167–73
  foreign policy 21–2, 24–7, 54–5, 60–63
  steps towards Asia 61–2
Millar, T.B. 54
Ministry of Foreign Affairs (Japan) 83–5, 90
MITI 84–5
Moerdani, General L.B. 175, 200–201
Moffatt, J.P. 15–16
Monroe Doctrine, for Australia 11, 12
multiculturalism 123–4, 211–12
Muraoka, Shigeo 85

New International Economic Order 70–71
New Zealand 75–6
Nixon, Richard 27, 63
North East Asia 77, 80–81
  see also East Asia
North-South dialogue 69–71
northern Australia, fears for 7–8

Ohira, Masayoshi 83
Okita, Saburo 83
One Nation party 104, 121, 128, 216
'open regionalism' 91

Pacific Basin project 82–3
Pacific Economic Cooperation Council (PECC) 83–4
Pacific economic regionalism 66, 82–7
Parkes, Sir Henry 8, 56
Peacock, Andrew 69
Pearce, Sir George 15–16
People's Republic of China 63, 65, 68, 92–3, 105, 219–20
Piesse, E.L. 13–14
Plimsoll, James 111
population size see vulnerability, sense of
Portugal 188–9, 202
Portuguese Timor
  Australian troops in 186–7, 191–3
  Japanese invasion 187–91
  see also East Timor
prejudice, ethnic and cultural 124
public opinion
  Australian nationality 34

Australia's Asian relations 104, 106, 211, 223, 232
  on Indonesia 4, 166, 178–9, 217–18

race consciousness 7, 12–13, 33, 34, 36
racist attitudes 10–11, 121–2
realism 67–8
refugees 124
region and regionalism
  East Asian sense of 147–50
  meaning for Australia 93–4, 101–3, 106–7, 136, 155–6
  see also APEC; Pacific economic regionalism
remoteness, Australia's sense of 5–6
Renouf, Alan 5
republic debate 136–7, 212
Robison, Richard 117–18
RSL 13
Russia, as threat 6, 10

Santa Cruz incident 202
Schultz, George 86
Scullin, J.H. 13
SEATO 23
Security Council 143
security fears 1–7
  see also vulnerability, sense of
security policy see foreign and defence policy
self-determination
  East Timor 204–7
  Portuguese Timor 196–9, 202, 203
Shedden, Frederick 57
Sheridan, Greg 99, 129
Singapore, fall of 39–42, 228
Singapore Strategy 38–41
Soeharto 90, 134–5, 173–4, 179–80
  East Timor issue 195–6, 202
  relationship with Keating 93, 105, 143, 176, 178–80
South East Asia
  communist threat to 26–7
  see also ASEAN
Soviet Union 68–9
Spender, P.C. 22–3
Sukarno 164, 167–9, 171–3
Sydney Olympic Games 120

Taiwan 220
Taliban 127
Terada, Takashi 149–50
Third World 69–71
Tiffen Rodney 206
Timor Gap Treaty 185
Tjan, Harry 196–8
trade 62
  disputes with EEC 78
  disputes with US 77–9, 106
  trade liberalization 84–5, 86

United Nations 59–60, 60
United Nations High Commissioner for Refugees 124
United States
  action against Taliban 127
  and APEC 86–7, 88
  Australia's security dependence on 10–11, 12, 19–20, 22, 42, 49–50, 61, 63
  free trade agreement with 157, 221
  Howard Government's alignment with 5, 125, 136, 220–221
  trade disputes with 77–9, 106
  and West Irian issue 169–71
  see also ANZUS Treaty

vulnerability, sense of 4–13, 16–17, 22, 28–9, 42, 54, 55, 71, 80, 211, 227–8
  communism and 5, 21–8
  population size and 2, 5–6, 22, 55, 230–231
  see also Japan: Australia's fear of

Wahid, Abdurrachman 130, 179, 207–8
Walker, David 5–6
Watt, Alan 59
West Irian issue 168–71
White Australia policy 55, 62, 66, 81, 120–1, 212
Whitlam, E.G. 27–8
Whitlam Government
  East Timor policy 194–5, 197–9, 203–4
  foreign policy 63–7, 194
  and Indonesia 175

Wilenski, Peter 99, 204
Woolcott, Richard 112, 197, 199–200, 204
World War I
  Australia's military performance 13, 37
  Peace Conference 11–12
  and sense of nationhood 33, 36
World War II 19–20
  and Australia's independence 49–50
  Australia's military performance 1–2, 36–8, 43–4, 48–9, 228–9
  Australia's military preparedness 38–9
  Australia's turning to the US 42–3, 46
  fall of Malaya/Singapore 39–42
  New Guinea campaign 43–4
  South West Pacific campaign 45–7, 49

'Yellow Peril' 11